CADOGAN

London Brussels

Travel	1
London: Introduction and Practical A–Z	11
London: Essential Sights	27
London: Central Neighbourhoods	51
London: Villages	87
London: Green Spaces	109
London: Shopping	119
London: Museums and Galleries	131
London: Children and Sport	141
London: Food, Hotels and Nightlife	145
Brussels: Introduction and Practical A–Z	181
Brussels: Essential Sights	193
Brussels: Area by Area	213
Brussels: Shopping	243
Brussels: Museums and Monuments	249
Brussels: Food, Hotels and Nightlife	257
Index	276

Cadogan Guides
West End House, 11 Hills Place, London W1R 1AH
becky.kendall@morrispub.co.uk

The Globe Pequot Press
6 Business Park Road, PO Box 833, Old Saybrook, Connecticut 06475–0833

Copyright © Andrew Gumbel and Antony Mason November 1999

Updated by: Ana de Roo (Brussels); Vanessa Letts, Linda McQueen, Jacqueline Chnéour, Gareth Mealing, Kate Paice, Dominique Shead, Mary-Ann Gallagher and Catherine Charles (London)

Book and cover design by Animage
Cover photographs © Ellen Rooney and Kicca Tommasi
Chapter title pages designed by Kicca Tommasi from photographs by Kicca Tommasi, Antony Mason, Linda McQueen, Catherine Charles, Jacqueline Chnéour and Mary-Ann Gallagher
Maps © Cadogan Guides, drawn by Map Creation Ltd

Editorial Director: Vicki Ingle
Series Editor: Linda McQueen
Editor: Dominique Shead
Indexing: Isobel McLean
Production: Book Production Services

A catalogue record for this book is available from the British Library
ISBN 1-86011-939-5

Printed and bound in Italy by LEGOPRINT

All rights reserved. No part of this publication may be reproduced, stored in a retrieval system, or transmitted, in any form or by any means, electronic or mechanical, including photocopying and recording, or by any information storage and retrieval system except as may be expressly permitted by the UK 1988 Copyright Design & Patents Act and the USA 1976 Copyright Act or in writing from the publisher. Requests for permission should be addressed to Cadogan Guides, West End House, 11 Hills Place, London W1R 1AH.

About the Authors

Andrew Gumbel was born in a distant corner of that great anonymous expanse, the London suburbs. He first decided he loved London at the age of 10, and has been trying to make sense of it ever since. A journalist as well as a travel writer, he has returned to London periodically between lengthy periods abroad as a foreign correspondent for *The Guardian* and *The Independent*. He also wrote the Cadogan guide to Berlin. He currently lives in Los Angeles.

Antony Mason is the author of some 40 books, which include biographies of great artists, children's atlases, and books on exploration, great civilizations, the Wild West, houseplants, volleyball, spying—as well as travel guides. He now lives and works in London, but for many years has been a frequent visitor to Brussels. So convinced is he of the virtues and charms of the Belgians that he has married one, and has since felt sufficiently qualified to write *The Xenophobe's Guide to the Belgians*, designed to cure xenophobes of any misguided prejudices.

Please help us to keep this guide up to date

We have done our best to ensure that the information in this guide is correct at the time of going to press. But places and facilities are constantly changing, and standards and prices in hotels and restaurants fluctuate. We would be delighted to receive any comments concerning existing entries or omissions, as well as suggestions for new features. Authors of the most helpful letters may be offered a copy of the Cadogan Guide of their choice.

> The author and publishers have made every effort to ensure the accuracy of the information in this book at the time of going to press. However they cannot accept any responsibility for any loss, injury or inconvenience resulting from the use of information contained in this guide.

Contents

Guide to the Guide vi

Travel 1–10

Getting to Europe from North America	2	Passports, Visas and Border Formalities	5
Between the Two Cities: London–Brussels–London	3	Getting Around London	6
Arrivals	4	Getting Around Brussels	8

London: Introduction 11–14

London: Practical A–Z 15–26

Calendar of Events	16	Post Offices	22
Consulates in London	18	Pronunciation	23
Crime and Police	18	Religion	23
Disabled Travellers	19	Smoking	24
Electricity	20	Students and Pensioners	24
Health	20	Telephones	24
London for Free	20	Time	25
Maps	21	Tipping	25
Money and Banks	21	Toilets	25
National Holidays	22	Tourist Information	26
Opening Hours	22	Where to Stay	29

London: Essential Sights 27–50

Albert Hall and Memorial	28	Natural History Museum	39
Aquarium	28	Science Museum	39
British Museum	29	St Paul's Cathedral	40
Buckingham Palace	32	Tate Gallery	42
Globe Theatre	33	Ten, Downing Street	43
Hampton Court	34	Tower Bridge	44
Houses of Parliament and Big Ben	35	Tower of London	44
Kensington Palace	37	Trafalgar Square	45
Millennium Dome	38	Victoria and Albert Museum	46
National Gallery	38	Westminster Abbey	49

London: Central Neighbourhoods   51–86

Bloomsbury	52	Piccadilly and Leicester Square	69
The City of London	55	Soho and Chinatown	73
Covent Garden	62	St James's and Royal London	76
Mayfair	66	The South Bank and Southwark	80

London: Villages   87–108

Notting Hill	89	Islington	100
Chelsea and the King's Road	92	Hampstead	102
Docklands	94	Richmond	104
Camden	99	Greenwich	106

London: Green Spaces   109–118

Battersea Park	100	Hyde Park	113
Chelsea Physic Garden	110	Kensington Gardens	114
Green Park	111	Kew Gardens	114
Greenwich Park	111	Regent's Park and London Zoo	116
Hampstead Heath	112	Richmond Park	117
Highgate Cemetery	112	St James's Park	117
Holland Park	113	Syon Park	118

London: Shopping   119–130

London: Museums and Galleries   131–140

London: Children and Sports   141–44

London: Food and Drink   145–60

London: Where to Stay   161–68

London: Entertainment and Nightlife   169–80

Brussels: Introduction   181–2

Brussels: Practical A–Z   183–92

Belgium: Key Facts and Figures	184	Emergencies	186
Children	184	Festivals and Events	186
Crime and Police	184	Gay Scene	187
Doctors and Pharmacies	185	Insurance, Language	188
Electricity	185	Money and Banks	189
Embassies and Consulates	185	Opening Hours, Post Offices	190

Contents

Brussels: Practical A–Z (cont'd)			183–92
Public Holidays	190	Time, Tipping	191
Telephones	190	Tourist Information	191

Brussels: Essential Sights			193–212
Atomium	194	Musée des Instruments de	
Cathédrale St-Michel	194	Musique	204
Centre Belge de la Bande		Musées Royaux des	
Dessinée	195	Beaux-Arts	204
The Grand' Place	196	Musée Wiertz	207
Manneken-Pis	199	Palais de Justice	208
Musée du Cinéma	200	Rue des Bouchers	209
Musée du Cinquantenaire	201	Tour Japonaise, Pavillon	
Musée Horta	202	Chinois, Japanese Art Museum	209
Musée de l'Hôtel Charlier	203	Waterloo	210

Brussels: Area by Area			213–42
The Grand' Place	214	The Sablon and Marolles	223
The Coudenberg and Parc de		North-central Brussels	229
Bruxelles	219	Quartier Léopold	237

Brussels: Shopping	243–48

Brussels: Museums and Monuments	249–56

Brussels: Food and Drink	257–62

Brussels: Where to Stay	263–68

Brussels: Entertainment and NIghtlife	269–75

Index	276–82

A Guide to the Guide

This guide is aimed at those who haven't much time to spend in these two great cities of Europe. Getting from one to the other couldn't be easier. The **Travel** chapter will tell you how to get to London and to Brussels, move between the two, and get around efficiently.

Each half of the book launches with a few **practical tips**, then gets right to the heart of the matter with an alphabetical list of **Essential Sights**—the big places you've heard about and seen in a thousand photos. This is followed with a chapter (or two) describing the city's key **Neighbourhoods**, or **Areas**—places which may not be full of museums but which have a distinct atmosphere of their own. If museums are your passion, though, you can find just what you want, from the imposing to the quirky, in the **Museums** chapter. **Shopping** gives you ideas on where to shop, from department stores to designer *couturiers* to buzzing markets. **Food and Drink**, **Where to Stay** and bang-up-to-date **Entertainment and Nightlife** listings ensure you get the best out of London and Brussels whatever your budget.

Getting to Europe from North America	2
Between the Two Cities: London–Brussels–London	3
Arrivals	4
Passports, Visas and Border Formalities	5

Travel

Getting Around London	6
Getting Around Brussels	8

Getting to Europe from North America

By Air to London

London is the spaghetti junction of the world's airways, with no fewer than five airports (at the last count) and planes from every conceivable airline zipping in from virtually every major city around the world. There should be no trouble finding a flight, even at the last moment, and you should be able to pick up a cheap deal without too much trouble. Shop around at several travel agents, and be prepared to consider Third World airlines as well as big names like British Airways, Qantas and the big North American carriers. North Americans wanting cheap flights to Europe can consult the worldwide web on: *www.travelocity.com*, or *www.lastminute.com*.

Travel times for direct flights are as follows: New York or Montreal 6 hours, Los Angeles 9 hours. The choice of airports is as follows:

Heathrow (✆ (020) 8759 4321), the largest of London's airports with four passenger terminals, is about 15 miles west of the centre. Terminal 1 is mainly for short-haul British Airways flights; Terminal 2 for the European services of non-British airlines; Terminal 3 for non-British long-haul services; and Terminal 4 for British Airways intercontinental flights and Concorde.

Gatwick (✆ (01293) 535353), with two terminals, is about 20 miles south of London and handles a lot of charter flights and the less prestigious airlines.

Stansted (✆ (01279) 680500) is the furthest from London, about 35 miles to the northeast, but in compensation is far and away the most pleasant. Only a few airlines, mostly arriving from continental Europe, use it for now, but it is likely to expand as pressure on Heathrow and Gatwick increases. Norman Foster's converted aircraft hangar design is pleasing to the eye and very efficient.

London City Airport (✆ (020) 7646 0000), about nine miles east of the centre, serves mainly business passengers arriving from continental Europe. It too is modern and pleasant.

Luton (✆ (01582) 405 100): If you are lucky, you will never go anywhere near Luton airport as long as you live. It is inefficient, overcrowded and unfriendly. Mostly it provides charter flights for British tourists heading for the sun, but there is just a chance a foreign travel agent will be mean enough to book you through there.

By Air to Brussels

As you might expect, Brussels, 'the capital of Europe', is well served by the world's airlines, jostling to harness the ceaseless ebb and flow of Eurocrats, multinational business travellers and a large population of expatriates—as well as tourists. There are many flights from all points of the globe, and they tend to be packed; if you are on a tight schedule, book early. International flights to Brussels arrive at Belgium's main airport at Zaventem, just 9 miles from the city centre.

There are direct flights from just about all the major gateway cities of the USA. Prices vary enormously but, to give some kind of yardstick, the round-trip price quoted by airlines for New York–Brussels is around $350–400 in the low season (winter), and rises to about $800 in the high season (summer). All fares are subject to additional airport taxes, which amount to about $40. Numerous agencies in the USA offer more competitive prices through charter flights or consolidated fares on scheduled flights; look in the travel pages of your Sunday newspaper.

Canadians are rather less well served: travellers have to take a two-stage journey, changing in the USA or in Europe to continue to Brussels.

Between the Two Cities: London–Brussels–London

By Air

The main carriers to Brussels are British Airways, reservations ✆ (0345) 222111, and the Belgian national airline Sabena, ✆ (020) 8780 1444. Each offers up to seven flights daily from London Heathrow, and there are daily flights from London Gatwick. Sabena also runs a daily service (except Saturdays) from London City Airport; British Midland flies direct from Heathrow.

The full London–Brussels fare for unrestricted economy travel is around £330 return. However, if your journey includes a Saturday night, prices for APEX fares drop to about £135–£145. In the low season this can drop to around £100. It is worth asking BA if they are running one of their occasional 'World Offers': return tickets for as little as £60, which must usually be booked at least a month in advance.

The flight from London to Brussels takes 60–70 mins. Since the check-in time is usually one hour before take-off, you will spend more time in the departure lounge than in the air—except at London City Airport, where the minimum check-in time is just 15 minutes. An airport tax of £10 is payable when you purchase your ticket.

By Rail

By far the quickest and most convenient way to reach Brussels is on the passenger-only train service run by Eurostar. There are usually eleven departures a day which, following the completion of the new-high speed line between Lille and Brussels, take 2 hours 40 minutes to travel from London Waterloo to the newly revamped Gare du Midi/Zuid Station in Brussels. Prices are on a par with its direct competitor air travel and vary between £129 for a standard economy fare to a full fare of £249. It is, however, well worth asking about any special deals that might be running. In the winter a weekend day return can be bought for as little as £69, rising to £79 if your stay includes a Saturday night. Passengers need to check in 20 minutes before departure.

The terminal is clean and modern and full of cafés and newspaper shops, a *bureau de change*, and there's even a small perfumery selling goods at discounts equivalent to the old 'duty-free' prices. If you want to travel in comfort, First Class offers wider seats and a meal.

Eurostar information and booking: ✆ (0990) 186 186 or in person at Waterloo station; web site: *www.eurostar.com*. If you will need help with baggage or assistance with walking, mention this at the time of booking.

Eurostar also offer **city break packages**: call ✆ (0845) 077 0777 for a brochure or ✆ (0870) 167 6767 to book.

There are two **long-stay car parks** at Waterloo: ✆ (020) 7620 0357 or ✆ (020) 7582 9944.

By Bus

The main carrier between London and Brussels is **National Express/Eurolines**, 52 Grosvenor Gardens, London SW1, ✆ (0990) 808080. Coaches depart from Victoria Coach

Station in central London and arrive at the Gare du Nord. There are usually three departures a day. The journey will take around 12 hours. Crossings are via Calais and cost £43 return in the low season rising to over £50 in summer.

By Car

You can take your car on a train through the Channel Tunnel with Eurotunnel (what used to be called 'Le Shuttle'), between Folkestone and Calais. The crossing under the Channel should only take 35 minutes, but in busy periods you may have to queue if you haven't booked. During the journey you can stay in the car or get out and stretch your legs and use the facilities. Prices fluctuate according to the season; call Eurotunnel on ✆ (0990) 353535.

The UK terminal is situated off junction 11a on the M20 whilst the French equivalent can be reached via junction 13 on the A16 motorway.

Arrivals

Arriving by Air in London

Heathrow: There is an excellent new direct **train** link from Heathrow to Paddington, the **Heathrow Express**, costing £10 one-way and taking a mere 15 minutes.

All Heathrow terminals link up with the **London Underground** system, which runs from 5.30am to midnight. The Piccadilly Line service gets you into the centre in about an hour for about £4.50. If you have a lot of luggage and your destination is not on the Piccadilly Line, it may be worth getting off at ⊖ Earls Court or ⊖ South Kensington and proceeding by taxi.

There is also a **bus** service from Heathrow, which provides far more space for luggage but is also less frequent, slower (depending on traffic), quite a bit more expensive (about £7) and only runs until 7pm (✆ (020) 7222 1234 for more information). The A1 goes to Victoria Coach Station, with stops on the way at Earl's Court, Harrods, Hyde Park Corner and Victoria railway station. The A2 goes to King's Cross with stops at the Kensington Hilton in Holland Park Avenue, Notting Hill Gate, Queensway, Paddington, Marble Arch and Russell Square.

If all this sounds like too much hassle, you can take a **taxi**, but it will set you back £30 or more and, if you arrive during the rush hour, could take as long as 90 minutes.

Gatwick: The most practical way into town is by the **Gatwick Express** train; this non-stop service to Victoria station (cost: £9.50) leaves every 15 minutes from 5am until 12am, and every hour for the rest of the night. Look out for the signs in your terminal. There is a bus to Victoria Coach Station called **Flightlink** (✆ (020) 8668 7261), which is cheaper but takes nearly three times as long. Don't even think about a taxi.

Stansted: Just pop down one floor, and you are on the railway platform for London Liverpool St. The journey takes 40–45 minutes and trains leave every half hour. The fare is £10.40.

London City: Bus services (tickets £5) leave for Canary Wharf in Docklands and for Liverpool St every 20 minutes or so. A taxi ride into the City of London costs around £12. There is an executive helicopter service; if you need to ask the price, don't take it.

Luton: Almost as far away from London as Stansted, and in much the same direction, the airport has no direct rail link to the city. You have to take an airport bus to the station and then take an invariably crowded Thameslink commuter train in to King's Cross (about £10).

Arriving by Air in Brussels

Taxis from Zaventem airport to the city centre cost between 1000 and 1400 BF, but taxis with an orange and white aeroplane sticker in the top right-hand corner of their windscreens offer special reduced rates, usually 25% off. It is, however, far cheaper to travel by train. Special train services run three times an hour throughout the day from around 5.40am to 11.40pm, and connect with the Gare du Nord and the Gare Centrale (some trains go on to the Gare du Midi). The journey takes 20 minutes to the Gare du Nord. A second-class return is 90 BF rising to 120 BF on weekends. There is also an hourly bus service to the Gare du Nord which takes 35 minutes; tickets are 75 BF.

Arriving by Train in London

Waterloo station is just south of the Thames and is on the **Underground**'s Northern line and Bakerloo line, either of which will take you straight into the West End in a matter of ten minutes. There is a direct link to the Underground from the international Eurostar terminal, about a five-minute walk inside the station; just follow the signs.

If you've got a lot of baggage it might be better to take a **taxi** to the centre, which will cost you from £5–£10; there's a taxi rank just as you exit the Eurostar gate. If you're taking a taxi to Waterloo from central London, make sure to specify the international terminal.

It's not a good idea to try to take a **bus** from or to Waterloo; the area just outside is a building site with the South Bank renovations and you would need to know where you were going.

Arriving by Train in Brussels

Eurostar trains arrive at the Gare du Midi/Zuid Station, which is on Line 2 of the métro network. The Pré-métro, part of the tram network that runs underground in the 'tram tunnel' on a north–south axis, also runs through the station. And it is situated at the conjunction of numerous overground tram lines (*see* map on inside back cover).

Passports, Visas and Border Formalities

London: Britain has opted not to join the eight-strong group of European countries practising an open-border policy (the so-called Schengen Group), so EU citizens will still have to bring their passports or identity cards. That means a few delays and detours (particularly at the Channel Tunnel terminus at Waterloo), but basically they can expect to breeze through immigration; there is even a separate queue for them to avoid hold-ups. Americans can expect a fair grilling, particularly at airports and particularly if you are not white. If you are a national of the United States, Canada, Australia, New Zealand, South Africa, Japan, Mexico or Switzerland, you won't need a **visa** to get into the country if you are just on holiday or on a business trip. Other nationalities should check with their local British consulate.

There are very few **customs** restrictions if you are coming from another EU country. Otherwise, the usual limits on alcohol, cigarettes and perfume apply (roughly speaking, half a dozen bottles of wine or one bottle of spirits, plus 200 cigarettes).

Brussels: UK citizens and other EU countries just need a valid passport for stays of up to 90 days. Americans, Canadians, Australians and New Zealanders need valid passports, but no visa is required. Strictly speaking you are supposed to be able to produce your passport or identity card at any time, so keep it with you.

Getting Around London

London Transport ✆ (020) 7222 1234, *www.londontransport.co.uk*

By Underground and DLR

London's **Underground** system (also known as the Tube) is 100 years old, and it shows. Creaky, unpunctual, smelly, unfriendly: it is everyone's favourite urban nightmare. The Tube is the most expensive city transport system in Europe, the most basic single adult ticket costing £1.40 (but *see* Tickets and Passes, p.7). For better or worse, though, it is still by far the quickest way to cross London and avoid the traffic, especially during office hours. Trains run from around 5.30am (7am on Sundays) until at least 11pm and as late as 1am on some lines (no service on Christmas Day).

The East End and Docklands, and from 2000 Greenwich also, are served by the **Docklands Light Railway**, or DLR, an overground monorail which links up with the Tube at Bank and Tower Hill (you can call the DLR 24-hour travel hotline for advice on journeys on ✆ (020) 7918 4000). DLR trains now run all week, until at least 11.30pm.

By Bus

London's buses are slightly cheaper than the Underground, and at least you can see trees and sky, as well as the life of the city zipping by. Since the bus system was deregulated, many different private companies have been running services all over town, but all are integrated into the London Transport network. Prices are based on the same zones as the Underground, and your best bet is to buy a Travelcard. If you plan to use the bus a lot, you should pick up a bus map, available from major Underground stations.

After midnight a large network of N-prefixed **night buses** takes over. You can get a map from Underground stations or just look on the bus stops for N numbers. The hub is Trafalgar Square. Note that One-Day Travelcards are not valid on night buses and you will have to pay.

There is a vast range of **tourist buses**, with stops all over central London. One useful one to know about is the Hop-on Hop-off, which takes you round all the main tourist sights of the centre and allows you to get on and off as many times as you like. Call ✆ (01708) 631122 for details of the route so you know where to catch it.

By Train

Overground trains around London are integrated into the London Transport system and can be useful for crossing large chunks of town, or else for accessing certain parts which the Underground neglects. Three useful services are the **Thameslink**, which starts at Luton Airport and snakes through West Hampstead, Kentish Town, King's Cross and Blackfriars through to the south London suburbs including Greenwich; the north London **Silverlink**, which starts in Richmond and goes through Kew Gardens, Hampstead and Highbury on its way through to the East End; and the quick and efficient **Waterloo and City** line between Waterloo and Bank. The rail lines are all marked on the larger Underground maps (called Journey Planners), and you don't have to pay extra if you have a Travelcard.

Information: ✆ (0345) 484950 or (020) 7222 1234.

Tickets and Passes (London)

The Underground fare system is organized in concentric zones, Zone 1 being the centre, and Zone 6 being the outermost ring including, among other things, Heathrow Airport. Pick up a map from any station and you will see that the lines are colour-coded to make them easier to follow.

The most practical kind of ticket is a £3.80 **One Day Travelcard**, which you can buy to cover as many zones as you need and which is valid on buses and overground trains as well. Daily Travelcards are available after 9.30am; weekly and monthly passes are available any time, although you'll need a passport photo to get these; Zone 1 tickets are now sold in useful **carnets** which cost £10 for 10 tickets (saving you £4). You can also buy a **Weekend Travelcard** for £5.70, less than the price of two One-Day Travelcards and valid for night buses on the first night.

Never ever travel beyond the zone or bus stop you have bought a ticket for. Even if you present yourself openly to the excess fares window, you will be liable for an instant £10 'penalty fare' (£5 on buses) and there's absolutely no sympathy to be gained from the steely staff.

By Taxi

Taxis are part of the mythology of London, perhaps because their drivers are the only people who can make sense of the great metropolitan labyrinth. Cabbies have to train for three years to take their qualifying exam, known as The Knowledge, in which they are expected to be able to locate every street, every major building and all the main tourist attractions as well as memorizing 468 basic routes. For years taxis conformed to a single sleek black design, but recently there have been some changes, notably the advent of advertising and different body colours. You can still recognize them, however, by the distinctive For Hire signs on the roof which light up in orange when the cab is free.

During the day it is easy to hail a taxi off the street, unless it's raining when they all disappear. All licensed cabs are metered. They are more expensive than in most cities, but you can be confident of getting to your destination by the quickest route. For lost property ✆ (020) 7833 0996. If you want to order a taxi, contact **Dial-A-Black-Cab**, ✆ (020) 7253 5000.

Black cabs are harder to find at night, and you may need to call a **minicab**. These tend to be cheaper, less reliable and occasionally a little hazardous. Some good ones are:

Atlas Cars, ✆ (020) 7602 1234.

Greater London Hire, ✆ (020) 8340 2450.

Town and Country Cabs, ✆ (020) 7622 6222, ✆ (020) 7622 6000, *www.taxi.co.uk*. For South and Central London: male or female drivers, as requested.

Lady Cabs, ✆ (020) 7254 3501, a specialist service run by women for women.

By Car

Traffic in London moves at an average of 11 miles an hour during the day, so you will be much better off forgetting about a car. Parking is also a huge problem. Car parks and meters are very expensive and can prove ruinous if you outstay your welcome—at least £30 for a parking ticket (or £60 if you leave it for longer than two weeks). Restrictions on parking, both on meters and on single yellow lines, vary wildly from borough to borough and catch out even switched-on Londoners by changing with no notice. If you're very unlucky you will have a nasty yellow clamp placed around one of your wheels. There is one even worse horror that could befall you, and that is having your car towed away altogether. Call ✆ (020) 7747 4747 to find out where your vehicle is and bring at least £135 in cash to the vehicle pound.

A car can nevertheless be a blessing in London, particularly for trips out of town. Familiarize yourself with the British Highway Code (available from newsagents) and take particular note of the strict drink-drive laws. You don't need to carry your driving papers with you, but if you are stopped you can be asked to show them at a police station within five days.

If you are hiring a car, you need to be over 21 and have at least one year's driving experience. Here are some addresses:

Hertz, ✆ (0990) 996699/ **Avis**, ✆ (0990) 900500, open 24 hours.

Supercars, 11c Greens End, SE18 6HX, ✆ (020) 8317 1414. Much cheaper.

On Two Wheels

The bicycle is a good mode of transport in London, if you can cope with the danger and bear the pollution. It is faster than going by car, at least during the day, and more pleasant than the Tube, especially if you make use of London's extensive parkland.

On Your Bike, 52–4 Tooley St (by London Bridge), ✆ (020) 7378 6669.

Dial-a-Bike, ✆ (020) 7828 4040, delivers to major hotels in London.

You could also telephone **The London Cycling Campaign**, ✆ (020) 7928 7220, for advice and maps of safe routes around the city.

By River

An excellent Riverbus service that used to ply the Thames all day suffered a sad demise in the summer of 1993; now you have to try your luck with a plethora of commercial companies that run services from Westminster Pier or Charing Cross Pier, both just south of Trafalgar Square. Services upriver to Greenwich and the Thames Barrier—the most attractive destinations—run every half-hour and take about 45–50 minutes (✆ (020) 7930 4097 for up-to-the-minute information). In the other direction, services downriver to Kew, Richmond and Hampton Court are more erratic and may not run more than four times a day (✆ (020) 7930 4721 for information).

Getting Around Brussels

By Métro

The Métro system in Brussels, constructed since 1965 and still being extended, has the fresh look of something new, and remains both clean and efficient. It has two lines: Line 1 crosses town on an east–west axis and Line 2 curls around the centre of the city. An additional service called the Pré-métro, which in fact is part of the tram network, runs underground in the 'tram tunnel' on a north–south axis, beneath the Boulevards Adolphe Max and Anspach.

To find your way around the Métro system you really need to consult a Métro map (there are maps posted in the stations, or see the map on the inside back cover of this guide). The direction of a train is indicated by the terminus towards which it is travelling, and this will be signalled on the platform and by a headcode (and by signs inside the carriages).

Tickets and Passes (Brussels)

Tickets for public transport in the Brussels area can be used on the tram, bus and Métro, which all form part of STIB (✆ 515 20 00). The price of an *aller simple*, for a single continuous journey, is 50 BF; this permits changes and is valid for one hour.

If you are making several journeys by public transport there is a five-journey card (*carte de cinq voyages*) for 240 BF, but the best buy is the 10-journey card (*carte de dix voyages*), which costs 320 BF. Alternatively, for 130 BF, you can buy a card that is valid for 24 hours (*carte de vingt-quatre heures*), during which time you can make as many journeys as you like. Also available from the Tourist Information Office in the Grand' Place is the Tourist Passport which will give you 24 hours' unrestricted travel and reduced admission to the city's museums and costs 220 BF. It is worth remembering that children over six years old have to pay adult prices. Single tickets and multiple journey cards are available from bus and tram drivers or at Métro stations and Brussels railway stations, at STIB information offices, at tourist offices (*see* p.191), and at newsagents displaying the STIB sign. When travelling with an STIB card, you have to validate it—which is to say, have it stamped with the time and date at the start of each part of a journey. As you board your tram or bus, or as you enter a Métro station, drop the ticket into the machine with the strip towards you, arrow downwards. The machine can tell if you are using your card to continue your journey on the same unit, or beginning a new journey. Don't be fooled that other passengers are not validating their tickets: they may well have passes.

By Tram

Brussels was once a city of trams: it grew with the tram age. Over the last two decades, however, the trams have been savagely axed and replaced by buses. This process has now more or less abated, and those tram routes that have survived look set to stay. It is a speedy and efficient way to travel—and for anyone from a city without trams it also has the novelty of its historic tradition.

The STIB public transport map shows the tram routes. Trams can be boarded only at designated tram stops (red signs). Note that they do not halt at all stops if no one is waiting to board: you can signal that you want to get off at the next stop by pressing one of the black or blue bell buttons on the wall of the tram. Trams, along with buses and the Métro system, operate from about 5.30am to midnight, but services are much reduced after 6pm at weekends.

By Bus

The bus network is now far more extensive than the tram network that it has largely usurped. Buses operate on the same ticket system as trams, and you have to validate your ticket on the bus at the start of your journey. Once you have got the hang of it, the bus system is a very effective way of getting around. The STIB public transport map marks all the routes and the stops, so it is easy to plan your journey and to feel confident about where to board and where to get off.

By Taxi

Taxis in Brussels are ordinary saloon cars with 'Taxi' written on the top. They can be hired only at a designated taxi rank (or by telephone), and cannot be hailed from the street. The fact that someone is registered as a taxi driver in Brussels does not guarantee that they know any more than just the key destinations and streets in the city: it helps to be able to supply as much information as possible yourself. Don't be surprised if your driver has to resort to a map.

A short journey will cost about 200 BF: this comprises the initial fee of 95 BF and then 38 BF per kilometre (it is advisable to check the meter on departure). It is normal to add 10–15 per cent as a tip, or round up to the nearest 50 BF.

Major Brussels taxi companies:
Autolux: ✆ 512 31 23 or 411 41 42
Taxis Bleus: ✆ 268 00 00
Taxis Oranges: ✆ 349 43 43
Taxis Verts: ✆ 349 49 49

By Car

Driving in Brussels is no more hair-raising than it is in any other major European city. Two points to watch out for are *priorité de droite* (from the right) and trams. Trams have priority and you have to get out of their way if you can. These days there are fewer roads where trams and cars jostle for position, but where they do, beware!

Parking is comparatively easy, especially in outlying districts. In the centre of town there is a fair number of underground car parks (follow the blue P signs) and parking meters (which take 5 BF and 20 BF coins).

On Two Wheels

Although cycling is a national sport and you will see *pelotons* of sleek cyclists on the open road, cyclists in Brussels are a rarity. This is probably an example of evolutionary adaptation: cyclists simply do not survive long enough to reproduce. Not recommended. If, however, you are determined to cycle, you could make use of a network of 'green' car-free routes devised by the green party Ecolo. Apply **Ecolo**, 12 Rue Charles VII, 1030 Brussels (150 BF). Bicycles can be hired from **Pro Velo**, 15 Rue de Londres, ✆ 502 73 55 (closed Mon) for about 100 BF per hour and 400 BF per day. Pro Velo also organizes guided cycling tours in groups of up to 23 persons, visiting the city centre, Art Nouveau houses, the parks and outlying woods and castles.

On Foot

Brussels is a compact city and most of the main museums and sights are within walking distance of the centre, the Grand' Place. There is no shortage of public transport around the centre, but walking is often quicker and more rewarding.

One word of warning: in Brussels pedestrian crossings appear to be there merely as a suggestion to drivers. Do not assume cars will stop at them for you. Given enough distance, drivers will reluctantly give way once you are on the crossing—but don't count on it. Foreign drivers also take note: other drivers do not expect you to stop at pedestrian crossings. If you do so in traffic, you are liable to incur the wrath of the driver behind you, if not an accident.

By Horse-drawn Carriage

During the summer months until September, and at weekends at either end of the season, authentic horse-drawn carriages are available for short tours of the city centre. Starting from Rue Charles Buls (off the Grand' Place), the usual tour goes to the Manneken-Pis, then around to the Bourse and across the Grand' Place itself. A 20-minute journey costs around 500 BF (for the carriage, irrespective of the number of passengers).

London: Introduction

> *Oh thou, resort and mart of all the earth*
> *Chequer'd with all complexions of mankind*
> *And spotted with all crimes, in whom I see*
> *Much that I love and more that I admire,*
> *And all that I abhor...*
>
> William Cowper, *The Task, Book III*
> (1785)

London, like all great cities, has a habit of going through drastic mood swings: grey, worthy and dull one minute, hip and ultra-modern the next. Down its long history it has been accused of everything from provincialism to irredeemable sinfulness; at times it has positively creaked under the weight of its own impossible size and complexity. At others, it has been hailed as everything a city could ever hope to be: a beacon of wealth, liberty, cosmopolitanism and artistic flair. And so, just when it was being written off as the crumbling capital of a dead empire, London has come roaring back to life. Freed from the shackles of empire and the bitter ideological divisions of the Thatcher years, it is enjoying a renaissance of extraordinary dimensions. London has recovered a belief in itself that would have seemed inconceivable even a decade ago, when gloom was perennially written on the hangdog faces of its citizens and the streets emptied as soon as the pubs closed. Now, in Soho or Notting Hill or Islington, you can barely move for people thronging to the latest designer shop, the newest art opening, or the hottest ethnic restaurant. The capital is being redefined by a new, highly creative generation of artists and designers iconoclastic enough to break down the fusty London of the past and rebuild it in their own image. Suddenly, everything seems possible and Londoners are embracing the changes with barely a whiff of scepticism or critical distance. The city invents and discards fads at an astonishing rate: rocket and shaved parmesan salad, the innovative food obsession of the mid-'90s, is already looking passé, along with Damien Hirst, Oasis and Vivienne Westwood. Old definitions no longer fit the new trends: sculpture and painting have given way to new mediums such as video art; the erstwhile household design guru Terence Conran, meanwhile, has moved beyond the restaurant business into gastrodomes, veritable palaces of food consumption in custom-made settings like an old tyre factory, say, or a sports car showroom. This new London has even contrived to pretend that the weather is better: pavement cafés and al fresco dining are the new watchwords, along with Italian coffee and Mediterranean clothing styles. No city in Europe is so desired, or so desirable.

Be warned, however. Amidst this creative frenzy, the old caveats about London still apply. It may be the most exciting city in Europe, but it is not the most beautiful, nor the easiest to get around. Indeed, there are times when it seems like one of those eccentric English aristocrats who deliberately dress in rags and forget to wash for weeks at a stretch. A city of its size is inevitably stricken with great swathes of dullness, not to mention air pollution, gridlocked traffic, creaky public transport, damp, ageing houses and all the other banal horrors of modern urban living. This is not a city that shouts its beauties from the rooftops, and many visitors who expect too much too quickly come away with a sense of bewildered disappointment.

There is an art to exploring London; you cannot only do the rounds of its celebrated sights and museums and say you have seen it all. You have to engage on a personal level, ferreting out neighbourhoods you feel at home in, finding little backstreets you can admire without necessarily looking for them in a guidebook, discovering the museums and theatres and pubs that give you a sense of personal satisfaction. Two visitors meeting after a week in London might discover that one had hung around wine bars in Kensington, taken a river trip to Hampton Court and shopped at Harrods, while the other had sought out Freud's house, done some sketching in the Tate Gallery and sat in pub theatres at lunchtime. They would not have visited the same city at all, but they would both have been to London.

Once you have got over the sheer vastness and inconvenience, once you have traced out your route around the labyrinth, the sense of diversity and discovery can be immensely liberating. Nobody can know all of London—not poets, not politicians, not even guidebook writers. You have to make up your own version of it. Out of the chaos you produce a personalized sense of order, your own map of the city. Pop out of an Underground station at random and you may well find yourself in the sort of anonymous urban wasteland the city's millions of commuters pass through every morning and night; it is just possible, however, that you will discover a charming unknown corner of the metropolis you can call your very own.

Orientation

The wit and raconteur Max Beerbohm once said that showing a visitor round London made him feel like Virgil accompanying Dante through the circles of hell. That may not sound like much of a compliment, but in one respect at least the observation is acute: the best way to orient yourself is to picture the city as a series of concentric circles. On the outside is limbo, that endless stretch of characterless suburbia that makes no sense to anyone except a mapmaker or a statistician; then comes the ring of inner suburbs, a zone of varied and often unexpected pleasures; finally, at the centre, is London's diabolical heart.

The centre is of course the part with most history, but that does not mean that it is necessarily the most interesting or most enjoyable to visit. What is central geographically may be only peripheral in terms of interest, and vice versa. As in Dante's *Inferno*, appearances can be deceptive. Certainly you should make sure you get to the National Gallery and St Paul's, but it would be a mistake to skip Hampstead, Greenwich or Kew just because they are not slap bang in the centre of town. In the same way, it would be foolish to spend too long in Mayfair or the City just because they happen to be where they are.

The Pick of London in a Weekend

There's nothing more dreary than spending a week in London going round museum after museum. Variety should be the watchword, whether this is your first time in the city or your 50th. Treat the following not as a list of must-sees to check off one by one, but rather a rich menu from which to pick the items that suit you best on the day:

First-time visitors

National Gallery, Westminster Abbey and Tate Gallery, Soho, British Museum, St Paul's, the South Bank, Victoria and Albert Museum, Portobello Market, Greenwich (including a boat ride down there).

Occasional visitors

Banqueting House and Houses of Parliament, the John Soane Museum, the Clink and Old St Thomas's Operating Theatre, the Wallace Collection, Holland Park, Hampstead, Kew Gardens, Hampton Court.

Residents

Spencer House and the Queen's Chapel, Westminster Hall and, if you can, the Foreign Office, Jeremy Bentham's corpse, St Etheldreda, Kensington Palace, Leighton House, Carlyle's House, Highgate Cemetery, Rotherhithe. Note: some of these are pretty tough to get into, but the effort will be well rewarded.

Not been back lately

To catch a whiff of the extraordinary changes in London, all you really have to do is stand in the middle of Soho in mid-evening and marvel at the variety, exuberance and sheer numbers of the people around you. Eat at Terence Conran's futuristic gastrodome, Mezzo, or grab some conveyor-belt sushi served by robots on Poland Street. Further afield, there is the irrepressible trendiness of Notting Hill. For sightseeing, the South Bank is a must, particularly the newly refurbished Oxo Tower, the rebuilt Globe Theatre and the developments at Butlers Wharf—this is the spirit of the new London. Look out, too, for looming Millennium projects and quirky new places like the Aquarium at County Hall.

Not been back in years

In addition to the above, you'll probably want to have a sniff round the Docklands, not just the monster tower at Canary Wharf, but also less obvious novelties like the riverfront at Rotherhithe. Go to the action-packed Science Museum which has changed beyond recognition. If you remember the strict old licensing laws, you'll get a buzz just sitting in a pub mid-afternoon and ordering a drink. As for eating, just about anywhere should come as a startlingly pleasant surprise; try a modern riverside location (the Blueprint Café, Butlers Wharf, or Canteen, Chelsea Harbour).

Can't stand all this new-fangled stuff

If what you want is good, old-fashioned London, St James's and Mayfair are the places to start. No doubt you'll stay in a favourite quiet hotel in South Kensington, or even one of the posher establishments in Mayfair, but that shouldn't stop you dropping in on Brown's or the Ritz for tea—ideal stopping-off points during shopping sprees on Jermyn Street (bespoke clothes, as well as marmalade and Earl Grey at Fortnum's). Once you've exhausted sights like Buckingham Palace and the Wallace Collection, you might want to stroll around Chelsea, meet the eccentric pensioners at the Royal Hospital, or even venture out to the fine Adam houses at Syon Park and Osterley. Back in town, there are cocktails at the Café Royal and enticing dinner options around Covent Garden at Simpson's, The Ivy and Rules.

Romantic London

Okay, this isn't Paris or Venice, but London is more romantic than you might think. Anthony Minghella's film Truly, Madly, Deeply highlighted the heart-wrenching pleasures of Kenwood (those great views of the metropolis over the Heath) and the pavement cafés on the South Bank (don't forget the foyer jazz and cosy book-browsing possibilities inside the National Theatre, either). For dreamy walks, Holland Park or the riverside at Richmond and Twickenham are perfect. Hampstead is London's dinkiest neighbourhood—visit Keats' house to relive the poet's romance with Fanny Brawne, and find yourselves a quiet nook in the atmospheric Holly Bush pub. Otherwise try kite-flying on Parliament Hill (more good views as well as bracing air), or the canal walks and Georgian rows of Canonbury (plus the romantic association of penniless Lord Compton and the rich local merchant's daughter). Hazlitt's is a charming, centrally located hotel, while Clarke's (on Kensington Church St) or Lemonia (in Camden) make fine settings for a romantic dinner.

Calendar of Events	16
Consulates in London	18
Crime and Police	18
Disabled Travellers	19
Electricity	20
Health	20
London for Free	20
Maps	21
Money and Banks	21
National Holidays	22
Opening Hours	22

London: Practical A–Z

Post Offices	22
Pronunciation	23
Religion	23
Smoking	24
Students and Pensioners	24
Telephones	24
Time	25
Tipping	25
Toilets	25
Tourist Information	26

Calendar of Events

Actual dates for nearly all the events listed below change every year. Numbers for checking are given where possible:

January

1 January	*New Year's day Parade* Display of 6,000 real-American majorettes starting from Parliament Square at 12pm and finishing in Berkeley Square at 3pm.
Early January	Harrods' after-Christmas sale starts.
Mid-January to early February	*Chinese New Year* celebrations around Gerrard St in Soho. Lots of food and colourful floats.

February

Shrove Tuesday *Soho and Great Spitalfields Pancake Day Races*. Sprints down Carnaby Street and Spitalfields, with participants tossing pancakes in a pan; ✆ (020) 7375 0441.

April

1 April	Check newspapers for April Fool's Day hoaxes.
Sat before Easter	*Oxford and Cambridge Boat Race*. Teams from the rival universities row their hearts out from Putney to Mortlake; ✆ (020) 7730 3488.
Easter Sunday	*Easter Day Parade* in Battersea Park, complete with funfair and sideshows.
Mid-April	*London Marathon* from Blackheath to The Mall; ✆ (020) 7620 4117 for details of route and how to enter.
Ascension Day	*Beating the Bounds*. Boys of St Dunstan's beat on the City's boundary markers with willow sticks in an ancient ritual. Starts at 3pm at All Hallows' by the Tower.

May

Early May	*Museums Week*—special events at 850 museums; www.museumsweek.co.uk
Late May	*Chelsea Flower Show* at the Royal Hospital Gardens. Funfairs on Hampstead Heath, Blackheath and Alexandra Park on Spring Bank Holiday Monday, Enquiries ✆ (020) 7630 7422, Tickets ✆ (0990) 344 444.

June

First Saturday	*Derby* horse race at Epsom racecourse, Surrey.
Early June	*Coin Street Festival*, Gabriel's Wharf, London SE1 (*see* p.83): buskers and free street performances. *Greenwich Festival*: concerts, theatre and children's events, plus fireworks on the opening night. Also, *Hampton Court Festival*, opera music and dance; ✆ (020) 7344 4444 (*see* pp.34–5). Also, *Beating the Retreat*, floodlit evening display by Queen's Household Division outside Buckingham Palace.
Second Saturday	*Trooping the Colour*. The Queen's Guards in a birthday parade for Ma'am. The date is chosen by the palace and is usually the second.

June (cont'd)	Saturday, but it does vary. It's difficult to get a ticket but people line The Mall to watch; ✆ (020) 7414 2497. *Spitalfields Festival.* Classical music in Christ Church, plus guided walks of the area; ✆ (020) 7375 0441.
Mid-June	*Royal Ascot.* Society horse races at Ascot in Berkshire.
Late June	*Henley Royal Regatta.* Rowers row on the Thames while very posh spectators get sozzled in their champagne tents.
Late June–early July	*Wimbledon* tennis championships. Box office ✆ (020) 8944 1066.
Late June to July	*City of London Festival*: classical concerts around the City; ✆ (020) 7377 0540.
June to August	*Summer Exhibition* at the Royal Academy (*see* p.72). More than 1,000 works by living artists.
June to September	*Kenwood Lakeside Concerts.* Open-air concerts at the top of Hampstead Heath every Saturday. Magical if the weather's good; ✆ (020) 7973 3427.

July

	Gay Pride Day, first week of July on Clapham Common, Also, *Hampton Court Flower Show;* ✆ (020) 7821 3042 (*see* p.34).
Mid-July	*Royal Military Tattoo* Military pageants in Earl's Court; ✆ (020) 7799 2323. Also, *Doggett's Coat and Badge Race*, a rowing contest from London Bridge to Cadogan Pier.
July to September	*The Proms* in the Albert Hall; ✆ (020) 7589 8212 (*see* p.28).

August

August to September	Buckingham Palace open to the public.
Last Sunday and Monday	*Notting Hill Carnival.* Steel bands, dancing and general Caribbean fun, occasionally broken up by police, around Portobello Rd and Ladbroke Grove (*see* p.90).

September

Mid-September	*Chelsea Antiques Fair*, ✆ (01444) 482514.
Third week	*Open House Weekend*, for info at 60p a minute: ✆ (0891) 600061. Houses and buildings which are normally closed to the public open up for free, also walking tours.
Late September	*Clog and Apron Race.* A sprint through Kew by gardening students in strange attire; ✆ (020) 8940 1171.

October

First Sunday	*Pearly Harvest Festival* at St Martin-in-the-Fields (*see* p.65). Lots of folklore cockneys in their button-splashed coats playing ukeleles.

November

5 November	*Bonfire Night.* Fireworks and bonfires, plus plenty of booze, in parks all over London (Highbury Fields and Battersea Park are good venues, but telephone the London Tourist Board ✆ (0839) 123456 or check

Early November	*Time Out* for details) to commemorate Guy Fawkes's attempt to blow up parliament in 1605.
	State Opening of Parliament. The Queen sets out from Buckingham Palace for Westminster where she reads out the government's programme for the forthcoming year. Crowds follow her around. Date varies a lot: check on ✆ (020) 7219 3107.
First Sunday	*London to Brighton Veteran Car Run.* Starts in Hyde Park; ✆ (01753) 681736 for details.
	London Film Festival, based at the NFT on the South Bank (*see* p.82) but with showings all over town; ✆ (020) 7815 1323.
Second Saturday	*Lord Mayor's Show.* The new Lord Mayor goes on a grand procession through the City in his 18th-century gilded coach. Most people stand around St Paul's to watch, but you can sit down if you ask the Pagent Master: ✆ (01992) 505 306.
Sunday nearest 11 November	*Remembrance Day Service* to commemorate war dead at the Cenotaph in Whitehall.
November to December	Christmas lights go on in Oxford Street, Regent Street, Bond Street and Trafalgar Square.
December	
31 December	New Year's celebrations beneath the Christmas tree in Trafalgar Square (*see* pp.45–6).

Consulates in London

You can always find the number of your consulate or embassy by calling directory enquiries (✆ 192). Here are a few:

US Embassy, 24 Grosvenor Square, ✆ (020) 7499 9000, open Mon–Fri 9–6. There is a 24-hour helpline for US citizens.

Australian High Commission, Australia House, The Strand, ✆ (020) 7379 4334, open Mon–Fri 9–5.15.

Canadian High Commission, 38 Grosvenor St, ✆ (020) 7258 6600, open Mon–Fri 8am–11am, with 24-hour telephone helpline.

Crime and Police

The British downmarket newspapers are full of lurid crime stories, usually involving children being attacked or abducted, or policemen being shot by crazed drug-dealers. Something of a siege mentality has set in, which is curious because serious crime in London has been stable for several decades. You won't be at greater risk in London than in any other biggish city in Europe; the greatest hazard is petty theft and pickpocketing, for which the usual precautions apply. Although usage is unmistakably on the increase, drugs are yet to become the kind of overwhelming crime problem they are in the United States or parts of southern Europe; firearms are extremely uncommon and even police officers do not carry them. Don't hang around lonely neighbourhoods late at night—Hackney or Tottenham spring to mind—and don't leave valuables in your hotel room. Women have a far more hassle-free time in London than in Rome or Madrid, and it is accepted as normal for a woman to be out on her own. They should watch out on the Underground, however, particularly late at night.

You'll find the authorities sometimes jumpy about the risk of terrorist attack, particularly in the City: waste-bins have been removed from the Underground, automatic luggage lockers have been taken out of railway stations and many buildings bristle with security guards. Don't let reports of terrorist bombs put you off coming to London, though. You are more likely to die on the aircraft into London than in an attack once you get here; and you stand a far greater chance of being run over outside your house than ever dying on an aircraft.

The police are usually friendly enough, although you might encounter suspicion or idle prejudice if you are Irish or black. If you need to go to the police to report a theft or other crime, simply visit your nearest station and you should receive a civil hearing—though you probably won't get your stolen goods back. In case of emergency, dial either ✆ 999 or ✆ 112. If you yourself get picked up by the police, you must insist, if you feel it necessary, on calling your embassy or consulate, or a lawyer if you know one. Keep your cool and remain polite at all times. Be particularly careful how you drive around Christmas time, as the drink-drive police are out in force.

Finally, to retrieve **lost property**, try the London Transport Lost Property Office at 200 Baker St, open weekday mornings only, ✆ (020) 7486 2496; or the Black Cab Lost Property Office, 15 Penton St, Islington, ✆ (020) 7833 0996, open Mon–Fri 9–4.

Disabled Travellers

London is reasonably wheelchair-conscious, certainly by comparison with the rest of Europe, and most of the major sights have proper access and help on hand if necessary. There are still problems, however, with the transport system and many theatres and cinemas. The London Tourist Board has a special leaflet which you can find in tourist offices called *Information for Wheelchair Users Visiting London* which covers hotels, tourists sights and transport. A fuller guide is *Access in London*, a booklet available at Books Etc on Charing Cross Road or by post from the Access Project at 39 Bradley Gardens, London W13 8HE (a donation of £7.50 for printing costs is requested). London Transport publishes *Access to the Underground* with information on lift-access to Tubes, available free from Tube stations or by post from the London Transport Unit for Disabled Passengers, 172 Buckingham Palace Road, London SW1W 9TN, ✆ (020) 7918 3312. Otherwise, bear the following addresses in mind:

Artsline, ✆ (020) 7388 2227. Free information on access to arts venues.
Holiday Care Service, ✆ (01293) 774535. Advice on hotels.
Shape, ✆ (020) 7700 8138. Offers cheap tickets for arts events.
Tripscope, ✆ (020) 8994 9294. Telephone helpline for people touring in London and the whole of Britain.

Finally **The Greater London Association for Disabled People** publishes a free *London Disability Guide*, available by post from 336 Brixton Road, London SW9 7AA.

Electricity

Britain uses three-prong square-pin plugs quite unlike anything else in Europe or North America. So far, the British government has resisted conforming to the rest of Europe on safety grounds—all British plugs have detachable fuses of three, five or 13 amps. So you will need an adaptor for any electrical device you bring in from abroad. The airport is as good a place as any to find one. Note also the electricity supply is 240 volts AC.

Health

Citizens of the European Union and some Commonwealth countries enjoy free medical care in Britain under the state National Health Service. The days when you could get free treatment on production of just a passport are probably over, so you'll need to fill out the appropriate paperwork before you leave home (in the EU the form is called an E111). Thus armed, the only things you will have to pay for are prescriptions and visits to the optician or dentist, although these should not cost more than a few pounds.

Anyone else, and that includes Americans, Africans, Indians and Canadians, should take out medical insurance.

If you need urgent medical treatment, you should head for one of the casualty departments (what in the United States are known as emergency rooms) of the major hospitals. These include St Thomas's on the South Bank, University College Hospital on Gower St in Bloomsbury, Guy's in Southwark, the Charing Cross Hospital on Fulham Palace Rd, Bart's in Smithfield and the Royal Free in Hampstead. You can call an ambulance by dialling ✆ 999 or ✆ 112.

Note also the following numbers:

Bliss Chemist, 5 Marble Arch. Stays open until midnight every day. Details of other late-opening chemists are available from police stations.

Dental Emergency Care Service, ✆ (020) 7935 4486. An advisory service open 24 hours which will direct you to the nearest clinic for emergency dental care.

London Rape Crisis Centre, ✆ (020) 7837 1600. Open 10am to 10pm at weekends and 6pm to 10 pm Mon-Fri.

Samaritans, ✆ (020) 7734 2800. Helpline for any emotional problems, open 24 hours.

Family Planning Association, ✆ (020) 7837 4044. Will tell you where your nearest family planning clinic is and give you advice on morning-after pills, abortions and so on.

London for Free

You'll hear plenty of moans about the high cost of living in London, so here as an antidote is a list of things to do without spending a single penny:

Museums and galleries: Many of London's best museums have traditionally been free, but it is turning into a losing battle because of wavering government commitment to the necessary subsidies. Museums still hanging on by their fingernails include the National Gallery, National Portrait Gallery, The RIBA Heinz Gallery, Tate Gallery (although it is considering charging for the new Museum of Modern Art at Bankside), British Museum, Dulwich Picture Gallery, Bethnal Green Museum of Childhood, The Percival David Foundation for Chinese Art, The

Royal College of Art, William Morris Gallery, Keats' House and the National Army Museum. The Victoria and Albert Museum, Museum of London, Natural History Museum, Science Museum and Imperial War Museum all waive their charge from 4.30pm–5.50pm.

Other sights: Churches, with the exception of Westminster Abbey and St Paul's Cathedral, are all free. So, too, are the Guildhall, the Changing of the Guard outside Buckingham Palace, court cases at The Old Bailey or The Royal Courts of Justice on the Strand, the Sunday afternoon haranguing sessions at Speakers' Corner and the more regular haranguing sessions at the Houses of Parliament. London's wonderful riverside walks and parks—St James's, Battersea Park, the 19th-century dinosaurs in Crystal Palace Park, Hampstead Heath, Hyde Park and Regent's Park—are always free. So also are the beautiful cemeteries in Kensal Green, Highgate, Brompton and the Pet Cemetery in Hyde Park.

Shopping: Some of the fancier delicatessens in Soho and St James's (for example, the cheese sellers Paxton and Whitfield in Jermyn Street) will give away free nibbles, although you are under some pressure to purchase something in return. Food markets (try Berwick Street for starters) sometimes knock down the price of fruit and vegetables at the end of the day so far that they are as good as free.

Entertainment: There are free foyer concerts at the National Theatre and Barbican in the early evening. Covent Garden boasts plenty of street theatre and music, although you should offer something as the hat comes round. If you turn up to concert or theatre venues at the interval, you will often find people leaving and if you ask nicely they will give you their tickets. Another option in the summer is to go up to Kenwood on Hampstead Heath on a Saturday evening. You can sit on the rolling hills and listen to the outdoor concerts there without actually paying to get in.

Maps

London is one city where wandering around clutching a map will not automatically mark you out as a visitor; few Londoners venture out of familiar territory without a copy of the *London A–Z Street Atlas*, an inch-thick book of maps with an index of street names to help you find your destination. Bus and Tube maps are available from most main Underground stations; the large Journey Planner maps show both Tube and British Rail links. Cyclists will find the *Central London Cyclists' Map* a helpful guide to the quickest, safest and most pleasant routes through London's traffic mayhem. Published by the London Cycling Campaign, it can be bought from their office at 228 Great Guildford Business Square, 30 Great Guildford St, London SE1 0HS, ✆ (020) 7928 7220 and from some bookshops and cycle shops.

Many other maps can be found at London's largest specialist map shop, **Stanford's**, 12–14 Long Acre, Covent Garden.

Money and Banks

The currency in Britain is the pound sterling, divided into 100 pence. You'll come across notes worth £5, £10, £20 and £50, and coins worth 1, 2, 5, 10, 20, 50 pence, £1 and £2. London is also fully up to speed on credit card technology, and many shops, restaurants and hotels will accept Visa, Mastercard or American Express for all but the smallest purchases.

Minimum banking hours are Mon–Fri 9.30am–3.30pm, although many banks in Central London stay open later and, in some cases, on Saturday morning too. Most branches have automatic cash dispensers open 24 hours a day; check the stickers to see if your card and usual PIN number will be accepted, although if you don't have a British card you can expect your bank to charge a commission fee for any transaction.

You can change travellers' cheques at any bank or bureau de change, but remember to bring a passport or similar ID along with you. By and large, the big banks offer a better rate and lower commission fees, but shop around. If you need non-British currency, *bureaux de change* will be more likely to stock it. Try:

American Express, 6 Haymarket, ✆ (020) 7930 4411.

Chequepoint, 548 Oxford St, and branches, ✆ (020) 7723 1005.

Thomas Cook, Victoria Station, Marble Arch and many other branches, ✆ (020) 7828 4442.

National Holidays

With the exception of Christmas and New Year's Day, Britain's national holidays, known as **bank holidays**, shift slightly every year to ensure they fall on a Monday. This avoids being 'cheated' out of holidays, as happens in continental Europe when they fall on the weekend, but it also leads to the absurdity of May Day being celebrated as late as 7 May. Banks and many businesses close down on bank holidays, but quite a few shops and most tourist attractions stay open. Public transport theoretically runs a Sunday service, but in practice tends to be very threadbare. The full list is: New Year's Day (plus the following Monday if it falls on a weekend), Good Friday, Easter Monday, May Day (first Monday in May), Spring Bank Holiday (last Monday in May), Summer Bank Holiday (last Monday in August), Christmas Day and the next day, known as Boxing Day (plus 27 December if one of them falls on a weekend).

Opening Hours

Traditionally, shops and offices stay open from around 9 to 5.30 or 6—significantly earlier than the rest of Europe. Pubs and bars still have fairly strict licensing rules and many of them will not serve alcohol after 11pm. Late opening for shops is becoming more and more common, however, particularly on Wednesdays and Thursdays, and Sunday trading is much more flexible than in the past: areas like Queensway and the Edgware Road, Hampstead, Greenwich, Tottenham Court Road and even most of the Oxford Street department stores are completely worth visiting.

Post Offices

Post offices are generally open Mon–Fri 9–5.30 and Sat 9–noon; avoid going at lunchtime as they can get very crowded. They are marked on most London maps (in the A–Z, for example, by a black star). You will be able to buy stamps at many newsagents'. Two of the biggest post offices are at 24 King William IV St next to Trafalgar Square (*open Mon–Sat 8–8*) and at King Edward St near St Paul's Cathedral. Both have stamp shops and a *poste restante* service, as well as a very useful mail collection on Sunday evenings.

Postcodes: London postcodes are fairly confusing, and rely on an intimate knowledge of city geography to be intelligible. Postcodes begin with a direction (W for West, WC for West Central, N for North, NW for Northwest, and so on) and a number from 1 to 28. The full postcode then adds a letter immediately after the number, followed by a space, a number and two more letters. So a postcode might read EC1R 3ER—gobbledygook to anyone but a post office computer. This book uses postcodes sparingly, preferring to indicate the geographical district.

Pronunciation

Modern English spelling was standardized at the end of the 18th century by a small group of educationalists who evidently thought it would be hilarious to make pronunciation as difficult as possible for the uninitiated. Foreign tourists are forever inviting ridicule by asking for Glawsister Road or South-walk; it is hardly their fault if they are merely following the written word. Here is a survival guide to some of London's more common spelling anomalies:

Written	Spoken
Balham	Bal'm
Berkeley Square	Barkly Square
Berwick St	**Ber**rick Street
Cadogan (Square or Guides)	Cad**ugg**an
Charing Cross	Charring Cross
Cheyne Walk	Chainy Walk
Chiswick	Chizzick
Cholmondeley Walk	Chumly Walk
Clapham	Clap'm
Dulwich	Dull Itch
Gloucester Road	Gloster Road
Greenwich	Gren Itch
Grosvenor Place	Grove-ner Place
Holborn	Hoe Burn
Leicester Square	Lester Square
London	Lun Don
Southwark	Suth'k
Thames	Tems
Wapping	Wopping
Woolwich	Wool Itch

Religion

The state religion in Britain is Anglicanism, a peculiar hybrid of Protestant theology and Catholic ritual that developed after Henry VIII broke with the Roman Church to divorce his first wife, Catherine of Aragon. The biggest **Anglican** churches are St Paul's Cathedral, which has the finest organ in London, and Westminster Abbey. If you want to attend a service, a smaller church may be more to your liking. Leaf through some of the churches in the index for ideas. The biggest **Catholic churches** are Westminster Cathedral (off Victoria St) and the Brompton Oratory near the South Kensington museums. A more intimate place is St Etheldreda's in Ely Place off Holborn Circus.

London also has a sizeable **Jewish community**, concentrated around Golders Green and Stamford Hill in north London. For information about services and activities contact the

Liberal Jewish Synagogue, 28 St John's Wood Road, NW8, ✆ (020) 7286 5181; West London Synagogue (Reform), 33 Seymour Place, W1, ✆ (020) 7723 4404; or the United Synagogue (Orthodox), Adler House, 735 High Road, N12, ✆ (020) 8343 8989.

The Pakistani immigrants of the 1950s, supplemented by Bengalis, Indians and Arabs from many countries, form the backbone of the **Islamic community**. The London Central Mosque at 146 Park Road near Regent's Park, ✆ (020) 7724 3363, is a magnificent building which also contains a library and nursery school. Another popular place for Friday prayers is the East London Mosque at 84–98 Whitechapel Road, ✆ (020) 7247 1357.

For other denominations, note the following addresses:

London Baptist Association, 1 Merchant St, Bow, ✆ (020) 8980 6818.

The Buddhist Society, 58 Eccleston Square, Pimlico, ✆ (020) 7834 5858.

Evangelical Alliance, Whitefield House, 186 Kennington Park Rd, ✆ (020) 7723 4787.

Greek Orthodox Cathedral, Aghia Sophia, Moscow Rd, Bayswater, ✆ (020) 7229 7260.

Hindu Centre, 7 Cedars Rd, Stratford, ✆ (020) 8534 8879.

Central Church of World Methodism, Central Hall, Storeys Gate, Westminster, ✆ (020) 7222 8010.

Assemblies of God Pentecostal Church, 141 Harrow Rd, ✆ (020) 7286 9261.

Religious Society of Friends (Quakers), Friends House, 173–77 Euston Road, ✆ (020) 7387 3601.

Smoking

Britain has caught on to the anti-smoking craze in a big way, and you will find total bans in theatres, cinemas, museums, buses and Underground stations. Most restaurants have non-smoking areas, and some bars and pubs are introducing a similar partition. If you are invited to someone's home, ask in advance if smoking will be tolerated. It is considered quite normal to send guests wanting a puff into the garden or street.

Students and Pensioners

Students and pensioners are entitled to discounts on transport passes, air and rail travel and entry to many museums and shows. You should have some appropriate ID; in the case of students, an ISIC card is the most practical and is recognized worldwide. Students with queries should address themselves to the University of London Union (ULU) in Malet St behind the British Museum, ✆ (020) 7580 9551.

Telephones

In this era of privatisation and information superhighways, telecommunications is becoming a highly competitive field, with more servers offering their services all the time. The two biggest companies remain British Telecom, the former national monopoly privatized in 1984, and Mercury, its most prominent competitor. Watch out whose phone you use if you buy a phonecard (they are company-specific but widely available, for example from newsagents). Cash, of course, works fine anywhere. For prices and information on cheap times to call, check with your local post office (the rates are constantly changing). Obviously, though, evenings and weekends are cheaper, particularly for international calls.

London phone numbers come with the prefix (020), which until April 2000 you must include even when dialling within the local area. Anyone calling from abroad must dial the country code 44, and then the prefix but without the first 0.

You can reach directory enquiries on ✆ 192. The general operator's number is 100, the international operator is on 155 and international directory enquiries are on 153. The international dialling code is 00, followed by the country code in question (1 for the United States and Canada, 353 for Ireland, 33 for France, 39 for Italy, 49 for Germany, 61 for Australia, 64 for New Zealand). You'll find a vast range of services in the phone book, from a speaking clock to an alarm call service. These are rather expensive, and you'll probably spend less buying a basic clock of your own. The emergency number for police, ambulance, or fire brigade is either ✆ 999 or ✆ 112.

Finally, Britain has peculiar telephone jacks that are wider than the US variety. If you need to plug in a telephone or computer, make sure you buy an adaptor, available at decent-sized general stores.

Time

Britain is one hour behind the rest of western Europe, just to be difficult. During the winter (roughly the end of October to the third week of March) it follows Greenwich Mean Time; in the summer it follows British Summer Time which is one hour ahead of GMT. After years of poor synchronisation, Britain has at last agreed to change its clocks at the same time as the rest of Europe and North America. New York is 5 hours behind London time, San Francisco 8 hours behind, while Tokyo and Sydney are 10 hours ahead.

Tipping

Britain does not have the United States' established tipping code, but 10–15 per cent is considered polite in restaurants, taxis, hairdressers' and the posher hotels.

Toilets

The old-fashioned underground public toilets are disappearing fast—and with good reason, given their dubious hygiene record and reputation for attracting gay men on the prowl for casual sex. In their stead you will find free-standing automatic 'Super-Loos' which are coin-operated (20p) and smell of cheap detergent (there is one, for example, in Leicester Square). Generally speaking, you'll have a more salubrious experience in pubs, bars and restaurants. If you don't want to buy anything, just pop in to the toilets discreetly, and nobody should give you a hard time.

Tourist Information

London is one of the tourist brochure capitals of the world; show one faint sign of interest and you will be inundated in glossy paper. The main tourist offices, which can also help you find accommodation, can be found at the Underground station for Heathrow Terminals 1, 2 and 3; at Liverpool St Underground station; on the forecourt of Victoria Station; and in the basement of Selfridge's department store on Oxford St. Many districts also have local tourist information offices, which can be excellent and provide guides to show you round for the appropriate fee. The centres at Greenwich (✆ (020) 8858 6376), Islington (✆ (020) 7278 8787) and Richmond (✆ (020) 8940 9125) also have accommodation services, but often don't even try to help you in high season. You'll have to visit their offices, as none of them takes phone bookings The London Tourist Board has a recorded telephone service with up-to-date information (© (0839) 123456); it is, however, rather expensive (up to 48p a minute, so look in the phone book or call (020) 7971 0026 first to find out exactly which recording you want to access). The Tourist Board also has a website on *www.LondonTown.com* with details on restaurants, shops, 3D maps and current attractions.

For more unusual tours of the city, contact the following: Supersky Trips, © (0345) 023842: panoramic views from a 400ft-high balloon tethered in Vauxhall Spring Gardens (open 10–dusk, seven days a week: £12 or £7.50 for children, for 15 mins); Open Top Taxi Tours, © (01525) 290800 (£15 for 2 hours if there are five of you, but £75 if you are alone): excellent tours of London in convertible taxis kitted out with sound systems, mini-fridges and instant cameras; Big City Scenic Flights, © (01275) 810767: expensive aeroplane flights 1000ft over London with in-flight commentary. There are any number of other guided tours, including guided walks. They are listed at tourist offices and in the pages of *Time Out.*

London: Essential Sights

Albert Hall and Memorial	28
Aquarium	28
British Museum	29
Buckingham Palace	32
Globe Theatre	33
Hampton Court	34
Houses of Parliament and Big Ben	35
Kensington Palace	37
Millennium Dome	38
National Gallery	38
Natural History Museum	39
Science Museum	39
St Paul's Cathedral	40
Tate Gallery	42
10, Downing Street	43
Tower Bridge	44
Tower of London	44
Trafalgar Square	45
Victoria and Albert Museum	46
Westminster Abbey	49

Albert Hall and Albert Memorial

Albert Hall

Kensington Gore; ⊖ South Kensington, High Street Kensington; bus 9, 10, 52. Call ℂ (020) 7589 8212 for details of concert programmes and other events.

As a concert venue the Albert Hall has one unforgivable flaw: an echo that has been the butt of jokes ever since the Bishop of London heard his prayers of blessing reverberate around the red-brick rotunda at the opening ceremony in 1871. The irascible conductor Sir Thomas Beecham remarked that the hall was fit for many things, but playing music was not one of them. But the Albert Hall is still well-loved. Visually, it is one of the more successful Victorian buildings in London, and the high frieze around the outside depicts the Triumph of Arts and Sciences—a most Albertian theme. The hall is huge (capacity 7,000 or more) and remarkably versatile; through the year it hosts symphony orchestras, rock bands, conferences, boxing matches and tennis tournaments. Every summer it becomes the headquarters of the Proms, a series of cheap concerts widely broadcast on radio and television, the last night of which, in early September, is a national institution, *see* p.173.

Albert Memorial

Kensington Gore, opposite the Albert Hall.

The notion of honouring Queen Victoria's beloved husband Albert with a memorial was mooted even before the prince's untimely death in 1861. His over-eager homage-payers had to bide their time, though, if only because Albert himself was adamantly opposed to the idea. 'It would disturb my rides in Rotten Row to see my own face staring at me,' he said, 'and if (as is very likely) it became an artistic monstrosity…it would upset my equanimity to be permanently ridiculed and laughed at in effigy.' As it turned out, the prince's fears were only too well founded. The widowed Queen Victoria launched a competition for a memorial the year after her husband's death and picked George Gilbert Scott, nabob of neo-Gothic excess. The 175ft-high monument he built is a bloated, over-decorated stone canopy housing an indifferent likeness of Albert reading a catalogue from the Great Exhibition by John Foley: a ponderous pickle of allegorical statuary and religious imagery decked out in far too much marble, mosaic panelling, enamel and polished stone, and now, after recent restoration, clad in startling resplendent gold to boot. It was a big hit with the Victorians and remained popular well into the 20th century. Osbert Sitwell described it in 1928 as 'that wistful, unique monument of widowhood'. It took a writer as cynical as Norman Douglas to puncture the myth. 'Is this the reward of conjugal virtue?' he wrote in 1945. 'Ye husbands, be unfaithful!'

London Aquarium

County Hall, Westminster Bridge Rd; ⊖ Waterloo, Westminster; bus 12, 53, 109; ℂ (020) 7967 8000, www.londonaquarium.co.uk

Open daily 10–6, last adm 5pm, holidays and summer till 6.30pm; adm.

To the left of Westminster Bridge, directly across the river from the Houses of Parliament, is **County Hall**, a grand grey stone public building in the pompous Edwardian 'Wrenaissance' style. Until 1986 it was the headquarters of the Greater London Council, the elected city government that proved such a threat to Margaret Thatcher that she abolished it.

County Hall has now been converted into a multi-purpose centre for residential housing, hotel accommodation and conferences. The basement already houses one of London's newer attractions, the **Aquarium**. Here, in spectacular three-storey fish tanks set among kitsch Roman ruins, you can say hello to sharks, stingray, octopus, sea bass, cuttlefish, umbrella-like jellyfish, pianha and wondrous shoals of sea bass, and even touch some of the gentler ones. The Aquarium is primarily entertainment and unfortunately fails to tell the visitor much about either the fish or the environment, but children will love it.

British Museum

Great Russell Street; ⊖ Tottenham Court Road; bus 7, 10, 24, 29, 134; ℂ (020) 7636 1555; www.british-museum.ac.uk

Open Mon–Sat 10–5, Sun 12–6; free; guided tours (adm) are available.

Back in the 1770s, the grumpy novelist Tobias Smollett complained that the fledgling British Museum was too empty and lacked a decent book collection. The museum has certainly made up for both deficiencies since. Stuffed with treasures gathered from the farthest reaches of the British Empire, and boasting one of the finest and fullest libraries in the world, it became an irresistible magnet for visitors and scholars of every temperament and interest. It is by far the most popular tourist attraction in London: triumphant proof that real quality beats the tackiness of the Tower of London or Madame Tussaud's any day.

There is more in the museum than can possibly be described below; what follows is a guide to its most famous and appealing artefacts. Your best strategy is to pick up a floor plan and make up your own mind what to see.

Between 1997 and 2000, the Museum has been organizing its most exciting and complicated reshuffle ever, as the British Library moves to new premises in St Pancras. The move (especially the removal of the Library's ugly postwar bookstacks) has liberated a massive 40 per cent of the Bloomsbury site for redevelopment. For the new British Library, *see* p.54.

Ground Floor

The Round Reading Room

Between 1997 and 2000 the Round Reading Room and the area around it will be completely redeveloped and still out of bounds to the general public.

This is one of the best loved rooms in the world, with a beautiful cavernous dome bigger in diameter than St Paul's or St Peter's in Rome. Although designed by Sydney Smirke, it was the brainchild of Sir Antonio Panizzi, an Italian exile who invented the systems for labelling and cataloguing that are used in libraries to this day. A steady stream of the world's political thinkers and revolutionaries came to this wonderfully spacious domed circular room, among them Marx (who wrote *Das Kapital* in Row G), Mazzini and Lenin. Other writers who have found inspiration, consolation and even, occasionally, love among its eighteen million tomes include Macaulay, Thackeray, Hardy, Dickens and Yeats.

Western Asia

Western Asian treasures are spread throughout the British Museum, but the most accessible, the Assyrian relics of Nineveh, Balawat and Nimrud, are here on the ground floor. The Assyrians, occupying an exposed area in what is now northern Iraq, constructed a civilization essentially built on war with their neighbours, especially the Babylonians, between the 9th and 7th centuries BC. Their palaces are decorated with figures of wild animals, mythical creatures and magic symbols as well as depictions of conical-helmeted soldiers at arms with their chariots, battering rams and pontoons. The most extraordinary artwork depicts a **royal lion hunt**; the dying animals, shot through with arrows, are sculpted with great emotional force.

Egypt

There are more lions here in the Egyptian sculpture gallery, this time red and black ones carved in granite and limestone for the tombs of Pharaohs; Ruskin described them as 'the noblest and truest carved lions I have ever seen'. Among the huge Pharaohs' heads and ornate sarcophagi, look for the likeness of Amenophis III, an 18th Dynasty ruler, and the gilded coffin containing Henutmehit, the Chantress of Amen-Re, from around 1290 BC. Many of the riddles of the ancient Egyptian world were solved through the **Rosetta Stone**, a slab of black basalt discovered by Napoleon's army in the Nile Delta in 1799, which by extraordinary good fortune reproduces the same text in three languages: Greek, demotic and Egyptian.

Greece

Two monuments overshadow the Greek collections: the Nereid Monument and the Elgin Marbles. The **Nereid Monument** is a reconstruction of a vast tomb found at the Greek colony of Xanthos in Asia Minor. Built like a temple with a pediment supported by Ionic columns, it is a stunning tribute to the Lycian chieftains who are buried there; it also features remarkable frieze sculptures.

As for the **Elgin Marbles**, they have aroused so much controversy for being in Britain rather than Greece that their artistic merit is sometimes entirely overlooked. The Elgin Marbles are the frieze reliefs from the Parthenon, the temple to Athena on top of the Acropolis, and are considered some of the finest sculptures of antiquity. Depicting a Panathenaic festival to commemorate Athena's birthday, they reveal a remarkable mastery of detail and human feeling. Lord Elgin, the British Ambassador to the Ottoman Empire, discovered the stones when he visited Athens in 1800. The Parthenon, from which the marbles came, had been half wrecked in a skirmish between the Turks and a Venetian fleet besieging them in 1687, when a supply of gunpowder kept in the building exploded and brought many of the colonnades crashing to the ground. Elgin obtained a licence from the Turkish Sultan in 1802 and proceeded to transport the treasures back home.

The British Museum has them displayed in a vast room giving an idea of the scale of the Parthenon itself.

Oriental Collections (halfway between Ground and Upper Floors)

These rooms cover a huge amount of ground, from Chinese Tang dynasty glazed tomb figures to Turkish and Syrian ceramic work, by way of Thai banner painting and religious monuments from India and Nepal. Perhaps the most impressive section for the non-specialist is the room devoted to South and Southeast Asia.

Upper Floor

Egypt (continued)

The display of **Egyptian mummies and sarcophagi** is the most popular section of the British Museum, no doubt for its addictive gruesomeness. Here is the Egyptian way of death in all its bizarre splendour: rows and rows of spongy bodies wrapped in bandages and surrounded by the prized belongings and favourite food of the deceased.

Western Asia (continued)

The collection is more eclectic here than downstairs: Bronze Age tools from Syria, a mosaic column from Tell-al-Ubaid, reliefs from Kapara's palace in Tell Halaf (now in northeastern Syria) as well as further relics from Nimrud (ivory carvings) and Nineveh (tablets from the royal library). The two highlights are a collection of magnificently preserved funerary busts from Palmyra dating from the 1st and 2nd centuries AD, and the extraordinary sculpture *The Ram in the Thicket* from Ur, the birthplace of Abraham.

The Italy of the Greeks, Etruscans and Romans

Have a look down the western staircase, which is adorned with a Roman mosaic. On the walls are more mosaic fragments, this time from Greek palaces in Halicarnassus, Ephesus and Carthage. The collections themselves are a bit of a mixed bag: Greek red-figure vases found in Lucania and Apulia in southern Italy (1400–1200 BC), a carved stone Etruscan sarcophagus found at Bomarzo north of Rome (3rd century BC) and plenty of bronze heads of Roman emperors. The highlight of the Roman collection, though, is the **Portland Vase**, so called because the Barberini family sold it to the Dukes of Portland. The vase, made around the time of the birth of Christ, is of cobalt-blue glass and coated in an opaque white glaze depicting the reclining figures of Peleus and Thetis, with Cupid and his love arrows hovering overhead.

Romano-British Section

The oldest and most gruesome exhibit here is **Lindow Man**, the shrivelled remains of an ancient Briton preserved down the centuries in a peat bog. The body, which has been dated between 300 BC and AD 100, shows evidence of extreme violence. All you see here is his torso and crushed head, freeze-dried like instant coffee, with a hologram giving you a better idea of what he originally looked like.

Excavations in Britain have provided more pleasant surprises, notably the **Mildenhall Treasure**, 34 remarkably well-preserved pieces of 4th-century silver tableware dug up from a field in Suffolk in 1942. There are some beautiful mosaics, the largest of them a 4th-century floor from Hinton St Mary in Dorset which appears to be Christian in inspiration.

Medieval Antiquities

Here you will find more extraordinary finds from digs around the British Isles. You should not miss the **Lewis chessmen**, a collection of 78 pieces in walrus ivory discovered in the remote Outer Hebrides in 1831. The farmer who first came across them fled thinking they were elves and fairies, and it was only the fortitude of his wife that persuaded him to go back for another look. The figures do not make up complete chess sets and are thought to have been left by a travelling salesman, possibly from Scandinavia, some time in the 12th century.

Prints and Drawings

The museum's vast collection is displayed in rotation. On a good day you can find Michelangelo's sketches for the roof of the Sistine chapel, etchings and sketches by Rembrandt and a large selection of anatomical studies by Albrecht Dürer. Look out, too, for William Hogarth's satirical engravings, notably *Gin Lane* which castigates the corrupting influence of drink on 18th-century London, and his extraordinary series on cruelty.

Buckingham Palace

> Buckingham Palace Road; ⊖ Green Park, Victoria; bus (closest stop Royal Mews) 2, 8, 16, 36, 38, 52, 73, 82; info ℂ (020) 7799 2331; ℂ (020) 7321 2233 to book in advance; www.royal.gov.uk
>
> Open Aug and Sept, at least until 2000, 9.30 daily for 1½-hour guided tours, last entry 4.15, ticket office closes at 4; adm exp. The ticket office, an elegant tent structure designed by architect Michael Hopkins, is at the western end of St James's Park just off the Mall, and the entrance is at Ambassadors' Court on the south side of the building.

On 7 August 1993, miracle of miracles, Buckingham Palace opened its doors to the public for the first time. For generations, royalists had invoked the need to preserve the mystery of the monarchy and refused, in the words of Walter Bagehot, to 'let daylight in upon its magic'. But by the early 1990s the British monarchy was in a crisis of quite astonishing proportions. Two royal marriages had broken up in quick succession, Princess Diana's struggles with bulimia and depression had been made glaringly public, Prince Charles had allegedly been taped telling his mistress on the telephone how he fantasized about being her tampon and, to top it all, half of Windsor Castle had burned down.

Little knowing the revelations and tragedies that were still to come, the Queen herself dubbed 1992, the year of most of these misfortunes, her '*annus horribilis*'. To rally public opinion back behind the monarchy she made two unprecedented concessions. The first was to agree to pay income tax for the first time. The second was to unveil some of the mysteries of Buckingham Palace for two months of the year, for an initial period of five years (now it will stay open until at least 2000). As a public relations coup, opening the doors of the queen's official residence proved less than spectacular. Quite a few newspaper critics, their knives already well sharpened by the preceding flurry of royal scandals, complained that the tour was impersonal, poorly put together and even boring. The public seemed more forgiving, fawning happily over every precious object listed in the official catalogue.

So what exactly is all the fuss about? What do you get to see? Certainly not a glimpse of the 'working palace' constantly alluded to by the Queen's public relations flaks. The tour takes in just 18 of Buckingham Palace's 661 rooms, and even these feel as though they have been stripped down to the bare minimum to ensure they are not sullied by the savage hordes. The original carpets are rolled away each summer and replaced with industrial-strength red Axminster rugs that clash awkwardly with the fake marble columns, greens, pinks and blues of the flock wallpapers and gold and cream ornamental ceilings.

The place feels hollow and spookily empty; in fact it is hard to imagine that anybody lives or works in such soulless surroundings. Perhaps it's just as well that there is no café or refreshment stall for the public, as the toilets are right at the end of the tour, in some tents in the Palace gardens. As for the personal touch, there is not so much as a photograph of the royal family on the whole tour, let alone a flesh-and-blood prince or princess to welcome the guests.

The tour route leads you to the inner courtyard and thence to the back part of the palace overlooking the gardens. The Grand Staircase, with its elegant wrought-iron banister, leads up to the first of the state rooms, the Green Drawing Room. The attractions are on the whole fairly obvious, and although there is no free groundplan to help you get your bearings the wardens are exceptionally helpful and friendly. All the rooms are filled with ostentatious chandeliers, somewhat chintzy furniture and ornate gilt and painted plaster ceilings. Whether you are in the Green, Blue or White Drawing Room you can't help feeling as though you are trapped in a Dairy Milk chocolate box. And the incidental decoration does not really improve as the tour goes on. The real highlight is the 155ft-long **Picture Gallery** (the third room on the tour) which is crammed from floor to ceiling with the cream of the royal collection of some 10,000 paintings. The walls are a bit crowded for comfort, but the gems stand out easily enough: Van Dyck's idealized portraits of Charles I, Rembrandt's *Lady with a Fan, Agatha Bas* and *The Shipbuilder and His Wife*, landscapes by Ruisdael, Poussin and Claude Lorrain, portraits by Frans Hals, Rubens' underwhelming *St George and the Dragon*, Albert Cuyp's *Landscape with a Negro Page*, and much more besides. Apart from Charles I, the only royal to receive anything like pictorial justice in Buckingham Palace is Victoria, whose family is cosily captured in Franz Winterhalter's 1846 portrait in the East Gallery (the room after the Picture Gallery).

The lower floor of the tour holds few new surprises, although you can have some fun in the 200ft **Marble Hall** with its yards of sculpture—look out for Canova's sensuous *Mars and Venus*, which George IV commissioned from Napoleon's pet artist after the British victory at Waterloo. A saunter through the **Bow Room** brings you out into the garden where Palace 'air hostesses' will deliver any bags and coats checked in at the beginning of the tour.

Here in the **garden** you may linger and enjoy some fine views, before moving on to the highlight of the tour which is the souvenir shop. In many ways this is the most telling part of the trip, with mugs and videos and other royal memorabilia displayed to the public in glass cabinets. At the top end of the scale, you can pick up a perfectly frightful crystal bowl or enamel box for roughly the same price as a dinner in a three-star restaurant. Better value (and more appetizing) are the Buckingham Palace Belgian chocolates moulded into the shape of the crown, or the attractive-looking Buckingham Palace gold tooth-mug, an ideal Christmas present for regally inclined mothers-in-law.

Globe Theatre

New Globe Walk; ⊖ Mansion House, Blackfriars, Borough; bus 149 to Southwark Bridge or to London Bridge, 35, 40, 43, 47, 48, 133, 149; ℂ (020) 7902 1400; box office ℂ (020) 7401 9919; http://shakespeares-globe.org

May–Sept 2 performances daily, tickets from £5; exhibition open daily Oct–April 10–5; May–Sept .30–12.30 only; adm.

The original Globe was in fact a few hundred feet away from this building site, on the corner of present-day Park Street and Southwark Bridge Road. When London's first playhouse, The Theatre, was forced to move off its premises in Finsbury Fields, just north of the City, in 1598, its manager Richard Burbage had it dismantled and reassembled here on Bankside where the Rose Theatre had taken root 12 years earlier. Shakespeare helped finance Burbage's enterprise and had many of his plays, including *Romeo and Juliet, King Lear, Othello, Macbeth* and *The Taming of the Shrew* performed in its famous O-shaped auditorium for the first time. Bankside was the perfect location for theatrical entertainment; all manner of pursuits not deemed proper across the river in the stiff-collared City had moved here, and the area was already notorious, among other things, for its taverns and its whorehouses.

The Globe never properly recovered from a fire in 1613 and was finally demolished during the Civil War. This reconstruction was the brainchild of the late American actor Sam Wanamaker, who devoted most of his retirement to realizing the scheme, which remained unfinished when he died in December 1993 at the age of 72. The theatre finally opened for business four years later, following a remarkable fund-raising effort in which actors, politicians and members of the general public volunteered to sponsor every last paving-slab and brick.

The construction is remarkably faithful to the original, from the distinctive red of its brickwork, to its all-wooden interior and thatched roof (the first of its kind to appear in London since the Great Fire of 1666). If you are in London during the summer you should try to see a performance (box office ✆ (020) 7401 9919) to appreciate the peculiarities of Elizabethan theatre. The huge stage, with its vast oak pillars holding up a canopy roof, juts out into the open area holding up to 500 standing members of the audience (known as groundlings). The rest of the public is seated on wooden benches in the circular galleries, giving a peculiar sense of intimacy and audience involvement. Again, there are a few concessions to modern sensibilities: the seating is more spacious and comfortable than in Shakespeare's day, and performances take place in the evening as well as the traditional afternoon slot.

Whether or not you come for a play, you can visit the **Shakespeare Globe Exhibition** which charts the building of both the original and the reconstructed theatre and offers a guided tour around the auditorium itself. Wanamaker's Globe is more than just a venue for authentic performances of Shakespeare, however: there is also a study centre and library, open to scholars and theatre performers.

Hampton Court

East Molesey, Surrey. If you don't travel by river (by far the most pleasant but slowest means), go by train from Waterloo to ≷ Hampton Court, or else catch a bus: the 267 comes from Hammersmith and the R68 from Richmond; ✆ (020) 8781 9500; www.hrp.org.uk

Open Mon 10.15–6, Tues–Sun 9.30–6, earlier closing mid-Oct–Mar; adm.

Hampton Court Palace is one of the finest Tudor buildings in England, a place that magnificently evokes the haphazard pleasures and cruel intrigues of Henry VIII's court. We are lucky to have it. Oliver Cromwell meant to sell off its treasures and let it go to pieces, but then fell in love with it and decided to live there himself. A generation later, Christopher Wren had every intention of razing it to the ground to build a new palace; only money problems and the death of Queen Mary prevented him from wreaking more damage than he did.

Hampton Court started as the power base of Henry VIII's most influential minister. Cardinal Thomas Wolsey bought the property from the Knights of St John in 1514, one year before he became Lord Chancellor of England. As his influence grew, so did the palace: at its zenith it contained 280 rooms and kept a staff of 500 busy, constantly entertaining dignitaries from around Europe. Seeing the grandeur to which his chief minister was rapidly allowing himself to become accustomed, Henry VIII grew nervous and threatened to knock Wolsey off his high perch. Wolsey responded in panic by offering Hampton Court to the monarch; Henry was unimpressed and at first snubbed him by refusing to take up residence there. Wolsey was then given the impossible task of asking the Pope to grant Henry a divorce from his wife, Catherine of Aragon. When he failed, his possessions were seized by the crown, he was arrested for high treason and eventually died as he was being escorted from his archbishopric in York to London.

Henry first got interested in Hampton Court as a love nest for himself and his new flame, Anne Boleyn. The two of them moved here even before Henry had annulled his first marriage and set about effacing every possible trace of Wolsey. They removed his coat of arms, since restored, from the main entrance arch and renamed it **Anne Boleyn's Gateway**—a magnificent red brick structure with octagonal towers at either end. In 1540, Henry added a remarkable astronomical clock, and renamed the main courtyard within Clock Court.

The mid-1530s were Hampton Court's heyday. Henry built the **Great Hall**, with its 60ft-high hammerbeam roof and its stained-glass windows, amended right up to the end of his life to include the crests of each of his wives, even the ones he repudiated or executed. The king also established the gardens, planting trees and shrubs, notably in the Pond Garden, and built a **real tennis court** which still survives in the outhouses at the northeastern end of the palace. Hampton Court began to turn sour for him after Jane Seymour died in 1538 while giving birth to his much anticipated son and heir, Edward.

For a century after Henry's death, Hampton Court continued to thrive. The Great Hall became a popular theatrical venue, and the state rooms filled with fine paintings, gold-encrusted tapestries, musical instruments and ornaments. Charles I built the gardens' fountains and lakes as well as the long waterway, originally cut to provide the palace with water at the expense of neighbouring communities. Charles also accumulated a vast collection of art including the wonderfully restored *Triumph of Caesar* series by Mantegna which hangs in its own gallery at the south end of the palace.

By the time William and Mary came to the throne, appreciation of Tudor architecture had waned considerably. The apartments at Hampton Court were considered old-fashioned and uncomfortable, and Christopher Wren was drafted in to build an entirely new palace to rival Louis XIV's extravaganza at Versailles—a project that, perhaps fortunately, never saw the light of day. The bulk of Wren's work is at the eastern end of the palace and centres around the cloisters of **Fountain Court**. The new apartments were decorated by the likes of Antonio Verrio, James Thornhill, Grinling Gibbons and Jean Tijou in sumptuous but stilted fashion; the **Chapel Royal** was also rebuilt, with only the Tudor vaulted ceiling surviving from the original. The best work carried out under William III was in the gardens, notably the lines of yew trees along the narrow strips of water, the herb garden (now beatifully restored) and the famous **maze**. Originally the maze was considered a religious penance to impress upon ordinary mortals the labyrinthine complications of a life in the service of Christ. Now it is a popular diversion, particularly for children too small to peer over the hedges to see what is coming next.

Houses of Parliament and Big Ben

> ⊖ *Westminster; buses 3, 11, 12, 24, 53, 77A, 88, 109 all go to Parliament Square.*
>
> To visit the **Houses of Parliament**, *you should head for St Stephen's entrance, which is roughly half way along the complex of buildings. Visiting arrangements for parliament are phenomenally complicated, and vary according to your nationality; you might well find that telephoning in advance (ⓒ (020) 7219 3000 , or ⓒ 7219 4272 for information on what is being debated) will avoid wasting time. If you turn up on spec, you must queue outside St Stephen's entrance; don't expect to sit down before 5pm. Note that both houses have long recesses, particularly in the summer, and that debates of particular public interest are likely to be very crowded.*

To see the rest of the Palace of Westminster (notably Westminster Hall) you need to apply for a permit about two months in advance from your MP or embassy. It's a good idea whatever your arrangements to bring your passport and leave behind any large bags or cameras. You should also dress reasonably formally. The one bit of good news is that the Houses of Parliament, once you get in, come free of charge.

The best way to approach the Palace of Westminster is to imagine it as a multi-layered onion. Most of today's building is the dizzy virtuoso work of Charles Barry and Augustus Pugin, two Victorian architects working at the height of their powers to replace the old parliament destroyed by fire in 1834.

The story of the palace begins with **Westminster Hall**, which has survived the centuries more or less intact. The hall was originally a banqueting chamber built by King William Rufus, the son of William the Conqueror, in 1097. The Hall was the meeting-place of the Grand Council, a committee of barons which discussed policy with the monarch in an early incarnation of parliament. Westminster Hall also became the nation's main law court. From about 1550, the lower house of parliament, known as the House of Commons, began meeting in St Stephen's Chapel in the main body of the palace. It may seem odd to convene parliament in a religious setting, but the juxtaposition is curiously appropriate: ever since the Reformation, parliament has been a symbol of the primacy of Protestantism in English politics. Pugin and Barry recognized this, and incorporated the chapel into their design. It was only when St Stephen's was destroyed in the Blitz that the House of Commons became an entirely secular chamber.

The inadequacies of the old Palace of Westminster were recognized as early as the 1820s. A new building might have been proposed there and then, but it took a calamity to spring them into action. On 16 October, 1834, the Clerk of Works, a Mr Richard Wibley, was asked to destroy several bundles of old talley-sticks in a cellar furnace. The fire raged out of control, and the whole palace was soon engulfed in flames. Augustus Pugin had been an eye-witness to the 1834 fire and revelled in every minute of it. He hated neoclassical architects and was only too happy to see their various improvements to the old parliament go up in smoke. Fearing that a neoclassical architect would be asked to design the new parliament, Pugin put his name forward and, although he was only 24 at the time, was named assistant to the older, more experienced Charles Barry. Theirs was a near perfect partnership. Barry sketched out the broad lines of the design, while Pugin attended to the details of ornamentation. Some of Pugin's work was lost in the bombing of the Second World War; you can nevertheless admire the sheer fervour of his imagination in the sculpted wood and stone, the stained glass, tiled floors, wallpaper and painted ceilings. Despite Pugin's rantings against the classicists, he was happy to go along with Barry's essentially classical design and Gothicize it to his heart's content. The Palace of Westminster's blend of architectural restraint (Barry) and decorative frenzy (Pugin) is one of its most appealing aspects.

Pugin went mad and died in 1852, and so never lived to work on the most famous feature of the new building, the clock tower at the eastern end known universally by the name of its giant bell, **Big Ben** (*visits to the clock must be arranged through an MP or serving member of the House of Lords, or, for horologists with a specific interest in the clock, directly through Chris Hillier on ℂ (020) 7219 4874*). Nowadays the clock is renowned for its accuracy and its resounding tolling of the hour, but the story of its construction is one of incredible incompetence and bungling. The 320ft-high clock tower was finished in 1854, but because of a bitter disagreement between the two clockmakers, Frederick Dent and Edmund Beckett Denison, there was nothing to put inside it for another three years. Finally a great bell made up according to Denison's instructions was dragged across Westminster Bridge by a cart and 16 horses. But, as it was being laid out ready for hoisting into position, a 4ft crack suddenly appeared. Similar embarrassments ensued over the next two years, until a functioning but still cracked bell was at last erected at the top of the tower. It remains defective to this day. As for the name, the most common explanation is that the bell was named after Sir Benjamin Hall, the unpopular Chief Commissioner of Works who had to explain all the muddles in his project to the House of Commons. Another theory has it that Big Ben was in fact Benjamin Caunt, a corpulent boxer who owned a pub a couple of hundred yards away in St Martin's Lane. The chimes, well-known around the world, are a bastardized version of the aria 'I Know That My Redeemer Liveth' from Handel's *Messiah*.

From the moment that Barry and Pugin's building opened in 1852, it set an entirely new tone to proceedings in parliament. It was no longer just a legislative assembly, it was a *club*. Like so many British institutions, parliament is a place of deeply embedded rituals, established by a ruling order intent on protecting itself and its idiosyncratic ways; even if the institution has changed, the rituals have survived out of a quirky fondness for the past. Whatever its modern way of functioning, parliament still *feels* like the exclusive terrain of upper-class men who drink and smoke cigars together and decide the fate of the nation in an atmosphere of elegant sparring.

Kensington Palace

Kensington Palace Gardens; ⊖ *Queensway, High Street Kensington, bus 12, 94 stopping to the north of the palace on Bayswater Road, and 9, 10, 52 stopping to the south on Kensington Road;* ℂ *(020) 7937 9561, www.royal.gov.uk*

Open April–Oct daily 10–5; Nov–Mar Wed–Sun 10–4; adm; includes small café.

Since the death of Princess Diana, Kensington Palace has become something of a shrine to her memory; this was where she, along with that other well-known royal divorcee Princess Margaret, lived after the failure of her marriage to Prince Charles. You won't be able to visit her private apartments, but the Palace offers other delights in their place.

The tour is divided into two sections: the historic apartments, and an exhibition of royal clothes including the coronation robes worn by monarchs from George II onwards. The most interesting aspect of the apartments is the decoration work by William Kent: a beautifully patterned ceiling in the Presence Chamber, some fine *trompe l'œil* murals of court scenes on the King's Staircase and painted episodes from the *Odyssey* on the ceiling of the King's Gallery. The Cupola Room plays clever optical tricks to make you believe the ceiling is taller and more rounded than it is; from the King's Drawing Room there is a fine view over Kensington Gardens, the Serpentine and Hyde Park.

The fashions in coronation garb charted by the special exhibition give a good reading of the changing status of the monarchy itself. The over-confident Georges wore ermine galore, particularly the profligate George IV who sported a ludicrously flamboyant white feather hat and a train as thick as a shag-pile carpet. William IV and Victoria, whose coronations went almost unnoticed by a populace more interested in democratic reform than regal pomp, were sober almost to the point of blandness. Edward VII, who helped restore the monarchy's image, showed renewed confidence with his bright military uniform and ermine mantle braided with gold.

Millennium Dome

⊖ North Greenwich (if open), ⇌ Greenwich. By far the pleasantest way of getting there will be via riverboat from Central London (Westminster Pier) or Greenwich, ✆ (0207) 930 4097 for sailing times.

Entry tickets must be pre-purchased, available from 22 September 1999 at Lottery outlets. Tickets can also be booked by phone, ✆ (0870) 606 2000, from travel operators, railway and bus stations, or at www.dome2000.co.uk. Adm very exp.

The Dome has cost £758m to build, more than half of which has been paid for by the public via The National Lottery. The enormous semi-sebaceous cyst is made of Teflon and fibreglass and supported by 12 steel masts attached to 70 kilometres of wire cable. It is big enough to hold two Wembley Stadiums, tall enough to sheath the whole of Nelson's Column, and strong enough for Superman to bounce on. Crunch time for Dome-hubris, however, comes on Domesday—31 December 1999—when the Dome opens for the first time to the general public and a sceptical British press. In the central arena inside, a live show with music by Peter Gabriel will be staged up to five times a day. Around this will be the fourteen 'Zones'—ranging from work, rest and play, to mind, body, spirit and a 'celebration of all things British' sponsored by Marks & Spencer.

The Dome has a life span of 30–100 years and its future remains uncertain, though several consortiums have already put in bids to buy it for use as film and TV studios. A more permanent fixture on the site should be the Millennium Village, a 'model village' of 1,400 sustainable homes nearby.

National Gallery

Trafalgar Square; ⊖ Charing Cross, Leicester Square; bus: very nearly all of London's day and night bus services go around Trafalgar Square; ✆ (020) 7747 2885.

Open daily 10–6, Wed 10–9; free.

The National Gallery is an astonishing collection of West European painting from the 13th to the early 20th centuries, including masterpieces from virtually every major school. Its great names include Leonardo da Vinci, Piero della Francesca, Van Eyck, Raphael, Titian, Veronese, Rubens, Poussin, Rembrandt, Velázquez, Caravaggio, Turner, Constable, Delacroix, Monet, Van Gogh, Cézanne and Picasso.

The National Gallery is very much a 19th-century phenomenon: a catalogue of paintings from the Grand Tradition reflecting the pride and power of the collector nation. Many of the gallery's masterpieces were bought in the Victorian era, particularly under its first director Charles Eastlake. The picture-buying has continued ever since; and although money has grown tighter in recent years the annual budget remains well over £2 million.

The first work of art, which most visitors miss, is a mosaic of Greta Garbo's head by Boris Anrep (1933) on the floor of the main entrance hall. Pick up a floor plan from the information desk and you'll see that the gallery's four wings each concentrate on a different historical period, starting with early medieval Italian painting in the new Sainsbury Wing and moving gradually eastwards towards the 20th century.

Rooms devoted to individual painters are clearly marked. At the entrance to each wing, you are given the names of the major paintings to look out for. The gallery is magnificently lit, with intelligent explanations displayed alongside each picture. There is a computer database in the Micro Gallery in the Sainsbury Wing, where you can look up and print out detailed information on pictures or artists. There are also organized lectures on individual pictures, as well as a changing special exhibition in the Sunley Room to the left of the central hall, where paintings from the collection are grouped to illustrate a specific theme. And if that is not enough for you, there are hundreds of minor paintings stored on lower floors available for public view.

Natural History Museum

Cromwell Road; ● *South Kensington; bus C1 from Victoria, 74 from Baker St, 14 from Tottenham Court Road;* ✆ *(020) 7938 9123; www.nhm.ac.uk*

Open 10–5.50 Mon–Sat, 11–5.50 Sun; adm but free after 4.30 Mon–Fri, children age 5–16 free.

This place looks for all the world like a cathedral, but you are soon jolted out of any notion that this is a place of worship by the giant dinosaur in the central hall. This skeletal creature, a 150-million-year-old plant-eating beast called a diplodocus, that warded off predators with its giant tusks and whiplash tail, really sums up what is best and worst about the Natural History Museum. Our prehistoric friend *looks* very impressive; the trouble is, he's a fake, just a cast. Ever since *Jurassic Park*, the **dinosaurs** have been the museum's main attraction. The special section devoted to them is long on history but short on real skeletons, though one display gives an intriguing list of theories on why prehistoric monsters died out.

Much of this museum resembles a science classroom. There are games explaining human perception and memory, interactive displays on creepy-crawlies and a politically correct **Ecology Gallery** explaining the importance of the rainforests in the world's ecosystem. All of this is fine for children, but not so great for adults. For grown-ups, the museum only really gets going with the **Bird Gallery**, featuring a remarkable collection of stuffed birds and wild animals from the 18th century onwards, and a geological section known as the **Earth Galleries**, which are filled with beautiful stones and gems, and where there's a chance to step inside the 'Earthquake Experience'. Right next to the Exhibition Road side-entrance you can really go for the broad view with an audio-visual experience called the **Story of the Universe**. Again, it is instructive, but not very inspiring. A newer part of the museum is the **Earth Lab Datasite**, an educational resource where you can investigate UK geology using an extensive on-line database.

Science Museum

Exhibition Road; ● *South Kensington; bus C1, 14, 74;* ✆ *(020) 7938 8080; www.nmsi.ac.uk*

Open daily 10–6; adm.

The Science Museum has done perhaps more than any other institution in London to make itself accessible and popular, undergoing constant updating and improvement. Children have always loved it; one of the latest gimmicks is to allow them to sleep at the museum overnight. Anyone between eight and eleven who brings a sleeping bag will be treated to an after-hours tour of the building, a choice of workshops and bedtime stories before lights out (children may also be accompanied by adults: phone the museum on ✆ (020) 7938 8008 for details).

For less privileged visitors, the best place to start is with the synopsis on the mezzanine above the **Ground Floor**, giving an overview of industrial and technological progress across the centuries. Here you can disabuse yourself of a few basic misconceptions: Jethro Tull was not just a bad 1970s heavy metal band but also an 18th-century agricultural pioneer who introduced rowcrop farming. Nearby, the Power section gives a brief history of engines including pioneering models by Boulton and Watt from the 1780s. Then comes a Space section, complete with Second World War V2 rocket and Apollo 10 command module. Beyond, the Land Transport section traces the history of automobiles from Stephenson's Rocket to the Morris mini, the latter bisected from top to bottom. One of the most recent additions is the Challenge of Materials, a new 'gallery of the future' whose centrepiece is a spectacular glass and steel bridge which spans the main hall of the museum, and whose exhibits celebrate British industry, manufacturing and design.

Moving up to the **First Floor** you come to one of the highlights for children, a gallery full of interactive games called the Launch Pad. Children are taken in groups at a time to be explained the rudiments of such diverse phenomena as bicycle gears and hangovers. For grown-ups the most fascinating section on this floor is Time Measurement, tracing the technology of clocks from the first Egyptian timepieces, based on water, to modern quartz and atomic clocks. Next to the tickers is Food for Thought, which explains everything you wanted to know about nutrition (and a few things you didn't—a group of see-through plastic vats, for example, demonstrating all too graphically how much urine, faeces and sweat a 10-year-old boy produces in a month).

The highlight of the **Second Floor** is the Chemistry section, exploring the history of the science through the discoveries of such pioneers as Priestley, Dalton, Davy and Faraday. Under Living Molecules you'll find Crick and Watson's metal-plate model of the structure of DNA. Further along the floor are displays on the development of computers and an overview of nuclear physics, as well as a beautiful collection of model ships. On the **Third Floor** most children head for the Flight Lab, featuring simulators, a wind tunnel and a mini hot air balloon. The main Flight section is a display of more than 20 historic aircraft, plus a collection of models and an ingenious air traffic control display. Equally intriguing is Optics, a collection of spectacles, telescopes, microscopes and the like, leading up to such modern developments as lasers and holograms. The **Fourth and Fifth Floors** are devoted to medicine.

Children in need of tiring out can be taken directly to the **Science of Sport** gallery, on the ground floor, where they can see a genuine £2 million Formula 1 McLaren, or practise rock-climbing an indoor mountain, try out their snowboarding skills or experience the thrills and spills of a simulated penalty shootout.

St Paul's Cathedral

St Paul's Churchyard; ↔ St Paul's; bus 8, 25, 242 from Oxford Street, 11, 15, 26 from the Strand, ℗ (020) 7236 4128, http://stpauls.london.anglican.org

Open Mon–Sat 8.30–4.30, last admission 4pm; adm.

St Paul's is more than just a cathedral or famous landmark. It is an icon for a whole city. Get to know St Paul's and you understand many of the ambitions and failings of London itself.

For nearly 1400 years, succeeding buildings on this site have sought to express the material confidence of a powerful capital while at the same time delineating its spiritual aspirations. Back in the 7th century, St Paul's was England's first major Christian temple; in its medieval incarnation it was the largest single building in the land. In the hands of Christopher Wren, who rebuilt it from scratch after the Great Fire, it was hailed as an architectural masterpiece. Since then St Paul's has dutifully propped up all the myths of the nation: as the burial place for heroes during the glory days of empire, as a symbol of British endurance during the Second World War when it miraculously survived the Blitz, or as the fairy-tale setting for Prince Charles's marriage to Lady Diana Spencer in 1981.

And yet St Paul's has often shared more with the commercial world outside its doors than with the spiritual world celebrated within. Back in the Middle Ages the cathedral was itself a kind of market, with horses parading down the nave and stallholders selling beer and vegetables to all-comers. Even today, the first thing confronting the swarms of tourists who come here is a cash register, a sign of St Paul's' peculiar ease in reconciling religious faith with the handling of money. It is a cool, cerebral place. While we admire Wren's pure lines and lofty vision, we feel little warmth or sense of a living church community. St Paul's is a monument to wealth first, and God second.

By the time of the Great Fire of London, old St Paul's was so dilapidated that several architects wanted to pull it down and rebuild it from scratch. Christopher Wren, commissioned to consider the cathedral's future in 1663, called it 'defective both in beauty and firmness...a heap of deformities that no judicious architect will think corrigible by any expense that can be laid out upon it.' He did not have to lobby long for the merits of demolition. On 4 September 1666, the first flames of the Great Fire of London reached St Paul's and proceeded to engulf it entirely.

Nothing was easy about the rebuilding. Wren initially used gunpowder to clear the wreck of old St Paul's but had to resort to battering rams instead after terrified locals complained of rogue pieces of stonework flying through their living-room windows. As for the design, Wren set his heart on building a dome in the manner of the great Italian Baroque churches. That idea, too, met stiff resistance—it was considered excessively Popish in those religiously sensitive times. You can see his magnificent 20ft oak replica of the Great Model on display in the crypt. Eventually the dome problem was solved through a mixture of guile and compromise. Wren submitted a third plan dispensing with a dome in favour of a steeple, and had it approved in 1675; in return the royal warrant giving him the go-ahead granted him the liberty 'to make some variations rather ornamental than essential, as from time to time he should see proper'. By the time the cathedral opened 35 years later, the dome was back, as were many of the architect's other rejected ideas.

The sheer imposing scale of St Paul's is apparent as soon as you approach the entrance at the west front. The broad **staircase** leads up to a two-tiered portico upheld by vast stone columns and flanked by two clocktowers. Dominating the high pediment in the centre is a statue of St Paul, with St Peter to his left and St James to his right. It is surely no coincidence that these three figures look down on the sovereign of the day, Queen Anne, whose statue stands on the ground outside the entrance. The ensemble, the work of a single artist, Francis Bird, forges a clear mystical link between the City, the crown and the church.

The **nave** is vast but remarkably simple in its symmetries; concentrate on the harmony of the architecture and try to blank out the largely hideous statuary and incidental decoration added well after Wren's time. As you walk beneath the dome, look down at the marble floor and you'll see the famous epitaph to Wren, added by his son after his death in 1723, '*Lector, si monumentam requiris, circumspice*' (Reader, if you seek a memorial, look around you).

Look, in particular, up towards the magnificent **dome**. This is something of an optical illusion, nowhere near as big on the inside as it is on the outside. In fact, Wren built a smaller second dome inside the first to keep the interior on a manageable scale. The story goes that the first stone used to construct the dome was a relic from the old St Paul's which by coincidence bore the Latin word *resurgam* (rise up). Wren took it as a good portent and had the word inscribed in the pediment above the south door, adorning it with an image of a phoenix rising from the ashes. You can climb up into the dome, or domes, from a staircase on the south side of the cathedral, in exchange for another cash contribution.

The first stopping-off point is the **Whispering Gallery** 100ft up, so called because you can murmur with your face turned towards the wall and be heard with crystal clarity on the other side of the dome, 107ft away. You can also admire James Thornhill's series of frescoes on the life of St Paul which stretch all the way around the gallery. Vertigo permitting, you can continue on up to the Stone Gallery, the Inner Golden Gallery and the Outer Golden Gallery, offering panoramic views over London from just below the ball and cross at a height of 365ft.

And so down to the **crypt** (entrance near the south door), whose highlight is undoubtedly Wren's Great Model (*see* above) and the fine exhibition that accompanies it. Most of the space, though, is taken up with tombs commemorating Britain's military leaders. Among the rows and rows of nonentities you can find the Duke of Wellington in his pompous porphyry casket and, directly beneath the dome, the black marble sarcophagus honouring Horatio Nelson. The Florentine sarcophagus, by Pietro Torrigiano, was originally commissioned by Cardinal Wolsey back in the 16th century, but was deemed too good for him and spent three centuries unused and neglected in Windsor Castle until Nelson's mourners unearthed it for his funeral in 1805.

Tate Gallery

Millbank; ● *Pimlico; bus 77A from Strand;* © *(020) 7887 8000, www.tate.org.uk*
Open daily 10–5.50; free, with guided tours Mon–Fri at 11, 12 noon, 2 and 3.

Founded at the end of the 19th century by the sugar baron Sir Henry Tate of Tate & Lyle fame, this is the second great London art collection after the National Gallery. In spring 2000 the collection will divide into two: 20th-century international art will move across the river to the massive new **Tate Gallery of Modern Art at Bankside** (*see* p.84); the gallery here will be renamed the **Tate Gallery of British Art** and the entire building will be devoted to a chronological survey of home-grown works from the Renaissance until now. This will vastly increase the proportion of art on display: for now, only 15 per cent of the Tate's total collection of over 5000 paintings and 50,000 drawings and sketches is viewable at one time.

If you're visiting the gallery before spring 2000, you will see a collection which breaks down clearly into three distinct parts: British art, 20th-century modern art, and James Stirling's attractive Clore Gallery extension, which opened in 1987 and contains an outstanding collection of paintings by the great 19th-century artist J.M.W. Turner.

Highlights of the Gallery

Room 2, which is almost entirely devoted to **Hogarth**'s finest satire, *O the Roast Beef of England*, a depiction of the greed and corruption of France.

Sir Joshua Reynolds, *Three Ladies Adoring a Term of Hymen*, which turns four upper-class English sisters into gossiping Greek nymphs with delicate complexions and dainty clothes.

Room 7, devoted to the terrifying Manichean world of **William Blake** (1757–1827), a man who turned his vivid Biblical and literary nightmares into extraordinarily enigmatic poetry, pen and ink watercolours and prints.

Victorian painting: starts with the Romantic John Constable and his lyrical depictions of Malvern Hall in Warwickshire and Salisbury Cathedral.

Pre-Raphaelites: among the works to look out for are Waterhouse's *Lady of Shalott*, Burne-Jones's *King Cophetua and the Beggar Maid* and Millais' *Ophelia*, floating lifelessly in a marshy brook. The best pieces here are by foreigners working in England, like the American James Whistler whose *Nocturne in Blue-Green* is a compelling cityscape of the Thames at Chelsea.

Turner Collection—the Clore Gallery. It is hard to pick out individual pictures, especially since the displays tend to change, but try to see some of the following: *Rome from the Vatican* (1820), an idealized portrait of the Eternal City reflecting many of Turner's artistic preoccupations; *Snow Storm: Steam-boat off a Harbour's Mouth*, a virtuoso whirl of chaos on the waves; *A City on a River at Sunset*, a gorgeous, warm study of sky and water, probably in Rouen; and *Peace—Burial at Sea*, a tribute to Turner's fellow painter David Wilkie in which light, mist and smoke mingle in Turner's typical sea setting.

Modern art: Highlights in the main modern galleries include Magritte's disturbing dreamscapes and the desolate cities of Giorgio de Chirico (*Uncertainty of the Poet*). Matisse dominates Room 24, particularly his early *Inattentive Reader* (1919) and his experiment with paper cut-outs, *The Snail* (which one of the guards insists is called the Snail because a tiny nick at the very top of the picture looks exactly like a snail making its way slowly across the picture). Abstract painting is well represented by Jackson Pollock and Mark Rothko; pop art by Roy Lichtenstein's comic-book *Whaam!* and Andy Warhol's *Marilyn Diptych* which parodies the movie superstar's transformation into a vulgar commodity.

10, Downing Street

Off Whitehall; ● *Westminster; bus 3, 11, 12, 24, 53, 77A, 88, 109*

Downing Street has been home to British Prime Ministers on and off since 1735. Unfortunately, you won't be able to sidle up to the famous Georgian front door at No.10 without a security pass; the best you can hope for is a glimpse through the heavy iron gates installed in 1990. Next door at No.11 is the Chancellor of the Exchequer, the British equivalent of treasury secretary or finance minister, and next door to him, at No.12, is the government whips' office, where the party in power keeps tabs on its members in parliament.

It is rather pleasing to think that this street, the scene of many a heated cabinet meeting and ministerial bollocking, was once an open venue for cock-fighting. A theatre dedicated to the proposition that encouraging animals to tear each other apart with spurs is just as entertaining as watching politicians doing the same thing in the Palace of Westminster stayed in business on this site alongside the Axe brewhouse until about 1675. It was only then that a rather modest building development, later to become the powerhouse of the British establishment, was undertaken by one George Downing, a slippery fellow who managed to spy for both Oliver Cromwell and Charles II during the Civil War and come out of it not only alive but stinking rich into the bargain. It was more accident than design that led to Downing Street's lasting fame. When the prime minister, Robert Walpole, succeeded a certain Mr Chicken as tenant in 1735 he never meant to establish No.10 as an official residence, and indeed many of his successors preferred to conduct the business of government from their more lavish homes elsewhere in London. Only in the early 19th century was 10 Downing Street kitted out with proper facilities, such as John Soane's sumptuous dining room; only in 1902 did it become the prime minister's home as well as office. The shortcomings of the place have never gone away, though; when Tony Blair became prime minister in 1997, he installed his family in the more spacious No.11 next door, swapping places with his unmarried Chancellor, Gordon Brown.

Tower Bridge

 ⊖ *Tower Hill; bus 42, 78 from the City, or 15 to the Tower of London*

Tower Bridge Experience, ℂ (020) 7403 3761. Open daily April–Oct 10–6.30, 9.30–6 Nov–Mar, last entry an hour and a quarter before closing; adm.

Tower Bridge is one of the great feats of late Victorian engineering, half suspension-bridge and half drawbridge, linked to two neo-Gothic towers. Designed by an engineer, John Wolfe-Barry, and an architect, Horace Jones, working in tandem, it has become one of London's most recognizable landmarks. Its fame was not exactly instant; indeed, at its opening in 1894, the critics found its evocation of medieval style crude. *The Builder* called it 'the most monstrous and preposterous architectural sham that we have ever known…an elaborate and costly make-believe.' There is still a reasonable case to be made that Tower Bridge is a kind of Victorian Disneyland, but time has mellowed its vulgarity and made it both awe-inspiring and loveable. Its two bascules, the arms that rise up to let tall ships through, weigh an astonishing 1000 tonnes each. Despite the decline of river freight traffic, the bridge still opens at least once a day on average; phone ahead (ℂ (020) 7403 3761) to find out the times. At the southern tower you can join the **Tower Bridge Experience**, a hi-tech retelling of the history of the bridge, plus a chance to enjoy the view from the overhead walkways and admire the giant Victorian hydraulic engines that once operated the bridge (it is now done with electric power).

Tower of London

Tower Hill; ⊖ *Tower Hill, bus 15; ℂ (020) 7709 0765 or 7680 9004; www.hrp.org.uk*

Open March–Oct, Mon–Sat 9–6 and Sun 10–6; Nov–Feb, Mon–Sat 9–5 and Sun 10–5, last adm all year round an hour before closing; adm expensive.

The Tower is one London sight that everyone knows but nobody particularly likes. Ever since the monarchy moved out in the early 17th century, the Tower has existed principally as a stronghold of historical nostalgia, a place that owes its appeal more to romantic notions of the past than to real past events. Modern Americans might want to compare it to the fantasy castles of Disneyland, especially if they follow the **Tower Hill Pageant** (entrance near All Hallows' Church), a 15-minute underground ghost train ride, complete with commentary, and nasty smells and sounds, past tableaux of famous episodes in London's history.

So what is the big attraction? First of all the site, which is one of the best preserved medieval castles in the world. The **White Tower**, the keep at the centre of the complex, dates back to William the Conqueror and includes the magnificent heavy round arches and groin vaults of the 13th-century **St John's Chapel**. More importantly, the Tower corresponds to every myth ever invented about England. Its history is packed with tales of royal pageantry, dastardly baronial plots, ghoulish tortures and gruesome executions. The Tower is still guarded by quaint liveried figures, the Beefeaters, who obligingly conduct their Ceremony of the Keys at 9.45 each evening. And, of course, the Tower contains the Crown Jewels.

Under Henry III the Tower expanded considerably and included for the first time a menagerie, complete with lions, leopards, a polar bear and an elephant. Prisoners were brought in from the river through **Traitor's Gate**, which you can still see today.

Inevitably, you also will be drawn towards the **Crown Jewels**. You'll probably have to share the spectacle with the entire adult population of Cleveland, Ohio, not to mention several thousand Euro-teenagers, but at least there is a decent attempt at crowd control, thanks to a relatively new conveyor-belt system. There are two main crowns: St Edward's Crown, a heavy, somewhat unwieldy piece used only during the coronation ceremony itself; and the golden Crown of State, encrusted with 3,000 gems, which was originally made for Queen Victoria and is still used for grand occasions such as the state opening of parliament. Next are the jewelled sword and spurs, also used to anoint the new monarch, followed by the orb, bracelets and two sceptres which symbolize the sovereign's secular and divine mission. The orb represents the spread of Christianity around the world, the sceptres forge the link between the monarch and his or her subjects, while the bracelets are an emblem of Britain's link to the Commonwealth. The Ring of Kingly Dignity is a sapphire mounted with rubies, while the Great Sword of State, the sovereign's symbolic personal weapon, is decorated with a lion and unicorn as well as the royal arms.

Trafalgar Square

Back in the 1810s and 1820s, when Britannia really did rule the waves and London was the capital of a burgeoning empire, a hitherto taboo concept suddenly came into fashion: urban planning. Previously it had been considered perfectly proper for London to develop organically according to the whims of private landowners. But then industrialization arrived, threatening to stifle the capital in factory smoke if the *laissez-faire* planning policy persisted. At the same time, Britain's victory in the Napoleonic Wars unleashed a broad desire for some decent monumental architecture. The Prince Regent, an ardent patron of grand building schemes, was only too happy to sponsor major projects, and soon architects were putting forward proposals for the wildest and most outlandish schemes.

It was in such an atmosphere that Trafalgar Square was first conceived. The Prince Regent (later crowned George IV) and his chosen architect, John Nash, wanted to create a vast open space glorifying the country's naval power which would also provide a focal point from which other urban projects could spread. It was a fine idea, but one that was destined to be cruelly truncated by the vagaries of history. George developed a reputation as a spendthrift and a philanderer, and as economic crisis gripped the nation in the mid-1820s all his dreams were brought to a halt by a hostile parliament. Nash was dismissed as soon as George died in 1830, and from then on Trafalgar Square was left at the mercy of successive parliamentary committees who argued for the best part of a generation over its final form.

Modern Trafalgar Square evolved partly out of a desire to raise the tone of the Charing Cross area. Nash pulled down the old King's Mews (incidentally, a fine Georgian building by William

Kent) to make room for his planned ensemble of grand classical buildings. But he never got to build them before his fall from grace. The whole Trafalgar Square project might have been abandoned had it not been for a lingering determination to bestow grand honours on Horatio Nelson, the country's legendary naval commander who had died at sea during the Battle of Trafalgar in 1805. In 1808, the essayist William Wood wrote a rousing eulogy of England 'proudly stemming the torrent of revolutionary frenzy', and proposed erecting a giant pyramid to his hero. Over the years 120 official proposals were submitted, including a myriad columns, pyramids and even a Coliseum. In the absence of a co-ordinating architect, however, the scheme made painfully slow progress. Where Nash had been extravagant, the special select committee of the House of Commons proved downright stingy. The new planners were not interested in producing monumental architecture unless it could be done on the cheap.

As for **Nelson's Column**, it did not see the light of day until 1843. The Corinthian column, topped by an unremarkable and scarcely visible likeness of Nelson in his admiral's three-cornered hat, by E.H. Baily, was erected on a sloping concrete basin prepared by the neoclassical architect Charles Barry. Railton based his design on a triumphalist precedent from ancient Rome, the Temple of Mars in the Forum of Augustus. The bronze bas-reliefs at the base of the column represent Nelson's four greatest victories, at Cape St Vincent, the Nile, Copenhagen and Trafalgar, while the surrounding statuary is of Nelson's generals. The two granite fountains at the base arrived in 1845, while the bronze lions, the most appealing feature of the ensemble, appeared a quarter of a century later.

Trafalgar Square is the point from which all measurements in London are drawn; there is a plaque indicating this on the corner of Charing Cross Road. On the eastern side of the square is South Africa House, where anti-apartheid protesters maintained a constant vigil through the latter part of Nelson Mandela's 26-year imprisonment. Next door is James Gibbs's church of St Martin-in-the-Fields. In the southeastern corner stands a lamp-post known as the smallest police station in the world, which contains a telephone linked up to police headquarters at Scotland Yard. On the western side, in a building designed by Robert Smirke, builder of the British Museum, is Canada House, home to the Canadian High Commission.

Victoria and Albert Museum

Cromwell Road and 2nd entrance on Exhibition Road; ⊖ *South Kensington, bus C1, 74, 14;* ℗ *(020) 7938 8500; www.vam.ac.uk*

Open Mon–Sun 10–5.45, in summer also Wed late view 6.30–9.30; adm, free after 4.30pm.

This huge, sprawling museum is nominally dedicated to applied art and design, but in fact even such a broad definition does not sufficiently cover the sheer vastness of its collections. Over the years it has become the nation's treasure trove. You could liken it to a magical chest in some long-forgotten attic; but the V&A has also kept bang up to date, displaying everything from Donatello to Dalí, from medieval reliquaries to Reebok sneakers. Its former director, Sir Roy Strong, once defined it as an 'extremely capacious handbag'. Unlike most large museums, you would be ill-advised to pick and choose your way around the V&A on a first visit. To get a proper feel of it, you should aim to get hopelessly lost along its seven miles of corridors.

Pick up a free **museum guide** at the reception desk. It tells you where the most famous exhibits are, and provides detailed maps of the two main floors, plus the six storeys of the Henry

Cole wing. There are guided tours through the day, which are recommended for an hour's concentrated stimulation. Neither the museum guides nor this book would be foolhardy enough to undertake an exhaustive description of the whole place: what follows is a broad-brush and personalized account of what to expect.

Highlights of the Museum

Level A: Dress

An enthralling starting point is the room dedicated to European fashion across history. Watch how the flamboyant clothes of the 17th and 18th century gradually grow more restricted by corsets and bodices, then become blander and fussier in the 19th century, turn morose in the 1930s and 1940s before exploding in new-found freedom and colour in the 1960s and beyond. Up a spiral staircase from the dress section are **Musical Instruments**, a range of historical music boxes, virginals and a Dutch giraffe piano with six percussion pedals, as well as the usual strings, wind and brass.

Italy 1400–1500

The V&A calls this the greatest collection of Renaissance sculpture outside Italy. The pieces here are so disparate they could have come from some glorified car boot sale held by the great churches of Tuscany and northern Italy. There are rood sculptures and reliefs, and beautifully decorated cassones in gilt and gesso; a *Neptune and Triton* by Giovanni Bernini and *Samson Slaying a Philistine* by Giovanni Bologna. The greatest treasures are two delicate reliefs by Donatello, the *Ascension With Christ Giving The Keys To St Peter*, which may have been commissioned for the Brancacci chapel in Santa Maria della Carmine in Florence, and a *Dead Christ Tended by Angels*, which may have been intended for Prato cathedral.

Poynter, Gamble and Morris Rooms

On your way through the Italian section you pass the world's first museum café-restaurant. Each of the three rooms is a rich, highly decorated example of Victorian design. The Poynter Room, originally the grill room, is decked out in blue tiles depicting idyllic country harvest scenes in between allegories of the seasons and the months of the year. The Gamble Room, used for the cold buffet, is a throwback to the Renaissance with its gold and blue tiles, enamelled metal ceiling and apt quotation from Ecclesiasticus around the walls: 'There is nothing better for a man than to eat and drink.' The last room is the work of William Morris, famous for the vegetal inspiration of his wallpaper designs.

Plaster Casts

Two rooms, straddling the altogether disappointing collection of fakes and forgeries, are devoted to near-perfect copies of some of the most famous sculptures and monuments in the world. The effect is altogether surreal: how can you get your mind around seeing Michelangelo's *David* and *Moses*, Ghiberti's *Gates of Paradise*, Trajan's Column from Rome, the *Puerta de la Gloria* from Santiago de Compostela and chunks of Bordeaux, Aix-en-Provence, Amiens, York and Nuremberg cathedrals all in one place?

Oriental Art

The central section of Level A is devoted to art from the Islamic world, India, China, Japan and Korea. The most famous piece is **Tipu's Tiger** in the Nehru Gallery of Indian Art. This is an adjustable wooden sculpture dating from 1790 in which a tiger can be seen mauling the neck of an English soldier. There are Indian sculptures of deities dating back to the 1st century BC, and paintings and artefacts giving an overview of two millennia of Indian decoration.

The Toshiba Gallery of **Japanese Art** boasts some particularly fine lacquer work: tables, trays and some amazing playing-card boxes. There are also some interesting ceramics, including a huge porcelain disc originally shown in Europe at the 1878 Paris Exhibition.

The **Chinese Art** section focuses principally on fine objects used in everyday life, particularly ceramics and a collection of ornaments and figurines used in burial ceremonies. Grander pieces include a large Ming dynasty canopied bed and a Qing dynasty embroidered hanging for a Buddhist temple. The **Korean Art** gallery also focuses on everyday objects, including some ancient metalwork, and ceramics from the Koryo and Choson dynasties that go back to the 9th century. Finally the section on **Art in the Islamic World** contains a pot pourri of carpets and prayer mats from Egypt and Turkey and finely decorated bowls and earthenware from Persia.

The Rest of Level A

Sandwiched in the middle of the oriental art sections is the **Medieval Treasury**, a beautiful collection of mainly religious artefacts from the 5th to the 15th century. The other remaining highlight of Level A is the **Raphael Cartoons**, sketches for the great religious and philosophical frescoes he painted for the Papal apartments in the Vatican. Dotted around the corridors of Level A are European works of all kinds dating from 1100 to 1800.

Level B: 20th Century Gallery

This series of altogether enthralling rooms is a far more engaging history of 20th-century design than the Design Museum at Butler's Wharf. The focus is on household furniture, but within that remit is everything from Marcel Breuer's pioneering Bauhaus chair to Salvador Dalí's totally frivolous lipstick-pink sofa in the shape of one of Mae West's kisses.

Tapestries

Beyond the 20th Century Gallery you have to walk through yards and yards of unexciting silver pots, metalwork and armour before reaching the tapestry collection and, in particular, the medieval series known as the **Devonshire Hunt**. Famed for their beauty, wealth of detail and high standard of preservation, these tapestries were commissioned in the 15th century for Hardwick Hall, a country mansion in southwestern England.

Henry Cole Wing

This wing, named after the museum's founding director, comes closest to the chest-in-the-attic analogy: much of what is in here is junk, particularly the painting section on the fourth floor, but a bit of patient burrowing will be well rewarded.

On the second floor is the **Frank Lloyd Wright Gallery**, a series of rooms dedicated to the great 20th-century American architect and figurehead of the modern movement. Floor three is reserved for special exhibitions of prints. Floor four is crammed with mediocre painting, much of it British. Skip past the fifth floor, which is a print library not open to the general public, and you come up to a light, airy exhibition of some of the best of British painting, including a clutch of Turners and a broad selection of the work of John Constable.

The glittering **glass gallery** at Room 131 shouldn't be missed either, with its staircase made entirely of green glass blocks.

Westminster Abbey

Parliament Square; ⊖ *Westminster; bus 3, 11, 12, 24, 53, 77A, 88, 109;*
✆ *(020) 7222 5152; www.westminster-abbey.org*

Admission to the Abbey is free for services or prayers. For visitors the nave is open Mon–Fri 9–4.45, last adm 3.45, and Sat 9–2.45, last adm 1.45; adm. Late night Weds 6–7.45pm, when amateur photos are allowed. The Cloisters are open daily 8–6; free. The Royal Chapels, Statesman's Aisle and Poets' Corner are open Mon–Fri, 9–4.45 and Sat, 9–2.45; adm. The Chapter House, Pyx Chamber and Undercroft Museum are open daily 10.30–4; adm. Guided tours conducted by the vergers are also available, call ✆ *(020) 7222 7110 to book.*

It is impossible to overestimate the symbolic importance of Westminster Abbey in English culture. This is where monarchs are crowned and buried, where the Anglican Church derives its deepest inspiration, and where the nation as a whole lionizes its artistic and political heroes. No other country invests so much importance in a single building.

Architecturally the abbey derives its inspiration from the great cathedrals at Reims and Amiens and the Sainte-Chapelle in Paris. 'A great French thought expressed in excellent English,' one epithet has it. The abbey's origins go back to the mists of the Dark Ages; it found a mystical patron in Edward the Confessor, saint and monarch; it was rebuilt from scratch in the finest Gothic traditions from the 13th until the 16th century; and it was completed in 1745. Thus the abbey spans virtually the whole of modern English history. To be buried there, or at least to have a plaque erected, is still the highest state honour for an English citizen. The tombs of the medieval kings and other relics bestow much of the legitimacy to which the modern monarchy can still lay claim. If St Paul's is a monument to the secular wealth of London, Westminster Abbey enshrines the mystical power of the crown.

It was Westminster's association with the crown that saved the abbey during the dissolution of the monasteries in the late 1530s, when it escaped with just a few smashed windows and broken ornaments. The royal connection made it a target during the Civil War, when Cromwell's army used it as a dormitory and smashed the altar rails. Cromwell succumbed to its lure once he was Lord Protector, however, and had himself buried in the abbey after his death in 1658. His body was dug up at the Restoration and eventually reburied at the foot of the gallows at Tyburn. After the Civil War, the abbey was once again given over to burials and coronations. Aside from royals, the place is stuffed with memorials to politicians (in the Statesman's Aisle), poets (in Poets' Corner), actors, scientists and engineers.

The coronation ceremony has become familiar around the world thanks to television re-runs of the investiture of Elizabeth II in 1953, the first coronation to be televised. But ceremonies have not always gone as smoothly as the establishment might have liked. Richard I had a bat swooping around his head during his ceremony, a sign perhaps of bad luck to come. Richard II lost a shoe in the Abbey, while James II's crown wobbled and nearly fell off during his parade down Whitehall. George IV was so weighed down by his outrageously extravagant coronation garb that he nearly fainted and had to be revived with smelling salts.

Pick up a floor plan at the entrance. Everything west of the choir screen is free; beyond is the old east end, now St Edward's Chapel; and beyond that the late Gothic extension including the Henry VII Chapel. The cloisters and Chapter House are off the end of the south transept.

The Nave

Measuring 103ft from floor to ceiling, the nave of Westminster Abbey is by far the tallest in England. But the nave is very long as well as high, giving an impression of general grandeur but not necessarily of loftiness. The columns, made of Purbeck marble, grow darker towards the ceiling, thus further deadening the effect of height. And the ceiling decorations push the eye not upwards, but along towards the altar. Overall, ornamentation is just as important as effects of perspective. As you come in, there is a 14th-century gilded painting of Richard II. The north aisle of the nave has become crowded with memorials and stones to politicians, earning the nickname **Statesman's Aisle**. Plenty of other walks of life are celebrated in this part of the abbey, notably scientists and engineers including Michael Faraday (a memorial tablet) and Sir Isaac Newton (a splendid monument against the choir screen by William Kent).

The Choir and St Edward's Chapel

The first attraction beyond the ticket counters, the choir screen, is a 19th-century reworking by Edward Blore of the gilded 13th-century original. Note the elegant black and white marble floor, and the heraldic shields commemorating the families who gave money to construct the abbey in the 13th century. Behind the High Altar is St Edward's Chapel, the epicentre of the abbey with its memorials to medieval kings around the Coronation Chair. Until November 1996, when it was finally removed to Edinburgh Castle, the simple gilded wooden chair contained the Stone of Scone, the most sacred symbol of the kings of Scotland, which was stolen by Edward I in 1279 and arrogantly kept for five and a bit centuries here in England.

Henry VII Chapel

The penny-pinching Henry VII managed one great feat of artistic patronage during his reign, this extraordinary fan-vaulted chapel which is nominally dedicated to the Virgin Mary but is in fact a glorification of the Tudor line of monarchs. Henrys VII and VIII, Edward VI, Mary and Elizabeth I are all buried here in style, along with a healthy sprinkling of their contemporaries and successors. Elizabeth shares her huge tomb with her embittered half-sister Mary in a curious after-death gesture of reconciliation. The bodies believed to be the two princes murdered in the Tower of London in 1483 also have a resting place here. The highlight of the chapel, though, is the decoration. The wondrous ceiling looks like an intricate mesh of finely spun cobwebs, while the wooden choirstalls are carved with exotic creatures and adorned with brilliantly colourful heraldic flags.

Poets' Corner

The south transept and the adjoining St Faith's Chapel are part of the original 13th-century abbey structure, and boast a series of wall paintings and some superbly sculpted figures of angels. Geoffrey Chaucer was buried in the south transept in 1400, and ever since other poets and writers have vied to have a place next to him after their deaths. When Edmund Spenser, author of *The Faerie Queen*, was buried in 1599, several writers tossed their unpublished manuscripts into the grave with him. His contemporary, the playwright Ben Jonson, asked modestly for a grave 'two feet by two feet' and consequently was buried upright. Few of the writers commemorated in Poets' Corner are actually interred here; among the 'genuine' ones are Dryden, Samuel Johnson, Sheridan, Browning and Tennyson. To free up more space in the increasingly crowded corner, the abbey authorities have recently installed a stained glass window with new memorials to parvenus such as Pope, Herrick and Wilde.

Bloomsbury	52
The City of London	55
Covent Garden	62
Mayfair	66
Piccadilly and Leicester Square	69
Soho and Chinatown	73
St James's and Royal London	76
The South Bank and Southwark	80

London: Central Neighbourhoods

Bloomsbury

⊖ *Holborn, Euston, Russell Square, Goodge Street, Warren Street*

Bloomsbury, according to William the Conqueror's survey *The Domesday Book*, started life as a breeding ground for pigs, but it has acquired a rather more **refined** pedigree since. Home to London University, the British Museum, the new British Library and countless bookshops and cafés, it is the **intellectual** heart of the capital. George Bernard Shaw, Giuseppe Mazzini, Marx and Lenin all found inspiration among the tomes of the Reading Room in the British Library. Bertrand Russell and Virginia Woolf helped form an intellectual movement here, the Bloomsbury Group, whose members invited each other for tea and gossip in the area's Georgian town houses. More recently, Bloomsbury has become a favoured location for the publishing trade and the new wave of independent television production companies. It is a **quiet**, slightly shabby but youthful quarter of London. Much of your energy will inevitably be devoted to the vast collections of the British Museum. But there's a good sprinkling of other curiosities as well, including some eccentric churches, a couple of interesting museums, and the jolly corpse of Jeremy Bentham sitting in a corner of University College.

52   London: Central Neighbourhoods

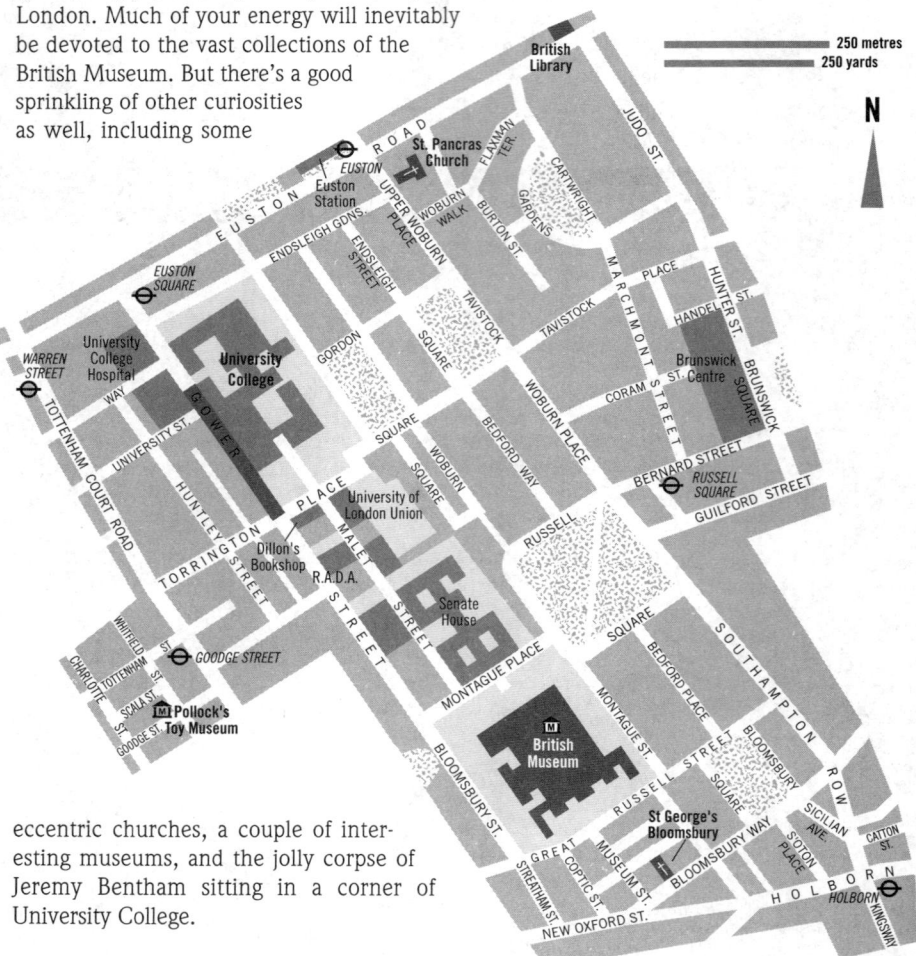

Bloomsbury Square

This was the original London housing development based on the leasehold system, and the model for the city's phenomenally rapid growth throughout the 18th and 19th centuries. Nowadays it is one of the more elegant squares in central London, with a ring of stately Georgian homes surrounding a flourishing garden. The square also has a plaque commemorating the **Bloomsbury Group**, a movement most often associated with its brightest member, the novelist Virginia Woolf, but which also included Woolf's husband Leonard, the novelist E.M. Forster, the economist John Maynard Keynes, the philosopher Bertrand Russell and the essayist Lytton Strachey. The group had no manifesto or specific aim; it was a loose association of like-minded intellectuals (most of them politically on the soft left) who met to exchange ideas. Following the teachings of the philosopher G.E. Moore, they believed that the appreciation of beautiful objects and the art of fine conversation were the keys to social progress.

Russell Square and the University of London

On the western side of the square looms **Senate House**, one of the spookiest buildings in London, which stands at the heart of the schools and colleges of the **University of London**.

The School of Oriental and African Studies (SOAS) sits in the northwest corner of Russell Square. On the corner of Malet Street is the students' union (ULU). If you happen to be a student yourself, you can use its good cheap bar. Halfway down Malet Street is **Birkbeck College**, which in 1823 became the first college in England to run evening courses for the working classes. It joined London University in 1920. Continuing down Torrington Place, you come to **Gower Street**, the blackened brick terraces of which sum up everything the Victorians disapproved of in Georgian building. Ruskin called it 'the *ne plus ultra* of ugliness in street architecture'. You can see what he meant: the sameness of the houses, relieved only by the occasional splash of paint on the lower storey, and the arrow-like straightness of the street. Along on the right, **University College** is a fine, if rather heavy, example of the Greek Revival style by William Wilkins, the architect of the National Gallery. Many Victorians hated the place, combining their dislike of classical architecture with their disapproval for what they called 'the godless College in Gower Street'. Visitors should head straight for the South Cloister in the far right-hand corner. Near the door is the glass cabinet with the stuffed body of **Jeremy Bentham**, the utilitarian philosopher and political reformer who died in 1832.

Cafés and Pubs

Museum Street Café, 47 Museum St. Overhyped but excellent bistro-style café with exquisitely presented home-made food.

The Coffee Gallery, 23 Museum St. Grilled aubergines, fishcakes with rocket, and scrumptious Sicilian salads.

Town House Brasserie, 24 Coptic St. Eclectic modern French 'fusion' food in smartish restaurant offering set lunch for £9.95, or an early bird menu, 2 courses for £5.

Bush & Field's Café, 49 Museum St. Great salt beef.

Wagamama, 4 Streatham St. Cheap, popular, delicious Japanese noodle ('ramen') bar—you might have to queue. £5–10.

Mandeer, 21 Hanway Place. Elegant but cheap vegetarian Indian restaurant a stone's throw from Tottenham Court Rd Tube, serving a fantastic value canteen-style lunch for under £5. Wonderful value.

Malabar Junction, 107 Great Russell Street. Set lunch from £3.50 in sleek but laid-back restaurant close to the British Museum.

Fitzroy Tavern, 16 Charlotte St. Drinking hole of the 1940s literati.

The British Library

Midland Street, ✆ (020) 7412 7332. Open Mon, Wed, Fri 9.30–6, Tues 9.30–8, Sat 9.30–5, Sun 11–5. Guided tours on certain days only; bookshops and a restaurant.

The history of this new building has been such a shambles that it came as a shock to most people when it finally opened, a decade late, in November 1997. Construction work on Colin St John Wilson's building began back in 1978 and took longer than the building of St Paul's cathedral. By the time it was completed, Wilson had overspent by £350 million, his practice had dissolved, and the building itself had been exposed to that peculiarly violent brand of venom that the British reserve for new architectural projects. Ironically, the building's most vicious critics have been stunned and delighted by the spectacular interior, with its vast scale, open tracts of white Travertine marble, and complex and fascinating spaces flooded with light. If the red brick exterior fills you with initial fear and loathing, remind yourself that the building is worth seeing for its three exhibition galleries and art treasures alone.

The big attraction is the library's vast number of **manuscripts**, from the sacred to the profane, from the delicate beauty of illuminated Bibles to the frenzied scrawl of Joyce's first draft of *Finnegan's Wake*; from musical scores to political documents, notebooks and private letters. Among the greatest treasures are the **Lindisfarne Gospels**, the work of a monk named Eadfrith who wrote and illuminated them on the island of Lindisfarne (also called Holy Island), off the northeastern coast of England, in honour of St Cuthbert. The other star exhibit is the **Magna Carta**. The British Library has two of the four surviving copies of this document, one of the founding texts of the modern democratic system signed by King John at Runnymede under pressure from his barons in 1215. Among the other manuscripts are Lenin's reapplication for a reader's ticket which he made under the pseudonym Jacob Richter. There is an extensive collection of literary manuscripts, including an illuminated version of Chaucer's *Canterbury Tales*, and—arguably the highlight—Lewis Carroll's beautifully neat handwriting and illustrations in the notebook version of *Alice in Wonderland*.

Stamp lovers should head for the **Philatelic Collections** which include first issues of nearly every stamp in the world from 1840 to 1890.

Also opening here from May 1998 will be the **British Library National Sound Archive** (*open Mon–Fri 10–5; free*). This wonderful collection includes early gramophones and record sleeves, and a series of priceless historical, literary and musical recordings: Florence Nightingale and Gladstone, Paul Robeson in a live performance of *Othello*, James Joyce reading from *Ulysses*, The Beatles interviewed by Jenny Everett, Charlie Parker's club performances (recorded on wire), and Stravinsky in rehearsal.

Pollock's Toy Museum

Corner of Scala St, ✆ (020) 7636 3452. Open Mon–Sat 10–5; very cheap adm.

Benjamin Pollock was the leading Victorian manufacturer of toy theatres, and this small but very attractive museum is based on the collection that he left. It's an atmospheric place, the four narrow floors connected by creaky staircases. The theatres are on the top floor, and exhibits also include board games, tin toys, puppets, wax dolls, teddy bears and dolls' houses.

Also see: The **British Museum**, p.29.
Onwards to: **Covent Garden**, p.62; **Tottenham Court Road shopping**, p.123.

The City of London

→ *Bank, St Paul's, Tower Hill, Mansion House, Monument, Barbican*
≈ *City Thameslink, Barbican, Fenchurch Street*

The City is the heart of London, the place where the whole heaving metropolis began, and yet there is something so strange about it that it scarcely seems to be part of London at all. Tens of thousands of commuters stream in each morning, the bankers, brokers and clerks that oil the wheels of this great centre of world finance, spilling out of Liverpool Street or crossing over London Bridge towards their jumble of gleaming high-rise offices. During the lunch hour, you can see them scurrying from office building to sandwich bar to post office, a look of studied intensity stamped on their harried faces. By early evening they have all vanished again, back to their townhouses and dormitory communities, leaving the streets and once-**monumental** buildings to slumber eerily in the silent gloom of the London night.

This is T.S. Eliot's 'Unreal City', a metropolis without inhabitants, a place of frenzied, seemingly mindless mechanical activity that the poet, back in the apocalyptic early 1920s, thought worthy of the lost souls of limbo. And yet it remains oddly fascinating, full of echoes of the time when it *was* London. Its streets still largely follow the medieval plan. Its fine churches and **ceremonial** buildings express all the contradictory emotions of a nation that built, and then lost, an entire empire. Its business is still trade, as it was in the 14th century, even if it is trade of a most abstract and arcane sort.

Wren's churches, and St Paul's Cathedral in particular, grace the skyline, but the area is also characterized by the bloody carcasses of Smithfield meat market and the grim legacy of Newgate prison, now converted into the Central Criminal Court.

At the other end of the Square Mile, the Tower of London is a striking relic of medieval London and a reminder of the constant **historical** struggle between wealth creation on the one hand and the jealous encroachment of political interests on the other. The City is a weekday place only, although you won't have any difficulty getting into the Tower or Guildhall on Saturday.

Temple Bar

In the Middle Ages this monument in Fleet Street was a barrier to control comings and goings into the City. So powerful were the City fathers that any unwelcome visitors were simply slung into the jail that stood on the site. The unlucky ones had their heads and pickled body parts displayed on spikes. Even the sovereign had to ask permission to pass this way, a tradition that has lasted in ritualistic form into the modern era. For 200 years an arched gateway designed by Wren marked this spot, but in 1878 it was removed because of traffic congestion and replaced with the present, rather modest monument by Horace Jones. The bronze **griffin** on top is one of the City's emblems, introduced by the Victorians who remembered that the griffins of mythology guarded over a hidden treasure of gold. They presumably forgot, however, that griffins also tore approaching humans to pieces as a punishment for their greed.

The City of London

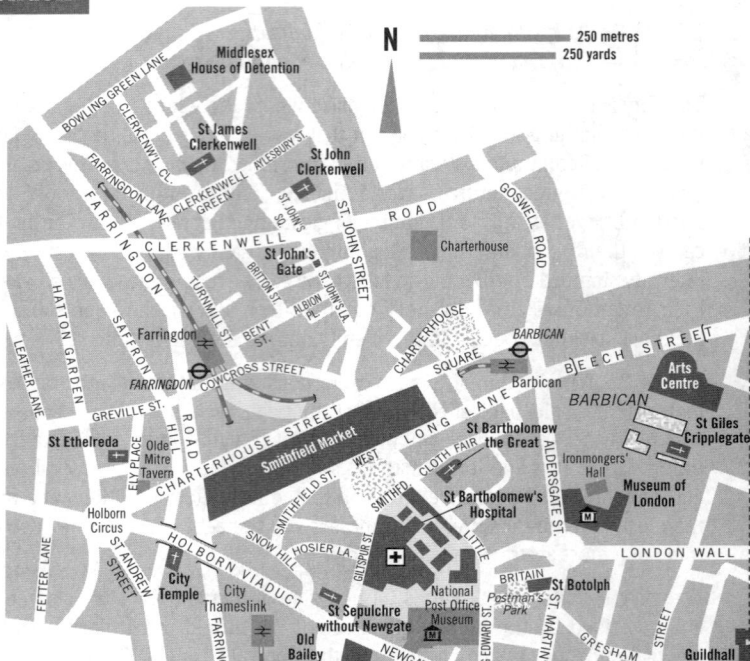

Mansion House

Mansion House, the official residence of the Lord Mayor of London, was intended to be something of a trend-setter, the first project of the Georgian era to be designed in Palladian style. There is a story that a design by Palladio himself was proposed but rejected because the 16th-century Italian master was a foreigner and a Papist. In the end George Dance's building, erected on the site of the old Stocks Market, was completed in 1752, nearly 40 years after the project was first put forward. The end result is not a tremendous success; the awkward shape of the surrounding square does not allow the eye to be drawn towards its grandiose portico, which in any case is top-heavy and unwieldy with its six Corinthian columns.

Unfortunately Mansion House is now almost always shut and more or less the only way to get in is to apply in writing for a minimum of 14 people two months in advance.

Cafés and Pubs

Dirty Dick's, 202 Bishopsgate. Dirty Dick was a dandy called Nathaniel Bentley. His fiancée died on the eve of their wedding in 1787, and he never washed again. When he died in 1809, the house was in ruins. Rebuilt in 1870, it's now a jolly cellar bar; lunch is well-cooked bar food from £5–8.

Reynier Wine Library, 43 Trinity Square. Wine cellar deep in the city where customers choose a bottle of wine from the comprehensive 'library', and down it with cheese and pâté from the simple but tasty £10 buffet. Lunch only from £13 upwards. *Open 10–6 Mon–Fri.*

Imperial City, basement of the Royal Exchange. A fine Chinese restaurant beneath vaulted brick ceilings. £16–35.

Obertelli's, 38 and 60 Lime St Passage. Sandwiches and café-style food. £3–6.

Poons in the City, 2 Minster Pavement. Stylish Chinese restaurant; lunch from £5 or £12 for the set meal.

The Place Below, St Mary-le-Bow, Cheapside. Award-winning, very popular, nutritious and vegetarian salads and soups in the basement undercroft of this historic City church. £3–7.

Simpson's of Cornhill, Cornhill. Traditional English food in a traditional eaterie off Cornhill: grills, bubble and squeak, steamed jam roll. £2–3 for starters, £5–7 for main courses

The Greenery, 5 Cowcross St. Healthy veggie snacks, salads and sandwiches. Restaurant and take-away sections. £2–4.

Fox and Anchor, 115 Charterhouse St. Famous Smithfield pub serving full breakfast (£7) and steak for lunch from £6–10.

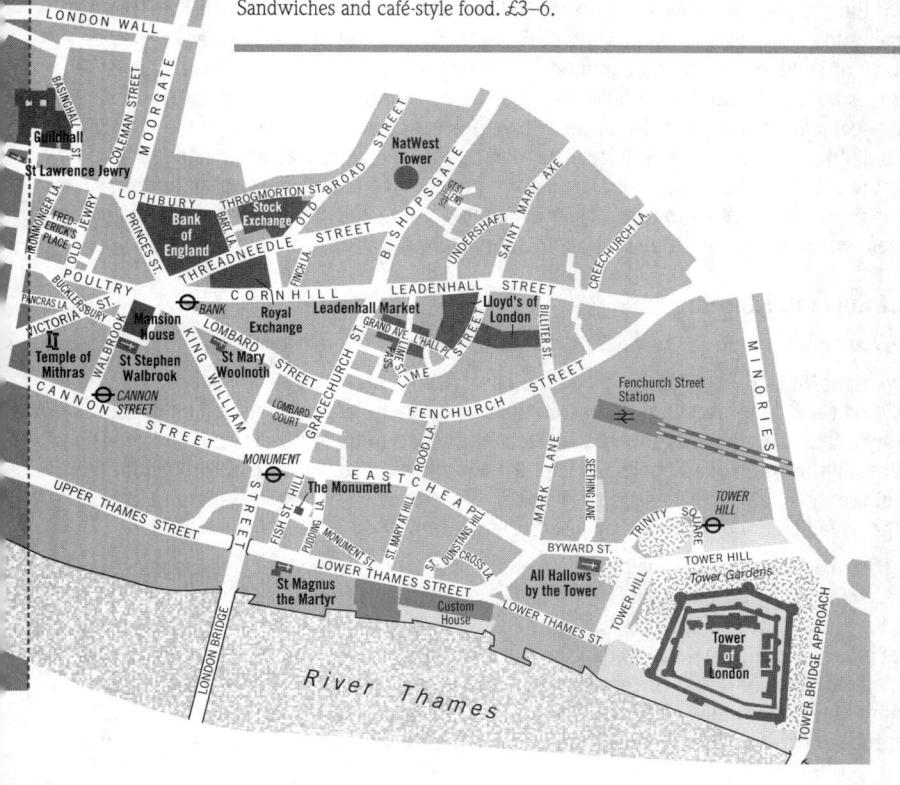

The City of London

Guildhall

Open 10–5 daily except on special occasions, closed Sun Oct–April; free.

The Guildhall is the seat of the City's government, headed by the Lord Mayor and his Sheriffs and Aldermen and composed principally of the 12 Great Livery Companies, or guilds, that nominally represent the City's trading interests. Nowadays the governing body, known as the Corporation of London, is little more than a borough council for the City, but back in the Middle Ages it wielded near-absolute power over the whole of London. Even kings could not touch it, since the guilds generated much of the nation's wealth and made sure everyone knew it. Henry III tried to impose direct rule on London in the 13th century but eventually gave up, describing the City fathers as 'nauseously rich'.

First built in the 15th century, architecturally the Guildhall has also retained much from the medieval era, despite the calamities of the Great Fire and the Blitz. The building nevertheless bears the marks of countless renovations. The pinnacled façade looking on to Guildhall Yard is a bizarre 18th-century concoction of classical, Gothic and even Indian styles.

You'll need to make an advance booking for a group to see the **crypt**, the most extensive of its kind left in London.

Royal Exchange

The eight huge Corinthian pillars give this building a sense of importance to which it can no longer lay claim. The Royal Exchange was once the trading centre of the City *par excellence*, home to all of London's stock and commodity exchanges, but it lost this crucial role in 1939 when it was bought by the Guardian Royal Exchange insurance company. It now houses a number of company offices. This is the third Royal Exchange building to occupy the site. The present building, designed by Sir William Tite, dates from 1844, a rare example of neoclassical architecture from the Victorian era. Tite's Exchange comes complete with an equestrian **statue of the Duke of Wellington**, made in suitably triumphalist fashion from the melted-down metal of French guns. There is also a memorial to the war dead of London.

Bank of England Museum

Open Mon–Fri 10–5; free; follow the building round into Bartholomew Lane.

The playwright Richard Sheridan described the Bank of England as 'an elderly lady in the City of great credit and long standing'. Its record as prudent guardian of the nation's finances is well known; it rescued London from bankruptcy at the end of the 17th century, resisted the temptations of the South Sea Bubble and kept the country's economy buoyant throughout the trauma of the Revolutionary wars against France. As the bank of last resort it played a crucial role in the development of Britain's capitalist system during the 18th and 19th centuries.

But the Bank has had a tough time of it in recent years, particularly since the abandonment of worldwide currency controls in the 1970s. The rise of virtually unfettered currency speculation has severely limited its control over the value of sterling. At the same time, the changing nature of international capital has made it increasingly hard for the Bank to monitor the activities of the commercial houses. In compensation, it has won independence from the Treasury and is now free to set interest rates as it sees fit. But even this role is under threat from the single European currency and the establishment of a pan-European central bank in Frankfurt.

Architecturally, the Bank has a distinctly mixed record. At the end of the 18th century Sir John Soane, that most quirky and original of English architects, came up with a magnificently intricate neoclassical design, a veritable treasure trove of inter-connecting rooms each with its own peculiarities of light and decoration. In 1925 the Bank governors decided they needed more space, and instead of considering an extension or a new building they simply demolished Soane's work and replaced it with an unimaginative multi-storey patchwork by Sir Herbert Baker. All that remains of Soane's original work is the secure curtain wall on the outer rim of the building and, thanks to a postwar reconstruction, the first room in the museum, the **Bank Stock Office**. Beneath Soane's vaulted roof, illuminated naturally through a series of skylights, the museum's displays recount the architectural fortunes of the Bank and show off some of the original mahogany counter-tops and oak ledger-rests. You are then led through a series of rooms, culminating in Herbert Baker's Rotunda, that give an account of the Bank's history.

The Old Bailey

The soaring gilt statue of Justice rising from the **roof** of the Old Bailey (*accessible via several flights of stairs only, open Mon–Fri, 10–1 and 2–when court rises, around 5, no cameras, large bags, drink, food, pagers, radios, mobile phones, etc., no children under 14, no cloakroom for bags; free*) has become such a potent symbol of temperance in the English legal system that it has eradicated virtually all memory of the barbarity once associated with this site. Until 1902 this place was Newgate Prison, one of the most gruesome of all jails, which Henry Fielding once described as a prototype for hell. Generations of prisoners were left here, quite literally, to rot; to this day judges wear posies of sweet-smelling flowers on special occasions as a grim reminder of the stench that used to emanate from the cold, filthy cells.

The mood now could not be more different. The nickname Old Bailey, referring to the alley running off Newgate Street, conveniently avoids all reference to the old prison. Ask about the place's history and you will be given a list, not of the horrors of incarceration, but of the famous names whose trials have taken place here: Oscar Wilde; the Edwardian wife-murderer Dr Crippen; and William Joyce, known as Lord Haw-Haw, who broadcast enemy propaganda from Nazi Germany during the Second World War.

You are welcome to attend a **court hearing** in one of the public galleries, although the tightly arranged wooden benches are not exactly designed for comfort. The rituals are similar to those of the civil courts, although the mood is inevitably more sombre.

St Mary-le-Bow

Wren almost certainly left the bulk of his church renovations to subordinates; it is hard to imagine that he had time to redesign all 52 himself. This church, however, bears all the signs of his own imprint. It is famous for two reasons. First for its massive, distinctive steeple, which soars 217ft into the sky, and secondly for its **Bow Bells** which have formed part of the mythology of London for centuries. It was their resounding peal that persuaded the fairytale Dick Whittington to turn again and return to London in search of fame and fortune. Ever since, the tradition has been that anyone born within earshot of the bells can call himself a true Londoner. There is a third, less well known, reason why you should visit St Mary-le-Bow: its magnificently preserved Norman **crypt**. Along with the Guildhall's, it is one of the few left in London.

Lloyd's Building

The City's most innovative and challenging building is Richard Rogers' design for **Lloyd's of London**, the world's biggest insurance market. On Leadenhall St itself, to the right, you can see a fine façade from the 1925 incarnation of Lloyd's. The entrance to the Richard Rogers building is on Lime St, the continuation of St Mary Axe, although since the IRA bombs of 1992 and 1993 the building has been closed to the public (*group visits can be organised via the Communications Department on ℂ (020) 7327 1000*).

Monument

Viewing platform, accessible by spiral staircase, open 10–5.40; adm; ℂ (020) 7626 2717.

The Monument commemorates the Great Fire of London. On its completion in 1677 it was the tallest free-standing column in the world; now it is so obscured by office buildings it is easy to miss. The view from the top is obscured by office buildings but still enjoyable.

St Etheldreda's

Ely Place.

Etheldreda was a 7th-century Anglo-Saxon princess who had the distressing habit of marrying and then refusing to sleep with her husbands. When husband number two, Prince Egfrith of Northumbria, finally lost patience with her and made unseemly advances, she withdrew into holy orders and founded a double monastery at Ely in Cambridgeshire. Seven years later, in 679, she was stricken with a tumour on her neck and died. None mourned Etheldreda more than her sister, the unfortunately named Sexburga, who campaigned ardently to have her sanctity recognized. In 695, Sexburga had Etheldreda's coffin opened and found that the tumour had quite vanished. Her skin was now quite unblemished. A miracle!

Etheldreda became Ely's special saint and was the obvious choice of patron for this double-storeyed church, built in the 13th century as part of the Bishop of Ely's palace. The Gothic **upper church** is a warm, lofty room with a fine wooden-beamed ceiling and huge stained-glass windows at each end. The east window, behind the altar, is particularly striking with its depiction of the Holy Trinity surrounded by the apostles and Anglo-Saxon and Celtic saints including Etheldreda herself. The west window is much starker, portraying the martyrdom of three Carthusian priors at Tyburn in 1535 with Christ hovering over them. Both windows date from after the Second World War; their predecessors were shattered by German bombs. Downstairs, the lower church or **crypt** is much simpler, no more than a room with a plain altar and little decoration.

Smithfield Market

Smithfield has come a long way since the 14th century, when cattle was slaughtered in front of the customers and witches boiled alive for the entertainment of the populace. This is still where Londoners come to buy their meat, but nowadays it is a civil, sanitized sort of place. The carcasses arrive ready-slaughtered and are stored in giant fridges so you'll barely see a speck of dirt or blood. The covered market halls have been refurbished and are surrounded by restaurants and pubs.

Leadenhall Market

Leadenhall Market is a pleasant surprise: a whiff of real life among the office blocks. It has considerable charm, plenty of bustle, often live music and excellent food, particularly meat, fish and cheese. The prices match the clientèle, many of them businessmen doing some inexpert and usually extravagant housekeeping on behalf of their wives stranded in suburbia; hence the popularity of game and exotic fish.

Barbican Centre

The Brave New World architecture of the Barbican comes straight out of the 1950s, all high-rise concrete and labyrinthine walkways. The City's only residential area worthy of the name, rebuilt after wartime bombing, would not be out of place in a 1960s television escape drama, though there are some advantages to living here: the leafy balconies, the forecourts and fountains.

The main reason for coming, apart from the dubious pleasure of gaping and shuddering, is a trip to the **Arts Centre**, home to the Royal Shakespeare Company, an art gallery (*open 10–6.45 except Tues to 5.45, Wed to 7.45, Sun 12–6.45; adm*), three cinemas, a concert hall and a semi-tropical conservatory (*on Level 3, irregular opening on Sun only, call © (020) 7638 4141 for more details*). On the way, you pass **St Giles Cripplegate** (*open Mon–Fri 9.30–5.30*), where John Milton was buried in 1674. The church itself, mostly built in the 16th century, escaped the 1666 fire but was destroyed by wartime bombs and faithfully rebuilt in the 1950s. A stretch of the Roman city wall can be seen just behind it.

Clerkenwell

By turns a centre for monks, clockmakers, gin manufacturers and Italian labourers, Clerkenwell has the feel of a cosy village with its squares, winding streets and pretty churches. Its proximity to the City made it an ideal headquarters for the knights of the Order of St John, who stayed here until the dissolution of the monasteries in the 1530s. Then in the early 17th century the digging of the New River put Clerkenwell on the main freshwater route into London and so attracted brewers and distillers. In the 19th century much of Clerkenwell was slumland, and the Victorians built forbidding prisons there to cope with the overflow from the city jails. After decades of neglect, it is now undergoing something of a revival, its grimy backstreets filling with offices, converted lofts and cheap, attractive cafés.

The sites of Clerkenwell are all within easy reach from the Green, which was often used in the 19th century as a starting point for protest marches. The **Marx Memorial Library** at Nos.37–8 (*open Mon 1–6, Tues–Thurs 1–8, Sat 10–1, closed Fri; non-members are welcome to look around for free but cannot use the library or its lending facility unless they pay a modest membership fee*) has the best private collection of radical literature in the city; Lenin wrote pamphlets here in 1902–3. Clerkenwell Close (off to the left) leads to the attractive yellow brick **St James's Church**, once part of a Benedictine nunnery but rebuilt many times. The steeple, the latest addition, dates from 1849. Further up the Close (follow the signposts) is the alarmingly Gothic **Middlesex House of Detention** (*open 10–6; adm*), the site of one of the area's notorious Victorian prisons, itself a conversion of an earlier prison.

Also see: **St Paul's Cathedral**, p.40; the **Museum of London**, p.135.
Onwards to: **Tower of London**, p.44; the **South Bank and Southwark**, p.80.

Covent Garden

Leicester Square, Covent Garden, Charing Cross, Tottenham Court Road

Covent Garden, home to the Royal Opera House and the converted fruit and vegetable market, is **teeming** with restaurants, natty boutiques and street performers. Sundays are rather quiet as the theatres are dark, but the market and shops are open. The Theatre Museum is shut on Mondays.

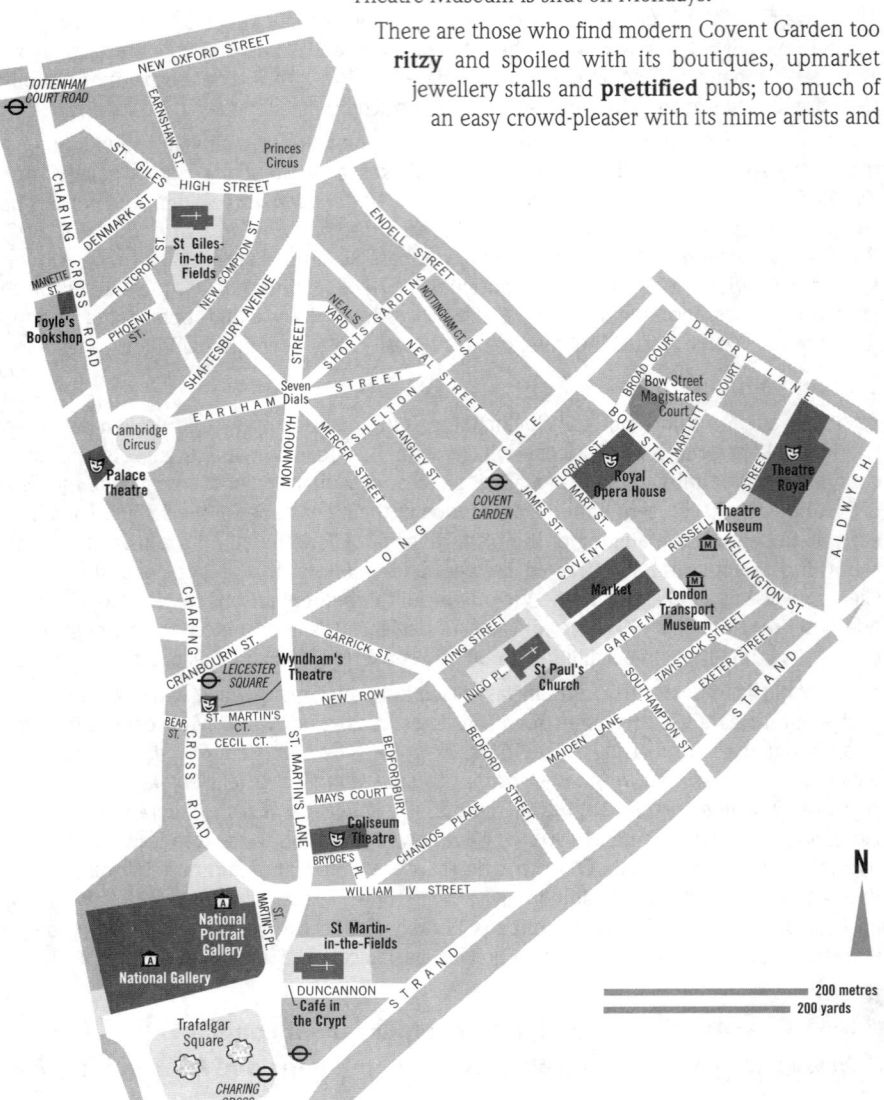

There are those who find modern Covent Garden too **ritzy** and spoiled with its boutiques, upmarket jewellery stalls and **prettified** pubs; too much of an easy crowd-pleaser with its mime artists and

62   London: Central Neighbourhoods

Cafés and Pubs

Belgo, 50 Earlham Street. Frites, mussels and Belgian beer, high-tech interior décor, and fashionable metropolitan crowd; lunch from £5–20.

Neal's Yard Dining Rooms, 14 Neal's Yard. Cheap, tasty and filling home-made vegetarian 'worldfood', from Mexican to Indian and African street food. £6–8 for a full meal.

Café in the Crypt, church of St Martin-in-the-Fields. Self service, hot and cold food in this atmospheric vaulted brick crypt. Main dishes around £5–7.

Food for Thought, Neal Street. One of London's first vegetarian cafés and still maintaining high standards. £5–£7.50.

Calabash, 38 King St. Come here for unusual and excellent dishes from all over Africa (grillled plantain, groundnut stew, etc.). Downstairs in the Africa Centre. Main dish £7–9.

Joe Allen, 13 Exeter Street. Great burgers (not on the menu; you have to know to ask!) and American-style food and monster puddings for grown-ups. Theatrically 'luvvie' in the evenings. Good Sunday brunch. £20–£25.

---

handclapping bands belting out yet another rendition of *I'm a Believer* or *The Boxer*; too much—heaven forbid—of a *tourist attraction*. Looking into the past, however, one should perhaps be relieved it is even half as pleasant as it is. When the wholesale fruit and vegetable market moved out to the south London suburbs in the 1970s, the London authorities initially wanted to build office blocks and a major roadway through here. Wouldn't that have been fun? It was the local traders and residents who saved Covent Garden with protests and petitions; it is also the locals who, by and large, have the run of the place today. Dig a little, and behind the obvious tourist draws are plenty of quieter, more discreet spots. If Covent Garden seems a little derivative, it is because it deliberately and self-consciously echoes its own past—a dash of Inigo Jones's original piazza with its street life and sideshows, several measures of Charles Fowler's covered market, plus plenty of the eating, drinking and general revelry that have always characterized this neighbourhood.

Covent Garden Market

With the loss of the original fruit and vegetable market, Covent Garden has undoubtedly lost its rough edges. The main hall, once littered with crates and stray vegetables, is now spick and span, while the Flower Market houses museums devoted to transport and the theatre. Unlike the disastrous redevelopment of Les Halles in Paris, however (see p.217), the place has not lost its soul. You can still buy roast chestnuts or a greasy baked potato from a street vendor as Dickens did, or watch clowns and jugglers performing in front of St Paul's where Punch and Judy shows first caught the public imagination in the 17th century.

In the lower level of the market is the wonderful **Cabaret Mechanical Theatre** (*open school holidays Mon–Sat 10–7, Sun 11–7; termtime Mon–Fri 10–6.30, Sat 10–7 and Sun 11–6.30; adm cheap, children under five free, award-winning website www.cabaret.co.uk*). This small and eccentric compendium of automata is guaranteed to amuse practically anyone from anywhere, instantly. On one side there's a quirky but jolly amusement arcade, with handmade machines costing 10–20p a go; on the other a fascinating exhibition of over 64 push-button automata. Tickets to the Exhibition are stamped by a wooden mechanical man; once you're inside, everything is push-button-operated and free.

Neal Street

This pedestrian alley is a pleasant throwback to the hippy era, all beads, home-made earrings and wholefood. While Carnaby Street, the in-place in the 1960s, has faltered and died, Neal Street, a development from the late 1970s, has survived largely thanks to its jolly shops and cheap vegetarian cafés. Turn left down Shorts Gardens and you come to distinctly New Age **Neal's Yard**, a tranquil triangular oasis planted with trees, and an excellent place to sit, away from the traffic fumes and confusion. There are plentiful cheap vegetarian eats here, a world food café, a beach café, an East-West herb shop, a groovy hairdresser's, a walk-in backrub parlour, an excellent bakery, a natural cosmetics shop, and the famous Neal's Yard Therapy Rooms, offering the gamut of 'alternative' therapies, from acupuncture to lymphatic drainage, from past-life counselling to 'rolfing'. As a last resort, there's a host of New Age shops stuffed with rainbow crystals, candles, incense, holograms and books on mystical healing. On your way in, don't miss the Heath Robinson clock above the Neal's Yard Wholefood Warehouse.

On the other side of Shorts Gardens is **Thomas Neal's Arcade**, filled with designer shops. With its wrought iron lamps and glass roof, this is another derivative piece of modern London architecture, this time a throwback to the arcaded emporia of the 19th century.

Royal Opera House

Two of the most famous London theatres are a mere stone's throw away: the **Theatre Royal Drury Lane**, which is not in Drury Lane but on the corner of Russell St and Catherine St (you can see it as you come out of the Theatre Museum to your right); and the **Royal Opera House**, better known simply as Covent Garden, which is off to the left down Bow St. Both buildings have been scourged by fire in their lives, and the Royal Opera House was razed to the ground in 1856, except for its portico.

Nowadays the drama focuses around the scaffolding, flying sparks, lunging cranes, exposed steel, concrete frames and girders and pungent circus smells as intensive construction works continue on a massive £230 million redevelopment of the opera house and an imaginative extension of the site surrounding it. These works are long overdue: the 1858 building has had no real maintenance since the 1960s, and the cramped and stifling back-stage facilities used by two separate companies (The Royal Ballet as well as The Royal Opera) and a leaking roof were in dire need of repair and technical updating. The redevelopment—by architects Jeremy Dixon and Edward Jones—will integrate the Opera House with Covent Garden market for the first time, replacing the Georgian houses on the north side of Russell Street with elegant glass and wrought iron shopping arcades (also containing cafés, restaurants and a box office) and a loggia walkway above, all based on Inigo Jones's original piazza. It is due to open in late 1999.

Bow Street Magistrates' Court

Opposite the entrance to the Opera House is the old **Bow Street Magistrates' Court** where the Fieldings, Henry and John, held court in the 18th century. Henry, who was a trained barrister as well as the author of *Tom Jones*, used his tenure here to set up the Bow Street Runners, an informal plainclothes police force that worked to crack down on underworld gangs and challenge the infamous official marshals, or 'thief-takers', who were usually in cahoots with the thieves themselves. The Runners proved remarkably effective and soon became famous throughout the land, particularly for their role in thwarting the Cato Street conspiracy in 1820. Until Robert Peel's uniformed 'bobbies' appeared in the 1830s, they were the closest thing to a police force that London had.

St Paul's Church

Inigo Place; church and gardens open Tues–Fri 9.30–4.30, services Sun 11am, ✆ (020) 7836 5221.

Don't be surprised if you feel you are sneaking up to this church from behind. That is exactly what you are doing. Properly speaking, St Paul's is part of the original Covent Garden piazza (*see* below) which Inigo Jones built in mock-Italian style in the 1630s. Jones made one crucial oversight, however. He and his low-church patron, the Earl of Bedford, thought they could get away with putting the altar of their church at the western end, so breaking with convention which insists it should be in the east. The Bishop of London, William Laud, ordered Jones to put the altar where it traditionally belongs, in this case flush against the planned main entrance. The interior is of disarming simplicity: a double square, 100ft by 50ft. St Paul's is one of the few pre-Great Fire buildings still left in London, and the only significant part of Inigo Jones's piazza still standing. St Paul's quickly won the affections of the theatre folk of Covent Garden, who preached here as well as attending services. They nicknamed it the Actors' Church, and several luminaries of the stage are buried here, including Ellen Terry, the *grande dame* of the late-Victorian theatre, whose ashes are marked by a plaque in the south wall.

St Martin-in-the-Fields

Open 8.30–6; free lunchtime concerts at 1.05pm on Mon, Tues, Fri, evening concerts at 7.30pm on Thurs, Fri and Sat; ✆ (020) 7930 1862.

The church of St Martin-in-the-Fields is the oldest building on Trafalgar Square, and the only one truly to benefit from the exposure the square affords; its curious combination of Greek temple façade and Baroque steeple catches the eye, even if the mix is a little awkward. Its churchyard, now a daytime junk market (*open daily 10–5.30*), contains the graves of Charles II's mistress Nell Gwynne and the 18th-century painters Reynolds and Hogarth. The church has become popular for its concerts and resident orchestra, the Academy of St Martin-in-the-Fields.

St Martin's Lane

Already you have stepped into London's theatreland, as the black strip at the bottom of the street signs says. The theatres along St Martin's Lane—the Albery and Duke of York's as well as the Coliseum—all date from the turn of the century and so were among the last great playhouses to be built in London. But as early as the 18th century the street was attracting such artistic residents as Joshua Reynolds, first president of the Royal Academy, and Thomas Chippendale, the furniture maker.

One of the main sites in St Martin's Lane is the distinctive globe of the **Coliseum** theatre (tickets and information, ✆ (020) 7632 8300), home to the excellent English National Opera. Built in 1904, this was the first theatre in England with a revolving stage. Now the whole place is under threat, with the government planning to move the ENO into Covent Garden along with the Royal Opera and Ballet. So catch it while you can.

Also see: **National Gallery**, p.38; **National Portrait Gallery**, p.132; **Trafalgar Square**, p.45; **London Transport Museum**, p.137; **Theatre Museum**, p.140.

Onwards to: **The City of London**, p.55; **Soho and Chinatown**, p.73; **Covent Garden shopping**, p.128.

Mayfair

◆ *Bond Street, Green Park, Piccadilly Circus*

The May Fair was once exactly that: an annual festival of eating, drinking, entertainments and (usually) debauchery that took place in the first two weeks of May. The custom began in 1686 when the area was in its infancy; by the middle of the 18th century, the neighbourhood had gone so far upmarket that the residents described the fair as 'that most pestilent nursery of impiety and vice' and made sure it was shut down for good. Mayfair has been pretty **staid** ever since, the preserve of London's *beau monde* who want nothing more than to be left alone. You will nevertheless notice, particularly around Curzon Street, some fine 18th-century houses and a few oddities. If you have ever played the London version of *Monopoly*, you will know that Oxford Street, Bond Street, Regent Street, Park Lane and Mayfair itself are the most expensive and desirable properties on the board. But Mayfair has not lived up to its early promise. It is cosmopolitan and **expensive**, but not really fashionable; **elegant** and well-maintained, but not sophisticated; central and self-important, but at the same time strangely quiet. In short, the place does not buzz.

So why visit at all? The main reason is a certain quirky charm which most visitors to the big shops of Oxford Street and Regent Street fail entirely to find. The eccentrically built jewellery shops on Old Bond Street, the bustle of Shepherd Market: these are all little-known curiosities within a stone's throw of the hordes that mill through London's main thoroughfares every day. Here in the heart of London you can enjoy a gentle stroll among Georgian mansions and fine shops, while having the streets virtually to yourself.

Bond Street

Two kinds of shopkeeper dominate Bond Street: jewellers and art dealers, whose gaudy if not always particularly attractive shop fronts make for a diverting stroll. **Old Bond Street**, the lower part of the thoroughfare, concentrates mainly on jewellery and includes all the well-known international names including Tiffany's at No.25 (note the distinctive gold-trimmed clock hanging above the entrance). Evidently these establishments have kept going through the recession thanks to the patronage of the Russian mafia, which has made London its main foreign outpost. Old Bond Street brought a rare piece of good luck to the inveterate 18th-century rake and gambler, Charles James Fox, who once made a bet with the Prince of Wales on the number of cats appearing on each side of the street. No fewer than 13 cats appeared on Fox's side, and none on the Prince of Wales's. Maybe, though, Fox should have taken his inauspicious number of cats as an omen and steered clear of the gambling dens of St James's, since he later went bankrupt and had to be bailed out by his father.

The turning on the left just after Stafford Street is the **Royal Arcade**. Built in 1879, it is one of the kitschier examples of the genre with caryatids painted orange and white above the entrance. Walk through the arcade to emerge on Albermarle Street. Across the road on the right is one of the entrances to **Brown's Hotel**. This old-fashioned hotel remains one of the quintessential addresses of aristocratic London. Founded by a former manservant in 1837, it retains the kind of service one imagines to have been quite commonplace in the houses of gentlemen of quality. Franklin and Eleanor Roosevelt spent their honeymoon here, while in room 36 the Dutch government declared war on Japan during the Second World War. Nowadays, the time to come is for tea when, for a slightly cheaper rate than the Ritz, you can

Cafés and Pubs

Boudin Blanc, 5 Trebeck St. Cheap French bistro food. Popular, atmospheric and good value with a two-course set lunch from £6.95.

Al Hamra, 31–33 Shepherd Market. Upmarket Lebanese fare. Delicious but rather expensive. £20–30.

Sofra, 18 Shepherd Street. Attractive, more relaxed Middle Eastern alternative to the above, this time Turkish. £16–21.

Da Corradi, 47 Curzon St. All-day breakfast in this high-quality Italian greasy spoon. £10.

Ye Grapes, Shepherd Market (no number). Attractive and popular pub tucked into the corner of the main square of the market.

Ristorante Italiano, 54 Curzon St. Quaintly old-world, much-loved restaurant from the 1950s, serving London literary types with good traditional Italian pasta and main courses; lunch from £15 closed lunchtimes on Sat and all Sun.

Mirabelle, 56 Curzon St, ✆ (020) 7499 4636. Incredible-value set lunch from £14.50 in this glamorous Marco Pierre White restaurant, popular with the smart set. Reserve.

---

fill up on scones and cucumber sandwiches and enjoy the attentions of demure waiters in tails. Dress smart or they won't let you in (*see* p.158).

New Bond Street, the top half towards Oxford Street, is the province of high-class designer clothes and accessory shops, plus also the showrooms of art dealers like Bernard Jacobson and Le Fevre (or, on Cork Street, Waddington and Victoria Miro). Sotheby's, the famous auctioneers, are at Nos.34–35 New Bond Street; above the front door is the oldest outdoor sculpture in London, an ancient Egyptian figure made of igneous rock dating back to 1600 BC.

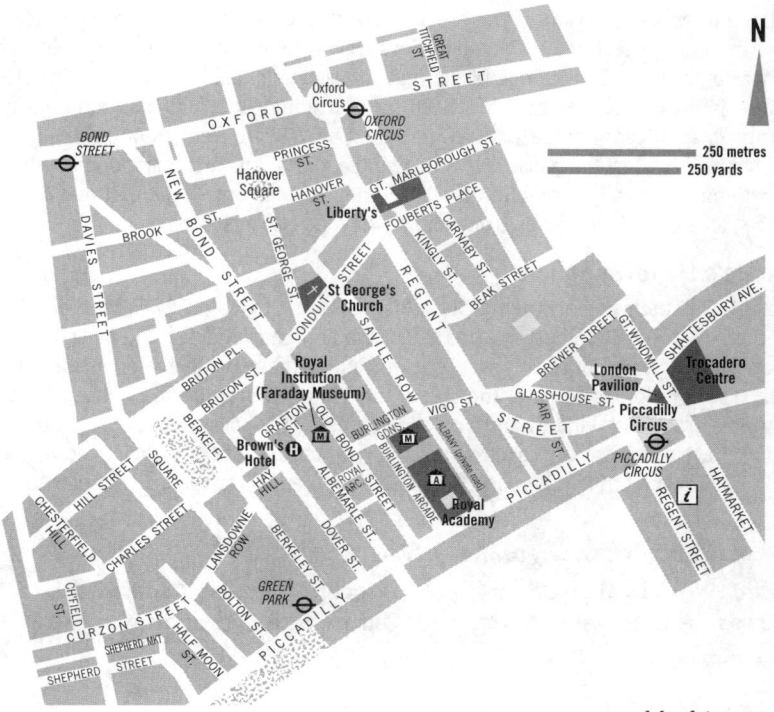

Royal Institution/Faraday Museum

21 Albermarle St. Open Mon–Fri, 10–6; adm.

This large, grand building, with its pompous façade based on the Temple of Antoninus in Rome, is to science what the Royal Academy is to the arts: the most prestigious association of professionals in the land. Founded in 1799, the Institution built up a formidable reputation thanks to early members such as Humphrey Davy (inventor of the Davy Lamp for detecting methane down mines) and his pupil, Michael Faraday. The small museum (the only part of the building regularly open to the public) is in fact Faraday's old laboratory where he carried out his pioneering experiments with electricity in the 1830s; his work is explained with the help of his original instruments and lab notes. The Royal Institution also organizes excellent lectures, including series specially designed for children.

Shepherd Market

There may not be any more May Fairs in Mayfair, but this enchanting warren of cafés, restaurants and small shops nevertheless comes as a nice surprise after all the stuffiness of its surroundings. Back in the 17th century, this was where the fire-eaters, jugglers, dwarves and boxers would entertain the crowds in early spring. The entrepreneur Edward Shepherd then turned the area into a market in 1735 (notice the attractive low Georgian buildings), and it has been a focus for rather more low-key entertainment ever since.

Berkeley Square

This is a key address for debutantes and aristocratic young bucks, who come for the annual Berkeley Square Charity Ball and vie to join the square's exclusive clubs and gaming houses. The chief interest to the visitor is the elegant row of Georgian houses on the west side. The highlight is No.44, described by Nikolaus Pevsner as 'the finest terraced house in London', which was built in 1742–4 for one of the royal household's maids of honour. Unfortunately the house is now a private casino called the Clermont Club, and its stunning interior, including a magnificent double staircase designed by William Kent, is out of bounds to the general public. They say the house is haunted by the ghost of its first major-domo, who can be heard coming down the stairs with his slight limp; one can only hope that one day he will spook the gamblers off the premises and allow everyone else a closer look.

St George's Hanover Square

A neoclassical church with a striking Corinthian portico, St George's was built in 1721–4 as part of the Fifty New Churches Act. It is the parish church of Mayfair and has proved enduringly popular as a venue for society weddings, including the match between Shelley and Mary Godwin. The interior, restored at the end of the Victorian era, has some fine 16th-century Flemish glass in the east window and a painting of the Last Supper above the altar attributed to William Kent. Notice also the cast-iron dogs in the porch; these once belonged to a shop in Conduit St and were brought here in 1940 after their original premises were bombed.

Also see: **Bond Street shopping**, p.122.

Onwards to: **Royal Academy**, p.72; **Piccadilly**, p.71; **Green Park**, p.111; **St James's and Royal London**, p.76; **Oxford Street shopping**, p.120.

Piccadilly and Leicester Square

⊖ *Leicester Square, Piccadilly Circus, Green Park*

The Piccadilly area has long been considered rather **vulgar**. The strange name derives from the fortunes of Robert Baker, a 17th-century tailor who made a fortune and built himself a mansion here on the proceeds in 1612. At the time, the land was totally undeveloped apart from a windmill (which inspired the name of the street leading off to the north of Piccadilly Circus, Great Windmill Street). Baker's peers thought his ostentation ridiculous and nicknamed his house Pickadilly Hall to remind him of his humble origins, a *pickadil* being a contemporary term for a shirt cuff or hem.

The development of St James's and Mayfair in the 18th century made Piccadilly one of the busiest thoroughfares in London. The area grew more **crowded** still in the late 19th century with the construction of Shaftesbury Avenue and a flurry of new theatres. Bus routes multiplied and an Underground station was constructed, followed by vast advertising hoardings on the side of the London Pavilion music hall. Virginia Woolf and others thought it was all marvellous, describing Piccadilly Circus as 'the heart of life...where everything desirable meets'. After the Second World War the ads went international—Coca Cola rather than Bovril—and **electric**, giving a touch of modernity to the 'swinging' city of Europe.

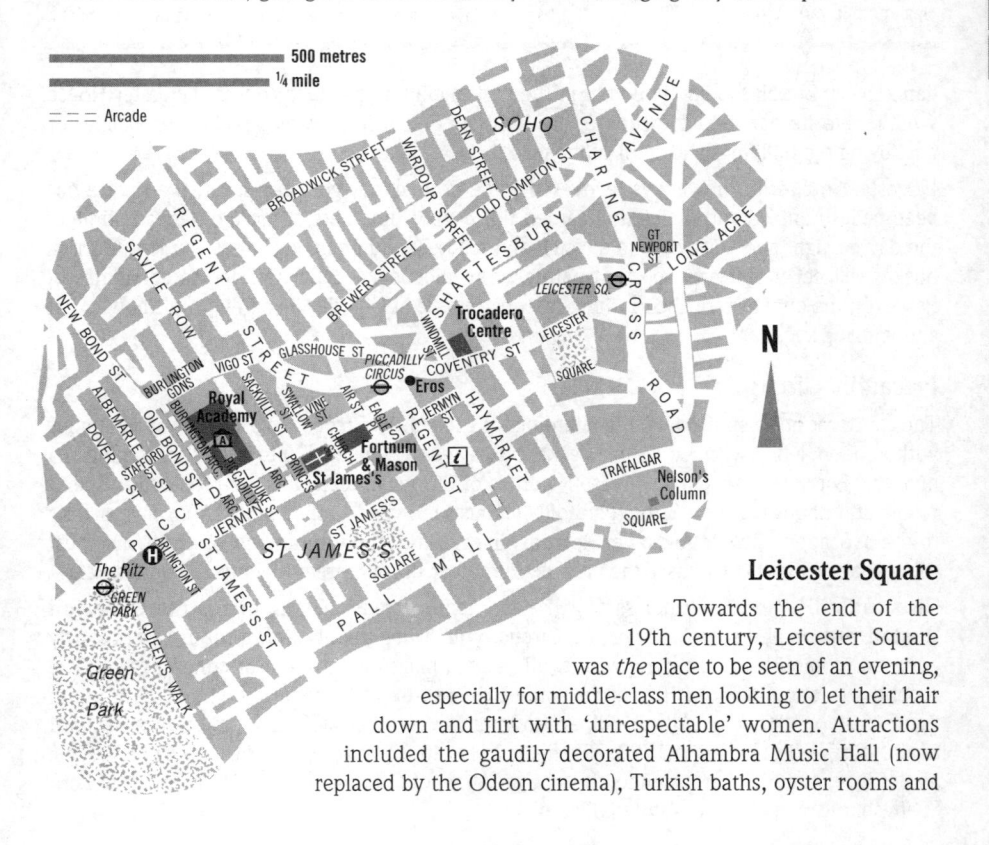

Leicester Square

Towards the end of the 19th century, Leicester Square was *the* place to be seen of an evening, especially for middle-class men looking to let their hair down and flirt with 'unrespectable' women. Attractions included the gaudily decorated Alhambra Music Hall (now replaced by the Odeon cinema), Turkish baths, oyster rooms and

Cafés and Tearooms

Photographers' Gallery Café, 5 Great Newport Street. This peaceful, friendly café in the tiny free gallery is filled with London's arty in-crowd eating bowls of healthy salad and home-made cakes and discussing creative endeavours over a cappuccino.

Café Rimini, Cranbourn Street. A gaggle of touristy cafés lines the south side of the street; this one stands out for excellent espresso and good falafel and sandwiches.

The Criterion, 224 Piccadilly (at Piccadilly Circus). Quality cuisine in a wondrous high decibel neo-Byzantine grotto; worth visiting for the interior alone. £14.95 for a two-course meal is one of London's better restaurant bargains.

Royal Academy Restaurant, Burlington House, Piccadilly. Self-service coffee, lunch and tea in an airy room. In summer there's a small café in the elegant courtyard. Open 10–5.30.

Fortnum & Mason, Jermyn Street and 181 Piccadilly. The luxury food shop has three traditional English restaurants, the posh Patio (£20 for a basic lunch menu; open til 6pm), the even posher Fountain on the ground floor (serving afternoon tea for £12.50; open till 8pm), and the St James's on the fourth (for a smart lunch from £16.95; open til 6pm). Something of a tourist trap and overpriced, but good nonetheless.

Ritz Hotel, 150 Piccadilly. Tea at the Ritz (a steep £24.50 a head) is a London institution, a challengingly priced indulgence that permits you to spend an hour or two immersed in an Edwardian paradise of gilded statues, ornate filigree roof decorations, interior waterfalls and exotic plants in the Palm Court. The food isn't bad either: cucumber or salmon sandwiches, plus scones with clotted cream and jam (a cheaper and less filling alternative to tea would be to have a cocktail at the bar).

---

dance halls. But all the fine buildings of the past, including the 17th-century Leicester House which gave its name to the square, are long gone. The Blitz was largely responsible for destroying the buildings and spirit of the place.

Leicester Square has nowadays recovered some of its happy-go-lucky spirit; the square has been pedestrianized and the central garden tidied up. Come here at more or less any time of the day or night and you will find a rough and ready crowd of cinema-goers, student tourists, buskers, street performers, portrait painters and pickpockets. For the dedicated sightseer, however, the only historical curiosity is a bronze statue of Charlie Chaplin with his bowler hat and walking stick.

Piccadilly Circus

The car horns and neon advertising hoardings of **Piccadilly Circus** have become synonymous with London, along with red double-decker buses and the Queen. Quite why is something of a mystery. For some inexplicable reason, hordes of European teenagers are prepared to spend whole afternoons trudging across Piccadilly Circus's crowded traffic islands, from Burger King to the Trocadero Centre to Tower Records, in search of the ultimate cheap thrill. The best thing about Piccadilly Circus is the view down Lower Regent Street towards St James's Park.

Two curiosities are nevertheless worth a moment's attention. The first is the **Criterion Restaurant** on the south side of the Circus, which has a long dining room sumptuously adorned in neo-Byzantine style, with a gilt ceiling, marble pillars and ornamental tiles. The second attraction of Piccadilly Circus is the **Eros statue** at its centre, a winged aluminium figure fashioned by Sir Alfred Gilbert in memory of the Victorian philanthropist Lord Shaftesbury and unveiled in 1893. The figure is not in fact supposed to be Eros, the cherubic god of love, at all; Gilbert intended it to be an Angel of Christian Charity, in memory of Lord Shaftesbury's work with destitute children.

Walking towards Leicester Square, on the north side of Coventry Street is the **London Pavilion**. This was once a music hall but has now been tarted up and revamped as the **Rock Circus** (*open 10–8, except Tues 11–8 and Fri and Sat 10–9; adm expensive*). This can be quite fun in a tacky sort of way—a sanitized history of rock'n'roll told with the help of wax figures from Madame Tussaud's and a vast array of lighting tricks, and a revolving theatre featuring an automaton of the Beatles. Right opposite the London Pavilion, with entrances on Great Windmill St, Coventry St and, round the back, on Shaftesbury Avenue, is the **Trocadero Centre**, a mélange of overpriced theme-u-rants, screaming kids and intimidating teenagers. Amidst the horrors, there are some thrilling and expensive virtual reality simulators, a dodgem ride (also thrilling and expensive) and a 3-D IMAX cinema.

Regent Street

Regent Street was once the finest street in London, although you might not think so to look at it now. In fact, all it boasts are a few fine shops (particularly men's clothes stores) and some rather stuffy, impersonal buildings livened up just once a year by the overhead display of electric Christmas decorations. The street could scarcely be further from the original plan, drawn up in 1813 by John Nash for the Prince Regent, which intended to bring revolutionary changes to the way London was organized. Nash's idea was to make Regent Street the main north-south artery linking the prince's residence at Carlton House on The Mall to the newly landscaped expanse of Regent's Park; as such it would have been the centrepiece of a carefully planned ensemble of squares, palaces and public thoroughfares.

One address that has not changed too much is the **Café Royal** at No.68 on the right-hand side of The Quadrant. A liveried doorman stands guard over one of the most fashionable addresses of the decadent years leading up to the First World War. Its extravagant mirrors, velvet seats and caryatid sculptures have remained more or less as they were when Oscar Wilde, Aubrey Beardsley and Edward, Prince of Wales, held court here in the naughty 1890s.

Piccadilly

From Piccadilly Circus to Green Park, this wide, straight, busy thoroughfare is the southern edge of Mayfair (*see* p.66) and it shows. Here you can find **Fortnum & Mason**, the ultimate old-fashioned luxury English food shop (✆ *(020) 7734 8040; open till 8pm with a good value afternoon tea for £16.50 from 3–5.30pm*), and the **Ritz Hotel**, where afternoon tea is a London institution. Small high-class shops can be found in the streets to either side: Jermyn Street and Savile Row (*see* p.124), and small, elegant shopping arcades.

St James's Piccadilly

> *Open daily, with lunchtime recitals and evening concerts; call ahead on* ✆ *(020) 7381 0441 for details.*

St James's (1684) seems curiously at odds with the rest of the neighbourhood, being totally unmarked by either pretension or exclusivity. Nowhere here do you see the trappings of wealth or snobbery; instead there is a flea market in the churchyard (*Wednesday–Saturday, with an antiques market on Tuesday*), a café (*open till 7; later if there's a concert*) in the annexe, a Centre for Healing, and a message of warm welcome on the noticeboard in the porch. Nevertheless, from an architectural point of view, St James's is an object lesson in effortless grace and charm. It is the only church that Christopher Wren built from scratch in

London (the others were all renovations or rebuildings on medieval sites), and as such most clearly expresses his vision of the church as a place where the relationship between the priest and his congregation should be demystified. St James's is airy and spacious, with the altar and pulpit in full view and accessible to all. An elegant gilded wooden gallery with rounded corners runs around the western end, supported by Corinthian pillars in plaster adorned with intricate decorations. There are some beautiful carvings by Grinling Gibbons, notably on the limewood reredos behind the altar (fruit and nature motifs) and on the stone font.

Royal Academy

Burlington House, Piccadilly, © (020) 7300 8000. Open 10–6 daily; adm.

In 1714, the third Earl of Burlington took a trip to Italy and, rather like Inigo Jones exactly one century earlier, came back an ardent convert to Palladian architecture. But where Jones failed to start a general trend, Lord Burlington succeeded triumphantly; Palladian buildings were soon sprouting all over London. One of the first was the earl's private residence here in Piccadilly, completed in 1720 to the designs of James Gibbs, Colen Campbell and the earl himself. The gate leads into a grand courtyard graced with a colonnade. The house was based on Palladio's Palazzo Porta in Vicenza, a classic exercise in harmony and simple lines.

Burlington House was lived in for more than a century, until the government bought it in 1854 to house the Royal Academy of Arts. It has been one of London's most important exhibition venues ever since, staging major retrospectives as well as the famed Summer Exhibition, a traditional but fairly underwhelming showcase for over a thousand amateur British artists.

The RA also has a permanent collection with works from each of its prestigious members (Reynolds, Gainsborough, Constable and Turner for starters), as well as a marble relief sculpture by Michelangelo of the *Madonna and Child with the Infant St John*. You won't get much sense of the original Palladian mansion, however, because the building was radically altered by the Victorian architect Sydney Smirke in 1872. The bronze statue in the centre of the courtyard is of Sir Joshua Reynolds, the founder of the Royal Academy, shown with palette and paintbrush. It dates from 1931.

Burlington Arcade

London never really went in for shopping arcades the way that Paris did at the beginning of the 19th century; nowhere in this city will you find the graceful iron and glasswork of the Parisian *passages* (*see* p.255), the precursors of the modern department store. Arcades nevertheless enjoyed a brief popularity in the final decade of George IV's life. The most famous is Burlington Arcade (1819), no doubt because of its top-hatted beadles who enforce the arcade's quaint rules: no whistling, no singing and no running. Originally it had a magnificent triple-arched entrance, but in 1931 the shopkeepers of the arcade demanded more girth to take deliveries, and the arches were destroyed. Nowadays it is elegant enough, its high-ceilinged halls decorated in green and white, and is home to upmarket shops.

Also see: **Jermyn Street and Savile Row shopping**, p.124; **Green Park**, p.111; **Faraday Museum**, p.68.

Onwards to: **Mayfair**, p.66; **Covent Garden**, p.73.

Soho and Chinatown

⊖ Leicester Square, Piccadilly Circus, Tottenham Court Road, Oxford Circus

Here, halfway between the clubbish pomp of Westminster and the venal frenzy of the City, is where Londoners come to enjoy themselves. Soho still thrives off its reputation as a seedy but **alluring** hang-out for **exotic** freaks and sozzled eccentrics who made the place famous after the Second World War. The establishment has always been suspicious of this area; the artistic community has never shown such squeamishness—indeed, this is the heart of London theatreland. Nowadays the sleaze is slowly disappearing, supplanted by the **flashy** cars and modish whims of the advertising and media darlings.

It was after the war that Soho really came into its own. In the 1950s it became the centre of the avant-garde in jazz, new writing, experimental theatre and cinema. In many ways Soho prefigured the social upheavals of the 1960s, creating a youth subculture based on rebellion, permissiveness, *joie de vivre*, booze and drugs. Above all, Soho developed its own community of intellectuals and eccentrics, people of all classes mingling, borrowing money off each other and getting pleasantly tippled in pubs or illicit 'near-beer' bars that stayed open outside the stringent licensing hours. Like all golden ages, 1950s Soho and its low life came to a somewhat sorry end. The liberalizations of the 1960s and 1970s brought peepshows and strip joints galore that nearly caused the destruction of the neighbourhood. The planning authorities, outraged by prostitutes openly soliciting on every street, threatened to bulldoze the whole district to make way for office blocks. It wasn't until the mid-1980s that new laws regulated the pornography business and Soho regained some of its spirit. The number of peepshows is strictly controlled, and most of the prostitutes now solicit via cards left in telephone booths. So attractive has Soho become that the trendies have inevitably moved in to join the fun. Not a week goes by without a new bar, a new restaurant, a new fad. Today it might be sushi served by robots, or caramelized onions; next week these will be passé and the new obsession will be pine-scrubbed noodle bars, or cafés that look like middle-class living rooms.

Soho Square

This was where Scott built his mansion, Monmouth House (long ago destroyed). A contemporary statue of Charles II by Caius Gabriel Cibber still stands in the square gardens, looking somewhat worse for wear behind a mock-Tudor toolshed which covers an underground air vent. On the north side of the square is the **French Protestant Church**, originally built for the Huguenots and then reworked by the Victorians in flamboyant neo-Gothic style. To the east is the red-brick tower of **St Patrick's Roman Catholic Church**, which holds weekly services for the local Spanish and Cantonese communities in their own languages.

Frith Street and Dean Street

The Frith Street Gallery at No.60 specialises in works on paper. In Frith Street you will also see **Ronnie Scott's** famous jazz club at No.47 (Scott, a jazz saxophonist, died in 1996, but his dingy basement club still gets high-profile bookings) and a plethora of restaurants including Jimmy's at No.23, a basement Greek café serving cheap moussaka and chips that has changed little since the Rolling Stones ate there in the 1960s.

Many phantoms also haunt Dean Street. No.49 is the **French House**, which became the official headquarters of the Free French forces under Charles de Gaulle during the Second

World War. Now it's a lively pub-cum-wine bar. Two clubs further down the street illustrate the changes in Soho since the 1950s. The Colony, at No.41, was once described as 'a place where the villains look like artists and the artists look like villains.' The Groucho—so called because of Groucho Marx's one-liner that he never wanted to join a club that would have him as a member —opened at No.44 in 1985 and has been a hit with the world of television, music, comedy, publishing and film ever since.

Quo Vadis, the restaurant at No.28, became instantly trendworthy in 1996 after it was bought from its original Italian owners by Marco Pierre White (famous London superchef) and Damien Hirst (Britpack conceptual artist-cum-restaurateur) and completed refurbished. Downstairs are works by Hirst and Marcus Harvey. Upstairs is where Karl Marx lived with his family from 1851–6 in a two-room attic flat in conditions of near abject penury (now a building site as it undergoes extensive refurbishments).

Cafés and Pubs

Mezzo, 100 Wardour Street. Ultra sophisticated brasserie food in massive restaurant owned and operated by interior designer Terence Conran; with a 2-course £8.50 before 7pm special.

Soupworks, 9 D'Arblay St. Huge variety of soups, from traditional to spicy Thai, hot and cold. £2–5.

Wagamama, 10A Lexington St. Busy and popular Japanese noodle restaurant, where you sit at long communal tables. Be prepared to queue. £5–10.

Mildred's, 58 Greek St. Classy vegetarian fare, including tostadas, stir-fries and delicious desserts. Very popular. Under £10.

Italian Graffiti, 163 Wardour St. Great Italian-style pizza and pastas in a friendly setting. £6–10.

Maison Bertaux, 28 Greek St. Mouthwatering French pastries. Lovely stopping-off point for excellent-value tea, gateaux and pastries.

Pâtisserie Valerie, 44 Old Compton St. More delicious croissants, cakes and savoury vol-au-vents. Very crowded and a bit self-consciously arty.

Bar Italia, 22 Frith St. Open 23 out of 24 hours, a Soho institution for everyone from after-hours clubbers to tourists: arguably the best espresso and cappuccino in town. Some snacks.

The New Diamond, 23 Lisle St. One of the best establishments in Chinatown (though there's not much to pick between them), with an enormous menu and seating on two floors. £7–18.

Old Compton Street and Wardour Street

In many ways Old Compton Street is the archetypal Soho street, as well as the heart of gay London. Here you'll find cafés like the Pâtisserie Valerie at No.44, restaurants, delicatessens, gay clubs and bars, and modest-looking newsagents stocking every conceivable title on the planet. Wardour Street, once known for its furniture and antique stores, is now occupied by film companies who advertise their forthcoming productions in the high glass windows on the left-hand side of the street.

Berwick Street Market and Brewer Street

Berwick Street Market (*open Mon–Sat 9–4*) always has beautifully fresh produce at incredibly low prices for central London. Ever since Jack Smith introduced the pineapple to London here in 1890, the market has also had a reputation for stocking unusual and exotic fruit and veg. The houses behind the stalls date, like the market itself, back to the 18th century. There's a couple of old pubs (The Blue Posts is the most salubrious), a scattering of noisy independent record stores and several excellent old-fashioned theatrical fabrics shops specializing in unusual silks, satins, velvets, Chinese printed silks and printed cottons, sold by the metre and the place to go if you're looking for something exotic for yourself or your sofa.

At the southern end of Berwick St is a poky passage called **Walker's Court**, dominated by peepshows and the London equivalent of the Moulin Rouge, Raymond's Revue Bar. Turn right into **Brewer Street**, the ultimate Soho mixture of sex-joints and eclectic shops. As you wander down it you will notice discreetly signposted peep-shows, an excellent fishmonger's, a well-stocked poster shop and, at No.67, the shop Anything Left-Handed.

Chinatown

London's Chinese population came mostly from Hong Kong in the 1950s and 1960s, victims not so much of the political upheavals in the region as the cruel fluctuations of the Asian rice market. Back then Gerrard Street, like the rest of Soho, was cheap and run-down and welcoming to foreigners. It took more than a generation for the new community to be fully accepted, however, and it was not until the 1970s that this street was pedestrianized and kitted out with decorative lamps and telephone boxes styled like pagodas—a spectacular backdrop to the Chinese New Year celebrations which take place here at the end of January or early February. Many of the older generation have only a rudimentary grip of English, and remain suspicious of their adoptive environment. The younger generation has integrated rather better; those born here are mockingly nicknamed BBCs (British-born children).

London's Chinatown is still very small—just Gerrard Street and Lisle Street really—and the trade is overwhelmingly in food and restaurants. There are a few craft shops, and there's always been a discreet illegal business in gambling—underground dens for mah-jong, pai-kau and fan tan. The eastern end of Gerrard St and Newport Place are crowded with Chinese supermarkets and craft shops, which are well worth poking around for a bargain.

Onwards to: **Covent Garden**, p.62; **Bloomsbury**, p.52; **Charing Cross Road shopping**, p.123; **Oxford Street shopping**, p.120.

St James's and Royal London

→ *Green Park, Charing Cross, Victoria*

St James's is the fairyland of London, a **peculiarly British** kind of looking-glass world where everyone eats thickly cut marmalade sandwiches and drinks tea from Fortnum & Mason, where the inhabitants are for the most part kindly middle-aged gentlemen with bespoke tailored suits and ruddy complexions, where shopkeepers are called purveyors and underlings wear livery coats. What's more, this **fairytale** comes with its very own queen, who lives in a palace surrounded by broad lush parks and guarded by toy soldiers in busby hats and red, blue and black uniforms. Everything is clean and beautiful in fairyland, even the roads, some of which have been coloured pink to add to the general feeling of well-being. St James's is the preserve of the **establishment**, not the vulgar money-making classes of the City but an older, rarefied pedigree which whiles away the hours in the drawing-rooms of fine houses and private clubs. It is a world that has been endlessly depicted and lampooned on film and on television; incredibly, it still exists.

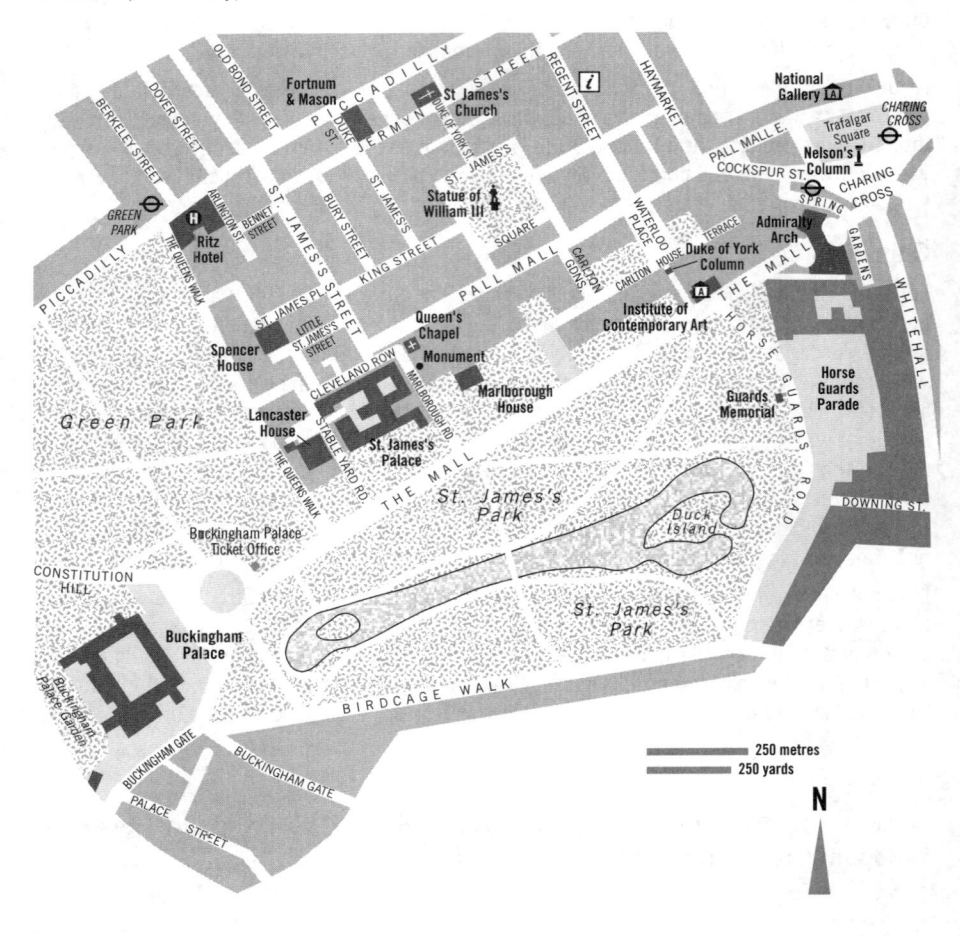

76   London: Central Neighbourhoods

The Mall

A sense of place, and occasion, is immediately invoked by the grand concave triple entrance of **Admiralty Arch**, the gateway to St James's and start of the long straight drive along The Mall up to Buckingham Palace. Passing through the arch, you'll appreciate the full splendour of St James's Park (*see* p.118) ahead to your left; notice, too, the white stone frontings to your right. These are part of **Carlton House Terrace**, the remnants of one of London's more lavish—and ultimately futile—building projects. In the early 18th century this site was home to Henry Boyle, Baron Carlton. The Prince of Wales (later George IV) decided he rather liked the place and hired the architect Henry Holland to spruce up the house to the standards of a royal palace. For 30 years Holland and his associates toiled away, adding Corinthian porticoes here, brown Siena marble columns there. One contemporary critic said the end result stood comparison with Versailles; that did not stop the extravagant George from declaring himself bored with the new palace and having most of it demolished. It was left to John Nash to salvage what he could from the wreckage of Carlton House and construct these elegant terraces in their place. They have housed many a club and eminent society in their time; now the most interesting address is No.12, the **Institute of Contemporary Arts**. Perhaps surprisingly given the setting, the ICA is a mecca for the 'Britpack' school of art, the pre-post-avant-garde and the obscure. There is a modest day membership fee to get into the main shows and the excellent café; otherwise you are restricted to the foyer and bookshop.

Horse Guards Parade (the Changing of the Guard)

The Horse Guards in question are the queen's very own knights in shining armour, properly known as the Household Division. Altogether, seven regiments are allocated the task of dressing up in chocolate-soldier costumes and parading in front of Buckingham Palace. Housed both here and at Wellington Barracks on the south side of the park are the Household Cavalry (look out for the horses), the Life Guards, the Blues and Royals, the Grenadiers, the Coldstream Guards and the Scots, Irish and Welsh guards. The best time to see them is on the first weekend in June, when they all take part in a grand parade in front of the Queen known as **Trooping the Colour**. Otherwise you can make do with the **Changing of the Guard** (*outside the Horse Guards at 11am daily or outside Buckingham Palace at 11.30am daily from May–Aug, and every other day the rest of the year*).

Cafés and Pubs

ICAfé, The Mall. Decent Italian bistro food inside the trendy arts centre, though you'll have to pay day membership (£1.50) to get in. £5–£10. Spicy 'street food' served after 5.30 at £2.50 a dish.

Spreads Café, 15a Pall Mall. Breakfasts, pasta and sandwiches to eat in or out. The least pretentious spot in St James's, next door to a shop selling large yachts. £4–5.

Wiltons, 55 Jermyn St, best to reserve in advance on ✆ (020) 7629 9955. English, strong on fish, in a setting resembling a gentleman's club. £30–40.

The Avenue, 7/9 St James's St. Attempt at a Manhattanesque sophisticates' restaurant serving elegant 'modern' food (crab and prawn galette, calf's liver, rabbit confit with fig chutney, their own fish fingers, etc.). The set lunch is especially good value: from £17.50 for two courses (✆ (020) 7321 2111 for reservations).

Quaglino's, 16 Bury St. Ferociously trendy Italian food in an ornate ballroom setting. £25 or so for lunch, reservations on ✆ (020) 7930 6767.

Pall Mall and Clubland

The street's curious name derives from an ancient Italian ball game called *palla a maglio*, literally ball and mallet. Charles II liked it so much that he built this pall mall alley close by St James's Palace.

If you enjoyed birdwatching in St James's Park, maybe you should pull your binoculars back out for some ornithological study of a different kind here in Pall Mall, the high street of London's **clubland**. The rare bird you are after is male, 50-ish and invariably well-dressed; he tends to stagger somewhat, especially after lunch, and looks rather like one of those old salt-of-the-earth types that Jack Hawkins or Trevor Howard used to play. The author and former club *maître d'* Anthony O'Connor has defined the London club as a place 'where a well-born buck can get away from worries, women and anything that even faintly smacks of business in a genteel atmosphere of good cigars, mulled claret and obsequious servants.' The end of the empire and the emancipation of domestic servants brought about a sharp decline in clubland: before the Second World War there were 120 clubs in London; now there are less than 40.

The **Athenaeum** on Waterloo Place, designed by Decimus Burton, is one of the best Greek Revival buildings in London, its frieze inspired by the relief sculptures from the Parthenon housed in the British Museum. The club was known in the 19th century as the haunt of the intellectual élite, which explains the gilt statue of Athena, goddess of wisdom, above the entrance and the Greek letters of Athena's name in the mosaic above the porch.

As you walk past the Athenaeum down Pall Mall, look out for the brass plates announcing a host of other clubs, including the Travellers', the Reform, the Royal Automobile, the United Oxford and Cambridge and the Army and Navy Club. The **Reform Club**, at Nos.104–5, is where Jules Verne's fictional hero Phineas Fogg made his wager and set out to travel around the world in 80 days.

St James's Street

Along with Pall Mall, St James's Street is clubland *par excellence*, although in the past it has enjoyed a less than irreproachable reputation because of its gambling dens. **White's**, the oldest London club may well have instituted the national mania for bets and betting in the mid-18th century when it ran books on everything from births and marriages to politics and death. White's was soon eclipsed, however, by **Brooks** down the road. One particularly obsessional gambler, Charles James Fox, ran up debts of £140,000 and was seen cadging money off the waiters at Brooks before his father, Lord Holland, stepped in to bail him out in 1781.

St James's Street has changed quite a bit in the 20th century. The bottom end, at the junction with Pall Mall, is dominated by two turn-of-the-century office buildings by Norman Shaw. There is an astonishing office block that resembles a bronze spaceship, currently unoccupied. More striking still is the **Economist Building** at Nos.25–7, a series of three concrete hexagonal towers designed by Peter and Alison Smithson for the weekly news magazine *The Economist* and completed in 1964. Much praised at the time, the building is certainly one of the more successful of London's experiments in 1960s modernism.

St James's Square

This square was where St James's turned from a mere adjunct to the royal palaces into a fashionable residential district in its own right. Just before the Great Fire of 1666, Charles II had granted a lease to Henry Jermyn, Earl of St Albans, charging him to build 'palaces fit for the dwelling of noblemen and persons of quality'. The result was to set the tone for nearly all of London's squares, creating a haven of privacy and seclusion. The equestrian statue in the middle is of William III; his horse has one hoof atop the molehill which caused the king's fatal riding accident in 1702. Nowadays there are no more private residences in the square's spacious, mainly Georgian houses; they have been replaced by a succession of clubs, eminent institutions and company offices.

St James's Palace

St James's Street. Closed to the public.

For more than 300 years this was the official residence of England's kings and queens; indeed, foreign ambassadors are still formally accredited to the Court of St James even though they are received, like every other official on royal business, at Buckingham Palace.

Although endowed with fine buildings (of which only the octagonal towers of the gatehouse survive), St James's Palace became known as a raucous place of ill manners and debauchery, particularly under Queen Anne and the early Hanoverians who used it to hold drunken banquets. Anne was well known for her unseemly appetite for food and drink, particularly brandy, and for the bodily noises she frequently emitted at table. Not suprisingly, the place soon came to be described as 'crazy, smoky and dirty'. The Prince Regent celebrated his disastrous marriage with Caroline of Brunswick here in 1795, spending his wedding night fully dressed in a drunken slumber in the fireplace of the bridal chamber. Soon afterwards he moved into Carlton House, and the palace's somewhat tarnished glory days were over. A fire destroyed most of the original buildings in 1809; the rebuilt courtyards now house offices for members of the royal household.

Spencer House

27 Queen's Walk, open Sun 10.30–5.30, last adm 4.45, except Jan and Aug; adm £6/£5. Visit by guided tour only; tours begin at regular intervals and last an hour.

This gracious Palladian mansion was born in sorrow: its original backer, Henry Bromley, ran out of money and shot himself moments after reading his will over with his lawyer. The site was then taken over by the Spencer family (ancestors of Princess Diana) who hired a bevy of architects including John Vardy and Robert Adam to produce one of the finest private houses in London. Completed in 1766, Spencer House boasts magnificent parquet floors, ornate plaster ceilings and a welter of gilded statues and furniture. The highlight is Vardy's Palm Room, in which the pillars are decorated as gilt palm trees with fronds stretching over the tops of the arched window bays. James Stuart's Painted Room features classical murals, graceful chandeliers and a fine, highly polished wooden floor. The whole house was renovated by its current owners, RIT Capital Partners, in 1990 and looks magnificent. Unfortunately only eight rooms are open to the public; the rest are kept for the pleasure of the financial executives who occupy it during the week.

Also see: **Buckingham Palace**, p.32; **St James's Park**, p.117; **Jermyn Street and Savile Row shopping**, p.124; **Green Park**, p.111.

Onwards to: **Piccadilly**, p.71; **Mayfair**, p.66.

The South Bank and Southwark

◉ *Waterloo, Embankment, London Bridge*

Southwark, the London borough stretching from Waterloo Bridge to the other side of Tower Bridge, has seen it all: butchers, leather-makers, whores, corrupt bishops, coach drivers, actors, bear-baiters, railwaymen and dockers. Shakespeare's Globe Theatre was here, and so was the notorious Marshalsea debtors' prison. It is one of the most **atmospheric** and **historic** parts of London, used over and over by the city's novelists, particularly Dickens.

In the 17th century, Bankside and the whole borough of Southwark were bywords for a raucous good time. The **boisterous** character of the area is easily explained by history. When the Romans first built London Bridge in AD 43, Southwark naturally developed as a small colony and market town opposite the City of London. As the City grew in wealth and importance, Southwark attracted some of the dirtier, more unpleasant trades that might have offended the rich merchants across the river. In 1556 Southwark came directly under the City's jurisdiction and cleaned up its act somewhat. The theatres made the available entertainment a little more thought-provoking, if only for a brief period. And then local industries sprang up: Bankside was bustling with wharves, breweries, foundries and glassworks.

Southwark remained a promising, if still raucous area until the mid-18th century, when the construction of Westminster Bridge and the first Blackfriars Bridge diminished its importance as the most accessible of London's southern satellites. The arrival of the railways in the Victorian era made it even more isolated, reducing it to no more than a row of warehouses stuck between the noisy train tracks. Further decline came after the Second World War, as the

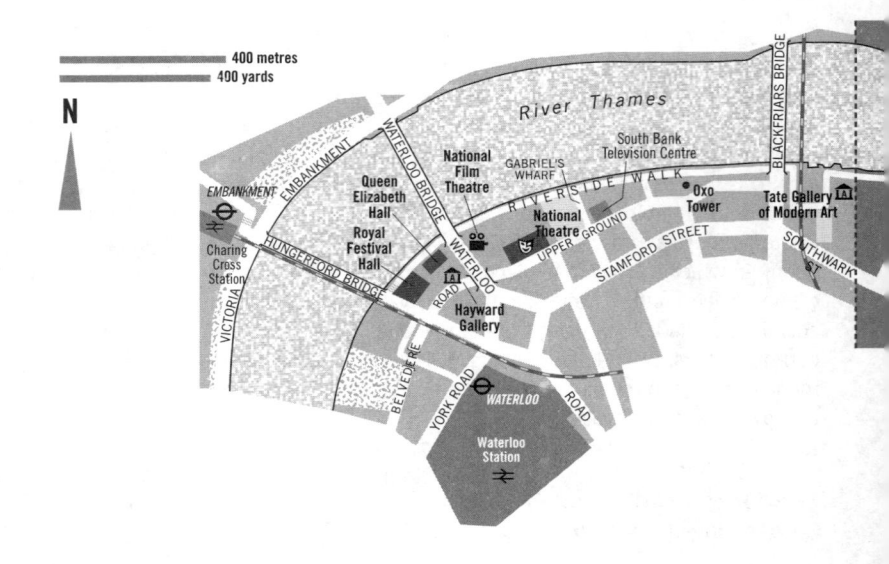

Cafés and Pubs

Gourmet Pizza Company, Gabriel's Wharf. Pizza with lovely views of the Thames from a riverside terrace. £4.75–8.50, with exotic toppings.

Doggett's Coat and Badge, 1 Blackfriars Bridge. Large, rambling renovated pub named after an annual boat race from London Bridge to Chelsea. Good beer, river views. Food so-so.

La Spezia, 33 Railway Approach. Typical Italian restaurant tucked away behind London Bridge station (it rattles!). £20–25.

Café Rouge, Hay's Galleria. Bustling café-brasserie in a converted wharf. £5–10 for a main course.

Blueprint Café, Design Museum, Butler's Wharf. Inventive and tasty Mediterranean cuisine attracting crowds from all over London. Worth booking (✆ 0171–378 7031). £20–25.

Fina Estampa, 150 Tooley Street. London's only Peruvian restaurant—tasty and delicious ceviche lunch from £15.

The Apprentice, 31 Shad Thames. A training school for Conran chefs and waiters—usually excellent gourmet food and extremely cheap, from £10.50.

The Fire Station, 150 Waterloo Rd. Renovated fire station opposite the Old Vic Theatre, serving fashionable modern British cuisine and Sunday roast lunches, from £10.95.

Le Pont de la Tour, Butler's Wharf. Sophisticated Conran-owned brasserie with spectacular views of the river and the City. Weekday set lunch from £28.50.

Oxo Tower: includes Bistrot 2—an informal café and bar serving cocktails and light snacks on the second floor, and the Oxo Tower Restaurant and Brasserie on the 8th floor, both managed by Harvey Nichols, with highly eclectic food. The Restaurant is more expensive and formal, with a good value but very filling set lunch for £26.50, the Brasserie and Bar cheaper and higher decibel. Both restaurants have wonderful views of the London skyline.

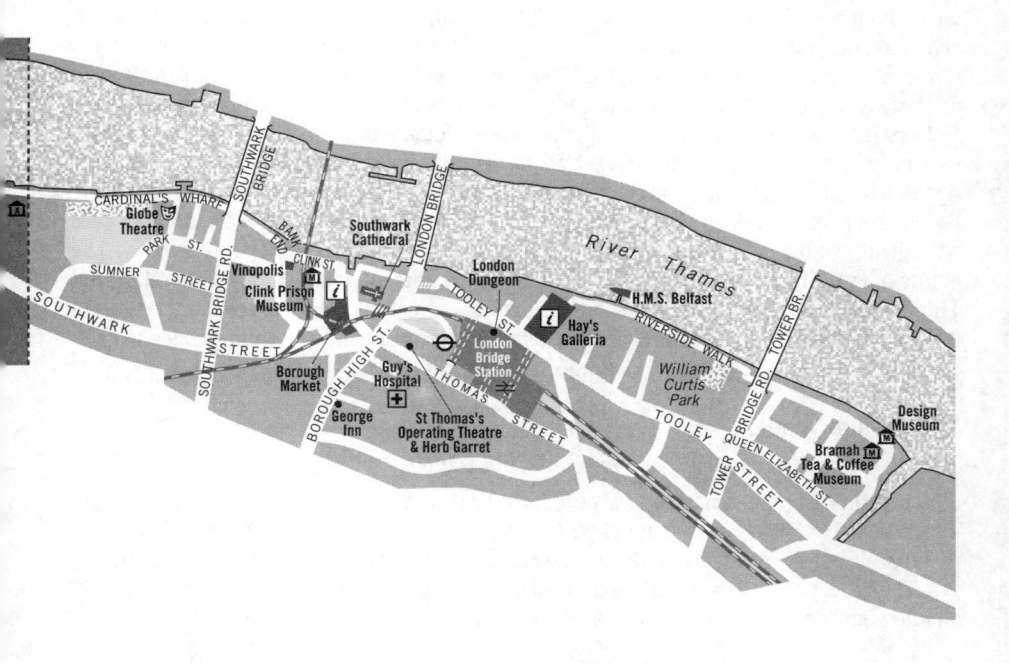

London docks became obsolete and the area's wharves and warehouses closed. Today, like so many neglected areas of London, it has only its past to turn to as a source of income, and is busy devoting itself to the heritage industry.

Nowadays, the atmosphere is very much intact, but in a wholly new form. The South Bank has become one of the most vibrant, fastest-changing parts of the city. Museums and arts venues have flourished where industrial life has curled up and died. Art galleries and restaurants have moved into the derelict wharves, and trendy new housing developments have livened up the old railway sidings. Even the Globe Theatre is back, not quite where it was in Shakespeare's day, but almost (see p.33). Best of all, these attractions are now linked by a wonderful river walkway stretching from Westminster Bridge to London Bridge and beyond—so you encounter little more than the distant rumble of traffic along the way.

The South Bank is where it will all be happening in the run up to the Millennium. Already, as these words are being written, the area is in a frenzy of refurbishment, rebuilding and future planning. So be prepared to see a few new and surprising apparitions along the route of this walk. Biggest and weirdest will be the **Millennium Wheel** just next to Westminster Bridge. The newly refurbished Oxo Tower will be graced with a **Floating Lido** right on its doorstep, complete with Olympic-length swimming pool, aquarium-lined changing rooms and retractable roof that can be converted into a sports arena or dance floor. At Bankside, the satanic old power station is being converted into the **Tate Gallery of Modern Art**, and plans are afoot to build another pedestrian river crossing designed by Norman Foster, **Bankside Bridge**, that will connect the new gallery to St Paul's Cathedral.

The South Bank Centre

From the outside, the buildings lying at the heart of the South Bank Centre look rather forbidding—lumps of dirty grey concrete streaked with rain, and proof if ever it was needed that concrete does not suit the English climate. Aesthetics apart, though, the South Bank works remarkably well as a cultural complex. The **Royal Festival Hall** is the South Bank's main concert venue, opened the same year; there's also the **National Film Theatre**, the **Hayward Gallery** (for major international exhibitions), **Queen Elizabeth Hall** and **Purcell Room** (also for concerts), and the three-stage Royal National Theatre. Everything is easily accessible, well-signposted and free of traffic. The concerts and plays are subsidized and tickets relatively cheap. People enjoy coming not just for the scheduled events, but also to hang out in the spacious halls with their plentiful cafés, occasional musicians, elegant bookstalls, piers and river views. The merits of the various venues are dealt with in 'Entertainment and Nightlife'. The **National Theatre** foyers have excellent bookshops, particularly for drama, as well as free live concerts in the early evenings. The **Festival Hall** has a varied programme of free lunchtime concerts.

Sadly, the entertaining **Museum of the Moving Image** is closed for restoration until 2003.

Millennium Wheel

Aka the 'London Eye', opening Jan 2000; adm £6.95, children £4.80.

This breathtaking construction is a peculiarly British take on the Giant Ferris Wheel in Vienna's famous Prater amusement park. The giant-size bicycle wheel will be solar- and wave-powered ; passengers will board 32 pod-like capsules to be taken a dizzying 450ft into the city sky. The wheel will be the fourth highest structure in London; each revolution will take 30 minutes, and views will stretch as far as Windsor to the west and Gravesend to the east.

IMAX Theatre

✆ (020) 7902 1234/1200. Open daily 11am–8.45pm, Sat and Sun 11am–10pm; adm £5–6.50.

Rising phoenix-like from a depressing roundabout outside Waterloo Station, this shiny £20m glass drum is the biggest, newest, most technically-advanced IMAX in Europe. Inside the 500-seat theatre 2 and 3D films are shown on a 10-storey screen via a projector the size of two small cars. For the time being the library consists of 125 films, ranging from the stupendous (documentaries such as *Into the Deep*, exploring the underwater coast of Southern California) to the wondrous and bizarre (Paul Cox's *Four Million Houseguests*—a fascinating journey via an illuminator super-microscope through a galaxy of giant-size carpets, rotting fruit and Velcro).

Gabriel's Wharf

This is an attractive square set back from the river. Formed by the backs of warehouses painted in *trompe l'œil* fashion to resemble house-fronts, it is occupied by sculpture, ceramics, fashion and jewellery workshops. There are some good cafés, bars and restaurants here if you want to stop for a drink.

Oxo Tower

Oxo, the stock cube people, neatly side-stepped the strict advertising regulations of the 1930s by working the letters 'OXO' into the design of the tower itself. In 1996 the Art Deco warehouse was magnificently restored by the Coin Street Community Builders, and it now contains over 30 retail units selling high quality textiles, furniture, clothing and jewellery at a fraction of West End prices (try Studio Fusion for the finest enamelled jewellery in the country). Above the workshops is a modestly priced café/bar (Bistrot 2) and several floors of co-op flats; at the very top is a free public viewing gallery with glitzy views of the London skyline, and the chi-chi Oxo Tower Restaurant and Brasserie.

Southwark Cathedral

You can enter through the modern annexe slightly to your left. Once inside, there is a café to the left and the cathedral entrance to the right.

Southwark Cathedral has a past almost as chequered as the neighbourhood, suffering fire, neglect and patchwork reconstruction over a history stretching back to the 7th century. It started life as the parish church of St Mary Overie (which despite the weird name merely means 'St Mary over the river'), built according to legend by the first boatman of Southwark to ferry gentlemen to and from the City. It burned down at least twice before being incorporated into a priory belonging to the Bishop of Winchester sometime around 1220. In the Civil War it was a bastion of Puritanism where preachers denounced the Bankside playhouses as offences to the Almighty. By the 19th century it had largely fallen to pieces, and the nave was rebuilt—twice as it turned out, since the first attempt was considered an appalling travesty. By the 20th century, with a little help from the restorers, Southwark was elevated to the rank of cathedral for the whole of south London. The architecture is still predominantly Gothic, particularly the choir, fine retro-choir and altar, making it something of a rarity in London. The tower is 15th-century, although the battlements and pinnacles weren't completed until 1689. The nave is the only significant portion from a later era, although you will also notice Victorian statues atop the reredos behind the altar.

Tate Gallery of Modern Art at Bankside Power Station

Opening May 2000; visitor's centre open most days 10–5, or by appointment on ✆ (020) 7401 7302.

Looking like a set from Fritz Lang's *Metropolis*, this dour fortress was designed by Sir Giles Gilbert Scott in 1947. The power station is now being gutted and flooded with natural light via a glass canopy designed by the Swiss architects Herzog & de Meuron. The glass roof will span the entire building, adding two floors to its height and giving visitors spectacular views across the City. The 100,000 square feet of galleries inside will house three temporary loan exhibitions a year plus the whole of the Tate's modern art collection (Picasso (*The Three Dancers*), Matisse (*The Snail*), Brancusi, Dalí, Pollock, Duchamp, Giacometti, Warhol (*Marilyn Diptych*), Hockney, etc). Contemporary art galleries clustering around the revamped station include the SE1 Gallery (near Southwark Bridge), Purdy Hicks and the innovative Jerwood Art Space.

Clink Prison Museum

Clink Street, ✆ (020) 7378 1558. Open daily approx 10–6; summer daily 10–10; adm.

The Clink was the Bishop of Winchester's private prison, where anyone who dared to challenge the extortion rackets he ran on Bankside would be locked up in gruesome conditions. For 400 years successive bishops acted as pimp to the local whores, known as Winchester Geese, and used the prison as dire punishment for any who tried to conceal their earnings, or work for somebody else. The name Clink is familiar enough nowadays as a synonym for jail; it derives from a Latin expression meaning, roughly speaking, 'kick the bucket', which gives a good indication of the fate a prisoner could expect inside.

The exhibition in this macabre museum highlights the cruelty of life in medieval Bankside, particularly the barbaric treatment of women both in prison and outside. Wives deemed too talkative would wear a scold's bridle, an iron gag shoved into their mouth and left there for days; sometimes the gag would be spiked. Crusaders off to the Holy Land would lock their womenfolk in chastity belts which prevented not only sexual contact but all genital hygiene. Women often died of infections or, if the belt was fitted while they were teenagers and still growing, of constriction of the pelvis. In 1537 Henry VIII ruled that women who murdered their husbands were to be boiled in a vat of oil; it was up to the executioner whether or not to boil the oil in advance.

George Inn

Goerge Inn Yard, off Borough High Street.

The coaching inns were like the railway stations that eventually superseded them, each one providing a transport service to a specific group of destinations. Unlike railway stations, however, the inns had no fixed timetable but functioned according to demand. As a result there was often a great deal of waiting to do, and the inns made up for this by ensuring a ready supply of draught ale for waiting passengers. The George Inn goes back to the 16th century, although the present buildings date from shortly after the Great Fire. It is an elegant terrace of small interconnecting wooden bars looking out on a quiet courtyard, where during the summer you can see morris dancing (an old English ritual which involves wearing folklore costumes festooned with bells) and open-air productions of Shakespeare.

St Thomas Operating Theatre Museum and Herb Garret

9a St Thomas's Street. Open Tues–Sun and most Mons 10–4; adm cheap.

The old church tower you enter used to be attached to the chapel of St Thomas's, one of the biggest hospitals in London, founded on this site back in the 12th century. The hospital moved to Lambeth in the 1860s to make way for London Bridge railway station, and all the old buildings except this one were destroyed. For a century the chapel was considered a mere curiosity, an unspectacular relic from a bygone age. Then, in 1956, a historian named Raymond Russell noticed a curious hole above the tower belfry. He squeezed through and discovered a garret containing a 19th-century operating theatre, the only one of its kind to have survived in the country. It was restored and in 1968 turned into a museum charting the tower's history, first as a medieval garret devoted to herbal remedies, then as an operating room attached to a women's ward in the next building. It is a fascinating, if grim place; nowhere else in London will you get such a graphic insight into the horrors of medicine before the modern age.

The museum also gives a lightning account of the history of apothecaries and of herbal and surgical medicine in London, accompanied by a display of gynaecological instruments that would not look out of place in a torture chamber.

The most famous woman in the hospital's history was Florence Nightingale, the legendary nurse of the Crimean War who set up London's first nursing school at St Thomas's in 1858.

London Bridge

'London Bridge is falling down,' goes the old nursery rhyme. Too right. London Bridge has fallen down so often that there's nothing left to see. No, it's not the one on all the postcards that opens in the middle (that's Tower Bridge), although God knows there are enough tourists who haven't realized this yet (and one American who, back in the 1960s, bought the previous incarnation of London Bridge and had it reconstructed stone for stone back home in Lake Havasu, Arizona—how disappointed his friends must have been). London Bridge stopped being interesting some time around 1661, when the spikes used to display the severed heads of criminals were finally removed. It ceased to be London's one and only river crossing about a century later with the construction of Westminster and Blackfriars Bridges. Now London Bridge is nothing more than a cantilevered lump of concrete with four busy lanes of traffic on top, just one nondescript bridge among many. And it hasn't fallen down for centuries. The only striking feature of London Bridge now is the building at the Southwark end, **One London Bridge**, a 1980s office complex in shining chrome and glass that links up with the dinky shops and restaurants of Hay's Galleria (*see* below).

Tower Bridge

Tower Bridge is one of the great feats of late Victorian engineering, half suspension-bridge and half drawbridge, linked to two neo-Gothic towers. Designed by an engineer, John Wolfe-Barry, and an architect, Horace Jones, working in tandem, it has become one of London's most recognizable landmarks. Its two bascules, the arms that rise up to let tall ships through, weigh an astonishing 1000 tonnes each. Despite the decline of river freight traffic, the bridge still opens at least once a day on average; phone ahead (✆ *(020) 7403 3761*) to find out the times. At the southern tower you can join the **Tower Bridge Experience** (*open Nov–Mar daily 10–last adm 5.15; April–Oct daily 9.30–last adm 4.45; adm*), a hi-tech retelling of the history of the bridge, plus a chance to enjoy the view from the overhead walkways.

London Dungeon

> *Nos.28–34 Tooley Street. Open summer daily 10–last adm 5.30; winter daily 10.30–last adm 4.30; adm exp.*

'Enter at your peril,' says the sign above the door. It is an appropriate warning for a museum that strives to make a spectator sport out of medieval torture but can only manage the ketchup-splattered inauthenticity of a 1950s Hammer horror movie. First of all, this is not a dungeon at all, but a converted warehouse underneath the arches of London Bridge station. Secondly, there is scarcely a genuine historical artefact in the place.

Hay's Galleria

London's oldest wharf dates back to 1651, but the present structure is dominated by the tall yellow brick façades of the Victorian dock buildings, covered with a barrel-vaulted glass roof to form a pleasant arcade of shops, cafés and restaurants. The best feature is the central fountain sculpture, *The Navigators* by David Kemp, a fantasy in which a Viking galley is overtaken by naval commanders, astronomers and modern sailors with half-umbrellas for hats.

Butler's Wharf and the Design Museum

> *Museum open daily 11.30–6, last adm 5.30; adm; ℡ (020) 7378 6055 for details of temporary exhibitions. Includes a Conran restaurant (The Blueprint Café).*

Created by Terence Conran and Stephen Bayley, the Design Museum is the only museum in the world devoted to industrial design and the cult of consumerism. A bower bird's shrine on the second floor showcases such mass production classics as the car (including designs by Le Corbusier from 1928), the vacuum (Dyson et al), early televisions and radios, telephones, tableware (by Enzo Mari) and chairs (by Charles and Ray Eames), while the ground floor is devoted to a diverse and diverting range of temporary exhibitions, from Porsche cars to Bosch washing machines. The museum is based in a disused warehouse which Conran and his partners rebuilt and—in a somewhat wistful homage to the International Style—painted white. Upstairs there are stunning views of Tower Bridge from the pricey Blueprint Café terrace.

The complex of buildings around the Design Museum is known as **Butler's Wharf**. As recently as the 1950s it was a hive of trade in commodities from tea and coffee to rubber, spices, wines and spirits. The rise of container shipping sounded the wharf's death knell; now only tourism and service industries can save it.

Vinopolis

> *1 Bank End, Clink Street, SE1, ℡ (020) 7940 8300, ⊖ Cannon St, Borough; bus 40, 133, 149. Open daily 10–5.30; adm.*

A brand-new museum on all imaginable aspects of wine culture, history and vineyards; five tastings included in the admission price. The *Cantina Vinopolis* restaurant will be joined in due course by a brasserie, coffee shop and wine bar and you can purchase the tipple of your choice in the Wine Warehouse.

Also see: **London Aquarium**, p.28; **Globe Theatre**, p.33; **Bramah Tea and Coffee Museum**, p.139; **Golden Hinde**, p.136.

Onwards to: **Docklands**, p.94; **The City of London**, p.55.

Notting Hill	89
Chelsea and the King's Road	92
Docklands	94
Camden	99
Islington	100
Hampstead	102
Richmond	104
Greenwich	106

London: Villages

London Villages

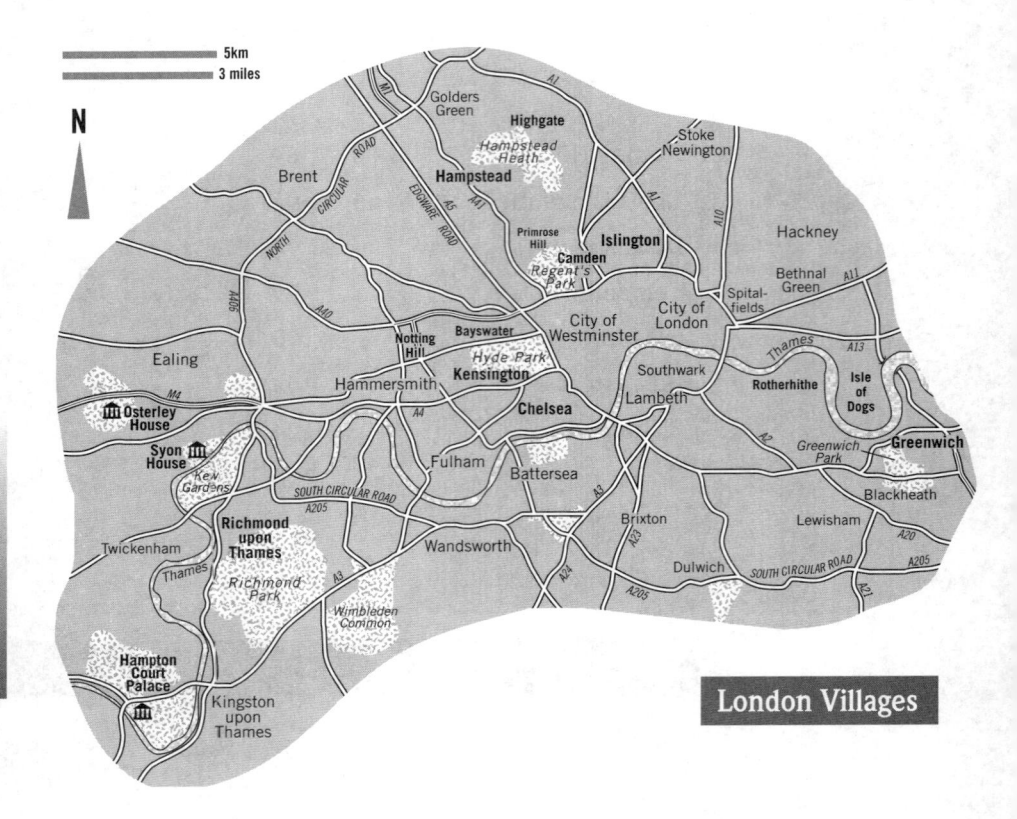

The London that stretches away beyond the centre is often described as a series of villages. Indeed, some of the geographical terms used to describe the various districts—Highgate Village, Camden Town, and so on—encourage this way of thinking, as though the outskirts of the city were a patchwork of truly autonomous communities separated by fields and trees.

To compare anything within the London urban area to village life is, of course, wishful thinking; there is little of a real village's close-knit sense of community, only hints of the unbroken greenery of the countryside, and none of the gossiping about the neighbours. It is important when visiting outer London, therefore, not to think that you are heading off into the sticks, as you might if you strayed 10 or 15 miles out of the centre of Paris or New York. Rather you should think of yourself as exploring another side of a multi-faceted city. Each outer satellite has a distinct identity of its own and a sense of integration with the whole.

Partly for this reason, the point at which central London ends and outer London begins is not easy to define. You might justifiably feel that Camden, Notting Hill and Chelsea are really part of the centre and do not belong in this section at all. The difference is that the wealth of history and culture is less focused. What you find instead is a sense of identity and atmosphere that can be described more usefully than an exhaustive list of tourist attractions.

The 'villages' below are arranged roughly in order of their distance from the city centre.

Notting Hill

⊖ *Notting Hill, Ladbroke Grove, Westbourne Park*
Buses 23, 12, 94, 27, 31, 52

Notting Hill conjures up many images: of imposing pastel-stuccoed or gleaming white terraced houses, of antiques dealers on the southern end of Portobello Road pulling a fast one on unsuspecting tourists; of young Caribbeans dancing in the streets during the annual carnival; of arty types standing in line outside the Gate cinema; of young people riffling through second-hand records and cheap jewellery underneath the A40 flyover; of Moroccans and Portuguese chatting away in the ethnic cafés of Golborne Road; of affluent professional families relaxing in their large gardens in Stanley Crescent or Lansdowne Rise. To say Notting Hill is a melting pot is both a cliché and an understatement. It has been an emblem of **multicultural** London ever since the big immigrant waves from the Caribbean in the 1950s.

Once considered irredeemably out of fashion, Notting Hill is now so **hip** with the liberal middle classes that it risks becoming as **exclusive** as the posh villas on Campden Hill on the south side of the main road. A rapid period of gentrification in the 1980s smartened things up but it has also created barriers of class and status that the neighbourhood had always previously sought to break down. The motorway flyover has created a neat divide between the spruced-up pastel-painted Victorian houses to the south (Notting Hill proper), and the high-rise 1960s council estates to the north (dismissively described as North Kensington).

Most recently, the success of the 1999 film *Notting Hill* has led to huge rent increases and is beginning to undercut the very nature of the area it sought to eulogize on celluloid; the small independent shops and cafés that made the area fun and different are being pushed out and replaced by the same chain shops and coffee bars that can be found anywhere.

Notting Hill 89

The Notting Hill Carnival

By the mid-1960s the Notting Hill Carnival, held on the last weekend in August, had become a permanent fixture. For two days each year, on the Sunday and Bank Holiday Monday, the streets throb with steel bands and soca music. The crowds sway giddily to the conga while balancing glasses of Jamaican draft stout and getting pleasantly high on some choice Caribbean weed. Everywhere is the tangy smell of saltfish, goat curry, fried plantain and patties. It is not always a peaceful affair. Relations between residents and police are tense at the best of times, and every few years that tension spills out at the carnival. Many of the middle-class residents of Notting Hill pack up the family Volvo and motor the hell out on Carnival weekend—not exactly eloquent testimony to their liberal credentials, but there you are. The impeccably liberal newspaper the *Guardian* once described the carnival as an 'all-singing, all-dancing Benetton advert viewed through a haze of marijuana', and included in its list of things to expect 'the contents of someone else's pitta bread dribbled down your back in the crush; vegetarian samosas embedded in the soles of your shoes; and a bassline that will reverberate through your ribcage for days'.

Notting Hill Gate and Around

Most visitors pile out of Notting Hill and head straight for Portobello Market. It's worth dallying for a while, though, to look at the pretty mews-style houses on **Uxbridge Street** and **Hillgate Street** behind the Gate cinema, and to head up **Campden Hill Road** to peek through the box hedges at the grandiose properties overlooking Holland Park. This is one of the most attractive residential areas in London, especially in the springtime when the small private gardens and trees are in bloom. It is also dotted with good restaurants and pubs like the Uxbridge Arms and Malabar on Uxbridge Street, and the Windsor Castle pub on Campden Hill Road.

Notting Hill Gate and **Pembridge Road** are a mixture of excellent second-hand record, book and computer stores, cheap chain restaurants and, towards Holland Park, sofabed stores, beauty salons and the posey Damien Hirst restaurant Pharmacy.

Portobello Road

Antiques market Sat (7am–5pm); fruit and vegetable market Mon–Sat till 5pm with early closing at 1pm on Thurs.

The antiques stalls start at the southern end of Portobello Road towards Notting Hill, and the rather shabbier furniture, food, jewellery, cheap records, books, postcards and funky bric-à-brac are at the north end, towards the A40 flyover. In between is a stretch of fruit and vegetable market popular with the whole community. The street is also lined with quirky, individual shops, some cheap, some expensive. Mingling among these counter-culture vultures are smarter, more self-conscious types on their way to the Travel Bookshop, Books for Cooks, Graham & Green, Ceramica Blue, Neal's Yard, the delicatessen Mr Christian or restaurants like 192 or Osteria Basilico on the side streets **Blenheim Crescent**, **Elgin Crescent** and **Kensington Park Road**.

Broadly speaking, the crowd gets more unorthodox and eclectic the further north you go. Under the flyover is a bric-à-brac and cheap clothes market, as well as vegetarian cafés and an indoor arcade called Portobello Green packed with young designers. Further north still, among

Cafés and Pubs

The Gallery, 5 Tavistock Rd. Unpretentious vegetarian, organic café.

Sausage and Mash Café, 268 Portobello Rd. Delicious, inventive speciality sausages and mash.

Market Bar, 240a Portobello Rd. Atmospheric wooden bar with a good Thai restaurant on the first floor.

Courtyard Café, 59a Portobello Rd. French-style sandwiches and salads and excellent coffee served in a hidden leafy courtyard. Profits go to charity.

Books for Cooks, 4 Blenheim Crescent. Test out their recipe books in the café. (You'll buy the book.)

Café Grove, 253a Portobello Rd. Popular terrace overlooking the market, serving good breakfasts and snacks.

Babushkas, 41 Tavistock Rd. Fashionable but laid-back bar with a garden for summer and cosy fires in winter.

The Pharmacy, 150 Notting Hill Gate. Restaurant/bar designed by Damien Hirst with clientele to match.

---

the ugly modern brick housing estates, you stumble across small art dealers, the excellent jazz shop Honest Jon's and the Spanish restaurant Galicia. Finally, off to the right is **Golborne Road**, a bustling short street divided between Portuguese and Moroccan communities.

Westbourne Grove and Ledbury Road

The Portobello Road end of **Westbourne Grove** is home to Agnès B, Tom's delicatessen, jewellery designer Dinny Hall and scores of antiques shops; in a traffic island you can't miss award-winning eau-de-Nil public toilet designed by Piers Gough, with one of London's best flower stalls attached. The Oxfam shop is one of London's best, with designer cast-offs. Further east towards Queensway are innovative home design shops like Aero, and Planet Organic, a wholefood emporium serving juices by the glass.

Ledbury Road is also packed with fashion and accessory designers, including Ghost (No.36), Molly K (63a), Lulu Guinness (66), Roger Doyle (38) and Nick Ashley (57).

Kensal Green Cemetery

> *Open Mon–Sat 9–5.30, Sun 10–5.30, closes an hour earlier in winter. Walk up Ladbroke Grove (several blocks) and turn left after the canal into Harrow Rd. The cemetery entrance, an imposing Doric arch, is opposite the William IV pub.*

The large entrance arch frames an avenue leading to the Anglican Chapel, itself adorned with Doric pillars and colonnades. The chapel stands atop a layered cake of underground burial chambers, some of which used to be served by a hydraulic lift. Around the rest of the cemetery are extraordinary testimonies to 19th-century delusions of grandeur: vast ornate tombs worthy of the Pharaohs, decorated with statues, incidental pillars and arches. What made Kensal Green such a hit was a decision by the Duke of Sussex, youngest brother of George IV, to eschew royal protocol and have himself buried among the people, so to speak. Eminent fellow-occupants include Thackeray, Trollope, Wilkie Collins, Leigh Hunt and the father and son engineering duo Marc and Isambard Kingdom Brunel.

Onwards to: **Kensington Gardens**, p.114; **High Street Kensington**, p.125; **Holland Park**, p.113.

Chelsea and the King's Road

◆ *Sloane Square, South Kensington*
Bus 137a, 19, 22, 239, 31, 49

Chelsea was an attractive riverside community long before it was ever integrated into greater London. The humanist and martyr Thomas More made the district fashionable by moving here in the 1520s, and soon every courtier worth his salt, even Henry VIII himself, was building a house near his. By the mid-19th century, Chelsea had turned into a **bustling** little village of intellectuals, artists, aesthetes and writers as well as war veterans—the so-called Chelsea pensioners who lived in the Royal Hospital built by Christopher Wren for Charles II.

Chelsea in the first half of the 20th century turned into little more than an annexe of South Kensington—a little more **classy** perhaps, a little more established, but just as snobbish and sterile. In the 1950s and 1960s, it became the refuge of the dying aristocracy, as films like Joseph Losey's *The Servant* (shot in Royal Avenue) showed to withering effect. In the 1980s, the sons and daughters of these last-ditch aristos mutated into a particularly underwhelming social animal known as the Sloane Ranger—a special kind of upper-class twit with deeply misguided delusions about being trendy. Male Sloanes wore corduroy trousers, striped shirts and tweed jackets, while the female of the species went in for frilly white shirts and pearls.

Chelsea's **artistic** streak never entirely disappeared, however, and in the 1960s and early 1970s it flourished with a vengeance along the King's Road. Like Carnaby Street in Soho, the King's Road let its hair down and filled with cafés and fashion shops selling mini-skirts and cheap jewellery. The Royal Court Theatre, opposite Peter Jones, came into its own as a venue for avant-garde writers like John Osborne (the original Angry Young Man), Edward Bond and Arnold Wesker. Mods, later replaced by punks, set the fashion tone for whole generations of young people.

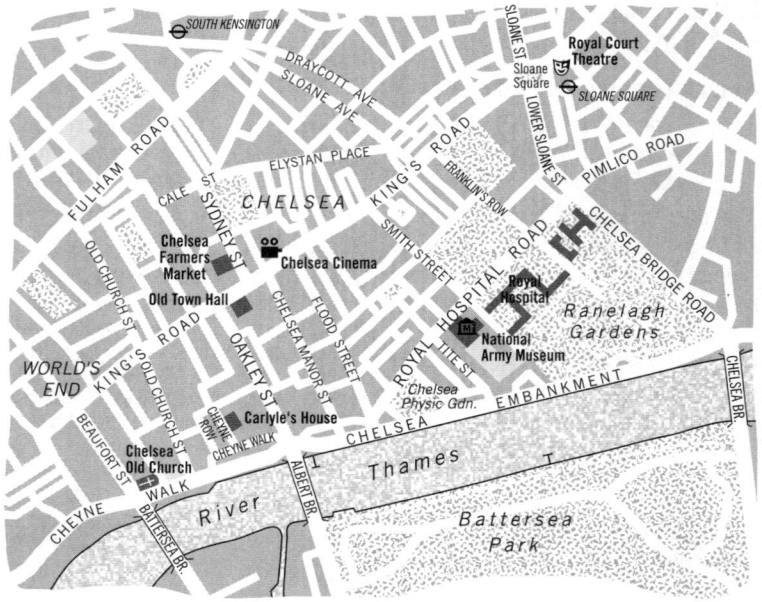

Cafés and Pubs

Habitat Café, King's Road. Airy, colourful room on the top of the shop, with big scrubbed wood tables and plants, and a daily Italian-inspired lunch menu, good coffee and scrumptious cakes.

King's Head and Eight Bells, 50 Cheyne Walk, Chelsea. Enjoy the antiques displays in this 16th-century building. There are views of the Battersea peace pagoda across the river.

Phene Arms, Phene St, off Oakley St. Small old pub with a courtyard garden in a quiet residential street, with surprisingly adventuous food.

Chelsea Kitchen, 98 King's Rd. Continental food and wine for less than £10.

Bluebird, 350 King's Rd. Part of the Conran empire, a converted 1930s garage containing a luxury food store, restaurant and café.

The King's Road

During the 1960s, old-fashioned shops were superseded by the likes of Terence Conran, who opened his first household store **Habitat** on the King's Road as a direct challenge to the fusty, old-fashioned goods then on sale at **Peter Jones** department store by Sloane Square. Meanwhile most of the boutiques have either gone upmarket or been replaced by generic highstreet chainstores. Some of the 1960s spirit lives on, however, in the delightfully sprawling **antiques markets** on the south side of the road. You might also want to take a look at the **Chelsea Farmer's Market**, Sydney Street, with its cafés and craft shops.

Chelsea Riverside

The heart of old Chelsea is down by the river. Either take the bus to Battersea Bridge, or walk down Old Church Street until you reach the water. Just to the left of the bridge is **Chelsea Old Church**, which preserves the memory of Sir Thomas More, author of the humanist tract *Utopia* and the first man to lose his head for standing up to Henry VIII over his break with the Pope. The church's history goes back to Norman times, but most of it was rebuilt in classical style in the 17th century. The churchyard has been converted into a small park..

Stretching to the east, just behind the Chelsea Embankment, are the delightful 18th-century brick houses of **Cheyne Walk**, one of London's most fashionable addresses for the past 200 years. Amongst the famous residents have been George Eliot, who died at No.4; Henry James, who spent the latter years of his life in Carlyle Mansions, a Victorian house standing just beyond the King's Head and Eight Bells pub; Whistler, who was living at No.101 when he produced some of his most extraordinary paintings of the Thames; and Turner, himself no mean painter of the Thames, who used No.119 as a retreat. The Queen's House at No.16 was shared during the 1860s by a trio of poets, Dante Gabriel Rossetti, Algernon Swinburne and George Meredith, who kept a whole bestiary of animals including some noisy peacocks.

The most interesting address, however, is 24 Cheyne Row just around the corner: **Carlyle's House** (*open April–Oct, Wed–Sun 11–4.30; adm*). Few houses in London evoke such a strong sense of period or personality as this redbrick Queen Anne building, where the historian Thomas Carlyle, author of *The French Revolution* and *Frederick the Great*, lived with his wife from 1834 until his death in 1881. It has been kept almost exactly as the Carlyles left it. Even the old man's hat still hangs on the peg in the entranceway.

> *Also see*: **Chelsea Physic Garden**, p.110; **King's Road shopping**, p.125.
> *Onwards to*: **Knightsbridge shopping**, p.126; **Battersea Park**, p.110.

Docklands

⊖ *Bank, Tower Hill, Wapping, Rotherhithe*

DLR *Tower Gateway, Shadwell, Canary Wharf, Mudchute, Island Gardens; ℂ (020) 7918 4000 for 24-hour travel information*

Buses: *100 from Liverpool Street for Wapping and Shadwell, P11 from Waterloo to London Bridge, D1 from London Bridge for the Isle of Dogs*

Boats *from Charing Cross or Westminster Pier every half-hour or so (less often in winter) 11am–5pm, stopping at London Bridge, St Katharine's Dock, Canary Wharf, Greenland Dock (in the Surrey Quays), Greenwich and the Thames Barrier. London Tourist Board recorded river service information line: ℂ 0839 123 432; Westminster Passenger Services: ℂ (020) 7930 4097; Thames Cruises (020) 7930 3373.*

Travelcards are valid on the DLR. A **Sail and Rail** *Ticket entitles you to a day's unlimited travel on the DLR plus a riverboat trip from Westminster or Greenwich Piers, and discounted entry to the London Aquarium at Westminster, the National Maritime Museum at Greenwich, The Royal Observatory and The Queen's House (see Greenwich, p.106).*

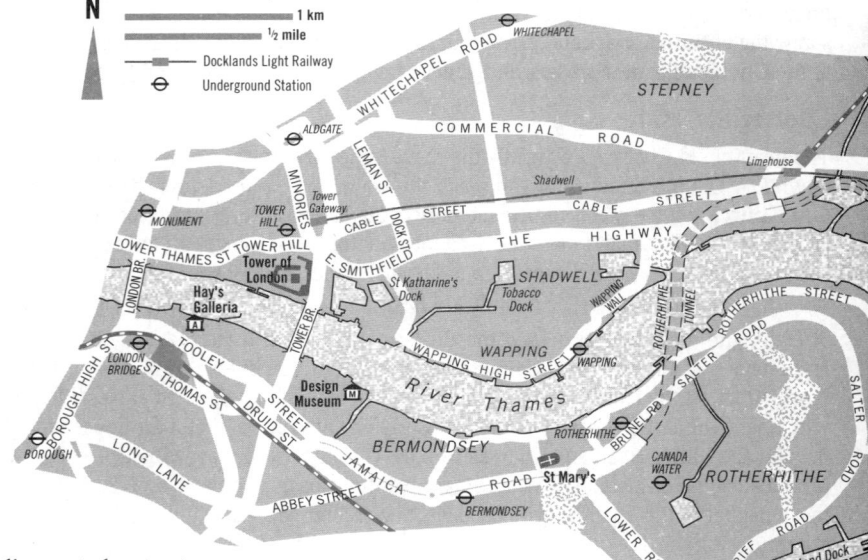

Free **street map** *of the area and other tourist information from the Tourist Board Centre at DLR Canary Wharf, or the potentially helpful roving Tourist Assistants employed by DLR.*

To head downriver from the Tower is to enter a different world— more in tune with the Emerald City in *The Wizard of Oz*. The converted Docklands show the face of a city of the future: a vision of **shimmering** high-rise glass and steel reflected in the lapping tides of the

River Thames, a Phoenix risen from the ashes of the derelict wharves and warehouses of a bygone age. It's **disorientating**, endlessly surprising, pock-marked by building sites, mud and cranes, and—in terms of sheer visual impact—extraordinarily **impressive**.

The Docklands were built in the 1980s without a shred of planning or civic sense and as a result were a spectacular financial flop. The development failed to respect its environment and the wishes of local people, many of whom were pushed out of their modest homes to make way for a higher-class breed of resident. Furthermore, nobody thought to provide proper services or adequate transport links, so the gleaming palaces were almost impossible to get to or live in. When recession struck at the end of the 1980s, hundreds of speculators went bust because they simply could not attract tenants. The place has become a bit of a ghost town: office blocks with bland reflective façades, impersonal shopping centres the same as you find in any New Town suburbia, luxury housing estates where the main luxury is a near-total absence of an identity.

The Docklands redevelopments continue out east all the way to London City Airport and beyond, featuring hi-tech office architecture by the likes of Richard Rogers and I. M. Pei,

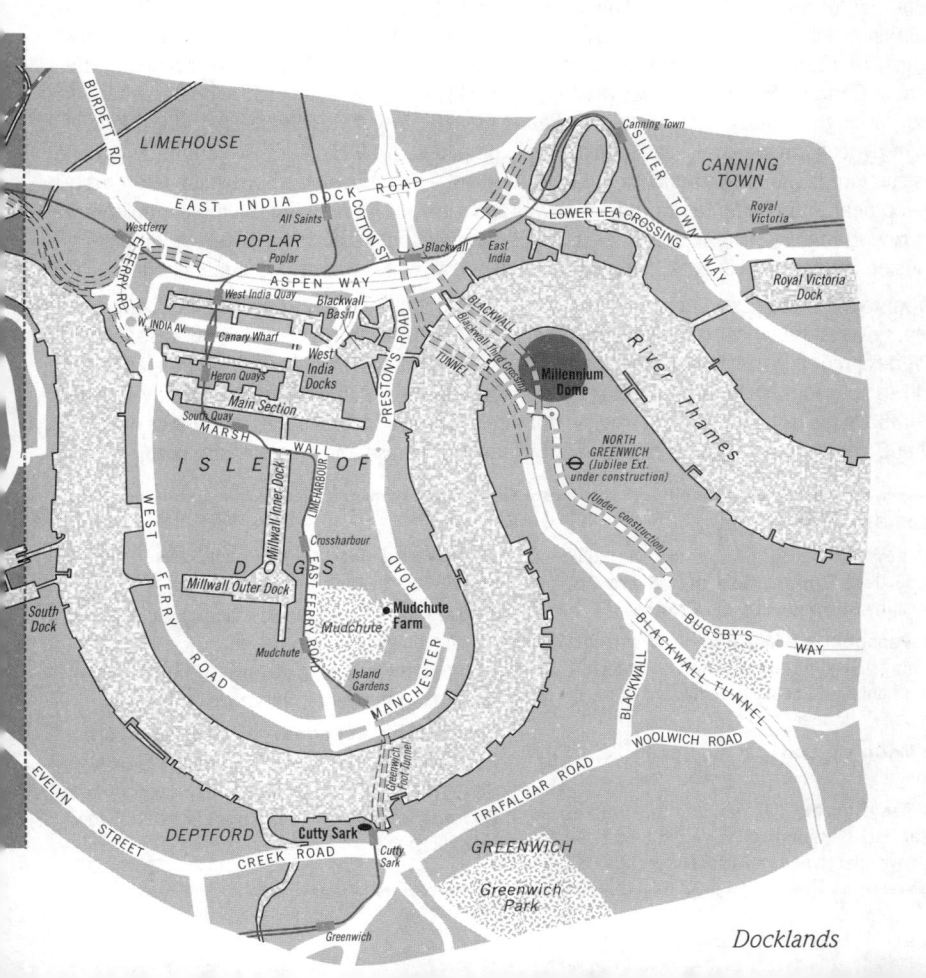

Docklands

which for the moment remain rather stranded as building works continue to develop an 'urban village' and a university campus on land where the Royal Docks used to be.

You can see a great deal of the Docklands by taking the overland **Docklands Light Railway** (DLR) from Bank or Tower Gateway to Island Gardens on the Isle of Dogs or Beckton. This elevated railway is like the futuristic monorail in Truffaut's *Farenheit 451*, the trains are computerized and quite eerily driverless. A ride on it—sitting next to the unmanned emergency driving position where you get panoramic views as you go, and getting on and off to explore—makes for an entertaining day out in itself. If you board at Tower Gateway on the hour between ten and four you are treated to a commentary on your trip all the way to Crossharbour.

The Isle of Dogs and Canary Wharf

The **Isle of Dogs** is a peninsula defined by a tight loop in the river and criss-crossed by artificial waterways. There is no hard evidence that it ever had any association with dogs, although there are folktales that the royal kennels were once kept here. Most likely, 'dogs' is a corruption of 'docks'; after all, that was what provided the area's livelihood from 1802 until the second half of the 20th century. The southern end of the Isle of Dogs is littered with failed upmarket residential estates as well as a sprinkling of older lower-class council houses. There's no mistaking the main attraction around here. The 812ft glass and steel tower block at the centre of **Canary Wharf** soars over the Docklands skyline, the flashing light atop its pyramidal apex winking 40 times a minute. Cesar Pelli's monster tower (*closed to visitors*), officially known by its address One Canada Square and completed in 1991 after just 18 months under construction, is the tallest building in London by far. This is Europe's largest single property development and clustered around the tower is a series of lower-lying buildings (mostly hi-tech reworkings by American architects of Edwardian styles), courtyards, shopping plazas, waterside footpaths, a car park, a fountain, incidental artworks and sculpted metal railings.

Continuity with the past is not its strong point, as traditionalists have been quick to point out. It bears no resemblance to the Canary Wharf of the 19th century, so called because it took deliveries predominantly from the Canary Islands. The Pelli tower is the first skyscraper in the world to be clad in stainless steel. It is 50 storeys high, has 32 passenger lifts, 3960 windows and 4388 steps in its four fire stairways. Building materials included 27,500 tonnes of steel, 500,000 bolts and a staggering 90,000 sq ft of Italian, Spanish and Guatemalan marble in the

Cafés and Pubs

Canary Wharf restaurants, inside the complex, include **Café Rouge**, **Gourmet Pizza Co**, and the healthy **Soup Opera** and **Cranks**.

The Prospect of Whitby, 57 Wapping Wall, charming pub with loads of history- starting in 1543. With a hangman's noose to remind us of the executions once held there.

The Widow's Son, outside Devon's Road DLR station, an inn with an interesting story.

The Mayflower, 117 Rotherhithe St, and the **Angel**, 101 Bermondsey Wall East. Both have fine views over the river, the Angel better for food.

Corney and Barrow, off Cabot Square, is shiny and you can sit outside.

Brera, Cabot Place West, deliciously sophisticated Italian sandwiches.

Chili's Grill & Bar, 2nd floor, Cabot Place East, serves a Texan lunch above Canary Wharf.

Babe Ruth's Legendary Eating Place, opposite Tobacco Dock, London's best themed restaurant.

Dickens Inn, St Katharine's Dock, where the food is pretty good if a little expensive.

lobby alone. Every feature is state-of-the-art. There are so many fax machines and photocopiers in the building that heating is quite unnecessary, even in the dead of winter. The fountain in Cabot Square is computer-controlled, adjusting the jet intensity according to wind strength so that passers-by never get splashed.

The **Storm Water Pumping Station** on Stewart Street off Marsh Wall is well worth a visit—but to get there you will have to get out at South Quay and walk along Marsh Wall (about 10–20 minutes). Built by John Outram in 1988, the enormous pump station looks like an outsized Chinsese temple, and is one of the most successful buildings in the Docklands.

Further south, **Mudchute** is one of a number of city farms dotted around east London, a 32-acre patchwork of vegetable allotments and open fields. A little further down Eastferry Road is **Island Gardens**, a small riverside park with an outstanding view across the river to Greenwich. You can walk over to Greenwich through the **foot tunnel** built in 1902 beneath the river, its two onion-domed brick towers marking the entrances at either end. The Light Railway has also decided to tunnel south under the river, and there is an extension to Cutty Sark, Greenwich and Lewisham due in time for the millennium.

Wapping

Until the 16th century, when the land around it was drained, Wapping was little more than a sliver of land hemmed in by swamps to the north and the river on the south. It has almost always been poor: John Stow described Wapping High Street in his *Survey of London* (1598) as 'a filthy strait passage, with alleys of small tenements or cottages'. Sailors made up the bulk of its modest population, later replaced by dockers. The waterfront near **Wapping Wall** known as **Execution Dock** earned its name because pirates and smugglers used to be hanged there and then displayed in chains for as long as it took for three tides to wash over them.

This was where some of the first failed luxury flats of the 1980s were built. Some of the architecture is truly dire, and although the area is now more or less fully inhabited Wapping still has no soul. The ambitious and attractively converted **Tobacco Dock** on The Highway, for example, is supposed to be a thriving new shopping centre, but in fact it is rather forlorn.

St Katharine's Dock looks benign enough now, with its yachts and cafés, but it was once one of the most callous of riverside developments. To build the docks and commodity warehouses here in the 1820s, the authorities knocked down 1250 houses and made more than 11,000 people homeless. For all that, the dock was not a great financial success and lost money until its closure in 1968. Now prettified with boats and bright paint, its walkways are linked with a series of attractive iron bridges. It is an obvious lunch spot after a hard morning's sightseeing at the Tower of London, along a signposted walkway. There is a free hour-long guided walk of the docker's way of life leaving on Saturdays at 1pm and 3pm from the East Gate of the Tower of London. Call London Walks, ✆ (020) 7624 3978, for details of others.

Opposite the Murdoch empire is Nicholas Hawksmoor's church **St George in the East** (1714–29) with its broad, tall tower with pepperpot turrets. The docks were heavily bombed during the Blitz, when the interior of St George was destroyed. It has now been redesigned as an intriguing hybrid—part church, part block of flats, part courtyard.

Limehouse

A more complete Hawksmoor church can be found a mile or so to the east, past Limehouse Basin off the Commercial Road. The chunky tower of **St Anne Limehouse** has been a guide to ships coming into London ever since it was completed in 1724. Named after the lime kilns which used to operate here, Limehouse bears the vestiges of the mini-Chinatown it was before the 1980s property bonanza and it has a little-publicized reputation for good cheap Chinese restaurants. In the 19th century the area was considered an iniquitous den of vice; this was where Oscar Wilde set the opium-smoking scene in his novel *The Picture of Dorian Gray*.

Rotherhithe

Rotherhithe was where the Pilgrim Fathers set out for America in their ship the *Mayflower* in 1620. You might think hordes of American tourists come to pay homage to their forefathers, but in fact Rotherhithe is a delightfully unspoiled, relatively unknown part of riverside London and one of the most successful of the Docklands redevelopments. The old warehouses have been repaired but not tarted up, the streets have been kept narrow, and the green in front of St Mary's Church lends an air of village-like cosiness.

Originally Rotherhithe was part of the estate of the great abbey of Bermondsey, which was destroyed at the Reformation. The monks used to drink in a tavern called The Salutation, since renamed **The Angel**. The present pub was built, probably in the 17th century, as a drinking haunt for sailors. The departure of the Pilgrim Fathers is commemorated in the **Mayflower** pub, which is partly built out of the broken up segments of the original ship and has a model of the vessel hanging outside its front door. Because of its tourist clientele, the pub is allowed to sell postage stamps, including American ones. This was probably the tavern where Captain Christopher Jones and his crew spent the night before their departure for the Americas. Within two years, the ship came back from its expedition, and Jones was eventually buried, along with the three co-owners of the *Mayflower*, in the churchyard of **St Mary's** opposite. The church itself, which was attractively rebuilt in the 18th century, contains a plaque to Jones as well as remains of the *Fighting Temeraire*, the battleship whose demise was so poignantly captured by Turner in his famous painting in the National Gallery.

Because of its isolation on a bend in the Thames, Rotherhithe became rather dilapidated after the Second World War. Its recent redevelopment, however, has attracted a modest number of artists and artisans, and by the river is an intriguing sculpture park called the **Knot Garden**.

Surrey Docks and Deptford

Southeast of Rotherhithe, if you can bear the noisy walk down Lower Road and off to the left down Redriff Road, are the old **Surrey Docks**, part of which have been converted into a yachting and pleasure-boat marina. Some of the hi-tech modern buildings are rather successful. **Greenland Dock** (used by the whaling trade in the 19th century) and **South Dock** are ideal for a stroll or a spot of rowing.

To the south is **Deptford**, famous as the place where Christopher Marlowe was stabbed to death in a tavern brawl in 1593 and where Peter the Great rode in a wheelbarrow in John Evelyn's garden during a state visit to the naval dockyard established there by Henry VIII.

Also see: **Millennium Dome**, p.38; **Tower of London**, p.44.

Onwards to: **Greenwich**, p.106; the **South Bank and Southwark**, p.80; the **City of London**, p.55.

Camden

● *Camden Town, Chalk Farm; bus 24, 29, 31*
Visit at the weekend to see the area at its liveliest.

Cafés and Pubs

Silks and Spice, 28 Chalk Farm Rd. Thai and Malaysian café-restaurant. Lunch from £4.95.

Crown and Goose, 100 Arlington Rd. Award-winning pub and wine bar with real ale, good food and friendly service.

Café Delancey, 3 Delancey St. Laid-back brasserie.

Dublin Castle, 94 Parkway. Rowdy but friendly Irish pub with live music.

Marine Ices, 8 Haverstock Hill, near ● Chalk Farm. Traditional old Italian ice cream restaurant, one of the best in all London.

Camden is above all its buzzing **open-air** market, or rather series of markets, that have sprung up around the canal and the surrounding streets. There is something for everyone: cheap clothes, pianos, herbal cures, tarot card readings, off-beat bookshops, furniture stores, pubs and lots and lots of restaurants. At the weekends, traffic comes to a standstill. The atmosphere is very **relaxed, young** but not overly self-conscious or trendy. You can easily spend hours sorting through the leatherwear and second-hand records, stopping for a drink or snack from a street stall; later, you can head off for a meal or a spot of dancing; or you can easily escape the crowds by strolling away along Regent's Canal. Camden's modern identity as a haven for artists and small shopkeepers was established in the 1970s, when the market started and the old Victorian warehouses were slowly converted into artists' studios, music venues and restaurants.

Markets and Shops

The nerve centre of the market is at **Camden Lock**, just next to the canal off Chalk Farm Road (the extension of Camden High Street). Some but not all of the stalls and shops stay open all week. In the middle of the market is a covered three-storey building with narrow staircases and passages selling jewellery and crafts; in the immediate vicinity are stalls selling clothes, antiques, books and records. The stalls then continue for about 500 yards up the Chalk Farm Road, in an area known as **The Stables**. **Chalk Farm Road** itself has interiors shops with an ethnic slant. Some of the most interesting shops are on **Camden High Street**, which is really a market unto itself; the Electric Ballroom nightclub doubles on Sundays as a bazaar for cheap designer fashions and jewellery. Finally, there is a fruit and veg market on **Inverness Street**, between the High Street and Gloucester Crescent, which is open Mon–Sat.

Jewish Museum

129–32 Albert St, (020) 7284 1997. Open Sun–Thurs 10–4; adm.

This celebration of Jewish life in England from the Middle Ages, formerly in Woburn House on Tavistock Square, is notable mostly for its collection of old ritual objects from London synagogues. The centrepiece is an elaborately carved 16th-century Venetian Synagogue Ark. There are also attractive illuminated marriage contracts and some Torah bells fashioned by the 18th-century silversmith Abraham Lopes de Oliveira.

Onwards to: **Regent's Park and London Zoo**, p.116.

Islington

⊖ *Angel,* ⊖/⇌ *Highbury and Islington*
Bus 19, 73

In the 1950s you wouldn't have found much in Islington apart from a clapped-out old music hall, a few eel and pie shops and an extended series of slummy terraced houses. How times have changed. Now it is one of the liveliest and trendiest districts in the capital, a Mecca for liberal-minded **arty** professionals, particularly writers and broadcasters, who live in attractively refurbished Georgian townhouses and eat out in expensive ethnic restaurants. The place is packed with pubs, cafés, designer bars and shops, and **alternative** theatres.

During the 1980s Islington was associated with a certain kind of earnest, occasionally radical left-wing politics that jarred completely with the prevailing Thatcherite ideology of free markets and individual responsibility. The borough council spent money on crèches and facilities for the disabled and was dismissed as a cabal of the 'loony left' for its pains. More recently, Islington has been taken to task in the right-wing press for spawning a more **comfortable** breed of liberal lefty who likes to discuss the meaning of socialism over a fancy plate of rocket and shaved parmesan. The occasion of this new wave of Islington-bashing has been the rise of Prime Minister Tony Blair, an Islingtonian of long standing.

In fact, the pleasures of Islington have been well known for centuries and were only seriously interrupted by the industrial revolution. In the 16th century it was popular as a royal hunting ground and noted for its pure spring water and good dairy farms. The open fields were dotted with well-appointed mansions, gardens and orchards. Elizabeth I used to meet her favourites here, and people from all walks of life came to enjoy the bowling greens, dance floors and taverns. The extension of Regent's Canal (here called the Grand Union Canal) and the advent of the railways in the 19th century did similar damage in Islington as it had in Camden; the attractive Georgian terraces which had sprung up in the district became dilapidated and dirty, as the local population, mostly made up of labourers, swelled uncontrollably. Soon Islington became a byword for everything that was *un*fashionable in London. In 1928, the novelist Evelyn Waugh ran away from Canonbury Square after just a few months in a rented house because he was fed up having to explain to his friends why he lived in such a backwater.

Just 20 years later, though, there was nothing marginal about Islington at all. The Camden Passage antiques market arrived in 1964, and pub theatres led by the King's Head on Upper Street began to flourish soon after. The old Collins Music Hall burned down and was replaced with the Screen on the Green cinema. Nowadays the changes in Islington come so fast it is hard to keep track of them: a Lebanese restaurant closes there, a Cuban bar opens here. The area retains a certain self-conscious shabbiness, but that is part of its charm. Islington doesn't have any tourist attractions in the traditional sense of the word, just bags of atmosphere. The best way to visit is to start at the Angel and work your way slowly northwards.

Camden Passage

Open Wed 7.30–5, Sat 9–5.30, some stalls open 10–5 other days, closed Mon

This is a cobbled row of elegant antiques shops and stalls, most of which open their doors on Wednesday mornings and Saturdays only. The market is ideal for browsing, since everything looks perfect and the prices of the furniture, prints, silverware and jewellery are probably too high to consider seriously for purchase.

Cafés and Pubs

Santa Fe, 75 Upper St. 'New Mexican' food (pot roast with garlic mash, quesadillas, lots of lime and chile, great desserts) in a large, bright, trendy bar/restaurant. Lunch £4–9.

King's Head, 115 Upper St. Great theatre pub with plush seats and bags of atmosphere.

Granita, 127 Upper St. *The* Islington restaurant and New Labour meeting place. Minimalist décor matched by trendy menu. Lunch served Wed–Sun 12.30–2.30. £15–20.

Pasha, 301 Upper St. Spicy Turkish food, with lots of choice including many vegetarian dishes. Set lunch menus from £5.

Upper Street Fish Shop, 324 Upper St. Perhaps the best fish'n'chips in London. From £2–3 takeaway; £12 for a 3-course sit-down menu.

Almeida Theatre Café, 7a Almeida St. Baguettes, soup, etc. from £2–3.

Angel of the North, 353 Upper St. Pleasant café serving breakfasts, salads, burgers. £5–8.

Upper Street

All the streets around here, from Upper Street across to St Peter's Street and down to City Road, are a delight for strollers—small, relatively traffic-free and packed with elegant houses, cafés and restaurants. The area to the east, along the Grand Union Canal, is particularly charming and dotted with pretty Georgian houses. In the 1950s and 1960s this was the distinctly unfashionable home of the playwright Joe Orton and his lover Kenneth Halliwell.

Just to the north, back on Upper Street, is the lumbering hulk of the **Business Design Centre**. This rather clumsy building is a redevelopment of the old Royal Agricultural Hall, a fine Victorian hangar made of iron and glass used for agricultural shows and industrial exhibitions. The Design Centre now hosts conferences, the Islington Art Fair and other odd art shows. On either side of the Design Centre, Upper St is packed with the restaurants and offbeat shops that characterize Islington, including several shops selling a fascinating variety of old furniture (try Castle Gibson, No.106a) and others even more miscellaneous, like After Noah (No.121), with its array of old and new lamps, clocks, soaps and old comics. Behind, on Liverpool Road, is **Chapel Market**, a lively fruit, veg and clothes market, open every day but Monday.

Triangular **Islington Green**, where Upper Street meets Essex Road, is more of a meeting place than a spot of any great beauty. Heading north on Upper St, you come to the **King's Head** theatre pub, which as a gimmick still counts money in the pre-decimal currency of pounds, shillings and pence (12 pence to a shilling, 20 shillings to a pound). The streets to the left of here, forming the beginning of the area known as Barnsbury, contain some fine Georgian townhouses. Theberton Street, not far from the pub, leads to the pale brick splendour of Gibson Square. One block further up is Almeida Street, home to the highly successful fringe theatre of the same name. The crowds and the trendiness factor gradually ebb away the further north you walk up Upper St. It is worth continuing for five minutes, past the town hall, to turn right on Canonbury Lane and explore one of the most unspoiled areas of Georgian housing in north London. The name **Canonbury** recalls Islington's roots as the burgh, or district, of the canons of the priory of St Bartholomew at Smithfield. Then, as now, the most imposing building in the neighbourhood was **Canonbury Tower** on Canonbury Place, a building of mythical reputation whose history goes back to pre-Roman times; no fewer than 24 ley lines meet at the point where the central pillar of its main staircase stands.

Onwards to: **Camden**, p.94; the **City of London**, p.55.

Hampstead

● *Hampstead, Belsize Park,* ⇌ *Hampstead Heath (Silverlink)*
Bus 24, 46, 210, 268

Hampstead is a pretty **hilltop** village of Georgian rows and Victorian mansions, surrounded by the vast expanse of the Heath. Throughout its history, it has provided a refuge when life in the city has become too much. John Constable came here and painted some distant cityscapes that were barely distinguishable in tone from his great rural idylls. No wonder: the air is so **pure** and the Heath so big and wild you can feel you are lost in the deep heart of the English countryside. Nowadays Hampstead has an unmistakable air of *established* comfort. More cosmopolitan than Camden and Islington, it is full of lively restaurants, bars and theatres frequented by its well-off, generally New Labour residents. But in contrast to its north London neighbours, Hampstead, for all its liberal credentials, is a staid and remarkably **conservative** place, everything carefully planned and lovingly looked after, from the window boxes in the Georgian houses on Holly Hill to the fish stall next to the community market.

Hampstead Village

The real pleasure of Hampstead village is in getting lost in the winding backstreets. Up near Whitestone Pond, Lower Terrace takes you past the entrance to **Judges Walk**, the legendary 'substitute' law court of the Great Plague which is now just a driveway to a couple of tumble-down houses. A little further down to the left is **Admiral's Walk**, which contains a splendid Georgian house with multi-levelled rooms and balconies, where at various times the novelist John Galsworthy and the architect George Gilbert Scott have taken up residence. At the other end of Admiral's Walk, Hampstead Grove takes you down to **Fenton House**, a splendid brick mansion dating from 1693 (☏ *(020) 7435 3471; open Sat and Sun 11–5, Wed–Fri 2–5; adm*). Aside from the elegant rooms and fine garden, the house has collections of early keyboard instruments and fine porcelain. At the bottom of Hampstead Grove, the narrow road up to the left is **Hollybush Hill**, a cul-de-sac lined with beautiful small houses including the 17th-century Hollybush pub. Just after the pub is a steep staircase plunging down towards Heath Street. Better, however, to retrace your steps and head down **Holly Walk**, another delightful cobbled path flanked by fine houses and a small flower-filled cemetery. At the bottom of the hill is **St John's**, an attractive 18th-century church with a tall tower and, inside, a balustraded gallery and a bust of Keats beside the lectern. Constable is buried in the churchyard. The road from the church back to Heath Street, called **Church Row**, is one of the most elegant lines of Georgian housing in London.

Heath Street is one of two Hampstead thoroughfares lined with fine shops, delicatessens, cafés and restaurants. The other, the **High Street**, can be reached through **Oriel Place**, which has an old plane tree growing in a minuscule patch of ground halfway along. Cross the High Street and you come into **Flask Walk** with its second-hand bookshops, galleries, children's boutiques, and posh tea and coffee merchant. Along with its continuation **Well Walk**, this is where fashionable folk came to take the Hampstead spa waters in the 18th century.

The Spaniards Inn

The 16th-century **Spaniards Inn** at the junction of Hampstead Lane and Spaniards Road, named after two Spanish proprietors who killed each other in a duel, owes its fame to the 18th-century highwayman Dick Turpin who used to stop for drinks here in between coach

Cafés and Pubs

Ye Olde White Bear, New End Square. Friendly pub in the maze of streets behind Hampstead tube. Food served outside and all day.

Toast, 51–53 Hampstead High St. Smart new restaurant/bar above Hampstead tube. Lunch from £15.

The Flask, Flask Walk. Rambling traditional pub behind flower-bedecked façade, just off the High Street.

Maison Blanc, 62a Hampstead High St. Chic pâtisserie serving excellent pastries and coffee.

Coffee Cup, 74 Hampstead High St. Much-loved but rather shabby café with seats outside.

The Crêperie, corner of Hampstead High St and Perrin's Lane. Tiny stall selling freshly made sweet and savoury crêpes.

Giraffe, 46 Rosslyn Hill. Funky café serving international menu accompanied by world music.

hold-ups. During the Gordon Riots of 1780, a group of mobsters dropped by on their way to Kenwood House, which they intended to destroy. The publican offered the rioters pint after pint of free beer and soon the men weren't in a fit state to walk to Kenwood, let alone burn it down. You can see their muskets hanging on the wall in the saloon bar.

Keats' House

> Wentworth Place, Keats Grove (walk down Hampstead High St and its continuation Rosslyn Hill, then turn left on to Downshire Hill and take the first right); ✆ (020) 7435 2062. Open April–Oct Mon–Fri 10–1 and 2–6, Sat 10–1 and 2–5 and Sun 2–5, and Nov–Mar Mon–Fri 1–5, Sat 10–1 and 2–5, and Sun 2–5; free.

The main attraction is the plum tree in the garden, under which Keats wrote *Ode to a Nightingale* in 1819 (if you think the tree looks a bit young, you're right; it is a replacement). In all, Keats spent only two years here as a lodger of Charles Armitage Brown, a literary critic specializing in Shakespeare's sonnets. It was nevertheless an eventful time. He produced some of his best and most famous work, fell in love with Fanny Brawne who lived in the other half of the house, and contracted the consumption that was to kill him two years later at the age of 25. Keats used one living room downstairs and one bedroom upstairs. Memorabilia are strewn in every room; these include a lock of Keats' hair and some of his manuscripts and books.

Kenwood House

> Hampstead Lane; entrance opposite Bishops Avenue; ✆ (020) 8348 1286. Open daily 10–6 April–Sept, closes 4pm in winter; free. For Hampstead Heath, see p.111.

The unpretentious atmosphere at Kenwood is a breath of fresh air after the stuffily earnest stately homes dotted around the rest of London. The expanse of the Heath rolls away to the south and its breathtaking views over Highgate and central London. Kenwood is famous for its summer concerts held by the lake at the bottom of the garden; the orchestra sits under a white awning and the audience watches from across the water. The house itself dates back to 1616 but was given a facelift by Robert Adam in the 1760s. He stuck on the white neoclassical façade, and reworked most of the interiors. The pictures, bequeathed by Lord Iveagh, include works by Rembrandt (a remarkable self-portrait), Vermeer (*The Guitar Player*), Van Dyck, Gainsborough, Guardi, Reynolds, Landseer and Turner.

Also see: **Hampstead Heath**, p.112; the **Freud Museum**, p.138.
Onwards to: **Highgate Cemetery**, p.112.

Richmond

⊖/≷ *Richmond*
Bus 65, 391

Richmond is a **tranquil**, affluent **riverside** community of attractive Georgian and neo-Georgian houses, flanked on all sides by wide expanses of greenery. On a sunny day it is an ideal place to walk along the river; the compact town centre beside Richmond Green has a pleasant **villagey** feel and there are plenty of cafés and riverside pubs. Richmond's sense of ommunity is such that it boasts not one but two theatres: the Richmond Theatre on the Green, and the Orange Tree near the station.

Richmond Palace and the Green

In medieval times, the focal point of the district was Shene Palace, a relatively modest manor house used as a lodge for the excellent hunting in the surrounding hills. The village green (today's Richmond Green) became a popular venue for pageants and jousting tournaments. Henry VII was so attached to the place that he changed its name from Shene to Richmond, after his earldom in Yorkshire, and entirely rebuilt the palace after a fire in 1497.

The new Richmond Palace must have been quite something, a riot of spires and turrets which you can see reconstructed as a model in the Richmond Town Hall's small **museum** (*entrance on Red Lion Street, ℂ (020) 8332 1141; open May–Oct only, Tues–Sat 11–5, and Sun 1–4; adm*). Sadly, almost nothing survives of medieval Richmond in real life. A charterhouse which stood a few hundred yards to the north was destroyed during the Reformation, and the palace followed suit immediately after Charles I's execution in 1649. All that remains is a stone gateway off Richmond Green, bearing Henry VII's coat of arms, and the palace wardrobe, or household office, to the left just inside Old Palace Yard.

Political upheaval could not disguise the basic attraction of Richmond, and by the early 18th century building had begun again in earnest. In Old Palace Yard is **Trumpeters' House**, an elegant mansion built by a pupil of Christopher Wren and subsequently used as a refuge for Prince Metternich after the upheavals in Vienna of 1848. Further fine Georgian houses are to be found in neighbouring streets, such as Old Palace Terrace and Maids of Honour Row.

The Riverside

Today, as ever, the biggest attraction of Richmond is the riverside, which boasts, amongst other things, the elegant five-arched **Richmond Bridge** dating from the 1770s. The houses on the north side have been extensively redeveloped as a neo-Georgian terrace of shops, restaurants and offices called **The Riverside**, opened in 1988. The architect responsible was Quinlan Terry, a chum of Prince Charles much in sympathy with the Prince's traditionalist leanings. Most critics were appalled by this piece of unadventurous pastiche, while Prince Charles called it 'an expression of harmony and proportion'. The development nevertheless does its job well enough, and on summer days its layered terraces descending towards the water are crowded with strollers, sunbathers and the spillover customers of the surrounding pubs. At the top of the bridge, Richmond Hill leads to wild Richmond Park, famous for its deer.

Cafés and Pubs

Bellini, 12 The Quadrant. Fish, pasta, *gnocchi* and singing waiters in flamboyant Italian eaterie (from £15).

Café Parisien, 7 Lower George St. Superior filled baguettes and toasted sandwiches; outdoor seating; exceptionally friendly service (from £5).

Pierre's Brasserie du Liban, 11–13 Petersham Rd. One of the best Lebanese restaurants in London (from £30); take-away sandwiches (from £3).

White Swan, 26 Old Palace Lane. Traditional riverside pub hidden in a tiny street of cottages.

Beeton's, 58 Hill Rise. Unusual modern British cuisine.

Caffè Mamma, 24 Hill Street. Superior pasta café decorated like an Italian courtyard.

White Cross Hotel, Richmond Waterside Ordinary pub fare, but a delightful spot. Crowded in summer.

Ham House

Ham Street, off Sandy Lane and Petersham Road; © (020) 8940 1950; bus 371 from Richmond. Grounds open Sat–Wed 10.30–6; adm; house open Sat–Wed 1–5; adm.

Ham House is one of the grandest surviving Jacobean mansions in London, a magnificent three-storey redbrick house that has been restored to something approaching its original splendour. Built in 1610 and nicknamed the 'sleeping beauty' for its tranquil position, it became the home of William Murray, a friend of Charles I, who as a child had acted as the future King's whipping boy. In gratitude, Charles offered the adult Murray a peerage (he became the Earl of Dysart) and all the property around Ham and Petersham including this house.

The highlight is the **Great Hall**, a wonderfully airy room decorated in blue, with a gallery overlooking the black and white checked floor. The rest of the house, some of which is still under reconstruction, boasts a profusion of tapestries, velvet drapes and plaster ornamentation on the staircases and ceilings. The gardens have retained their original 17th-century formal layout; the hedges and rows of trees intriguingly conceal the house from the river, lending an air of mystery and anticipated pleasure as you approach from the ferry stop.

Marble Hill House

Richmond Road, Twickenham; © (020) 8892 5115; ≥ St Margaret's; bus 490, 33, R70 from Richmond. Open April–Oct daily 10–6, Nov–Mar Wed–Sun 10–4; adm.

From the Twickenham side of Richmond Bridge you can enjoy a delightful mile-long walk along a stretch of the Thames that seems almost entirely rural. Marble Hill House is a simple white Palladian villa built in 1729 for Henrietta Howard, the 'exceedingly respectable and respected' mistress of George II. Henrietta could not stand the pressure of life at court, where she had to negotiate a tricky path between her lover and her influential husband, and so with a little help from the royal purse she set up home here, some 10 miles out of central London. The house is rather empty, having been neglected for 200 years and depleted of most of its furniture. But the park is open and very green, affording the broadest possible view of the river. A series of annual open-air concerts is staged here every summer; it is a delightful venue when the weather holds.

Also see: **Richmond Park**, p.117.
Onwards to: **Kew Gardens**, p.114; **Syon Park**, p.118.

Greenwich

> ⊖ *Jubilee line (North Greenwich) should be completed late 1999*
> ⇌ *Greenwich (a bit off to the west) or Maze Hill (a bit off to the east) from Charing Cross, Cannon St and London Bridge.* **DLR** *to North Greenwich*
> **Bus** *53 and 188 from Trafalagar Square and Waterloo*
> *By* **boat** *from Charing Cross, Tower and Westminster Piers daily*

Greenwich has been a place of pleasure since the 15th century, when Henry V's brother, Duke Humphrey of Gloucester, built the first royal palace. While neighbouring districts like Deptford and Woolwich have always had to live by their wits and the hard graft of building and unloading ships, Greenwich has concentrated on **idle pleasures** like hunting and jousting, or rarefied pursuits like astronomy. Thanks to the contributions of Jones, Wren, Hawksmoor and Vanbrugh, it also boasts a remarkable **architectural** heritage, evident from the moment you look up from the ferry pier. It is an ensemble of great grace and proportion, which in recent years has spawned an **affluent** community of middle-class Londoners in fine Georgian houses up Crooms Hill or on the grassy verges of Greenwich Park and Blackheath.

Henry VIII was born at Greenwich and, after a boyhood spent jousting, hunting and attending balls, never lost affection for the place. Henry married his first wife, Catherine of Aragon, in the palace's private chapel and watched in frustration and rage as six of their seven children—four of them the boys he so desired—died here within a few weeks of their birth. The latter half of Henry's reign, when Hampton Court took over as the 'in' palace, saw a decline at Greenwich. Edward VI was sent here to convalesce in 1553. Queen Elizabeth I came here occasionally, and it was here that Sir Walter Ralegh magnanimously threw his cloak on a 'plashy place' (i.e. a puddle) so Her Majesty would not get her feet muddy. But it was the Stuarts who breathed new life into Greenwich with the fine buildings we see today.

The village is mobbed at weekends by bargain-hunters coming for the markets: crafts in the covered market off Nelson Road, and antiques, bric-a-brac, and vintage clothing around Stockwell Street.

Royal Naval College

> *King William Walk, on the site of the old Palace of Placentia. Open daily 10–4; free. The Pepys Building inside the college is home to the Millennium Visitors' Centre (open Mon–Fri 11–7, Sat–Sun 10–6) until Oct 1999 when the tourist information office will move here.*

Charles II's first thought when he restored the monarchy was to rebuild Placentia, but he didn't have the money and gave up soon after the foundation stone was laid. Queen Mary had another idea after she witnessed the terrible wounds inflicted on British sailors at the battle of La Hogue in 1692: she commissioned Christopher Wren to clear the ruins of the old palace and build a naval hospital. Mary and Wren did not enjoy an altogether happy collaboration, since Mary insisted that the Queen's House should be visible from the river (something that was never the case when Placentia was still standing), and that the path of the Deptford to Woolwich road, which at the time ran through the middle of the building site, should be undisturbed. As a result, Wren and his successors, Hawksmoor and Vanbrugh, were obliged rather against their will to come up with a design based on four entirely separate buildings, with its majestic neoclassical façades overlooking the river and pepper-pot towers at the back.

Cafés and Pubs

Bar du Musée, 17 Nelson Rd. French-style bar with a garden, good wines and a mellow ambience.

Spread Eagle, 2 Stockwell St. Small, plush, friendly restaurant serving delicious traditional English food, with a French twist. Good value menu.

Time Bar and Restaurant, 7a College Approach. This new sleek and spacious loft-style bar also functions as a gallery. The restaurant serves excellent modern British cuisine.

North Pole, 131 Greenwich High St. Fashionable bar and restaurant dishing up good modern European food to a cheerful crowd.

Peter's Café, 21 Greenwich Church St. Easy-going café serving cream teas, cakes and lunches. Tiny terrace.

Saigon, 16 Nelson Rd. Long-standing Vietnamese.

Goddard's Ye Old Pie House, 45 Greenwich Church St (no phone). Local haunt serving great pie and mash.

The hospital was eventually closed, and the Royal Naval College moved here in 1873. Now it is to house the University of Greenwich from the autumn of 1999. Only the chapel and Painted Hall are open to the public. The former is based on a design by Wren, but was entirely refurbished by James Stuart after a fire in 1779. It has an intricate plaster-moulded ceiling, and a fine painting of *St Paul at Melita* by Benjamin West above the altar. The **Painted Hall** is a magnificent ensemble of three rooms painted in opulent style by James Thornhill, the man who also decorated the cupola of St Paul's.

Queen's House and National Maritime Museum

Romney Road. Open daily 10–5; adm. Combined ticket for attractions available.

The **Queen's House** (undergoing repairs until late 1999) was Inigo Jones's first experiment in Palladian architecture after his return from Italy in 1615. James I's wife Anne of Denmark was the queen in question, who wanted her own private villa as an extension to the Palace of Placentia. For years after Anne's death in 1619 the house languished unfinished, but the project was taken up again by Queen Henrietta Maria in 1629. So happy was she with the final result, completed in 1640, that she nicknamed it her 'house of delights' and returned to live in it as the Queen Mother after the Restoration. The building is a textbook exercise in Palladian classicism—simple and sober on the outside, and full of 'licentious imaginacy', as Jones put it, on the inside. Much of the decay which the Queen's House suffered in the 18th and 19th centuries has been reversed, thanks to a recent restoration bringing the building back to something close to its 1660s state. The centrepiece is the **Great Hall**, a perfect 40ft cube immediately inside the main entrance with an elegant gallery at first floor level. Note the **Tulip Staircase** at the eastern end of the hall, a wrought-iron helix staircase which twists its way up to the Queen's Bedroom. This was the first open-well staircase to be built in England. The floral decorations on its banister are not tulips at all, but fleurs-de-lys.

The **National Maritime Museum** has recently re-opened after a £40,000,000 overhaul and is now the most up-to date museum in the UK. A whole floor is devoted to interactive learning, ostensibly for kids, but everyone seems to enjoy shooting water pistols or blowing hair-dryers at model ships. The courtyard has been glassed over to airily accommodate the larger exhibits: an enormous propeller, a container, even a yacht. Historical memorabilia, particularly that of Napolean's era, still features but the focus has shifted from past history to an engagingly energetic portrayal of the high-tech world of modern shipping.

Old Royal Observatory

> *Greenwich Park. Open daily 10–5; adm. Combined tickets for major attractions available. For the park itself, see p.111.*

Greenwich is, of course, a time as well as a place; Greenwich Mean Time, as measured at this observatory, has synchronized the world's watches and guided the world's ships since 1884. The first two things you see on approaching the museum entrance are the metal plaque marking 0° longitude and, next to it, a large red ball on a stick that lowers every day at 1pm precisely as a symbol of the accuracy and universality of GMT.

Why Greenwich? First, because this was where England's first Astronomer Royal, John Flamsteed, decided to build his home and observatory in 1675. And secondly, because Flamsteed and his successors did more than anyone to solve the oldest navigational problem in the book: how to measure longitude. Measuring latitude was relatively easy, as it could be ascertained from the angle of the Pole Star to the horizon. But longitude was something else. Scientists knew what they needed: a dependable and portable watch or clock with which to work it out. But for anything other than the shortest journeys no such timepiece existed. In 1754, parliament issued a Longitude Act, offering a reward of £20,000 to the person who could crack the problem. The first proposals ranged from the sublime to the ridiculous. It was a Yorkshire clockmaker called John Harrison who eventually broke the impasse. He constructed his first marine clock in 1730 and continued perfecting it all his life; by the time he came up with the prize-winning model in 1772 he was 79 years old. Captain Cook took Harrison's clock to Australia and called it his 'trusty friend'. The museum takes the history of navigation and time up to the present, including the 1884 Washington conference that selected Greenwich as the Prime Meridian, and the invention of atomic clocks based on the nine billion vibrations per second of a caesium atom. The observatory itself is also worthy of note, particularly Flamsteed's original observatory, the **Octagon Room**, designed by Christopher Wren.

The *Cutty Sark* and the *Gipsy Moth IV*

> *On the quay by the ferry pier; open daily 10–5; adm. Combined tickets for major attractions available.*

Much is made of the *Cutty Sark* as the last of the great tea clippers that plied the route from England to the Far East. Built in 1869, it was certainly one of the fastest sailboats of its time, winning the annual clippers' race in 1871. Its commercial usefulness was rather limited, however, since steam ships soon took over the bulk of maritime trade, and the opening of the Suez Canal took a lot of the time pressure off merchant vessels. The greatest pleasure afforded by the *Cutty Sark* now is its magnificent gilded teak fittings, the rigging on its three masts and its fine collection of figureheads and other maritime memorabilia. The name, by the way, comes from Robert Burns's poem *Tam O'Shanter*, in which a witch called Nellie is described as wearing only a *cutty sark*, a corruption of the French *courte chemise*, or short shirt. You'll notice the female figurehead on the prow is dressed in this manner. Next to the Cutty Sark, the *Gipsy Moth IV* was the ketch in which the British mariner Sir Francis Chichester made his solo round-the-world voyage in 1966–7, completing the trip in nine months and one day.

Also see: **Greenwich Park**, p.111; **Fan Museum**, p.140; **Dome**, p.30.
Onwards to: **Docklands**, p.94.

Battersea Park	110
Chelsea Physic Garden	110
Green Park	111
Greenwich Park	111
Hampstead Heath	112
Highgate Cemetery	112
Holland Park	113
Hyde Park	113
Kensington Gardens	114
Kew Gardens	114
Regent's Park and London Zoo	116
Richmond Park	117
St James's Park	117
Syon Park	118

London: Green Spaces

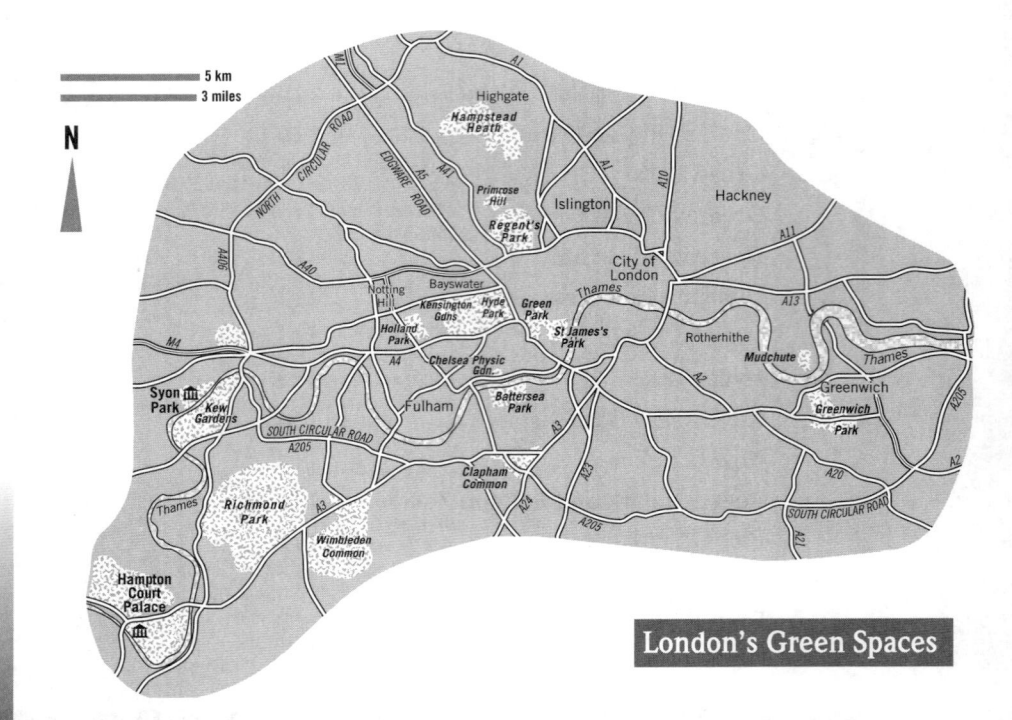

London's Green Spaces

Battersea Park

≋ *Battersea Park (from Victoria), Queenstown Road (from Waterloo)*
⊖ *Vauxhall and then bus 344 or 44;* ⊖ *Sloane Square and then bus 19 or 49*

Battersea Park is an all-action activity centre with a café, children's zoo, tennis courts, a bowling green and a running track. Although opened by Queen Victoria in 1853, the park really came into its own in 1951 when it was one of the centrepieces of the Festival of Britain. Near the boating lake at the southern end is a Henry Moore statue entitled ***Three Standing Figures***. Near the river, about two-thirds of the way over towards Albert Bridge, is the **Battersea Peace Pagoda**, built by a group of Japanese Buddhist monks in 1985 and now one of London's most distinctive riverside landmarks.

Chelsea Physic Garden

✆ *(020) 7352 5646; Cheyne Walk; enter from the back on Swan Walk. Open April–Oct Wed 2–5 and Sun 2–6; adm.*

⊖ *Sloane Square then a walk: Lower Sloane St, and left down to the end of Royal Hospital Road.*

This wonderfully unusual garden of rare trees, plants, herbs and seeds has a history stretching back to 1676 when it was founded by the Apothecaries' Company. Some of England's first cedar trees were cultivated here in the 1680s and the hardiest of them lasted until 1903. In the 1730s the Physic Garden sent out the seeds that allowed James Oglethorpe, the colonist of

Georgia, to sow the southern United States' first cotton fields. Among the wonders still visible today are the world's first rock garden, built in 1772 with old bits of stone from the Tower of London, a Chinese willow pattern tree, and a 30ft-high olive tree that once produced seven pounds of olives in a season (something of a miracle in rainy old England). The statue in the garden is of Sir Hans Sloane, the physician and philanthropist who saved the gardens from bankruptcy in 1722. Sir Hans owned large tracts of Chelsea (hence the number of streets named after him) and built up a huge collection of art and antiquities that were bequeathed to the nation after his death and provided the foundation of the **British Museum** (see p.29).

Also see: **Chelsea and the King's Road**, p.92.

Green Park

⊖ *Green Park, Hyde Park Corner*
Bus 8, 9, 14, 19, 22, 38.

This pleasantly undulating expanse, which is green all year round, has much the same history as St James's Park (*see* p.117). It was originally a burial ground for Queen Matilda's lepers (and, in deference to the dead beneath it, has never been planted with flowers). Henry VIII made it a royal park, and Charles II laid out its walkways. Green Park, like its neighbour, was a haunt of trouble-makers and duellists in the 18th century. On one occasion, Count Alfieri returned to the nearby Haymarket Theatre for the last act of a play after sustaining a duelling wound to his arm from Lord Ligonier, his mistress's husband. Deckchairs can be hired and you can pop next door to tea at the Ritz (*see* p.158).

Also see **Buckingham Palace**, p.32.

Greenwich Park

≋ *Greenwich*
⊖ *North Greenwich (from 2000)*
DLR to Island Gardens and then foot tunnel to Greenwich.

The park, along with Blackheath beyond, was the hunting ground that attracted Duke Humphrey to Greenwich back in the 15th century. It has been tamed considerably since then, particularly under Charles II who hired the great French landscape gardener André Le Nôtre, of Versailles fame, to help lay it out anew in the 1660s. There is no evidence Le Nôtre ever visited the site for himself; indeed to judge from the way the park falls away abruptly at the bottom it looks as though he didn't even realize it was on a hill. It is nevertheless an elegant place, unusually continental in its formality. Sadly, the deer that used to roam freely are confined to The Wilderness on the southeastern edge; they were isolated after a 19th-century stroller was gored and killed during the rutting season. On Chesterfield Walk, just beyond Croomshill Gate is **Ranger's House** (*open daily 9–1 and 2–6, earlier closing in winter*), an elegant mansion dating from 1699 which is no longer the residence of the park ranger but instead holds a collection of musical instruments and 17th-century portraits. On the opposite side of the park, at 121 Maze Hill, is the eccentric **Vanbrugh Castle**, where the eponymous architect lived for six years until his death in 1725. It is not open to the public.

Right in the centre of the park is a **statue of General Wolfe**, who died fighting the French in Quebec in 1759 and is buried at St Alfege's. Note the shrapnel scars, and then look out across the Thames: you quickly appreciate what a perfect bombing route towards the Docklands this was for German aircraft during the Blitz. The **Old Royal Observatory** (see p.108) is next to the statue.

Also see: **Greenwich**, p.106.

Hampstead Heath

⇌ *Hampstead Heath, Gospel Oak*
⊖ *Hampstead, Belsize Park*
Bus 24 from Trafalgar Square, 268, C11

Hampstead Heath is so big and wild you can easily feel you are lost in the deep heart of the English countryside, yet there are amazing views over London. At the top (north) end is the superbly located, unpretentious white neoclassical **Kenwood House** (*see* p.103), famous for its idyllic summer concerts held by the lake at the bottom of the garden; the orchestra sits under a white awning and the audience watches from across the water. The hill down from Kenwood leads to **Highgate Ponds**, a series of open-air pools segregated by sex to encourage nude bathing. The ladies' pool, discreetly hidden behind some thick bushes, is nearest the top just off Millfield Lane; the men's pools are alongside the path nearer Highgate Road. Right down at the bottom of the Heath, should you stray that far, is **Parliament Hill**, site of an ancient barrow where the rebel queen Boudicca (Boadicea) is rumoured to have been buried. The view from the hill, no more than a bump compared to the heights of Kenwood, is rather disappointing, but the wind the site attracts is ideal for kite-flying.

Also see: **Hampstead**, p.102.

Highgate Cemetery

⊖ *Archway, Highgate*
Bus 271, 210

To reach the entrance to the cemetery, start in Highgate High Street and turn right down the steep narrow hill called Swains Lane. At the bottom there are patches of gravel on either side of the road. To the right is the grand arched entrance to the western cemetery (open for guided tours only, usually every two hours during the afternoon, ✆ (020) 8340 1834; adm), and to the left is the more mundane iron grille leading to the eastern cemetery (open daily 10–5, closes at 4pm in the winter; free).

Highgate Cemetery has been a tourist attraction ever since it opened in 1839, both for its magnificent funereal Victorian architecture and for its views. 'In such a place the aspect of death is softened,' wrote the *Lady's Newspaper* in 1850. The **western side** is the older and more splendid of the two halves, a maze of winding paths leading to an avenue of mock-Egyptian columns and obelisks, and a hemicycle of tombs around a cedar of Lebanon. Winding roads and footpaths lead up to the so-called Egyptian Avenue, which you enter through an arch flanked with obelisks and mock-Egyptian columns. The avenue leads beneath a bridge to the Circle of Lebanon, a complex of tombs constructed on each side of a circular path with a magnificent cedar tree in the middle. The spire of St Michael's parish church looms above at the top of Swain's Lane. The guide will point out the eminent dead occupying these hallowed tombs; they include the chemist Michael Faraday and the poet Christina Rossetti.

The **eastern cemetery**, which opened in 1857 to cope with the overload of coffins from across the road, is altogether wilder and spookier (it features in Bram Stoker's *Dracula*) where the cracked tombstones are covered in creepers and ivy. Here you can roam around at will. Most people head straight for the large black bust of Karl Marx marking the place where the much-maligned philosopher was buried in 1883. The eastern cemetery contains a sprinkling of other left-wing revolutionaries, mainly from the Third World, plus the remains of novelist Mary Ann Evans (a.k.a. George Eliot) and the radical conservative thinker Herbert Spencer who died in 1903.

Holland Park

● *Holland Park, High Street Kensington*
Bus 94 (north side) from Oxford Street and Piccadilly, 9, 10, 49, 27 (south side)
Open daily 7.30am until half an hour before sunset. The best way to enter is through the wooded northern end. Take Holland Walk, a path opposite Holland Park Underground station, and look out for the first turning into the park, which is on the right after about 300 yards.

Holland Park turns reality on its head: it seems much bigger, much wilder, much more remote than it really is. Covering only about 40 acres (a fraction of the size of Kensington Gardens, for example), it feels like something out of a magical children's story, a maze of winding paths, wooded hideaways, rolling fields and formal gardens, wild flowers and birds. The park is what remains of the estate of **Holland House**, a grand Jacobean mansion devastated during the Second World War, which survives only in truncated form, about two-thirds of the way down towards Kensington High Street. You can see some of the ground-floor stonework of the original building, but little else. The east wing has been entirely rebuilt as a **youth hostel** (a wonderful place to stay if you are a student, *see* p.168), while part of the ruined main house has been converted into an open-air theatre with an summer season of opera (*see* p.173).

Around the house to the north is a series of formal gardens, all different in style, including the peaceful **Kyoto Garden** with its still lake, lawns lined with gentle blooms, and a square Elizabethan-style herb garden. On the south side is a calm terrace **café** overlooking a cricket pitch and tennis courts. Wild woodland areas surround the park on its outer edges. Wherever you walk, you will be startled by wild rabbits and peacocks and begged at by almost tame squirrels used to tourists and their sandwiches. Take nuts if you don't want to feel guilty.

Also see: **Leighton House**, p.134.

Hyde Park

● *Hyde Park Corner, Marble Arch, Lancaster Gate, Knightsbridge*
Bus 12, 94 (north side), 9, 10, 52 (south side), 10, 2, 16, 36, 73, 74, 82 (east side).

Hyde Park is a remarkably large expanse of greenery for the centre of a big city. This end is rather hilly and open, giving views of the posh hotels along Park Lane up to Marble Arch. There are more trees towards Kensington Gardens, as the stretch beyond the Serpentine lake is known. **Rotten Row** is the sandy horse path running along the southern edge. Its name is a corruption of the French *route du roi* (royal road).

Hyde Park started out as part of the Westminster Abbey estate, a breeding ground for deer, boar and wild bulls. When Henry VIII dissolved the monasteries, he decided to keep it as a private hunting ground; it was not opened to the public until the beginning of the 17th century. William III hung lamps along Rotten Row to deter highwaymen while he made his way from Kensington Palace to St James's, instituting the idea of street-lighting in London. The park was a favourite hang-out for crooks of all kinds, and even George II was once robbed of his purse, watch and buckles while out walking. In the course of the 18th century it also became London's most popular duelling ground.

In 1730 Queen Caroline created the **Serpentine** by having the underground Westbourne river dammed. The L-shaped lake is still the park's most prominent feature, famous for its New Year's Day swims which are open to anyone foolhardy enough to jump into the freezing winter water (some years the swimmers have to break the ice before they start). The Serpentine has provided the focus for many other events, from funfairs to political demonstrations. The northeastern end of Hyde Park remains the only place in Britain where demonstrators can assemble without police permission, a concession made in 1872 in a truce between the Metropolitan Police and a succession of angry demonstrators. The spot is known as **Speaker's Corner**, and every Sunday afternoon you can hear impassioned crackpots droning on for hours about the moral turpitude of the world. Despite the fame of Speaker's Corner, it is hardly an impressive symbol of free speech. Microphones are banned, and most of the words are drowned out by the traffic on Park Lane. Nobody takes the place seriously, particularly in this media-saturated era. You can talk all you like, Speakers' Corner says; just make sure nobody can hear you.

Kensington Gardens

⊖ *Queensway, Bayswater, Lancaster Gate, High Street Kensington*
Bus 12, 94 (north side) 9, 10, 52 (south side)

The Serpentine divides Hyde Park from the westerly Kensington Gardens, originally the grounds of Kensington Palace (*see* p.37) with its **Round Pond** where you can play with model boats. George Frampton's famous statue of **Peter Pan** is by the lakeside towards the Bayswater Road. On the south side of the park, just behind the Albert Memorial (*see* p.28), is an attractive area of bushes and flowering plants known as the **Flower Walk**, and near the Serpentine is the **Serpentine Gallery**, famous for its shows of modern art. On summer weekends the park throngs with locals on rollerblades and playing ballgames.

Kew Gardens

⊖ *Kew Gardens*
⇌ *Kew Bridge (from Waterloo)*
Bus 391 from West Kensington, 190 from West Brompton

✆ *(020) 8940 1171; www.kew.org. Gardens open 9.30–dusk; adm. The glasshouses and other buildings open at 9.30am as well but close at 5.30. Guided tours in the summer at 11am. There are several entrances to Kew Gardens, the most useful being the Victoria Gate on Kew Road, where guidebooks and free leaflets are available at the visitor centre and shop. Take sturdy shoes as there are around 300 acres of gardens to explore. Pick up a free map at Queen Victoria Gate, which will locate all the major sites for you. It is also colour-coded for easier use.*

For the visitor, Kew is a place of many wonders: 38,000 different plant species, some of them entirely extinct in the wild; vast glasshouses, historic houses and buildings and, above all, acres and acres of beautifully tended parkland, some of it wonderfully wild and remote, with views up and down the Thames. All year round, Kew provides a glorious array of colours: flowering cherries and crocuses in spring; roses and tulip trees in summer; belladonna lilies, heather and darkening leaves in autumn; strawberry trees and witch hazels in winter.

The Royal Botanical Gardens at Kew have always been more than a collection of trees, flowers and plants; they are more like a giant vegetable laboratory, sucking up new information about the botanical world and, through the power of their research, influencing the course of human history in all sorts of unexpected ways. In the 19th century, Kew's laboratories first isolated quinine and, realizing it was an efficient natural antidote to malaria, recommended putting it in the tonic water with which the colonial administrators of India and Malaya diluted their gin. Kew was also involved in the development of commercial rubber and helped produce artificial fibres like rayon and acetate. It is now actively researching plant substances for the treatment of AIDS. In these days of receding rainforests and dwindling numbers of species of all kinds, Kew also does vital work in cataloguing and preserving plant types and developing new, genetically engineered hybrids that stand a better chance of survival in the wild.

In the 18th century, Kew was part of the royal estates that stretched down as far as Richmond. Princess Augusta, the mother of George III, first had the idea of laying a botanical garden in the grounds of **Kew Palace** where she lived. This elegantly gabled two-storey Jacobean mansion (*open April–Sept 11–5.30 daily only; separate adm*) so endeared itself to George II and his wife Queen Caroline a generation before Augusta that they leased it for 99 years, for 'the rent of £100 and a fat doe'. The botanical garden was at first of only incidental importance to Kew; George III spent his energies commissioning a series of follies and outhouses from the architect William Chambers. These included three pseudo-classical temples, a ruined Roman arch, the handsome Wren-like Orangery, and—most striking of all—the **Pagoda**. Chambers took his inspiration for this ten-storey octagonal tower from a visit to China in his youth. When finished in 1762, it was the most accurate rendering of Chinese architecture in Europe—although to be truly accurate it should have had an odd number of storeys.

The botanical garden began to grow thanks to the enthusiasm of its keeper, Sir Joseph Banks, who organized Kew's first foreign plant-hunting expeditions and set about cultivating rare species. Banks's was nevertheless a small-scale enterprise, and Kew did not really take off until 1840 when it was handed over from the royal family to the state, opened to the public and expanded to more than 200 acres. The first director of the new public gardens, Sir William Hooker, put Kew on a firm scientific and research footing. Hooker's most lasting architectural influence was to commission two great glasshouses from Decimus Burton. The **Palm House** (1844–8) is a wondrous structure of curvilinear iron and glass, with a two-storey dome as its centrepiece. The **Temperate House**, built in the early 1860s and modified right up to 1898, is far bigger but more conventional in structure, using straight panes and iron rods to achieve its great height and width.

William Hooker's son Joseph took over as director in 1865 and established the **Jodrell Laboratory** to enhance Kew's research credentials. He also encouraged a young artist called Marianne North to set up a special gallery to display her collection of 832 botanical paintings based on her travels around the globe between 1871 and 1885 (left of Victoria Gate).

In this century, a number of new glasshouses have been added to the park, including the **Princess of Wales Conservatory**, containing Kew's collection of tropical herbaceous plants not least of which the incredible Titan Arum, which at two metres high is one of the largest flowers in the world. The newly refurbished **Museum No.1** contains Kew's fascinating 'Plants + People' exhibition of wood and plant materials which have been made into useful materials for man—a 200-year-old shirt made out of pineapple fibres, from the Caribbean, and an incredible collection of Japanese lacquer boxes.

Regent's Park and London Zoo

> ✆ *Baker St (for the boating lake and theatre), Regent's Park (for the theatre), Great Portland St (for the theatre), Mornington Crescent, Camden Town (for the zoo). Bus C2 from Oxford Circus (for east side), 13, 82, 113 and 274 (for west side).*

Regent's Park is the most ornate of London's open spaces, a delightful mixture of icing-sugar terraces, wildlife, lakes and broad expanses of greenery. It is the most rigorously planned of London's parks, the brainchild of George IV's favourite architect, John Nash, who conceived it as a landscaped estate on which to build several dozen pleasure palaces for the aristocracy. It was meant to be the culmination of a vast city rebuilding project, of which the centrepiece was Regent Street. Nash's dreams of a new London, endowing the city with a full sense of aristocratic majesty, were tempered by a succession of objections and financial problems; Regent's Park, however, perhaps comes closest to embodying the spirit of his plans. His stuccoed terraces around the perimeter of the park are at once imposing and playful; the handful of grand mansions inside the park exude the same air of nonchalant, summery elegance as the hunting villas and parks on the outskirts of central Rome; the park itself is beautifully manicured, giving it a curious air of exclusivity even though it is open to all; most delightfully, for the visitor, it is remarkably empty.

Within the Inner Circle of the park is **Queen Mary's Rose Garden**, a magnificent array of flowers and plants of all kinds. At the north end is the **Open Air Theatre** *(open May–Sept, ✆ (020) 7486 2431)*, a magical sylvan setting for summer productions of *A Midsummer Night's Dream* and *As You Like It*. On the west side of the Inner Circle (find the path next to the open air theatre) is the **Boating Lake**, a wonderfully romantic stretch of water where you can rent boats of all kinds for a balmy summer afternoon's idle dreaming.

London Zoo

> *London Zoo ✆ (020) 7722 3333; open April–Oct 10–5.30, Nov–Mar 10–4; adm exp.*

The Zoological Gardens in Regent's Park were where the term 'zoo' originated. The abbreviation, which first surfaced in the late 1860s, was immortalized in a music-hall song of the time beginning: 'Walking in the zoo is the OK thing to do'. In these post-colonial, animally-correct times, zoos are not quite as OK as they used to be. But London Zoo has responded to debate about its role with some energy. The **Bear Mountain**, once horribly overcrowded and a place of abject misery, has been redeveloped, and houses just two bears. The delightful new **Children's Zoo** is built entirely out of sustainable materials, with a Camel House whose roof is planted with wild flowers and grass seed, a wonderful touch paddock, barn, and pet care centre. A new Lottery-funded **Conservation Centre**, with exhibitions explaining eco systems and animal diversity, opened in mid-1998.

One of the attractions of visiting the zoo now is the fine array of well-designed animal houses—the penguin pool by Lubetkin and Tecton (1936), Lord Snowdon's spectacular polygonal aviary (1964), Hugh Casson's elephant and rhino pavilion (1965) or the recently built Macaw Aviary. On your way round you will be invited to 'adopt' any animal that takes your particular fancy. Pay £20 for an exotic breed of cockroach, £6,000 for an elephant, or £30 for a part share in *any* animal, and you are assured the beast will be fed and nurtured for a year. Your name will also go on a plaque beside the animal's enclosure—you'll see plenty of these already in place.

Richmond Park

⊖ *Richmond*
Bus 65 and 391, 337

At 2470 acres, Richmond is the largest urban park in Britain and one of the least spoiled in London. A few medieval oaks survive, as do many of the varieties of wildlife that medieval royal parties would have hunted. The deer are what make Richmond Park famous—around 350 fallow deer and 250 red deer, which do so well in the heart of London that there is an annual cull—but there are also hares, rabbits and weasels. Richmond Park also has two ponds for anglers, five cricket pitches, two golf courses, no fewer than 24 football grounds and numerous cycle paths.

At the top of Richmond Hill near the park entrance is the **Star and Garter Home**, once a humble tavern which rose to be one of the most fashionable addresses in outer London. Its Assembly Room was the setting for many a 19th-century wedding reception, and its modest bedrooms housed everyone from common wayfarers to continental royalty. In the 1860s the tavern was revamped as an imitation French Renaissance chateau, a project as unpopular as it was extravagant, and one that led to the establishment's demise at the turn of the 20th century. Used as a hostel for disabled soldiers after the First World War, it is now an old people's home. Few can enjoy its enviable views over Richmond and the river; it, however, is all too visible for a mile or more in each direction along the Thames towpath.

Also see: **Richmond**, p.104.

St James's Park

⊖ *St James's Park*
bus (to Whitehall): 3, 11, 12, 24, 53, 77A, 88, 109

The dreamy expanse of St James's Park explains much about the spirit of the neighbourhood. Certainly it seems perfectly spruce nowadays, even rather romantic in a restrained sort of way, with its tree-lined pond and proliferation of city wildlife; but its elegance is a cunning artifice created to overcome centuries of turbulence and squalor.

Back in the early 12th century, Queen Matilda founded a women's leper colony on the site of what is now St James's Palace. By the mid-15th century leprosy had subsided and the hospital was turned into a special kind of nunnery; special because its young occupants were better known for administering to the flesh rather than to the spirit of the eminent men who called on them.

These so-called *bordels du roi* were closed by Henry VIII, who built St James's Palace in their place and drained the marsh to create a nursery for his deer. The first formal gardens were laid out under James I, who installed, among other things, an aviary (hence the name of the street on the south side, Birdcage Walk) and a menagerie of wild beasts including two crocodiles. The setting was romantic enough for Charles II to use it as a rendezvous with his mistress, Nell Gwynne; unfortunately it also attracted upper-class hooligans in search of both trouble and rumpy-pumpy with the local whores.

In 1672 Lord Rochester described the park as a place of 'buggeries, rapes and incest', a state of affairs not improved even after a decree issued by Queen Anne banning dogs, hogs, menials, beggars and 'rude boys' from the premises. James Boswell lost his virginity to a whore in St James's Park on 20 March 1763, an experience which brought him 'but a dull satisfaction'. It was only under George IV that the park developed its present dignity. George landscaped the lake as we see it today and added gas lighting to deter the ladies of the night. The sex-crazed aristocrat gave way to an altogether gentler breed, the birdwatcher, as St James's filled with more than 30 ornithological species. Look out for the pelicans, ducks, geese and gulls which have made the lake their home.

Also see: **St James's and Royal London**, p.76.

Syon Park

London Road, Isleworth, with another entrance off Park Road near the riverfront.

Open April–Sept Wed–Sun 11–4.15, Oct–Dec Sun 11–4.15, gardens open 10am–dusk daily; adm.

Across the river from Kew Gardens, officially in Isleworth, is Syon Park, not so much a stately home as a kind of theme park *à l'anglaise*. Here in the large if rather empty park stretching down to the river are a butterfly house, a vintage car museum and a gardening centre housed beneath an impressive Victorian domed conservatory made of gunmetal and Portland stone.

The house itself, built in crenellated stone around a quadrangle, was once part of a monastery, but was seized by Henry VIII for his own private use after his break with the Roman church. He locked up his fifth wife, Catherine Howard, in Syon House before her execution on adultery charges; a few years later the gods got their revenge when a band of dogs discovered the half-open coffin containing Henry's remains and chewed on them all night long. Since 1594 Syon Park has belonged to the Percy family, holders of the Duchy of Northumberland. At first they let it slowly decline, but then in 1762 Robert Adam was commissioned to rework the interior, and the landscape architect Capability Brown was set to work on the grounds.

The house is particularly successful, using only the bare bones of the original structure to create a sumptuous classical atmosphere. The highlights are the Great Hall, which makes up for the unevenness of the floor with a series of small steps embellished with Doric columns, and the ante-room, which has a lavishly gilded plasterwork ceiling and a multi-coloured marble floor. Osbert Sitwell once said this room was 'as superb as any Roman interior in the palaces of the Caesars'.

Oxford Street	120
Regent Street	121
Bond Street	122
Tottenham Court Road	123
Charing Cross Road	123
Jermyn Street and Savile Row	124
High Street Kensington	125
King's Road	125
Knightsbridge and Brompton Cross	126
Covent Garden	128
Markets	129

London: Shopping

London...a kind of emporium for the whole earth.

Joseph Addison

London has been a cosmopolitan place to shop since the Romans traded their pottery and olive oil for cloth, furs and gold back in the 1st century AD. Until comparatively recently the best shopping was for the rich, channelled through prestigious department stores such as Harrods, or smaller establishments in St James's and South Kensington offering exceptional service and attention to detail. The Carnaby Street spirit of the 1960s changed that, and now you can find cheap clothes and jewellery, unusual music and exotic food all over town in flea markets and gaily coloured shops. Carnaby Street itself, regrettably, has long since sold its soul to the cause of tourist kitsch, but you will find its successors in Covent Garden, down the King's Road, around Notting Hill and at Camden Lock market.

A note on VAT: if you leave Britain for a non-EU country within six months of arriving, you are entitled to a refund on the Value Added Tax, or VAT, that you have paid on any goods you have bought from shops displaying a 'tax free for tourists' sign. You must pick up a form in the shop where you make your purchase, and then hand it in at the airport when you leave the country. Since the rate of VAT is 17.5 per cent, this is well worth the hassle, especially with larger items.

Opening hours: Traditionally, shops stay open from around 9 to 5.30 or 6—significantly earlier than the rest of Europe. Late opening for shops is becoming more and more common, however, particularly on Wednesdays and Thursdays, and Sunday trading is much more flexible than in the past: areas like Queensway and the Edgware Road, Hampstead, Greenwich, Tottenham Court Road and most of the Oxford Street department stores are worth visiting.

Oxford Street

Oxford Street is forever packed with shoppers and tourists, for whom its wide pavements and large department stores symbolize the very essence of the big city. This rather puzzling mystique is not really borne out by the reality, which is impersonal, uniform and unremittingly grey. In 1825 John Wilson Croker called Oxford Street 'thou lengthy street of ceaseless din', and the description still applies; even if cars have been banned during the daytime, there is still plenty of noise from the zillions of buses and taxis.

The most prestigious address, a few blocks off to the right beyond Duke Street, is **Selfridge's**, which for sheer size and range of goods is the closest rival in London to Harrods. The other department stores such as Debenhams, D.H. Evans and **John Lewis**, and outsize outlets of high street regulars like **Marks & Spencer**, River Island and The Gap, are not as much fun (or as cheap) as the specialist shops dotted around more intimate parts of London, but they do offer a one-stop shopping day. Most are open Sunday, except John Lewis.

Off and behind Oxford Street are a few side streets with interesting small stores: at the Selfridge's/Bond Street end try walking down **South Molton Street**, **Davies Street**, **St Christopher's Place**, **James Street**, **Duke Street** and **Wigmore Street**, and past Oxford Circus there's **Great Portland Street** and **Argyll Street**, and pedestrianised **Carnaby Street**, which bears no traces of its 60s heyday but still has some odd little one-offs and its own array of even tinier side-alleys.

Selfridge's, 400 Oxford St. Classic department store. There are also perfume and make-up demonstrations and a travel agent's in the basement.

Marks & Spencer, 458 Oxford St and branches all over London. Suppliers of cheap, comfortable clothes and underwear to the nation—and the worldd. Don't overlook the food section, either, with excellent pre-prepared dishes and stunningly good ice-cream that beats Haägen Dazs for both quality and price.

John Lewis, Oxford Street. With its slogan 'Never knowingly undersold', this cheerful and efficient department store promises to refund the difference if you find anything cheaper elsewhere. Well-stocked departments of household goods and accessories, and for decades one of London's largest retailers of dressmaking and furnishing fabrics and haberdashery. *Not open Sundays.*

Borders, 197 Oxford St. Huge branch of the US book and music shop, with readings, performances and a coffee shop. *Open till 11pm and on Sundays.*

H.R. Higgins, 79 Duke St. Purveyor of fine coffee to Her Majesty the Queen. Evokes the atmosphere of the old Jacobean coffee houses.

South Molton Drug Store, 64 South Molton St. Cheap end-of-line cosmetics.

Electrum Gallery, 21 South Molton St. Classic jewellery from around the world—at a price.

Browns, 23–7 South Molton St. Centre of a burgeoning empire of fashion shops along this bijou pedestrian street off Oxford Street. Lots of famous labels, not all of them unaffordable.

Vivienne Westwood, 6 Davies St. The punk queen of British fashion offers real clothes as well as eccentric pieces of tailoring art.

Gray's Antique Markets, 58 Davies St. An enclosed antiques market with over 200 dealers in a large Victorian building. Mainly silverware, glassware, jewellery, toys, ancient artefacts and china. Some odder stalls, such as Wheels of Steel model train sets stall or Pete McAskie's Dinky toys. The Thimble Society of London is a stall dedicated to antique and modern thimbles.

James Smith and Sons, 53 New Oxford St. Fend off the British weather with a trip to this Victorian shop dedicated to umbrellas. Also stocks walking sticks, often with carved handles.

Sonico, 47 Oxford St. Jeans galore at competitive prices.

NikeTown, Oxford Circus. Supermodel sports shop full of loud music, encouraging slogans ('Life is a Verb') and weird sculptures.

TopShop, Oxford Circus. Haven of cheap trendy gear for style-obsessed but cash-poor teenage girls.

A.K. Mowbrays, 28 Margaret St (basement of Waterstone's). Excellent religious bookshop.

Forbidden Planet, 71 New Oxford St. The best sci-fi bookshop around.

Muji, 26 Carnaby St and 187 Oxford St. Minimalist Japanese paper, fabric, fashion and edible goods.

Lush, 40 Carnaby St. You can smell this shop from yards away! Handmade soaps and toiletries using only natural ingredients.

Storm, 21 Carnaby St and 6 Gees Court. Unusual modern watches as well as fashion, sunglasses, lava lamps and so on.

Cerex, 11 Carnaby Street St. Inexpensive young-style shoes.

Octopus, 28 Carnaby Street St. All kinds of gifts and gimmicks: lamps made of brightly coloured rubber, bags with holograms on, glasses mounted on toy cars. Great fun.

Regent Street

Regent Street was once the finest street in London, although you might not think so to look at it now. In fact, all it boasts are a few fine shops (particularly men's clothes stores), the new *Cheers* theme-u-rant (at 72 Regent Street, overpriced and depressingly anonymous) and some rather stuffy, impersonal buildings livened up just once a year by the overhead display of electric Christmas decorations.

One address that has not changed too much is the **Café Royal** at No.68. If you're feeling tired, this is a good stopping off point for a cocktail or afternoon tea from 3pm–5pm.

Liberty, Regent St. A labyrinth of a store with warm wooden interiors. Famous for print scarves, also good for fashion, china, rugs and glass.

Dickins and Jones, Regent St. Department store for counties matrons. Very strong on cosmetics.

Aquascutum, 100 Regent St. Raincoats, cashmere scarves and endless sober suits. Clothes to last, not look hip in.

Boosey and Hawkes, 295 Regent St. Classical music.

Crabtree and Evelyn, 239 Regent St. Herbs and fruit scents, all beautifully packaged. Ideal for gift-hunting.

L'Occitane, 237 Regent St. Provençal herbs and fruit scents, also all beautifully packaged. Also ideal for gift-hunting.

Teddy Bear Shop, 153 Regent St, W1. Sells handmade (English) teddy bears. Traditional ones as well as more modern varieties.

Hamley's, 188 Regent St. London's biggest toy emporium.

Zara, Regent St. Stylish Spanish fashion store chain.

Grant & Cutler, 55-7 Great Marlborough St, off Regent Street. Uneven, but nevertheless the best bookshop in London for obscure and not so obscure foreign-language books.

The European Bookshop, 5 Warwick St, off Regent St. Makes up for Grant and Cutler's deficiencies, especially in French literature in which it excels.

Bond Street

Two kinds of shopkeeper dominate Bond Street: jewellers and art dealers, whose gaudy if not always particularly attractive shop fronts make for a diverting stroll. **Old Bond Street**, the lower part of the thoroughfare, concentrates mainly on jewellery and includes all the well-known international names including **Tiffany's** at No.25 and **Chatila** at No.22.

At the top of Albermarle St is the ultimate shop for country gents, **Asprey's**, whose windows are packed with rifles, shooting-sticks and waders. If you walk through the shop to the Bond Street side you can also enjoy its extraordinary collection of military jewellery, including tanks and fighter jets made of gold and silver.

New Bond Street is famous for the showrooms of art dealers like Bernard Jacobson and Le Fevre (or, round the corner on Cork Street, Waddington and Victoria Miro). **Sotheby's**, the famous auctioneers, are at Nos. 34-35 New Bond Street.

Fenwick's, New Bond St. One of the more old-fashioned, very English-traditional department stores, strong on accessories and women's clothes.

Church's, 163 New Bond St. Solid, sober shoes to last half a lifetime.

Miu Miu, 123 New Bond St. The funkier offspring of Prada.

Calvin Klein, 55 New Bond St. (opposite Miu Miu). Famous for jeans, underwear and scents.

Donna Karan, 20 New Bond St. and **DKNY**, 27 Old Bond St. Trendy streetwear for women. DKNY includes a café.

Mulberry, 41 New Bond St. Traditional high-quality bags and leather goods, stamped with the recognisable mulberry tree symbol.

Yves Saint Laurent, 137 New Bond St.

Hermès, 155 New Bond St. Source of the famous scarves and accessories.

Louis Vuitton, 17 New Bond St. The famous monogrammed bags are back in trend.

Smithson, Stylish stationery for the swish set; uninspired designs but good quality paper, and fountain pens that will last a lifetime.

Bulgari, 172 New Bond St. Top Italian jewellery.

Chanel, 173 New Bond St for jewellery and 26 Old Bond Street for everything else.

The Spy Shop, 26 Conduit St. Everything you need for surveillance!

Tottenham Court Road

As late as the 1870s, cows grazed along this road which is now all too crowded with traffic. Its main attractions are its furniture stores—**Heals** (very classy and upmarket), **Habitat** (cheaper but duller) and shop after anonymous shop specializing in sofa-beds and futons—and its **discount computer and hi-fi** shops. Visit plenty of shops, ask to see write-ups in the trade magazines to back up the recommendations and haggle the price down as far as you can. North Americans will find prices rather high, but Europeans will be astounded at how cheap everything is. Most shops open Sundays. Only a couple of specific addresses to recommend:

Habitat, 196 Tottenham Court Rd. Everything for the house, from glasses and corkscrews to fitted cabinets. Cheap and practical.

Heal's, 196 Tottenham Court Rd. Upmarket sister to Habitat, with innovative designs.

Hi-fi Care, 245 Tottenham Court Rd. Accessories shop. Very useful for extension cords, speaker cable and all those other things you can't usually find.

Charing Cross Road

Charing Cross Road is the traditional centre of the London **book** trade, although the pressure of high rents is pushing many original establishments out into other areas. The once-gentlemanly publishing and book trade has become something of a cut-throat environment. Stores no longer stock the eclectic range of titles that they once did, preferring to focus on titles they know will sell in large numbers. On the plus side, many assistants still give expert advice on titles and subjects. Browsing is not only tolerated, it is welcomed.

The most famous bookshop on the street is **Foyle's**, at No.119. Don't be deluded by its reputation, however, which dates from the inter-war years: inside it is a chaotic, antiquated mess. Foyle's fame largely rests on the boast that you can find any book at all on its well-thumbed shelves. Sure you can, as long as you have about 36 hours to spare and the patience of a saint.

The modern chains just down the road, **Books Etc** and **Waterstone's**, are far more efficient general stores. Charing Cross Road's charm, however, lies in higgledy-piggledy secondhand bookshops such as **Quinto** (think *84 Charing Cross Road*) or its specialist shops. Collet's, the celebrated left-wing bookshop at No.66 where radicals lectured on revolution in the 1930s, sadly went bankrupt in 1993. However, the expensive art bookshop **Zwemmer's**, at Nos.76–80, is still going and so are places like the **Silver Moon Women's Bookshop** at No.64–8 and small specialist bookshops come and go.

Waterstones, 121–5 Charing Cross Rd and many branches. Probably the best chain overall, with an outstanding selection at every branch.

Books Etc, 120 Charing Cross Rd and many branches. The most commercial of the quality chains, but strong on crime fiction and film screenplays. Charing Cross Rd has a permanent bargain basement.

Travellers' Bookshop, 25 Cecil Court, off Charing Cross Rd. Atmospheric shop in a Georgian building, with a broad range of travel titles.

Silver Moon, 64–8 Charing Cross Rd. Specialist women's bookshop.

Zwemmer, 80 Charing Cross Rd. London's leading art bookshop.

Murder One, 71–3 Charing Cross Rd. New and secondhand genre fiction, mainly science fiction and crime.

Henry Pordes, 58–60 Charing Cross Rd. One of many secondhand and antiquarian booksellers on the Charing Cross Rd and its offshoot, Cecil Court.

Jermyn Street and Savile Row

Jermyn Street which boasts some of the fanciest shopping in town. Royal and aristocratic patronage has showered down over the years on the old-fashioned emporia lining it. The names of the establishments hark back to another era: Turnbull and Asser the shirtmakers, George Trumper, barber and perfumer, or Bates the hatter (the full spectrum, from flat caps to bowlers). The shop assistants more closely resemble manservants from the great aristocratic houses of the past than paid employees of ongoing business concerns. Deference and attention to detail are the watchwords, sometimes pushed to rather absurd extremes. At Trumpers clients are still asked, at the end of a haircut, if Sir would like 'anything for the weekend' (a wonderfully euphemistic way of avoiding any mention of the dread word 'condom'). Anyone buying a shirt is in for a treat of careful measuring, discreet compliments and nonchalant chitchat about the fluctuating quality of modern cloth (try Harvie and Hudson at No.97, with its attractive mid-Victorian fronting).

Jermyn Street also has several galleries selling old prints, silverware and antiques. Another fine establishment is **Paxton and Whitfield** the cheese-seller at No.93, where the freshest cuts of the day are advertised on a blackboard behind the counter and samples of unusual cheese types are offered for tasting with water biscuits.

Along Jermyn St you pass two arcades lined with more purveyors of quality goods: first Princes Arcade, with its brown and white décor and then, after Duke St, the lower-ceilinged, green and white Piccadilly Arcade. Halfway between them is the back entrance to **Fortnum & Mason**, the ultimate old-fashioned English food shop (*open till 8pm with a good value afternoon tea for £16.50 from 3–5.15pm*).

North of Piccadilly is the quintessential address for men's bespoke tailoring, **Savile Row**. Classic menswear like **Hardy Amies** can still be found here, although the styles on offer are beginning to look impossibly old-fashioned; suffice to say that one of the biggest contemporary fans is the puddingy French politician Edouard Balladur. The street has hit hard times recently, although you'll still find some atmospherically traditional establishments, and you can see tailors working away in the basements as you pass.

Also north of Piccadilly is **Burlington Arcade**, which contains a host of little shops seling Irish linens, old pens, leather, pashmina shawls, antique and modern costume jewellery, perfumes and accessories.

Gieves and Hawkes, 1 Savile Row. One of the last gentlemen's outfitters in Savile Row. Unwavering attention to detail, atmospherically traditional.

Turnbull and Asser, 69–72 Jermyn St. One of many old-fashioned clothing boutiques on Jermyn Street, with lots of shirts and silk ties.

Paxton and Whitfield, 93 Jermyn St. Impeccable, old-fashioned cheese shop with specials of the day and nibbles at the counter.

Floris, 89 Jermyn St. Old-fashioned, long established perfume shop.

Taylor of Old Bond Street, 74 Jermyn St. Old-fashioned barber paraphernalia: shaving brushes and so on.

Davidoff, 65 Jermyn St. Fine cigars.

Bates, 21a Jermyn St. Men's hatter, with straw Panamas and other traditional styles.

Immaculate House, Burlington Arcade. All manner of strange and wonderful objects for the home.

Au Bon Pain, Burlington Arcade. Bakery café.

High Street Kensington

This is a really fun place to shop, and not that expensive either; it's really a mini Oxford Street, more compact and less busy. It's got its very own department store, **Barker's**, recently completely redesigned and especially good for cosmetics and furniture and Christmas goods.

There are big branches of **Marks & Spencer**, **BHS** and **Boots**. At the western end of the High Street are all the women's fashion chains (**H&M**, **Kookai**, **Jigsaw**, **Warehouse**, **Hobbs**, **Monsoon**, **French Connection**) and a selection of shoe shops, but also a large branch of the booksellers **Waterstone's**. Turn right from the Underground station to find trendier clothes shops, notably the discount designer emporium Hype DF and, almost directly opposite, the bazaar-like **Kensington Market**. For antiques, look around the lower end of **Kensington Church Street** and the cobbled passage, **Church Walk**, that snakes behind the Victorian-era St Mary Abbots church. Late night shopping day is Thursday.

Muji, 157 Kensington High Street and branches. Minimalist Japanese store selling kitchen equipment and stationery.

Crabtree and Evelyn, 6 Kensington Church St and branches. Herbs and fruit scents, all beautifully packaged. Ideal for gift-hunting.

Amazon, many branches at the bottom of Kensington Church St. Well-loved by locals for its discounted and end-of-line men's and women's clothes.

Cologne & Cotton, 39 Kensington Church St. Luxury linen for the stylish bedroom, mostly in tasteful white, cream and blues.

What Katy Did, 49 Kensington Church St. Cute kiddie clothes.

Hype DF, 26–40 Kensington High St. Indoor market-style showcase for young designer talent, a place to snatch the trendy stuff before it becomes really trendy (and expensive).

Howard Jones, 43 Kensington Church St. Silver and enamel gifts.

Inventory, 26 Kensington High St. Huge selection of cheap and cheerful household goods over three floors: from bathroom goods to candles.

Urban Outfitters, 36 Kensington High St. Kitsch, young and fun, but you have to be fit to climb the stairs to the cool café.

Claire's Accessories, 171 Kensington High St. Pink ribbons, plastic earrings and hairslides: a little girl's paradise.

Past Times, 179 Kensington High St. Gift shop trading on nostalgia for the British past in all its incarnations. Not as tacky as it sounds.

Snow and Rock, 188 Kensington High St. Everything necessary for skiing and mountaineering.

Ehrmann's, Lancer Square, off Kensington Church St. A vast range of tapestry kits and equipment: make your own medieval cushion.

King's Road

Like Carnaby Street in Soho, the King's Road let its hair down and filled with cafés and fashion shops selling mini-skirts and cheap jewellery. Old-fashioned shops, including the delightfully named toilet-maker Thomas Crapper, were superseded by the likes of Terence Conran, who opened his first household store Habitat on the King's Road as a direct challenge to the fusty, old-fashioned goods then on sale at **Peter Jones** on Sloane Square.

Nowadays, most of the boutiques have either gone upmarket or been replaced by generic high-street chainstores. Some of the1960s spirit lives on, however, in the delightfully sprawling antiques markets on the south side of the road: **Antiquarius** at No.137, the **Chenil Galleries** at No.181–3 and the **Chelsea Antiques Market** at No.253. You might also want to take a look at the **Chelsea Farmer's Market**, with its cafés and craft shops just off the King's Road on Sydney Street. Behind the King's Road to the north, Cale Street and Elystan Place have nice little shops and a certain charm. For a map of the area, *see* p.92.

Chelsea Antiques Market, 245–253 King's Rd. All sorts of antiques.

Designer Sale Studio, 241 King's Rd. Last season's collections at up to 70% off.

Monsoon, 33d King's Rd and branches. Strong-coloured cotton clothes with an oriental influence. Mostly for women. Unusual homewares department in this branch.

Rococo, 321 King's Rd. Zany chocolate shop; an Aladdin's cave of edible delights.

Habitat. Everything for the house, from glasses and corkscrews to fitted cabinets. Cheap and practical. Good café for people-watching.

Heal's, 196 Tottenham Court Rd and 234 King's Rd. Upmarket sister to Habitat, with innovative designs for furniture, beds, lighting, etc.

Daisy and Tom, 181–83 King's Rd. Children's emporium, complete with hairdressing salon, carousel, toys, clothes and shoes.

Designer's Guild, 269 King's Rd. Bright and colourful textiles, linens, pottery and furniture. At the cutting edge of the lime-green revolution.

Steinberg & Tolkein, 193 King's Rd. Vintage clothing and accessories beloved by the 'in-crowd'.

Brora, 344 King's Rd. Scottish cashmere, tweed and wool with a modern twist.

The Holding Company, 241 King's Rd. A wealth of storage solutions for every room in the home or office.

Bluebird, 350 King's Rd. Part of the Conran empire, a converted 1930s garage containing a luxury food store, cookware shop, flower stall, restaurant and café.

Peter Jones, Sloane Square. A West London institution; a branch of John Lewis renowned for wedding lists and Chelsea 'ladies who lunch'.

Chelsea Town Hall, corner of Manor Street and King's Rd. Venue for antique sales and craft fairs.

The Chelsea Courtyard, Sydney Street. Pleasant haven from the main drag, with Bikepark, a bike shop where you can buy, hire and park bikes and get them repaired; an antiques centre; and the only authentic Vietnamese street barrow in London.

John Sandoe Books, 10–11 Blacklands Terrace, just off the King's Rd. An old-fashioned, higgledy-piggledy bookshop with knowledgeable staff.

Boy London/Ad Hoc, 153 King's Rd. OTT selection of fun, kitsch clothing and clubbing accessories.

American Classics, 400 King's Rd. All you need for that authentic 'street' look.

R. Soles, 109a King's Rd. Cowboy boot heaven.

L'Artisan Parfumeur, 17 Cale St. Beautifully gift-wrapped, elegant scents and colognes..

V.V Rouleaux, 54 Sloane Square, just behind Peter Jones. An irresistible shop filled to the ceiling with rolls of ribbon and brocade.

Knightsbridge and Brompton Cross

It was the Great Exhibition that turned Knightsbridge into the birthplace of the late Victorian department store. **Harvey Nichols**, the most stylish (and the absolute favourite of Patsy and Edina in *Absolutely Fabulous*), is on the corner of Sloane Street and Knightsbridge. Harvey Nicks is justly famous for its weird and wonderful window displays, and fifth floor food halls, where swishly packaged exotica of every description are sold under an equally exotic steel panelled corrugated canopy with views of the Knightsbridge skyline. (If you need a break, coffee or even a drink, it's well worth making a short detour from here to the food hall's glamorous café and bar).

The most famous department store of all, **Harrods**, is on the Brompton Road. Nowadays it is often mentioned in the same breath as the name of its owner, Mohammed Fayed—Egyptian tycoon, failed candidate for British citizenship and father of the ill-fated Dodi, last companion of Princess Diana. But its pedigree stretches back much further to the glory days of the 19th century. The vast, terracotta-fronted palace that Harrods now occupies was built in the first five years of the 20th century, at much the same time as the first modern luxury hotels like the Savoy and the Ritz. Indeed Harrods is itself in some ways more like a five-star hotel than a mere shop; service and indulgence towards the customer are paramount, and no request is ever too much trouble. The place is kitted out to provide a fitting welcome to the noblest of princes; particularly striking are the Food Halls with their beautiful food displays and Edwardian Art Nouveau tiles in the Meat Hall depicting hunting scenes. As you wander around, you are serenaded alternately by a harpist and a piano player. You'll find just about anything on its six floors, just as long as money is no object.

Both **Brompton Road** and **Sloane Street** parade classy designer shops, some of them too scary to enter. Nicole Farhi, Dior, Christian Lacroix, Chanel, Gucci, Kenzo and a clutch of others stretch down Sloane Street, while beyond Harrods in the Brompton Road you will find Emporio Armani and Issey Miyake. The streets behind Harrods have hidden treasures, and halfway down Brompton Road to the left is **Beauchamp Place**, lined with tiny exclusive shops selling anything from underwear to jewellery to designer cast-offs. Yet around the many exits of Knightsbridge tube are branches of Monsoon and Miss Selfridge, Jigsaw and Laura Ashley as well.

Harrods, Brompton Rd. A shopping institution of such proportions that it demands to be seen. Whether you want to buy anything is another matter. Exotic foods, kitchenware, silverware and toys are all excellent, clothes rather less so. Look out for bargains on mundane things like CDs during the sales.

Harvey Nichols, 109–125 Knightsbridge. High-class fashionwear, plus an excellent food hall and café on the fifth floor.

Scotch House, 2 Brompton Rd. Classic woollens, from socks to knitted ties, plus Scottish kilts and all the paraphernalia.

Descamps, 197 Sloane St. Fine French linen.

Gant USA, 17 Brompton Rd. American sportswear.

Graff, 55 Brompton Rd. Very expensive jewellery.

Space NK Apothecary, 305 Brompton Rd. Make-up and beauty products not available elsewhere: Nars, Kiehl's, Stila.

The Outlet, Brompton Rd. Discounted designer wear.

Emporio Armani, 191 Brompton Rd. Elegant cuts from the king of classic Italian tailoring.

Rigby and Peller, 2 Hans Road. Sublime underwear.

La Bottega del San Lorenzo, 23 Beauchamp Place. Divine Italian deli.

Isabell Kristensen, 33 Beauchamp Place. Ballgowns.

Mulberry, 185 Brompton Road. Classic English leather bags and luggage with the distinctive logo.

Brompton Cross

Further along the Brompton Road is a small enclave of shops and restaurants at the start of the Fulham Road known as Brompton Cross. The most striking building at its centre is Terence Conran's remarkable Art Nouveau **Michelin Building** (at No.61), which he renovated in the 1980s complete with glass cupolas and car-themed mosaics to create offices, a Conran Shop and the Bibendum restaurant and Oyster Bar.

Behind and parallel to the Brompton Road, first left off Draycott Avenue, **Walton Street**, like Beauchamp Place, is a quiet enclave of unmissable classy little shops.

Conran Shop, Michelin House, 81 Fulham Road. Baskets, chairs, lighting, even notebooks are all beautifully designed and presented in this tremendous Art Deco building.

Voyage, 115 and 175 Fulham Road. Bouncers decide whether you're elegant or trendy enough to be allowed in this designer clothes store.

Formes, 313 Fulham Road. Fashion for pregnant women.

The Ringmaker, 191–3 Fulham Road. Huge jeweller's with stylish designs.

Divertimenti, 139 Fulham Road. Pots and pans of the highest quality and inventiveness.

Agnès B, Fulham Road. One branch of the women's design shop: clothes and make-up.

Czech and Speake, 125 Fulham Road. Incense burning by the door lures you into this haven of scents for the body and home.

Jerry's Home Store, 163–7 Fulham Road. American household goods and food, including shiny chrome 50s blenders and ice-cream machines and authentic brownie mixes.

Dinny Hall, 54 Fulham Road. Resin and silver earrings from this trend-setting jewellery designer.

Bentley's, 190 Walton Street. Leather goods and luggage.

Maman Deux, 79 Walton Street. For the street-smart baby.

Jo Malone, 154 Walton St. Her own range of toiletries from the queen of the facial. Delectable and now legendary products for the face and body.

Nôm, 150 Walton St. Calm Japanese style for the home.

Sam de Teran, 151 Fulham Rd. Sailing, skiing and sports gear.

The Room, 158 Walton Street. Beautiful homewares that are almost works of art.

Cox and Power, 95 Walton St. Flamboyant modern jewellery.

Farmacia di Santa Maria Novella, 117 Walton St. Italian hand-milled soaps and fragrances.

Covent Garden

Apart from the market, there are many shops that make this a rewarding area to take your credit card. Neal Street, Seven Dials and the streets radiating from it, Thomas Neal's Arcade, Long Acre, New Row and the streets around the market are the places to head for.

The Astrology Shop, 78 Neal St. Have your personal horoscope done; also books, CDs and astrological objects.

Red or Dead, 43 Neal St. Trendy British shoe shop that now also sells clothes.

Janet Fitch, 37 Neal Street and 1 The Market. Jewellery shop with work by different designers.

Sam Walker, 33 Neal Street. Vintage clothing.

The Tea House, 15a Neal St. All kinds of teas from around the world: herbal, green, organic and fruit.

Neal Street East, 5 Neal St. An oriental emporium of books, clothes and home decorating ideas.

Michiko Koshino, 70 Neal St. Glad rags suitable for the high-class club circuit. Cool and dazzling.

Ray's Jazz Shop, 180 Shaftesbury Ave. Old classic LPs and new CDs on jazz and blues.

Neal's Yard Wholefood Warehouse, off Shorts Gardens. Organic everything.

Neal's Yard Remedies, 15 Neal's Yard. Lots of oils and homoeopathic remedies, all very natural.

Neal's Yard Dairy, 17 Shorts Gardens. More than 70 varieties of cheese, matured and served with love.

Duffer of St George, 29 Shorts Gardens. Very trendy menswear store, selling street-/clubwear.

Dress Circle, 57 Monmouth St. 'The greatest showbiz shop in the world', they claim, with sheet music, scores, books, posters and CDs.

Natural Leather, 33 Monmouth St. Leather jackets, jeans and bags.

Muji, 39 Shelton St, and branches. Minimalist Japanese store selling kitchen equipment and stationery.

Stanfords, 12–14 Long Acre. Map specialist, indispensable if you are travelling to the Third World where maps are virtually non-existent. Also travel guides, travel literature and walking guides.

Dillons Art Bookshop, 8 Long Acre. Books on art; also cards and postcards.

Nicole Farhi, 12 Long Acre and Unit 4, East Piazza. Stylish, elegant clothes for women.

Jones, 13 Floral St. At the cutting edge of fashion; here Gaultier and Galliano are old hat.

Paul Smith, 40–4 Floral St, Covent Garden. High-class gloss on the bovver-boy look. Mostly for men, but there is now a women's collection too.

The Tintin Shop, 34 Floral St. Books, videos and T-shirts.

Oasis, 13 James St and branches. Stylish, fashionable womenswear at reasonable prices.

Culpeper Herbalists, 8 The Market. Herbs, spices, bath salts and pot-pourri, mostly taken from homegrown sources.

Segar & Snuff Parlour, The Market. A tiny shop selling pipes, lighters, and hand-rolled cigars from Cuba.

Ordning & Reda, 21 New Row. Stylish, colourful, Swedish-designed stationery and office accessories.

Vertigo Galleries, 29 Bedfordbury. Vintage movie posters.

The Africa Centre, 38 King St. African crafts; also a restaurant/café.

Dr Martens Department Store, 1–4 King St. Four floors of DMs for men, women and children; also sells clothing.

Crime in Store, 4 Bedford St. Specialist crime and mystery bookshop, including many US titles unavailable elsewhere in Britain.

Penhaligon's, 41 Wellington St. Own-brand eau de toilette and other fragrances. Also delicious air freshener sprays.

Markets

Street markets are one of the best things about London. They are where the city comes alive, showing off the vitality and variety of the neighbourhoods lucky enough to have them. Some, such as Covent Garden and Portoballo, are described in the main sections of this book; what follows is a list of what to expect and details of opening hours.

Berwick Street, Soho. Outstanding fruit and veg (*open every day except Sun, with lunchtime closing on Wed*). See p.75.

Brick Lane, Whitechapel (*open Sun morning*). Very popular market where East End barrows try to offload their junk, especially furniture and old books. Keep a hard nose and you can haggle a real bargain.

Brixton, Electric Avenue (*open daily except Sun, with lunchtime closing on Wed*). London's biggest Caribbean market, with music, exotic vegetables, goats' meat and wafting spices.

Camden Lock, between Camden High St and Chalk Farm Rd (*open Sat and Sun*). A weekend institution, with an array of books, clothes, records and assorted antiques by the canal. Huge crowds guarantee a festive atmosphere, and there are lots of excellent refreshments on hand.

Camden Passage, Islington (*open Wed and Sat only*). High-class antiques market in a quiet street next to the bustle of Upper St.

Chapel Market, Islington (*closed Mon and at lunchtime on Thurs and Sun*). An exuberant north London food market, with excellent fish and, as a sideline, lots of household goods and cheap clothes.

Columbia Road (*off the Hackney Road about three-quarters of a mile north of Liverpool St Station, open 8am–1pm Sun morning*): Columbia market was set up in 1869 as a covered food market set in a vast neo-Gothic palace. The traders preferred to do their business on the street, however, and the venture failed. The shortlived market building was knocked down in 1958 to make room for the lively, modern, highly successful flower market. As well as a wide range of cut flowers and pot plants, you can buy home-made bread and farmhouse cheeses and enjoy the small cafés that line the street.

Earlham St, Earlham St, Covent Gdn, between Shaftesbury Ave and Seven Dials (*Mon–Sat 10–4*). Extraordinary flowers, and secondhand clothes.

Greenwich, College Approach, Greenwich (*Sat and Sun only*). Lots of crafts, books, furniture and coins and medals. Worth a detour.

Petticoat Lane, Middlesex St, Whitechapel (*open Sun morning*). Leather, cheap fashion and household goods at London's most famous Sunday market. Look out for the jellied eel and whelk sellers on the fringes.

Portobello Road, Notting Hill (*open Mon–Sat, with lunchtime closing Thurs; antiques Sat only*). Perhaps the most atmospheric market in London. The southern end is stuffed with antique dealers, while the northern end is a mixed bag of design shops, cafés, food stalls, jewellery stands, record stores and more. Has a real neighbourhood feel, culminating in the wonderful half-Portuguese, half-Moroccan Golborne Road. *See* p.90.

St James's, St James's Churchyard, Piccadilly (*Tues antiques, Wed–Sun 10–6*). Lots of books, old prints, coins and medals on a Tuesday, and ethnic crafts the rest of the time.

South Bank, Riverside Walk, in front of the NFT (*Sat and Sun*). Secondhand books and prints along the riverside, open rain or shine.

Art Collections	132
Design and the Decorative Arts	133
Historical, Political and Military	135
Science, Medicine and Technology	136
Famous Homes	137
Religion	138
One-offs	139

London: Museums and Galleries

Summer Exhibition

Art Collections

Courtauld Institute, Somerset House, The Strand, WC2, ℡ (020) 7873 2526. ⊖ *Covent Gdn, Temple.* Open Mon–Sat 10–6, Sun 2–6; adm; full disabled access, café, entrance is to the right on the way in to Somerset House.

Somerset House was the first Renaissance palace in England, built for one of the biggest thugs in the country's history. In 1547 the Duke of Somerset was named Lord Protector for the new king, nine-year-old Edward VI, and set about building a home grand enough to match his overweening ambitions. He knocked down two bishops' palaces, an inn of chancery and a church to make room for his super-palace, and pillaged two more churches to provide the stone. Such a man could not last long, and Somerset was executed in 1552. But his palace lived on, at least for a while, as a residence for royalty and a venue for peace conferences. It fell out of fashion in the 17th and 18th centuries and, despite boasting a chapel by Inigo Jones and the first example of parquet flooring in Europe, was demolished in the 1770s. The replacement, used to house a succession of Royal Societies, various public records and the Inland Revenue service, is a fine Georgian building by William Chambers.

Somerset House's chief attraction is the Courtauld Institute, with its exquisite collection of paintings, particularly of Impressionists and post-impressionists. Most of the paintings were a bequest by the philanthropist Samuel Courtauld, who also set up a school of fine art affiliated to London University. An elegant staircase leads to 11 smallish rooms spread over two floors. There is a magnificent *Adam and Eve* by Lucas Cranach the Elder, some fine Rubens including his early masterpiece *The Descent from the Cross*, and a roomful of unusual 18th-century Italian art including a series of Tiepolos. The Impressionists include a copy by the artist of Manet's *Le Déjeuner sur l'Herbe*, some wonderful Degas studies of dancers and moody Cézanne landscapes. Highlights from the 20th century include Kokoschka, Modigliani and some excellent contemporary British works donated in the early 1980s.

Estorick Collection of Italian Art, Northampton Lodge, 39a Canonbury Square, N1, ℡ (020) 7704 9522, ⊖ *Highbury & Islington.* Open Wed–Sat 11–6, Sun 12–5; cheap adm. Fascinating private collection of Italian art, mainly futurist painters including Balla, Boccioni and Carra. With a library, café and shop.

Kenwood House, Hampstead Lane, NW3, ℡ (020) 8348 1286, ⊖ *Hampstead, Highgate.* Open daily 10–6; Oct–Mar daily 10–4. See p.103.

National Gallery, St Martin's Lane, WC2, ℡ (020) 7747 2885, ⊖ *Charing Cross, Leicester Sq.* Open daily 10–6, Wed 10–9; free. See p.38

National Portrait Gallery, St Martin's Lane, WC2, ℡ (020) 7306 0055, ⊖ *Charing Cross, Leicester Square.* Open daily 10–6; free.

This gallery is unique, and a true oddity. Unique, because no other Western country has ever assembled a similar collection of portraits of the glorious names populating its history. Odd, because the kings, generals, ministers, pioneers, inventors and artists on display here have not been chosen according to the quality of the painting—in fact some of it is downright lousy. They are here because the Victorian aristocrats who originally founded the gallery believed that it would serve as a stern kind of history lesson. The gallery is a forceful argument for Thomas Carlyle's view that the history of the world is 'but the biography of great men', and that the proper duty of the lower orders is to shut up and be grateful. Don't be too surprised, then, to find that in here you will see no revolutionaries, few union leaders, few true dissidents.

The gallery has far more pictures than space: over 9,000 portraits with only five narrow floors to exhibit them (a café on the roof is planned for 2002). You only get to see a small, rotating fraction—check the computer database provided. Chronologically, the collection starts at the top with the Tudor age and works its way down towards the present day, with a magnificent new 20th-century wing designed by Piers Gough. The best paintings, technically speaking, are probably Holbein's vividly life-like versions of Henrys VII and VIII and Sir Thomas More. There are also magnificent renditions of the 19th-century prime ministers Disraeli and Gladstone by Millais, self-portraits by Hogarth and Reynolds, a distinctly ambivalent Churchill by Walter Sickert (all yellows and greens) and a Cubist

T.S. Eliot by Jacob Epstein. Some of the portraits are so reverent as to be absurd. Lawrence of Arabia appears in stone effigy like some medieval king imbued with divine powers, and Jacques-Emile Blanche's James Joyce looks ludicrously respectable in a smart suit in front of an orderly writing desk.

Percival David Foundation of Chinese Art, 53 Gordon Square, WC1, ☏ (020) 7387 3909, ⊖ *Euston Sq. Open Mon–Fri 10.30–5; free.* This fine collection of imperial porcelain is named after the philanthropic collector who acquired its treasures. With its extensive library and superb ceramics, this is a vital stopping-off point for China scholars. The vases, which are beautifully documented and dated, range from the Sung dynasty of the 10th century up to the Qing dynasty of the 18th.

Royal Academy, Burlington House, Piccadilly, W1, ☏ (020) 7300 8000, ⊖ *Green Park, Piccadilly. Open daily 10–6; adm. See* p.72.

Tate Gallery, Millbank, SW1, ☏ (020) 7887 8000, ⊖ *Pimlico. Open daily 10–5.50; free. See* p.42.

The Wallace Collection, Hertford House, Manchester Square, behind Oxford St, W1, ☏ (020) 7935 0687, ⊖ *Marble Arch, Bond Street. Open Mon–Sat 10–5, Sun 2–5; free, donations welcome.* One could not hope for a more perfect monument to 18th-century aristocratic life than the Wallace Collection, a sumptuous array of painting, porcelain and furniture housed in a period mansion called Hertford House. It is the location that makes it, the wonderfully uplifting feeling as you glide up the staircases with their gilded wrought-iron banisters and wander from one elegant, well-lit room to another. The collection is the result of several generations of accumulation by the Hertford family, whose link with the art world had already begun in the mid-18th century, when the first Marquess of Hertford patronized Joshua Reynolds. Richard Wallace, who gave his name to the collection (as well as designing the Paris drinking fountains that still bear his name), was the bastard son of the fourth Marquess and acted as agent for his father in all his transactions. He later bequeathed the whole lot to the state, on condition that it remain on public view in central London.

Highlights include works by Frans Hals (*The Laughing Cavalier*), Rembrandt (*Titus*), Rubens (*Christ's Charge to Peter* and *The Holy Family*), Poussin (*Dance to the Music of Time*) and Titian (an extraordinary rendition of *Perseus and Andromeda* in which the Greek hero tumbles towards the open jaws of the sea monster with only his sword and shield to save him). Take your time around the rest of the collection to take in the finely carved wardrobes inlaid with tortoiseshell and gilt bronze, the delicate porcelain and any number of eccentric *objets d'art*.

Whitechapel Art Gallery, Whitechapel High St, ☏ (020) 7522 7888, ⊖ *Aldgate East. Open Tues–Sun 11–5; free.* A lively gallery focusing on contemporary and avant-garde work, housed in an interesting Art Nouveau building designed by Charles Harrison Townsend at the turn of the 20th century. It was the brainchild of Samuel Barnett, a local vicar who believed education could help eradicate the appalling poverty in the East End. Jackson Pollock and David Hockney both held exhibitions here early in their careers.

Design and the Decorative Arts

Clockmakers' Museum, Guildhall Library, Aldermanbury, EC2, ☏ (020) 7606 3030, ⊖ *Bank, Mansion House. Open Mon–Fri 9.30–4.45.* Here you'll find more than 700 timepieces of all shapes and sizes belonging to the Worshipful Company of Clockmakers. Look out for the silver skull watch said to have belonged to Mary, Queen of Scots, and the wrist watch worn by Edmund Hillary during the first recorded ascent of Mount Everest in 1953.

Commonwealth Institute, Kensington High Street, W8, ☏ (020) 7371 3530, ⊖ *High Street Kensington; bus 49, 9, 10, 27. Open daily 10–5;* adm. The shimmering green hyperboloid roof, made of Zambian copper, is only the first of many surprises at this highly imaginative cultural centre celebrating the diversity and imagination of Britain's former colonies, now grouped together as the Commonwealth. There are three floors of galleries, each dealing with a different country, where you can pluck a sitar, sit on a snowmobile or watch a model demonstrating the digestive system of a New Zealand cow. Children love it. The Institute also has a lively programme of lectures, concerts and art exhibitions; a shop jam-packed with craft work; and a restaurant offering indigenous dishes from around the Commonwealth. A new 'interactive' attraction called The Commonwealth Experience is a vertiginous and quite scary simulated helicopter ride over a rather more visible Malaysia than in real life.

Crafts Council Gallery, 44a Pentonville Rd, E3, ✆ (020) 7278 7700, ⊖ *Angel; bus 19, 38, 73. Open Tues–Sat 11–6, Sun 2–6; free.* Excellent exhibition of modern British crafts.

Design Museum, Butler's Wharf, SE1, ✆ (020) 7403 6933, ⊖ *Tower Hill. Open Mon–Fri 11.30–6, Sat and Sun 12–6. See* p.86.

Geffrye Museum, Kingsland Rd, E2, ✆ (020) 7739 9893, ⊖ *Old Street then bus 243. Open Tues–Sat 10–5, Sun 2–5; free.* A thoroughly absorbing series of reconstructions of British living rooms from Tudor times to the present, housed in a row of former almshouses, with a new extension focusing on design.

Leighton House, 12 Holland Park Rd, W14, ✆ (020) 7602 3316, ⊖ *Holland Park, High Street Kensington; bus 9, 10, 27, 49. Open Mon–Sat 11–5.30; free.* This apparently straightforward red-brick house opens into a grand extravaganza of escapist late Victorian interior design. Lord Leighton, one of the Pre-Raphaelite painters, used his imagination, his not inconsiderable funds and the inspiration of a number of friends to create an astonishing Oriental palace here in his London home. The highlight is undoubtedly the Arab Hall, which has a stained-glass cupola, a fountain spurting out of the richly decorated mosaic floor and glorious painted floral tiles which Leighton and his friends picked up in Rhodes, Cairo and Damascus. Dotted around the downstairs reception rooms, among the paintings of Leighton and his contemporaries Millais and Burne-Jones, are highly ornate details including Cairene lattice-work alcoves and marble columns decorated in burnished gold. *See also* p.112.

Sir John Soane's Museum, 12–14 Lincoln's Inn Fields, WC2, ✆ (020) 7430 0175, ⊖ *Holborn. Open Tues–Sat 10–5, with a £3 guided tour—which is free to students—on Saturdays at 2.30 and with visits by candlelight on the first Tuesday of each month from 6–9; free, but any donations are gratefully accepted.* John Soane (1753–1837) was a great English eccentric and also one of the great architects of his age. He was a fanatical student of antiquity, and one of the towering figures of the neoclassical movement in Britain. One contemporary described him as 'personal to the point of perversity'. Soane did not seem unduly bothered by the relative paucity of high-profile commissions; he stayed busy throughout his professional life and won a formidable reputation as a lecturer. In later life he bought up and converted three adjacent houses here in Lincoln's Inn Fields, adapting each room to his quirky style and filling them with objects from his remarkable art collection. In 1833 (four years before his death in 1837), Soane saw through a private Act of Parliament in which he bequeathed the whole collection to the public, with the stipulation that the museum should be maintained forever as it was on the day of Soane's death.

One of the highlights is the Picture Room on the ground floor, containing two great satirical series of paintings by Hogarth: *The Rake's Progress*, which follows the rise and fall of a degenerate young man from the moment he comes into his inheritance to his untimely end in the madhouse, and *The Election*, four scenes satirizing the greed and corruption surrounding political ambition. The Picture Room also includes studies by Piranesi and architectural drawings by Soane himself. Soane's other prized exhibit is the sarcophagus of the Egyptian Pharaoh Seti I (1303–1290 BC) in the Sepulchral Chamber in the basement. This is the finest example of a sarcophagus you can see outside Egypt, beautifully preserved and covered in hieroglyphics honouring Osiris and Ra and adorned with a painted figure of the goddess Nut, to whom Seti had pledged allegiance, on the inside.

It would be a mistake, however, to visit this museum merely for its artistic highlights. Every room yields surprises, whether it is the enormous collection of plaster casts Soane made from classical models, or the classical colonnade running along the upstairs corridor, or simply the amazing ambiguities of light, which Soane manipulated so intriguingly in every area of the house with the aid of concave and then convex mirrors.

Victoria and Albert Museum, Cromwell Rd, SW7, ✆ (020) 7938 8500, ⊖ *South Kensington. Open Mon–Sun 10–5.45, summer Wed late view 6.30–9.30; adm, free after 4.30pm. See* p.46.

William Morris Gallery, Lloyd Park, Forest Rd, E17, ✆ (020) 7527 3782, ⊖ *Walthamstow Central*. *Open Tues–Sat 10–1 and 2–5, plus first Sun in the month 10–noon and 2–5; free.* A long way to go to see William Morris's childhood home and its fascinating exhibition on his life and work. Lots of Arts and Crafts wallpaper, stained glass, tiles and carpets. There is also an interesting collection of pre-Raphaelite paintings and drawings by Burne-Jones and Rossetti, plus a few Rodin sculptures.

Historical, Political and Military

Bank of England Museum, Bartholomew Lane, Threadneedle St, EC2, ✆ (020) 7601 5545, ⊖ *Bank. Open Mon–Fri 10–5; April–Sept Sun 11–5; free.* See p.58.

Cabinet War Rooms, Clive Steps, King Charles St, SW1 (entrance Horse Guards Rd), ✆ 0171 930 6961, ⊖ *Westminster. Open daily 9.30–5.50, last adm 5.15; adm.* Winston Churchill had the basement of a number of government buildings converted in preparation for war in 1938, and he, his cabinet and 500 civil servants worked here throughout the conflict, protected from the bombing by several layers of thick concrete. The floor below the present exhibition contained a canteen, hospital, shooting range and sleeping quarters. Churchill, whose office was a converted broom cupboard, kept a direct line open to President Roosevelt in Washington; all other telephone connections were operated from an unwieldy old-fashioned switchboard and scrambled, for perverse reasons of security, via Selfridge's department store. The War Rooms, with their Spartan period furniture and maps marking the British Empire in red, are a magnificent evocation of the wartime atmosphere. A pity, then, that the curators do not allow the place simply to speak for itself.

Clink Prison Museum, 1 Clink St, SE1, ✆ (020) 7403 6515, ⊖ *Borough; bus 40, 133, 149. Open daily 10–6; June–Sept 10am–10pm. adm.* See p.84.

Imperial War Museum, Lambeth Rd, SE1, ✆ (020) 7416 5329, ⊖ *Lambeth North. Open daily 10–6; adm but free after 4.30pm.* Until the First World War this was the site of the notorious Bethlehem Royal Hospital for the insane, better known as Bedlam, where inmates were kept like zoo animals in cages and cells. The building is now used to illustrate Britain's wartime experiences from 1914 to the present day. Despite the intimidating pair of artillery cannon at the entrance, this museum does everything it can to illustrate the human side of war, not just the military hardware. Certainly, there are plenty of Zeppelins, Lancaster bombers, Cruise missile launchers—there is even a distasteful flight simulator for which visitors cough up extra money to 'experience' a World War Two bombing mission. Fortunately there are also exhibits on rationing and air raids, sound and light shows illustrating the terrors and privations of life in a First World War trench, and artworks including Henry Moore's drawings of London during the Blitz. Try as it might, however, the museum ultimately fails to convey the sheer barbaric awfulness of war and can't help wrapping the experiences it depicts in a coat of patriotic nostalgia.

Kensington Palace, Kensington Gardens, W8, ✆ (020) 7937 9561, ⊖ *High Street Kensignton, Queensway. Open Mar–Oct daily 10–6; Nov–Ferb Wed–Sun 10–3.* See p.37.

Museum of London, 150 London Wall, EC2, ✆ (020) 7600 3699, ⊖ *St Paul's. Open Tues–Sat 10–5.50, Sun 12–5.50; adm, free after 4.30pm.* This ambitious and fast-changing museum sets out to tell the story of London from prehistoric times to the present, drawing on a vast collection of documents and historical relics. It is an ideal place to come if you want to familiarize yourself with the basic facts about the city. It is also a tremendous resource for students and researchers. The museum is very strong on early history, particularly the Roman era, and gives a rich impression of life in the 19th century. It also has an imaginative section on contemporary London. In other areas, perhaps inevitably, the museum is a bit patchy, since the quality of the displays varies according to the illustrative material available. The main problem, in the end, is that the museum's archive of documents is far richer than its collection of artefacts. That said, the museum is never boring. It is beautifully laid out over three descending levels. There are lucid explanations of the historical evidence yielded by lumps of Roman paving stone and recovered coinage. One angled window cleverly gives you a view down on to a piece of Roman wall (AD 200) on the ground outside. Many of the best displays in the rest of the museum are reconstructions of contemporary buildings: a 16th-century grocer's shop, a cell at Newgate Prison, a Victorian pub, a Second World War bedroom kitted out with a protective cage called a Morrison shelter. The museum also has a magnificent range of clothing, giving an insight into changing fashions since the 17th century. The undisputed centrepiece, though, is the **Lord Mayor's Coach**. Built in 1757 in blazing red and burnished gold, the coach is still used every November for the investiture of the new Lord Mayor. It looks the sort of thing Prince Charming might have used to drive Cinderella home; it is covered in allegorical paintings depicting both the virtues of modesty and the glories of wealth.

National Maritime Museum, Romney Rd, Greenwich, SE10, ✆ (020) 8312 6565, ⇌ *Maze Hill (from Charing Cross)*. *Open daily 10–5; adm. See* p.107.

Royal Naval College, King William Walk, SE10, ✆ (020) 8858 2154, ⇌ *Greenwich; DLR Island Gdns; by river to Greenwich Pier; bus 188. Open*

Fri–Wed 10–5, Thurs 2.30–5, Sat and Sun 12–5; free. See p.106.

Winston Churchill's Britain at War Museum, 64–66 Tooley Street, SE1, ✆ (020) 7403 3171, ⊖ *London Bridge; bus 47, P11. Open daily 10–4.30; adm exp*. This is the kind of museum you could cook up out of a recipe book. Take a popular subject (the Second World War), add plenty of period memorabilia (books, clothes, newspaper cuttings, radio broadcasts, etc.), mix in a couple of set-piece reconstructions (an Underground station during an air raid and a bombed-out house) and top with lashings of patriotism (Vera Lynn singing *There'll Always Be An England*). There is not a drop of originality about the place. You'll see all of it, and more, at the Cabinet War Rooms in Whitehall.

The *Golden Hinde*, St Mary Overie's Dock, Clink Street, ✆ (0541) 505 041, ⊖ *Borough; bus 40, 133, 149. Open daily 9–sunset; adm cheap; tea and coffee available*. A perfect replica of the galleon used by Sir Francis Drake to circumnavigate the world in 1580. The original rotted away in a berth in Deptford, and the reconstruction you see here is a working galleon which has sailed many more miles across the world than its progenitor. A crew of 15 lives aboard the ship.

Science, Medicine and Technology

National Postal Museum, King Edward St, EC1, in the post office in King Edward Building on the left-hand side of the road, ✆ (020) 7239 5420, ⊖ *St Paul's. Open Mon–Fri 9.30–4.30; free*. This is a stamp collector's wet dream: three floors of postal memorabilia, from rare stamps to uniforms, Bantams (the motorbikes used for delivering telegrams) and red and green post boxes dating back to the 1850s.

Brunel Engine House, St Marychurch St, SE16, ⊖ *Rotherhithe; bus 47, P11, 188. Open by appointment on* ✆ *(020) 7252 0059 or* ✆ *(020) 8748 3534; adm*. Rotherhithe acquired a new cause for celebrity in the early 19th century, when Marc Isambard Brunel made it the starting point for the first tunnel to run beneath the Thames. Brunel was born in France and fled the Revolution with a forged passport. Although a talented engineer—he invented a system of pulley blocks still remembered today—he had no financial sense and spent far too

much of his own money on his work. The Duke of Wellington had to haul him out of debtors' prison to start the tunnel from Rotherhithe to Wapping. The job took 18 years, from 1825 to 1843, and nearly ended in disaster on five separate occasions when the roof caved in. You can see the bright red pump that Brunel used to suck out the water, as well as a number of other memorabilia at the Brunel Engine House. The Thames Tunnel is now used by the East London Underground line; it is not to be confused with the adjacent Rotherhithe Tunnel, built for road traffic in 1908.

Faraday Museum, Albemarle St, W1, ✆ (020) 7409 2992, ⊖ *Green Park. Open Mon–Fri 9–5; adm*. The Royal Institution building, with its pompous façade based on the Temple of Antoninus in Rome, is to science what the Royal Academy is to the arts: the most prestigious association of professionals in the land. Founded in 1799, the Institution built up a formidable reputation thanks to early members such as Humphrey Davy (inventor of the Davy Lamp for detecting methane down mines) and his pupil, Michael Faraday. The small museum (the only part of the building regularly open to the public) is in fact Faraday's old laboratory where he carried out his pioneering experiments with electricity in the 1830s; his work is explained with the help of his original instruments and lab notes. The Royal Institution also organizes excellent lectures, including series specially designed for children.

Florence Nightingale Museum, 2 Lambeth Palace Rd, SE1, ✆ (020) 7620 0374, ⊖ *Lambeth North, Waterloo; bus 507. Open Tues–Sun 10–5, last adm 4; adm*. You won't learn much more about the founder of modern nursing here than at the Old St Thomas's Operating Theatre (*see* p.85), but the museum nevertheless builds up a vivid image of her life and times. Here are the letters, childhood books and personal trophies that the 'Lady with the Lamp' brought back from the Crimean War. You can also see a reconstructed ward from the Crimea, contemporary nurses' uniforms and some of the equipment they used. 'Nursing is a progressive art, in which to stand still is to go back,' Florence Nightingale said towards the end of her long life (she died, aged 90, in 1910). Her influence is still being felt today.

London Planetarium, Marylebone Rd, NW1, ✆ (020) 7935 6861, ⊖ *Baker Street. Open June–Aug daily 9.30–5, Sept–May daily 12.20–5; adm. A joint ticket is available with Madame Tussaud's.* If you have children, you might enjoy the Planetarium, with its exciting and informative laser, sound and light show projected over a vast dome-shaped auditorium via a high-tech Digistar Mark 2 projector. The show explains how the solar system works, what the galaxy and the Milky Way are (apart from the chocolate bars you chomped in the queue), how earthquakes and volcanoes happen, and more.

London Transport Museum, 39 Wellington St, WC2, ✆ (020) 7379 6344, ⊖ *Covent Garden. Open Sun–Thurs and Sat 10–6, Fri 11–6; adm, full disabled access*. Londoners like to grumble about London Transport, but in their heart of hearts they are really rather fascinated by it. This cheerful museum celebrates everything that is excellent about the system, from the red London Routemaster bus to the London Underground map, designed in 1931 by Harry Beck, and never surpassed. In the main gallery, a glass walkway takes you past a series of historic buses, trams and steam locomotives, including the oldest surviving double-decker horse tram. In adjoining galleries you can see an original watercolour of Beck's Underground map, and a superb collection of Art Deco period posters. There's a simulated Tube train driving seat, actors dressed in period costume, educational 'Action Zones' and a museum shop. The museum also organizes a programme of talks and events (including a regular tour and lecture on London's disused Tube stations)

Natural History Museum, Cromwell Rd, SW7, ✆ (020) 7938 9123, ⊖ *South Kensington. Open Mon–Sat 10–5.50, Sun 11–5.50. See* p.39.

Royal Observatory, Greenwich Park, SE10, ✆ (020) 8858 4422, ⇌ *Maze Hill (from Charing Cross); bus 188. Open daily 10–5. See* p.108.

Science Museum, Exhibition Rd, SW7, ✆ (020) 7938 8080, ⊖ *South Kensington. Open daily 10–6. See* p.39.

St Thomas's Operating Theatre Museum, 9a St Thomas St, SE1, ✆ (020) 7955 4791, ⊖ *London Br. Open Tues–Sun 10.30–4.45; adm. See* p.85.

Thames Barrier Visitor Centre, Unity Way, SE18, ✆ (020) 8854 1373, ⇌ *Charlton; by river from Westminster Pier; bus 188 then bus 472. Open Mon–Fri 10–5, Sat and Sun 10.30–5.30; adm*. A brief history of flooding in London, and an explanation on how the barrier works.

Famous Homes

Apsley House, Hyde Park Corner, W1, ✆ (020) 7499 5676, ⊖ *Hyde Park Corner. Open Tues–Sun 11–5; adm*. Wellington was given this house as a reward for his victories against the French, and he modestly dubbed it No.1 London (its real address being the more prosaic 149 Piccadilly). Robert Adam had built it half a century earlier for Henry Bathurst, a man generally reckoned to be the most incompetent Lord Chancellor of the 18th century. The Iron Duke succeeded in defacing Adam's original work, covering the brick walls with Bath stone, adding the awkward Corinthian portico at the front and ripping out much of the interior with the help of the architects Benjamin and Philip Wyatt. You feel the coldness of a man who terrified most who met him and who, according to legend, once defused a mounting riot in Hyde Park with a single crack of his whip. Sadly the museum does not own a pair of Wellington boots, the man's greatest legacy to the 20th century. The highlight is indubitably Canova's double-life-size sculpture of Napoleon, which Wellington stole from the Louvre after its megalomaniac subject rejected it.

Carlyle's House, 24 Cheyne Row, SW3, ✆ (020) 7352 7087, ⊖ *Sloane Square then bus 19, 22. Open April–Oct Wed–Sun 11–5; adm. See* p.93.

Dickens' House, 49 Doughty St, WC1, ✆ (020) 7405 2127, ⊖ *Russell Sq, Chancery Lane. Open Mon–Sat 10–5; adm.* The only one of Dickens's many London homes to survive. The furnishings have been drafted in from other Dickens homes; really just a collection of hallowed objects.

Dr Johnson's House, 17 Gough Square, EC4, ✆ (020) 7353 3745, ⊖ *Blackfriars, Temple. Open Mon–Sat 11–5.30 and 11–5 Oct–April; cheap adm.* This is the elegant 17th-century house where the Doctor lived from 1748 to 1759. For many of those years he was busy compiling his famous dictionary, the first of its kind in the English language. He worked in the attic, sitting in a rickety three-legged chair and ordering about his six clerks, who must have had a tough time coping with his boundless energies and inexhaustible wit. Boswell said the attic looked like a counting house. The chief legacy of the dictionary to modern lexicographers is its scrupulous references to literary texts.

But it is also full of jokey definitions that poke fun at anyone and everyone, including Johnson himself; a lexicographer is defined as 'a writer of dictionaries, a harmless drudge'. The dictionary, published in 1755, made Johnson's reputation as both a serious academic and a great wit. The house is of interest more for its atmosphere than its contents.

Freud's House, 20 Maresfield Gardens, NW3, ✆ (020) 7435 2002, ⊖ *Finchley Road; bus 46. Open Wed–Sun 12–5; adm.* This is the house where Freud set up his last home after fleeing the Nazis in Vienna in 1938. Six rooms have been left untouched since the founder of psychoanalysis died of throat cancer on the eve of the Second World War. Of greatest interest is the couch where his patients lay during sessions—if, that is, it is not on loan to another museum. You can also see Freud's collections of furniture and artefacts, including some extraordinary phalluses, and watch the home movies he made of his family and dog at home in Vienna in the increasingly dark days of the 1930s.

Hogarth's House, Hogarth Lane, Chiswick, W4, ✆ (020) 8994 6757, ⊖ *Turnham Green. Open Tues–Fri 1–5, Sat 1–6; winter closed 1hr earlier; closed Jan; adm.* This was where the great 18th-century painter and satirist, in the last 15 years of his life, came to get away from it all—hard to believe, given the current traffic level. It is no more than a curiosity, since the house itself is unspectacular and contains only prints of his most famous works, not the originals which are elsewhere.

Keats's House, Wentworth House, Keats Grove, NW3, ✆ (020) 7435 2062, ⊖ *Hampstead. Open April–Oct Mon–Fri 10–1 and 2–6, Sat 10–1 and 2–5 and Sun 2–5, and Nov–Mar Mon–Fri 1–5, Sat 10–1 and 2–5, and Sun 2–5; free. See* p.103.

Religion

Freemason's Hall, Great Queen St, WC2, ✆ (020) 7831 9811, ⊖ *Covent Garden. Open Mon–Fri 10–5 and Sat 1pm, guided tour only; free.* An intriguing PR exercise stressing Freemasonry's principles of truth and brotherly love. Lots of regalia but no elucidation of those handshakes. 'It is not a secret society,' explains a leaflet. Right, and the Pope's not Catholic.

Wesley's House, Wesley Chapel, 49 City Rd, EC1, ✆ (020) 7253 2262, ⊖ *Moorgate. Open Mon–Sat 10–4, Sun 12–2; adm.* John Wesley's house, and the nonconformist chapel he built next door in 1778, with columns made from the masts of ships donated by George III. Lots of missionary paraphernalia, and the world's first electric chair (invented by Wesley).

Jewish Museum, 129–32 Albert Street, NW1, ✆ (020) 7284 1997, ⊖ *Camden Town. Open Sun–Thurs 10–4; adm. See* p.99.

One-offs

BBC Experience, Broadcasting House, Portland Place, W1, ✆ (0870) 603 0304, ⊖ *Oxford Circus*. *Open daily 10–4.30, Mon 11–4.30; tour takes 2hrs; adm on the pricey side.* This rather grim 1930s building is the nerve centre of the British Broadcasting Corporation, better known by its initials, BBC. The Beeb (or Auntie as it is sometimes referred to) used to run its main radio operations here. There never used to be much for the visitor to see around here, but now the broadcasting grandees have thought fit to provide something called 'The BBC Experience'. This includes a guided tour of the building, a look at a collection of Marconi's earliest radio equipment, a shop and café, and various inevitable interactive displays in which visitors have the opportunity to direct a soap opera, read the weather forecast or 'be' a sports commentator.

Bethnal Green Museum of Childhood, Cambridge Heath Road, E2, ✆ (020) 8980 2415, ⊖ *Bethnal Green. Open Mon–Thurs, Sat 10–5.50 and Sun 2.30–5.50; free.* This extension of the Victoria and Albert Museum is housed in the building once known as the Brompton Boilers where the decorative arts collections were kept during the 1850s (you'll notice the very Victorian mosaic frieze on the outside depicting Agriculture, Art and Science). Inside are some extraordinarily intricate children's toys, notably dolls' houses, train sets, puppet theatres and board games; a shame, however, that they are displayed in such gloomy cabinets. (Cambridge Heath Road, incidentally, leads up to the East End extension of the Grand Union Canal and the western end of Victoria Park, the biggest piece of greenery in east London).

Bramah Tea and Coffee Museum, Maguire St, Butler's Wharf, SE1, ✆ (020) 7378 0222, ⊖ *Tower Hill, London Bridge; bus 47, 188, P11. Open daily 10–6; adm cheap.* Coffee arrived in London in the 1640s and quickly became popular among the traders and brokers of the City. 'It is a very good help to digestion, quickens the spirit and is good against sore eyes,' remarked one contemporary quaffer. Coffee was very much a man's drink; indeed for a long time women were not admitted to coffee houses at all. They were expected to drink tea, which arrived in Europe at roughly the same time. This full fresh-flavoured museum was set up by a commodity broker, Edward Bramah, with his amazing collection of over 1,000 tea and coffee pots which tell the intricate history of the commodities, from the 17th and 18th century coffeehouses which spawned the Stock Exchange and Lloyds Insurance, to that most elegiac of 20th-century inventions, the mass-produced tea bag. A more authentic brew is made in the two cafés, and the shop sells a choice selection of leaf-teas.

Dennis Severs' House at **18 Folgate Street**, E1, ✆ (020) 7247 4013 for times and booking, ⊖ *Liverpool Street. Open first Sun in the month 2–5pm; adm; and also for evening performances three times a week with a special Silent Night on the first Monday of each month when the house is lit by candles and no one speaks, so that a 'silent poetry' is created; adm exp.* This is not so much a house as a theatre, a place which offers a glimpse back into the past not by showing off well-preserved artefacts and objects in the way that National Trust homes do, but by forcing you to feel your way into the atmosphere of bygone eras, from neoclassical to romantic. Inside, each room is a living tableau, a lovingly constructed still-life time machine, where sheets are rumpled, candle wax is congealed on the floor and last week's vegetables sit half-eaten on the tables. The master of ceremonies is Dennis Severs himself, a mildly eccentric ex-pat American lawyer who dropped out of the southern Californian rat race in the late 1970s and bought this house as a way of getting back in touch with himself and with the past. In his startlingly original evening performances (for which you should book several weeks in advance since only eight people can attend at a time), Mr Severs evokes the lives of five generations of occupants of the house, the fictional Jervis family, through a mixture of sound effects, light, still-life décor and sheer acting bravado. Emma Thompson came here to prepare for *Sense and Sensibility*. The effect is almost that of a seance. Mr Severs calls this 'perceiving the space between the eye and what you see'. Or, to quote his motto, *aut visum aut non*—you either see it or you don't.

Fan Museum, 12 Croom's Hill, SE10, ☏ (020) 8858 8789, ⇌ Greenwich. DLR Island Gdns. By river to Greenwich Pier; bus 188. Open Tues–Sat 11–4.30 and Sun 12–4.30; adm. Delightful collection of fans from the 17th century to the present.

London Aquarium, County Hall, Waterloo, SE1, ☏ (020) 7967 8000, ⊖ Waterloo, Westminster. Open daily 10–5. See p.28.

Madame Tussaud's, Marylebone Rd, NW1, ☏ (020) 7935 6861, ⊖ Baker Street. Open May–Sept daily 9–5.30, with slightly later opening the rest of the year; adm exp. There is no escaping the horrendous queues, which are little shorter in the winter. Nearly three million people put themselves through the crush each year, although it is hard to see why—the only thing you can say in the end about a waxwork is whether it is lifelike or not—and most of the film stars, politicians and famous villains here fare pretty indifferently. Back in the 19th century, of course, waxworks made more sense as they provided the only opportunity for ordinary people to catch a glimpse of the rich and famous, albeit in effigy. Marie Tussaud was a Swiss model-maker who trained with her uncle by making death masks of the victims of the revolutionary Terror in France. Her hallmarks were her attention to detail, particularly in the costumes, and her efforts to keep the exhibition bang up to date with the latest celebrities and figures in the news. One of Madame Tussaud's most inspired ideas, the **Chamber of Horrors**, survives to this day. The final section of Madame Tussaud's is called the **Spirit of London**, a funfair-type ride in a modified black cab featuring illustrations of London's history from the Great Fire to the swinging 1960s.

Museum of Garden History, St Mary's, Lambeth Palace Rd, SE1, ☏ (020) 7261 1891, ⊖ Westminster; bus 77, 159, 170, 507. Open Mon–Fri 10.30–4; free (donations welcome). The plants on display were first gathered by Charles I's gardener John Tradescant, who is buried in the churchwith his son. You can also see gardening tools dating back to the ancient world. The church, largely rebuilt in 1852 but still based on its 14th-century precedent, is curious for other reasons too. It contains the only full-immersion font in London. It is the last resting place of Captain Bligh, of *Mutiny on the Bounty* fame. And in the south chapel is a stained-glass window commemorating a medieval pedlar who grew rich when his dog unearthed great treasure while scratching around one day on a piece of waste land in the area. The pedlar left an acre of land to the parish when he died, but asked for the window for him and his dog in return.

Sherlock Holmes Museum, 221b Baker St, NW1, ☏ (020) 7935 8866, ⊖ Baker Street. Open daily 9.30–6; adm. The museum *says* its address is 221b Baker St, and certainly looks convincing enough to be the supersleuth's consulting rooms. Unfortunately, though, it is really No.239; the building encompassing No.221b (which never actually existed as a self-contained address) is the glass-and-concrete headquarters of the Abbey National Building Society. The museum is a lot of fun, if you enter into its spirit of artifice. You are greeted at the door by either a housekeeper or a policeman. Most entertaining of all is the folder containing Sherlock Holmes's fan mail.

Theatre Museum, Tavistock St, Covent Garden, WC2, ☏ (020) 7836 2330/7836 7891, ⊖ Covent Garden. Open Tues–Sun 11–7; phone to check time of tours; adm. This museum is confusingly laid out; by far the best way to see it is to join one of the very informative guided tours led by actors three times a day and free with the price of admission. A vast number of exhibits cover the history of the English stage from the Elizabethan public playhouses to the rise of the National Theatre, illustrated by period costumes and plenty of model theatres. Unfortunately all this wonderful stuff—from Edmund Kean's death mask to the psychedelic hand-printed costumes used by the Diaghilev Ballets Russes to premiere 'The Rite of Spring' in Paris in 1913—is displayed behind the smudged glass of dully lit fish tanks. Rather more engaging fun is to be had by submitting yourself to the free make-up displays; you may have noticed some eccentric-looking people with werewolf faces or Mr Hyde expressions on your way in.

Vinopolis, 1 Bank End, Clink Street, SE1, ☏ (020) 7940 8300, ⊖ Cannon St, Borough; bus 40, 133, 149. Open daily 10–5.30; adm. See p.86.

Children's Activities	142
Child-minding Services	143
Sport	143
Taking Part	143
Spectator Sports	144

London: Children and Sports

Children's Activities

Children have traditionally come somewhere beneath dogs and horses on the scale of human affection in England. The prevailing view is that children should be neither seen nor heard in public. If some pubs, bars and restaurants now admit children, and even provide high chairs and nappy-changing facilities, it is more out of a sense of obligation than any real enthusiasm. Nevertheless, there is plenty to keep children occupied and amused in London. Aside from the ideas listed below, you can find out more through **Kidsline** on ✆ (020) 7222 8070 (*open during school summer holidays 8am–4pm*), or the London Tourist Board's **what's on for children line** on ✆ 0839 123 404 (*recorded information*).

Among the most popular and absorbing sights for children are: the **Science Museum** (where they can even spend the night), the Natural History Museum, the Commonwealth Institute and the three museums devoted to the younger generation: Pollock's Toy Museum in Fitzrovia, the Bethnal Green Museum of Childhood, the Cabaret Mechanical Theatre in Covent Garden, and the London Toy and Model Museum in Bayswater. For gore and ghoulishness, if you want to avoid the queues at such crowd-pullers as the London Dungeon and Madame Tussaud's, try instead the Clink Exhibition in Southwark or the **Tower of London**.

To keep the kids entertained there are many: **funfairs** in the parks during the summer (*see Time Out*); Punch and Judy shows at Covent Garden; children's films at the National Film Theatre, the Barbican and the ICA. At Christmas time there are **pantomimes** galore all over London. During the rest of the year there are children's shows at the following theatres:

Little Angel Theatre, 14 Dagmar Passage, Islington, N1, ✆ (020) 7226 1787. ⊖ *Highbury & Islington/Angel*. A delightful puppet theatre. *Closed Aug.*

Polka Theatre for Children, 240 The Broadway, Wimbledon, SW19, ✆ (020) 8543 0363. ⊖ *Wimbledon*. A complex for the under-13s including the main theatre, a playground, two shops with cheap toys and an adventure room for under-5s. *Closed Sept.*

Unicorn Theatre for Children, 6 Great Newport St, Covent Garden, WC2, ✆ (020) 7836 3334. ⊖ *Leicester Square*. London's oldest children's theatre.

Rainforest Café, 20 Shaftesbury Avenue, W1, ✆ (020) 7434 3111. ⊖ *Piccadilly Circus*. Exciting rainforest eating place which will delight children, and an inspired alternative to the ubiquitous McDonald's. (Not only for children.) Top floor is a retail area.

No lack of outlets to shop *for* kids: for most emergency toy or clothing needs you should be satisfied by the many branches of the Early Learning Centre, Mothercare, Toys R Us, Next, Baby Gap or Gap for Kids. As for shopping *with* kids, here are a few key destinations:

Borders, 203 Oxford St, W1, ✆ 0171 292 1600. ⊖ *Oxford Circus*. American bookstore on five floors; excellent children's section with places to sit and read, and storytelling sessions (call for details); nice café on the same floor.

Davenports Magic Shop, Charing Cross Underground Shopping Arcade, WC2, ✆ 0171 836 0408. ⊖ *Charing Cross*. Masks, practical jokes and hardware for magicians.

Disney Store, 140–144 Regent St, W1, ✆ 0171 287 6558. ⊖ *Piccadilly Circus*. Anything Disney you or your kids could possibly desire, and more.

Hamleys, 188 Regent St, W1, ✆ 0171 494 2000. ⊖ *Oxford Circus*. One of the world's great toyshops with loads of puzzles, computer games, teddy bears and gadgets. The escalators alone can keep kids happy for hours. Expensive, though.

London Doll's House Co., 29 The Market, Covent Garden, WC1, ✆ 0171 240 2288. ⊖ *Covent Garden*. Everything for your child's doll at this delightful basement boutique.

Child-minding Services

Childminders, 6 Nottingham St, W1, ✆ (020) 7935 3000. An agency with a network of babysitters, nurses and infant teachers.

Universal Aunts, ✆ (020) 7738 8937. Provides babysitters, entertainers, people to meet children off trains, and guides to take children round London.

Pippa Pop-Ins, 430 Fulham Rd, SW6, ✆ (020) 7385 2458. This award-winning hotel for 2–12 year olds provides a crèche, nursery school and babysitting services.

Sports

London is rich in sports facilities and venues thanks to its extensive parkland and plentiful supply of ponds, reservoirs and lakes. It boasts several first-rate venues, including Wembley for soccer, Twickenham for rugby, Crystal Palace for athletics, Lord's and the Oval for cricket, and the mythical lawns of Wimbledon for tennis. For any sporting query, whether for spectating or taking part, call **Sportsline**, ✆ (020) 7222 8000.

Taking Part

For health fanatics in need of a workout, the **public sports centres** run by all London boroughs usually have good facilities—ask Sportsline for the most convenient one.

There are some superb outdoor venues for **swimming**, notably the Highgate and Hampstead Ponds on Hampstead Heath. The Hampstead Pond, which is mixed-sex, is best reached from East Heath Road. The single-sex Highgate Ponds are accessible from Millfield Lane. Other council-run lidos worth trying are Tooting, Brixton and Parliament Hill (lidos are large unheated open-air pools, usually built in the 1930s).

There are **tennis** courts in virtually every London park—check with Sportsline for details and booking procedure. Battersea Park has some of the cheapest courts, while Holland Park has the trendiest. Most charge a membership fee, but this may entitle you to play at other London venues. Often you have to book in person.

Queens Ice Skating Club, 17 Queensway, W2, ✆ (020) 7229 0172. ⊖ *Queensway*. Lessons, ice discos and more at London's most famous club. Also ten pin bowling.

Regent's Park Boating Lake, ✆ (020) 7486 4759. ⊖ *Baker Street*. Rent a boat during the summer and idle away a few hours on either the large adult or the tiny children's lake between the Inner and the Outer Circle of Regent's Park. Cheap and wonderful.

Ross Nye Stables, 8 Bathurst Mews, Bayswater, W2, ✆ (020) 7262 3791. ⊖ *Lancaster Gate*. For riding in Hyde Park. *Horses on holiday mid-July–early Sept.*

Rowans Ten Pin Bowling, 10 Stroud Green Road, Finsbury Park, N4, ℡ (020) 8800 1950. ⊖ *Finsbury Park*. For a little late-night exercise.

Wimbledon Village Stables, 24a/b High Street, Wimbledon Village, SW19, ℡ (020) 8946 8579. ⊖ *Wimbledon*. Good for beginners, with the whole of Wimbledon Common and Richmond Park in which to roam free.

Spectator Sports

A game surely invented to be incomprehensible to the uninitiated, **cricket** incites great passions in its most ardent fans and sheer tedium in nearly everyone else. It would be foolhardy to attempt an explanation of the rules, which defy description, at least on paper. Atmosphere's the thing, and a visit to Lord's or the Oval usually provides plenty of good drink and conversation as well as an introduction to the world of silly mid-offs, follow-ons, googlies, chinamen, long legs and short legs.

Rougher and more complex than soccer, **rugby** football involves hand as well as foot contact and is played with an ovoid ball. Still an essential part of the summer season, the Wimbledon lawn **tennis** championships take place in the last week of June and the first week of July. The men warm up a couple of weeks' earlier in competition at the smaller Queens Club.

All England Lawn Tennis Club, Church Road, Wimbledon, SW19, ℡ (020) 8944 1066. ⊖ *Southfields*. You'll need to apply nine months in advance for a seat on Centre or Number One Court during the championships—they're allocated by ballot. However, if you turn up early in the competition you'll see plenty of action on the outside courts, and can still enjoy strawberries and cream under the pale English sun.

Crystal Palace Sports Arena, Ledrington Road, SE19, ℡ 0181 778 0131. ⇌ *Crystal Palace*. Venue for national and international athletics events.

Highbury Stadium, Avenell Road, N5, ℡ (020) 7704 4000. ⊖ *Arsenal*. Home to Arsenal (the Gunners), Tottenham's arch-rival.

Lord's Cricket Ground, St John's Wood Road, NW8, ℡ (020) 7289 1611. ⊖ *St John's Wood*. The most famous cricket venue in the world, and home to the original governing body of the sport, the Marylebone Cricket Club (MCC), as well as the local county side, Middlesex.

The Oval, Kennington, SE11, ℡ (020) 7582 7764. ⊖ *Oval*. Home to Surrey, this vast pitch usually hosts the last Test match of the summer.

Queens Club, 14 Palliser Road, W14, 0171 385 3421. ⊖ *Baron's Court*. One-week men's competition just before Wimbledon gives a good idea of who's on form to win the big one. Some tickets available on the day.

Twickenham Stadium, Rugby Road, Twickenham, in southwest London, ℡ (020) 8892 2000. ⇌ *Twickenham*. International rugby fixtures and cup finals.

Wembley Stadium, Stadium Way, northwest London, ℡ (020) 8902 0902. ⇌ *Wembley Stadium*/⊖ *Wembley Park*. Major international soccer fixtures and cup finals. Also venue for pop concerts.

White Hart Lane, 748 High Road, N17, ℡ (020) 8365 5050. ⇌ *White Hart Lane*. Home to Tottenham Hotspur (Spurs), Arsenal's arch-rival.

Restaurants	146
Cafés, Teahouses and Snack Food	157
Pubs	158

London: Food and Drink

Food, Glorious Food

Nice manners, shame about the food: nothing about the English has traditionally left foreigners so aghast as their dining habits. The horror stories are legion: of wobbly, green-tinged custard, of vegetables boiled until they are blue, of white bread so vile you can roll it into little balls and use it as schoolroom ammunition, of rice pudding so sickly and overcooked it makes you gag. No wonder visitors from abroad have often contemplated packing a few home goodies to keep the wolf from the door.

In fact, you can put away your prejudices; London is now one of the great gastronomic centres on the planet. Never in its history has the city been so cosmopolitan, and never has there been such a wide variety of cuisines to sample. Its cutting-edge chefs are treated like superstars as they vie to reproduce, and improve on, the best that world cooking can offer. London boasts the best Indian food outside of India, and the best Chinese food in Europe. There are excellent Caribbean restaurants, Lebanese restaurants, Italian, Greek and Spanish restaurants, Polish, Hungarian and Russian restaurants. Even the British restaurants aren't bad, and some of them are outstanding.

Restaurants

London restaurants tend to take lunch orders between 12.30 and 2pm, and dinner orders between 7 and 10pm, although you'll find cafés and brasseries that stay open all afternoon and accept orders until 11pm or even later. Listed restaurants are open every day for lunch and dinner unless indicated otherwise. Soho and Covent Garden are undoubtedly the most fertile areas, although there are excellent selections in Notting Hill, Fulham, Camden Town, Islington and Hampstead.

The one drawback is money—eating out in London is an expensive pleasure. There are some incredible bargains to be had, but overall you are lucky to get away with much less than £25–35 per head for a decent evening meal, roughly half as much again as you would in Paris, Rome or a number of North American cities. One reason for this is the wine, which can be cripplingly expensive without being especially reliable: watch out. Meal prices should be inclusive of tax (VAT), but an extra cover charge (no more than £2) may be added in swankier places. Look carefully to see if service is included. If not, leave an extra 10–15 per cent of the total, preferably in cash. As for prices, the lists below divide restaurants into the following categories, according to the price of a full meal with wine and service:

∞∞∞∞∞	*luxury*	more than £50
∞∞∞∞	*expensive*	£35–50
∞∞∞	*moderate*	£25–35
∞∞	*inexpensive*	£15–25
∞	*cheap*	under £15

All but the cheapest establishments will take cheques or credit cards. If you are paying with plastic, the total box will inevitably be left for you to fill, in anticipation of a fat tip. Don't feel under any pressure, especially if service is already included.

Soho

- **Alastair Little**, 49 Frith St, W1, ✆ (020) 7734 5183 (*closed Sun and Sat lunchtime*). One of the first and also the best of nouvelle British cuisine restaurants. The simplicity of the ingredients is echoed by the positively bare-essentialist decor. The menu changes according to what's fresh in the market.

- **The Gay Hussar**, 2 Greek St, W1, ✆ (020) 7437 0973 (*closed Sun*). Velvet-upholstered Hungarian restaurant, famous for its wild cherry soup, goulash and dumplings, served on thick red-and-white china. The stylish, intimate setting is much beloved by the old left of British politics. The unchanging menu is calorific and filling.

- **L'Escargot**, 48 Greek St, W1, ✆ (020) 7437 2679 (*closed Sat lunch, all day Sun*). This one-time bulwark of the Soho scene has reopened under new management, serving high quality, classic French food under the gaze of high modern art (Picassos, Mirós, Chagalls). The first-floor dining room is more formal than the magnolia room below, but both serve exquisite dishes in daring sauces. A speciality is *feuilleté* of snails served with bacon.

- **Vasco and Piero's Pavilion**, 15 Poland St, W1, ✆ (020) 7437 8774. Sophisticated, friendly Italian restaurant serving immaculately presented dishes, e.g. grilled breast of guinea-fowl with juniper berries. Cheaper two- or three-course set menus. Truffles from Umbria available in season.

- **Sri Siam**, 16 Old Compton St, W1, ✆ (020) 7434 3544. Modern, minimalist and hip, a combination unusual in a Thai restaurant. The sleek, cream walls, adorned here and there by banana and palm leaf themes, host throngs of diners in the evening, although it can be empty at lunch.

- **Café Fish**, 36–40 Rupert St, SW1, ✆ (020) 7287 8989 (*closed Sat lunch, all day Sun*). Although there is an underlying old French character to this bustling bistro, the accent is fish, obviously. And you can order fish and shellfish in most cooked forms, be it chargrilled, steamed, *meunière* or fried, or sometimes even marinated.

- **The Criterion**, 224 Piccadilly, W1, ✆ (020) 7930 0488. (*Closed Sun lunch.*) A magnificent, Art Deco, gold mosaic interior, opened in 1870 and recently re-launched with Marco Pierre White as chef. The place has seen much drama—suffragettes met here in the 1910s when women were not allowed into pubs. While the service is sometimes impatient and the room crowded, the food is exquisite without being exotic.

- **Fung Shing**, 15 Lisle St, WC2, ✆ (020) 7437 1539. Beautiful, delicate, mainly Cantonese Chinese food, served with style in a bright lemon, blond-wood-panelled dining room; there is also an airy veranda at the back. The menu includes some more traditional Chinese dishes. One of the classic dishes is braised suckling pig.

- **Mezzo**, 100 Wardour St, W1, ✆ (020) 7314 4000. Reputedly one of the biggest, trendiest restaurants in Europe, which opened in 1995 to loud acclaim by the media, partly because of the prestige of the designer and owner, Sir Terence Conran. The basement restaurant is overpriced, and the service is erratic, but the place definitely has style. Prepare for noise. A high standard of cooking: fillet of beef, pesto and *pommes frites*; salmon, pickled eggplant and yoghurt. *Closed upstairs on Sundays.*

- **The Sugar Club**, 21 Warwick St, Soho, W1R, ✆ (020) 7437 7776. One of the hippest places in London. Globally inspired dishes with particularly good contrasting textures and tastes, e.g. grilled scallops with sweet chilli sauce and crème fraîche.

- **Little Italy**, 21 Frith St, W1, ✆ (020) 7734 4737. An offshoot of the famous Bar Italia, which was for many years the only place selling real espresso in London. The restaurant has a comparable authenticity that some of the more fashionable places may lack. Photographs of boxers adorn the walls.

- **Dell'Ugo**, 56 Frith St, W1, ✆ (020) 7734 8300. A big statue sticks out of one of the windows. A three-storey building, each level being a separate, different restaurant. The ground floor hosts a fashion-conscious under-30s crowd. The upper floors are calmer and serve more serious dishes.

∞ **Quo Vadis**, 26–29 Dean St, W1, ✆ (020) 7437 9585. Lime green airy interiors with meticulous table decoration. Positively serene compared with the new, trendy bustling bistros. Features spoof 'Brit Art' by chef-turned-artist Marco Pierre White, inspired in the wake of his recent and highly publicized fall-out by ex-partner Damien Hirst. French food with Mediterranean influences.

∞ **Frith Street Restaurant**, 64 Frith St, W1, ✆ (020) 7734 4545 (*closed Sat and Sun lunch*). Modern Provençal food served in a cool interior of aquamarine walls, wood floors and comfortable leather chairs.

∞ **The Lexington**, 45 Lexington St, W1, ✆ (020) 7434 3401 (*closed Sat lunch, Sun*). Modern European food: 2 course set menu for £10 which includes broad-shouldered dishes like roast pheasant and chorizo or suckling pig with butter bean and morel stew. Warm, purple and faintly psychedelic with modern art. Jazz pianist at night.

∞ **Andrew Edmunds**, 46 Lexington St, W1, ✆ (020) 7437 5708. Simple, beautifully prepared dishes at low prices. Queues at the door, which makes the service understandably frenzied. Old-fashioned frontage, hard benches and restless sawdust effect belie the modern ethos and originality of the cooking. Menus change weekly.

∞ **Randall & Aubin**, 16 Brewer St, W1, ✆ (020) 7287 4447. An old Victorian butcher's shop converted into an oyster and champagne bar, with a rôtisserie; the original tiled interior has been preserved. Specializes in seafood and spit-roasts, also langoustines, crabs, whelks—the ingredients can be made into sandwiches to order.

∞ **The Red Fort**, 77 Dean St, W1, ✆ (020) 7437 2115. Northern Indian restaurant. Excellent Tandoori and Mogul specialities such as quail and a Rajasthani smoked kebab of fresh salmon. Recently refurbished decor has upped the prices. Indian food festivals occasion special menus.

∞ **French House Dining Rooms**, 49 Dean St, W1, ✆ (020) 7437 2477 (*closed Sun*). Dark, worn wooden rooms above a pub of the same name. Atmospheric, 1920s ambience, much frequented by literati. Excellent British food, e.g. smoked eel salad, ox tongue, guinea fowl, confit of duck.

∞ **Kulu Kulu**, 76 Brewer St, W1, ✆ (020) 7734 7316. Sushi is hand-made at this busy Japanese eating spot. A long, narrow conveyor belt runs along the counter and the food is served on colour-coded plates.

∞ **Tokyo Diner**, 2 Newport Place, W1, ✆ (020) 7287 8777 (*open from 12 every day—all year*). Japanese fast food—sushi and Japanese curries. One of the cheapest Japanese eateries in London. Noodles (about £6), *donburi*—rice and various toppings (£4–£6). Ingredients are fresh and crisply cooked. Good service, authentic décor, no tips.

∞ **Soho Spice**, 124–126 Wardour St, W1, ✆ (020) 7434 0808. One of the few Indian restaurants in Soho. Radiant blue, orange and magenta colour scheme makes for a modern Indian look. Genial service; also a bar.

∞ **Poon's**, 27 Lisle St, W1, ✆ (020) 7437 4549. Recently expanded, this has lost some of its chaotic caffness. Famous for high-quality 'wind-dried' meats—especially the duck.

∞ **Jimmy's**, 23 Frith St, W1, ✆ (020) 7437 9521. Moussaka and chips, as eaten by the Rolling Stones, among others, in the 1960s, is a mainstay of this basement Soho institution. Unchanging décor, green lino and cheap prices for standard Greek Cypriot dishes, like *tarama*, *afelia* and the like. Cosy in winter, hot in summer.

∞ **Mildred's**, 58 Greek St, W1, ✆ (020) 7494 1634 (*open till 11*). Eclectic wholesome vegetarian fare from Brazilian casserole to Chinese black bean vegetables and vegetarian sausages. Vegan daily specials. Also seasonal organic produce and even organic wines. Good Sunday brunch.

∞ **Cranks**, 8 Marshall St, W1, ✆ (020) 7437 9431. Popular, pioneering vegetarian restaurant with several branches around London. Warm, apricotty interiors. Good vegetarian food—roasted vegetables and couscous—and tasty salads, quiches, pies. Self-service.

- **Wagamama**, 10A Lexington St, W1, ✆ (020) 7292 0990. Wagamama, now an institution in Bloomsbury, has opened a new branch in Soho. The philosophy of this Japanese noodle bar is 'positive eating, positive living'. Hi-tech, efficient, fast service on long communal tables. Long queues do not diminish the experience.
- **Café España**, 63 Old Compton St, W1, ✆ (020) 7494 1271. Plain, authentic little Spanish restaurant—a far cry from self-conscious, un-Spanish tapas bars that have cropped up all over London. Good generous portions of Galician and Castilian dishes, emphasizing fish.

Covent Garden

- **The Ivy**, 1 West St, WC2, ✆ (020) 7836 4751. The moody oak panels and stained glass dating from the 1920s are offset by vibrant modern paintings. The menu caters for elaborate as well as tamer tastes. Salmon fishcakes on a bed of leaf spinach is a signature dish. Takes orders from 12–3 and 5–12, which ensures a diverse clientèle, but particularly popular amongst the theatre comers and goers as well as the players.
- **Simpsons**, 100 Strand, WC2, ✆ (020) 7836 9112. The ultimate, old-fashioned English restaurant, ideal if you like your roast beef and Yorkshire pudding served by deferential, tail-coated waiters in an aristocratic environment. Once a gentlemen's club and also a chess club, the ethos of which is preserved and refined. Also serves 'The Great British Breakfast' which includes the 'ten deadly sins' of liver, black pudding, sausages and the like.
- **Christophers**, 18 Wellington St, WC2, ✆ (020) 7240 4222. The opulent curved stone staircase in the foyer recalls a 19th-century pleasure dome—reinforced when one realizes that this was once London's first licensed casino (and later a high-class brothel). Up the stairs, in the dining hall, a more restrained elegance pervades. As an American restaurant, the menu emphasizes steaks and grills, but there are also seafood inspirations.
- **Rules**, 35 Maiden Lane, WC2, ✆ (020) 7836 5314 (*open all day*). The oldest restaurant in London (established 1798), with a long history of serving aristocrats as well as actors. Formal and determinedly old-fashioned, panelled in dark wood and decorated with hunting regalia. Specializes in game of the season: even rarities such as snipe, ptarmigan and woodcock. Dress smart.
- **Mon Plaisir**, 21 Monmouth St, WC2, ✆ (020) 7836 7243. Jumbled, old bohemian charm, reminiscent of a convivial Rive Gauche brasserie, and a cluttered yet capacious dining area, thronged with rushing, Gallic waiters. Appetizing French provincial dishes, especially seafood.
- **Bertorelli's**, 44a Floral St, WC2, ✆ (020) 7836 3969 (*closed Sun*). Conveniently located for opera-goers, 'Bert's' serves a broad range of proven Italian favourites, but also a more radical catalogue of Italian dishes, like *maltagliati* served with pumpkin, cream, chorizo, or antipasti of deep-fried mozzarella.
- **Orso**, 27 Wellington St, WC2, ✆ (020) 7240 5269 (*open all day*). High quality Italian fare, served in a graceful, terracotta, Venetian dining room. Mainly Tuscan food, interestingly and daringly interpreted, like pizza with goat's cheese and roasted garlic and oregano, or *puntarelle* with anchovy dressing.
- **Joe Allen**, 13 Exeter St, WC2, ✆ (020) 7836 0651. Started out as an American restaurant, serving hamburgers and steaks, but now embraces modern British and European too. The result is a long menu, lacking character—but there are some delights, particularly if you're into monster puddings. Joe Allen's is traditionally a venue to be seen in and also for star-gazers. Rollicking atmosphere with last orders at 12.45am.
- **Café des Amis du Vin**, 11–14 Hanover Place, WC2, ✆ (020) 7379 3444 (*closed Sun*). A cheap, quiet French brasserie, favoured by theatre goers. Caters for all tastes, from omelettes to stuffed trout. More formal upstairs dining room. A little pedestrian, but solid. Service can be slow.

Calabash, Africa Centre, 38 King St, WC2, ✆ (020) 7836 1976 (*closed Sat lunch, all day Sun*). Dishes from all over Africa are served at this basement restaurant under the Africa Centre. A surprisingly institutional feel pervades the dining room, partly because of the collegey canteen. *Egusi* (stew of beef, melon, shrimps cooked in palm oil) from Nigeria, couscous from the Maghreb, *dioumbre* (okra stew) from Ivory Coast, with lots of fried plantain.

Bloomsbury/Fitzrovia

Nico Central, 35 Gt Portland St, W1, ✆ (020) 7436 8846 (*closed Sat lunch, Sun*). Although this restaurant is no longer run by Nico Ladenis, the standards, as well as the good deals in the set menus, remain. Mostly Provençal-inspired creations. Sometimes smallish portions, but beautifully cooked, with interesting ideas such as boudin blanc with caramelized apple galette, and red snapper with couscous. Dream puddings.

Museum Street Café, 47 Museum St, WC1, ✆ (020) 7405 3211 (*closed Sat, Sun*). Sleek and spartan, emphasizing the '90s predilection for scarce décor. Excellent, unusual items, though standards are reputedly variable. Sample dishes include salad with *confit* of guinea fowl with roasted beets and walnut vinaigrette, and penne with roasted red peppers and basil cream.

Gonbei, 151 King's Cross Rd, WC1, ✆ (020) 7278 0619 (*closed Sun*). One of London's cheaper, but still excellent, Japanese restaurants. Only open in the evening (*6–11*). Delicious set dinners; also à la carte choices. Sushi is particularly recommended, as is noodle soup with tempura.

Elena's L'Etoile, 30 Charlotte St, W1, ✆ (020) 7636 1496 (*closed Sat lunch, all day Sun*). This historic Fitzrovian locale has appropriated Elena Salvoni's name to its title in tribute to her personal contribution to the Etoile. Faded grandeur and old photographs of fêted regulars serve as the backdrop. But the menu is no longer only traditional French fare: some modern touches especially in the Eastern influence of some recipes.

Alfred, 245 Shaftsbury Ave, WC2, ✆ (020) 7240 2566 (*closed Sat lunch, all day Sun*). A modern angle on old British favourites. Stark, no-nonsense décor with duck egg blue and nut brown walls and formica tabletops. This serves to underline the delicacy of the cooking. Straightforward dishes like roast pork combine with imaginative accompaniments.

Mandeer, 8 Bloomsbury Way, W1, ✆ (020) 7242 6202 (*closed Sun*). Appetizing vegetarian food from Gujarat and Punjab, including puffed lotus seeds and tofu curry. The place has been serving vegetarian dishes of this ilk since 1961. There are about five *thalis*—complete meals.

Townhouse Brasserie, 24 Coptic St, WC1, ✆ (020) 7636 2731. A fusion of modern French and international cooking, e.g. seafood tempura in French batter. Somewhat cramped quarters even though there is plenty of space. Fizzing and boozy atmosphere, and huge portions.

Chutneys, 133–5 Drummond St, NW1, ✆ (020) 7388 0604 (*unlicensed*). One of several extraordinarily cheap, vegetarian Indian restaurants along this narrow street just behind Euston Station. Watch out for unexpectedly high service charges.

Wagamama, 4 Streatham St, ✆ (020) 7323 9223. *See* under Soho, p.149.

October Gallery Café, 24 Old Gloucester St, WC1, ✆ (020) 7242 7367. Eclectic inspiration from around the world; busy, cosy and friendly. Two- or three-course meals for highly reasonable prices. A limited choice—but usually a vegetarian option. A courtyard to skulk in in summertime.

Marylebone

Stephen Bull, 5–7 Blandford St, W1, ✆ (020) 7486 9696 (*closed Sat lunch, all day Sun*). An excellent, original voice amongst the multi-faceted strains of modern European cooking. Bull believes strongly in simplicity in cooking, and emphasizes fresh ingredients and unfussy, non-gimmicky presentation. The result is highly sophisticated.

- **Singapore Garden**, 154–6 Gloucester Place, NW1, ✆ (020) 7723 8233. A spacious, light basement venue under Regent's Park Hotel, serving Singaporean food. Sometimes very hot, but successful seafood dishes. The service is very friendly, the environment a touch staid. Try the fried seaweed and squid and the mild fish curry.
- **Sea Shell**, 49–51 Lisson Grove, NW1, ✆ (020) 7723 8703. Arguably the best fish and chips in town. Fresh and crisp. Fine home-made fish cakes and, more's the rarity, home-made tartare sauce. Clean and attractive. Café-style eating as well as takeaway.

Mayfair/St James's

- **Connaught Hotel Grill Room**, Carlos Place, W1, ✆ (020) 7499 7070 (*closed Sat afternoon*). Steaks, grills, as well as unusual French delicacies are a treat in this most exclusive of surroundings. High quality but not wildly adventurous. A fine, apple-green room, chandeliers, banquettes. Serious but friendly waiters with impeccable sensitivity.
- **Le Gavroche**, 43 Upper Brook St, W1, ✆ (020) 7408 0881 (*closed Sat, Sun*). Albert Roux is one of the most revered cooks in Britain, the first this side of the Channel to win three Michelin stars. He has now delegated the cuisine to his son, Michel, but standards are still de luxe. Extraordinary creativity, from the sautéed scallops to the coffee cup desert. It doesn't come cheap.
- **Suntory**, 72–3 St. James's St, SW1, ✆ (020) 7409 0201 (*closed Sun lunch*). One of the best, most expensive Japanese restaurants in town, with a Michelin star and also prices to remind you of the fact. You can eat in the old-fashioned, paper screened dining room— or in a private room. Very delicate sushi.
- **Al Hamra**, 31–33 Shepherd Market, W1, ✆ (020) 7493 1954. Sophisticated if rather overpriced Middle Eastern restaurant in the heart of the cosmopolitan chic of Shepherd Market, where you can sit 'out' in the summer months. Select a meze of different dishes from the 48 delicacies.
- **The Greenhouse**, 27a Hay's Mews, W1, ✆ (020) 7499 3331 (*closed Sat lunch*). The principal idea behind this restaurant was to resurrect stale old English recipes into new categories. Liver and bacon or sponge pudding may sound dull, but they come to life here. Signature dishes include fillet of smoked haddock with Welsh rarebit.
- **The Square**, 6–10 Bruton St, W1, ✆ (020) 7839 8787 (*closed Sat, Sun lunch*). The Square has moved to a new Mayfair address, equally sleek and modern. Constantly changing menu, with strong emphasis on fish. Try the delicious seared tuna with niçoise dressing.
- **Le Caprice**, Arlington House, Arlington St, SW1, ✆ (020) 7629 2239. Fashion victims crowd this modish but imaginative restaurant. Essentially 'modern British' food, but eclectic choice, with lovely starters such as squash risotto.
- **Quaglino's**, 16 Bury St, SW1, ✆ (020) 7930 6767. Modern, designer restaurant in a converted, sunken ballroom, mainly Italian menu. Polished and gleaming, it is another facet of the growing Conran empire. The menu is equally design conscious, although there is a large choice. Good shellfish.
- **Sofra**, 18 Shepherd Market, W1, ✆ (020) 7493 3320. Excellent Turkish restaurant with all the usual meze dishes, a crushed wheat salad and delicious sticky filled pastries. An emphasis on fresh ingredients ensures high quality at reasonable prices.
- **Mulligans'**, 13–14 Cork St, W1, ✆ (020) 7409 1370 (*closed Sat lunch, all day Sun*). Hearty Irish cooking, but a new management has incorporated lighter dishes (such as smoked fish, or blue cashel cheese and artichoke and spinach salad), especially at lunch time. But you can still find beef cooked in Guinness. Wicked puddings.
- **Down Mexico Way**, 25 Swallow St, W1, ✆ (020) 7437 9895 (*open from 12 noon everyday*). London does not excel in Mexican food but this is one of the better addresses in town. Fish with chilli and almond, and lime-cooked chicken provide welcome variations on the usual enchiladas.

∞ **Condotti's**, 4 Mill St, W1, ✆ (020) 7499 1308. A smart pizza parlour with white linen table-cloths and chic waitresses. Otherwise the pizzas are regular and juicy as opposed to thin and crusty. At lunchtime it is full of business clients, but in the evening it jollies up.

Kensington

∞∞∞ **Clarke's**, 124 Kensington Church St, W8, ✆ (020) 7221 9225 (*closed Sat, Sun*). A Californian restaurant to the extent that there is an emphasis on fresh produce. The set menu changes nightly, including salad of roasted pigeon with water cress, blood orange and black truffle dressing, and chargrilled turbot with chilli and roasted garlic mayonnaise. Small, intimate, nearly prissy room, but cooking is precise and professional.

∞ **Phoenicia**, 11–13 Abingdon Rd, W8, ✆ (020) 7937 0120. Swish, carpeted Lebanese restaurant attracting smartly dressed customers. Delicious meze selections—excellent *basturma* (smoked, cured Lebanese beef) and falafel—but portions can be modest. Makes much of pudding too: a variety of fresh cream and pastry dishes are given a dousing in aromatic syrups.

∞ **Wódka**, 12 St. Alban's Grove, W8, ✆ (020) 7937 6513 (*closed Sat, Sun lunch*). This site has been a Polish restaurant since the 1950s—but the current proprietor of this newish venture is intent on modernizing the image of Eastern European food in London. Plain interior with jazz backdrop. A list of 30 different vodkas and *eaux de vie*; also a daily changing set lunch at low prices. The result is both classy and professional.

∞ **Cambio de Tercio**, 163 Old Brompton Rd, SW5, ✆ (020) 7244 8970. Exuberant contemporary Spanish cooking: delicate paella, skate wings, salt cod, octopus. Intensely popular; best to book ahead. Strong references to the bullring in the decorative theme. Some real tapas too to start with— *jamón serrano* with *fino* or *manzanilla*.

∞ **The Gate**, 51 Queen Caroline St, Hammersmith, W6, ✆ (020) 8748 6932 (*closed Sat lunch, all day Sun*). First-rate vegetarian restaurant with mouth-watering fennel mousse, wild mushroom cannelloni and teriyaki aubergine. Sunflower walls and a leafy courtyard make an attractive ambiance.

○ **Polish Air Force Association Club and Restaurant**, 14 Collingham Gardens, SW5, ✆ (020) 7741 4052. Set three-course meal from £5.20. Atmospheric basement club founded after the War, filled with flying memorabilia, catering to local Poles but welcoming visitors. Hearty Polish cooking: *pierogis*, sauerkraut, meatballs: also *golonka* (pig's knuckle), and jam pancakes.

Chelsea and Fulham

∞∞∞ **La Tante Claire**, Wilton Place, Knightsbridge, SW3, ✆ (020) 7823 2003 (*closed Sat, Sun*). Classic French cuisine, with three Michelin stars to its name. Lots of goose, foie gras and duck, as well as other Gascon-inspired compositions.

∞∞∞ **Bibendum**, Michelin House, 81 Fulham Rd, SW3, ✆ (020) 7581 5817. Excelling in ultra-rich French regional food, set in the sumptuously restored art deco Michelin building (ex-headquarters of the tyre manufacturers, designed by an untrained architect in 1905, and restored by Conran in 1987). The oyster bar downstairs, with a shorter fish-oriented menu, is cheaper though less grand.

∞∞∞ **River Café**, Thames Wharf Studios, Rainville Rd, W6, ✆ (020) 7381 8824 (*closed Sun dinner*). Simple, very tasty Italian food in a splendid riverside setting designed by Richard Rogers—and then re-designed by him. Rogers' wife, Ruthie, and her friend Rose Gray, are the chief chefs—and they have written a series of influential cookbooks.

∞∞∞ **Bombay Brasserie**, Courtfield Close, Courtfield Rd, SW7, ✆ (020) 7370 4040. Near Gloucester Rd. Unlike most Indian restaurants in London, this is posh, in sumptuous colonial décor, and gastronomically flawless. Largely north Indian menu, including some unusual tandoori dishes. Beautiful veranda.

- **Canteen**, Unit 4G, Harbour Yard, Chelsea Harbour, SW10, ℡ (020) 7351 7330. Part owned by the actor, Michael Caine, a resident of the harbour. Post-modern setting with playing-card upholstery. Dishes include *velouté* of artichokes, spinach and chestnut ravioli, and peppered duck breast, roast baby vegetables and pineapple *jus*.
- **Ken Lo's Memories of China**, 67–69 Ebury St, SW1, ℡ (020) 7730 7734 (*closed Sun lunch*). Minimalist décor, but maximalist cooking. Ken Lo, one of Britain's best-known Chinese restaurateurs, who died a few years ago, founded this esteemed establishment which offers a stunning gastronomic tour of China to delight your eyes and satisfy every stomach. His daughter, Jenny Lo, has opened a similiarly impressive Chinese eatery, building on her father's inspiration, at Jenny Lo's Tea House, 14 Eccleston St, SW1, ℡ (020) 7259 0399.
- **Del Buongustaio**, 283 Putney Bridge Rd, SW15, ℡ (020) 8780 9361 (*closed Sat lunch*). Tasty Italian regional specialities at very reasonable prices. Emphasis on seasonality: monthly changing menus, knowledgeably researched, e.g. baked goat with prosciutto and roasted vegetables.
- **La Delizia**, 63–65 Chelsea Manor St, Sydney St, SW3, ℡ (020) 7376 5411. Good pizzeria with attractive outdoor seating and elegant indoor rooms. Often very crowded.
- **Montana**, 125 Dawes Rd, SW6, ℡ (020) 7385 9500. Cooking from the American southwest: subtle chilli flavours, and lots of cumin, squash, tortilla and pumpkin. Some highly original combinations such as Navajo rabbit and fig *quesadilla*. Sophisticated blue and purple colour scheme.
- **Chelsea Kitchen**, 98 King's Rd, SW3, ℡ (020) 7589 1330. Continental food and wine for less than £10. Known since the 1960s as a jostling, student joint for knockdown prices.
- **Stockpot**, 6 Basil St, SW3, ℡ (020) 7589 8627. Three-course meals for not much more than a fiver. Strains of school dinner. Hardly makes pretensions at culinary art, but the quality isn't actually bad.

Notting Hill

- **Leiths**, 92 Kensington Park Road, W11, ℡ (020) 7229 4481 (*closed all day Sun, lunch Sat–Mon*). An ultra-neutral environment, verging on the bland. This is doubtless to emphasize that the culinary delights on offer are not to be competed with. Presentation is as expert as the combination of ingredients. Roasted scallops and spiced lemon couscous amount to high art.
- **192**, 192 Kensington Park Rd, W11, ℡ (020) 7229 0482. Once the early stamping ground of embryonic chefs such as Alastair Little. Now a very trendy French brasserie where food plays second fiddle to the posing: models and actors and the like come in their droves. Dishes include sea bass on samphire with *beurre blanc* and chives; duck confit with mash and apple sauce.
- **Alastair Little**, 136A Lancaster Rd, W11, ℡ (020) 7243 2220 (*closed Sun*). New branch of famous Soho establishment (*see above*). Even more minimalist, but food just as marvellous.
- **Pharmacy Bar and Restaurant**, 150 Notting Hill Gate, W11, ℡ (020) 7221 2442. The ultimate in tasteful conceptual art: a restaurant and café/cocktail lounge designed by formaldehyde artist Damien Hirst, with the help of a few consignments of pill-boxes and specimen jars from St Mary's Hospital, Paddington. Waiters are dressed in hospital gowns designed by Prada. A small menu, and a trendy, arty crowd.
- **Dakota**, 127 Ledbury Rd, ℡ (020) 7792 9191 (*closed Sun*). Increasingly popular amongst the great and the good of Notting Hill, this is one of the best in the area. Modern, elegant US cuisine boasting an impressive (delicious corn bread) menu. Impeccable service.
- **The Cow Dining Room**, 89 Westbourne Park Road, W2, ℡ (020) 7221 0021. The relaxed, almost countrified atmosphere at the upstairs rooms above the trendy pub (of the same name) belies the precision cooking. Global inspiration but strong French strain, particularly in the sauces.

∞ **Orsino**, 119 Portland Rd, W11, ✆ (020) 7221 3299. Sibling restaurant to Orso's and thus shares many of the latter's characteristics. Terracotta walls, Venetian blinds and simple but innovative cooking with Tuscan roots, like veal escalopes with sun dried tomatoes, sage and white wine.

∞ **Veronica's**, 3 Hereford Rd, W2, ✆ (020) 7229 5079 (*closed Sat lunch, all day Sun*). A restaurant that has unearthed historical and regional British dishes—spring lamb with crabmeat or calf's liver and beetroot—and even relaunched recipes that date from the 14th century, sometimes adapting them to more modern tastes. Elizabethan puddings.

∞ **First Floor**, 186 Portobello Rd, W11, ✆ (020) 7243 0072. Fantastical—some might say pretentious—upmarket brasserie above a loud drinking place with interesting concoctions, and verging on the weird with coffee-smoked ostrich fillet with mango sushi. The room itself is a haven of calm.

∞ **Kensington Place**, 201 Kensington Church St, W8, ✆ (020) 7727 3184. Sleek, airy, noisy, modern dining room with bold garden frescoes and 'eclectic European' cuisine. The highest quality ingredients; venison, sirloin steak, wild sea trout, sorrel omelette. Full of publishers lunching out with their favoured writers and journalists.

∞ **Malabar**, 27 Uxbridge St, W8, ✆ (020) 7727 8800. Quiet northern Indian restaurant with sumptuous, but unchanging choices. Very popular with Notting Hill regulars. Modern and wooden inside with whitewashed alcoves. Dishes are served on large, shiny stainless-steel plates. Sleek, deferential waiters all dressed in black.

∞ **Galicia**, 323 Portobello Rd, W10, ✆ (020) 8969 3539. Galicia jostles with a rum mixture of authentic 'Gallego' locals and a trendy crowd of 'Gatey Mates' (Notting Hill Gate fashion fiends). But the produce, the waiters and the 'feel' are uncannily real.

∞ **Mega Kalamaras**, 66 Inverness Mews, W2, ✆ (020) 7727 9122. A high-quality, very friendly Greek restaurant. Good seafood and a wide variety of vegetarian dishes as well as the hearty meat standards. Its smaller, cheaper twin Micro Kalamaras is in a basement next door.

∞ **Anonimato**, 12 All Saints Road, W11, ✆ (020) 7243 2808. Imaginative, inventive menu drawing on the unusual and the familiar (ostrich, seafood, ravioli). Blends trendy Italian and Pacific elements in airy, unfrenetic surroundings.

∞ **Mas Café**, 6–8 All Saints Rd, W11, ✆ (020) 7243 0969 (*closed lunch Mon–Fri*). Swinging, bustling, loud, ultra-trendy restaurant. Starts buzzing late. Mediterranean food like baby squid; definite high-quality spicy cooking to boot.

∞ **Khans**, 13–15 Westbourne Grove, W2, ✆ (020) 7727 5420. Hectic, helter skelter Indian restaurant; frantic waiters collide with waiting queues. Noise drowns intimacy, and yet the main dining room preserves its charm—painted clouds waft all about you and palm trees act as columns. Delicious food.

∞ **Osteria Basilico**, 29 Kensington Park Rd, W11, ✆ (020) 7727 9372. Intensely popular, hence intensely noisy restaurant with warm ochre walls. New wave Italian dishes that are now becoming the norm, like spaghetti with fresh lobster and tomato, and linguini with spiced salami, parmesan, tomato and basil. Wooden kitchen tables and chairs, and echoey floors. Brazen staff.

∞ **Palio**, 175 Westbourne Grove, W11, ✆ (020) 7221 6624. Cool yellow and black décor with big round staircase winding through to the first floor; jazz wafts through the rooms; dark and intimate and yet noisy. Italian food in bold combinations.

∞ **Geales**, 2 Farmer St, W8, ✆ (020) 7727 7528 (*closed Mon*). Superior fish and chips (deep-fried in beef dripping for a touch of class). Very busy.

∞ **Standard Indian Restaurant**, 23–4 Westbourne Grove, W11, ✆ (020) 7229 0600. First-rate tandoori restaurant with excellent pickles and friendly service. Unassuming name and room belie the high quality of the food.

- **Brasserie du Marché aux Puces**, 349 Portobello Rd, W10, ✆ (020) 8968 5828 (*open all day*). Inventive, café-style restaurant (the name means flea-market brasserie, as it's near Portobello market). Serves eclectic menu including an extraordinary haggis in filo pastry with quince purée. Old-fashioned but popular.
- **Casa Santana**, 44 Golborne Rd, W10, ✆ (020) 8968 8764. Neighbourhood Portuguese restaurant (Madeiran to be precise)—meat stews and smoked cod—with bags of character and good food. Triumphant desserts and Madeiran beers.
- **Mandola**, 139–141 Westbourne Grove, W11, ✆ (020) 7229 4734 (*unlicensed*). Delightful Sudanese restaurant which has had to expand to cope with demand. Simple wooden décor with a few African exotica. Strong Arabic overtones to the dishes: *filfilia* (mixed vegetable stew), *addas* (lentil stew dressed with caramelised garlic.
- **Satay House**, 13 Sale Place, W2, ✆ (020) 7723 6763 (*closed Mon*). Small, intimate shop front serving delicious Malaysian food—most of the customers appear to be Malaysian which suggests authenticity. Strong flavours and a broad range of delicious recipes, chargrilled, baked and marinated. Karaoke on a Saturday night in the basement is popular amongst Malaysians too. Photographs of Malay pop stars adorn the walls downstairs.
- **Rôtisserie Jules**, 133A Notting Hill Gate, W11, ✆ (020) 7221 3331 (*closed Sat lunch, all day Sun*). A very welcome new venture in cheap but good restaurants. Good free-range chicken and other meats, with huge portions. Three courses for a very modest bill. Two other branches in Bute St, SW7, and 338 King's Rd, SW3.
- **Calzone**, 2A Kensington Park Rd, W11, ✆ (020) 7243 2003 (*open all day from 10am*). Wide thin-crust pizzas. The antidote to Pizza Express (whose pizzas are juicier)—particularly if you dislike chain restaurants. Calzone is situated in an interesting, curved glass-fronted room overlooking the juncture of four roads.
- **Manzara**, 24 Pembridge Rd, W11, ✆ (020) 7727 3062 (*open all day*). Good, cheap Turkish restaurant with a wide selection of meze dishes. Sometimes sloppily cooked—as in oily or overdone—but good value and some definitely tasty, fresh choices.

Camden

- **Café Delancey**, 3 Delancey St, NW1, ✆ (020) 7387 1985 (*open all day*). Charming, discreet French restaurant with robust, attractively presented dishes. Caters for all types. Brasserie food: venison but also snacks and soups.
- **Lemonia**, 89 Regent's Park Rd, Primrose Hill, NW1, ✆ (020) 7586 7454 (*closed Sat lunch and Sun eve*). Popular Greek Cypriot restaurant with a delightful conservatory for simulated *al fresco* dining in the summer. Very high standard Greek food, especially fish, although a particularly good *spanako pita* with fresh mint.
- **Vegetarian Cottage**, 91 Haverstock Hill, NW3, ✆ (020) 7586 1257 (*evenings only, closed Tues*). Excellent vegetarian Chinese restaurant, with inventive dishes including 'duckling' made entirely of soya, and water chestnut pudding. Essentially seeks to provide Buddhist vegetarian dishes—sometimes variable, but wonderful when good.
- **Camacheira**, 43 Pratt St, Camden, NW1, ✆ (020) 7485 7266. Portuguese cuisine, with a strong emphasis on meaty dishes, especially lamb, chicken and veal. Main courses start at £6.45.
- **Cheng Du**, 9 Parkway, Camden, NW1, ✆ (020) 7485 8058. Spicy Chinese Szechuan cooking in the heart of Camden. Often mixes Szechuan with more modern Chinese cooking. Attentive service.

Hampstead

- **Café des Arts**, 82 Hampstead High St, NW3, ✆ (020) 7435 3608. Classy French cooking and a beautiful 17th-century building make this one of the most appealing restaurants in north London. An open fire and wooden panelling impart warmth.

∞ **Byron**, 3A Downshire Hill, NW1, ✆ (020) 7435 3544. Elegant English restaurant with good fishcakes and trimmings and excellent traditional Sunday lunches. Romantic Georgian townhouse setting, and long swirling taffeta curtains give a stagey feel. Cheap lunches in the week.

Islington

∞ **Granita**, 127 Upper St, N1, ✆ (020) 7226 3222 (*closed Mon and Tues lunchtime*). Eclectic Islington restaurant, with imaginative polenta, fish and meat dishes. Tony Blair is reputed to have dined here with Gordon Brown when they decided who should go for the leadership of the Labour Party in 1994.

∞ **Anna's Place**, 90 Mildmay Park, N1, ✆ (020) 7249 9379 (*closed Sat eve, all day Sun*). A real oddity: a Swedish restaurant, and one that has made a mark on the local community. Lots of marinated fish and meat, plus home-made bread. Book in advance, especially for the terrace tables which are especially delectable in summer and heated in winter. Cottagey interior.

∞ **Upper St Fish Shop**, 324 Upper St, N1, ✆ (020) 7359 1401 (*closed Sun*). Superior chippie with the option of grilled or poached fish as well as the traditional deep-fried. Plain wood panelled walls decorated with pictures of the mop-like former house dog, Hugo. House special is halibut.

Smithfield/East End

∞ **Quality Chop House**, 94 Farringdon Rd, EC1, ✆ (020) 7837 5093 (*closed Sat lunch*). Superior English specialities like fishcakes, game pie and roast lamb, though a modern Mediterranean influence has crept on to the menu. All served in the highly atmospheric rooms of a former 19th-century working-class men's club.

∞ **Stephen Bull**, Smithfields, 71 St. John St, EC1, ✆ (020) 7490 1750 (*closed Sat lunch*) Innovative Mediterranean cooking, especially good fish and seafood. Strong Spanish influence, as well as Latin American *ceviches*.

∞ **St John**, 26 St. John St, EC1, ✆ (020) 7251 0848 (*closed Sat lunch, all day Sun*). A converted smokehouse, still with an industrial feel to it. Hearty, meaty, ingenious British cooking with a difference: every conceivable part of the animal (trotters, oxheart, bone barrow) is presented in interesting dishes. No fussiness, crisp vegetables.

∞ **Alba**, 107 Whitecross St, EC1, ✆ (020) 7588 1798 (*closed Sat, Sun*). Quietly excellent Italian restaurant, specializing in polenta, risotto and other northern or Piedmontese dishes. Pink and minimalist inside.

∞ **The Peasant**, 240 St John St, EC1, ✆ (020) 7336 7726. A gaudy pub converted into an interesting restaurant—the aim being to make country food sophisticated, with delicious results. Upstairs you move from purple and blue Victoriana (the pub décor) to a white, pristine, wooden room. The food has Italian leanings.

∞ **F. Cooke**, 9 Broadway Market, E8, ✆ (020) 7254 6458 (*open all day, closed Sun*). An authentic East End pie and mash shop that goes back nearly 100 years. The present owner, Bob Cooke, is grandson of the first.

∞ **Nazrul**, 130 Brick Lane, E1, ✆ (020) 7247 2505 (*open late*). One of a number of incredibly cheap, unlicensed Bengali Indian restaurants on and around Brick Lane. Getting a little too well-known for its own good, but still outstanding value.

South of the River

∞∞∞ **Le Pont de la Tour**, Butlers Wharf, 36d Shad Thames, SE1, ✆ (020) 7403 8403 (*closed Sat lunch*). The flagship of Terence Conran's little restaurant empire at Butlers Wharf, with high-class French food and views of the river, Tower Bridge and the City. Everything, even the bread, is homemade. Chic but relaxed.

∞ **RSJ**, 13a Coin St, SE1, ✆ (020) 7928 4554 (*closed Sat lunch, all day Sun*). Flamboyant, innovative French cooking, with a certain amount of global influence from Thailand and elsewhere. Extremely popular. Delightful upper rooms.

∞ **Blueprint Café**, Design Museum, Butlers Wharf, Shad Thames, SE1, ℡ (020) 7378 7031 (*closed Sun eve*). French and Italian food at the Pont de la Tour's less expensive sister establishment. Recently refurbished to include a new conservatory to emphasize the terrific views over the river and Tower Bridge, as well as Canary Wharf.

∞ **Buchan's**, 62–4 Battersea Bridge Rd, SW11, ℡ (020) 7228 0888. Just over Battersea Bridge, a popular wine bar and restaurant with a Scottish slant. The seasonal menu ranges from steaks, pheasant and wild boar to seafood, soufflés and salads.

∞ **Ransome's Dock**, 35 Parkgate Rd, Battersea, SW11, ℡ (020) 7223 1611. With its canal-side view, this periwinkle-blue converted warehouse provides an inventive modern-English menu with seasonal dishes. Good-value lunch and monthly changing menu. Reliable good cooking. Relaxed.

∞ **Riva**, 169 Church Rd, Barnes, SW13, ℡ (020) 8748 0434. It is worth making the journey to this foodie shrine, where the variations on Italian recipes are of a high standard: San Daniele ham and pears, bresaola with goat's cheese.

∞ **The Fire Station**, 150 Waterloo Rd, SE1, ℡ (020) 7620 2226. This former fire station has had its basic features preserved and been converted into an extremely fashionable restaurant, just opposite the Old Vic theatre. Serves excellent warm salads and Mediterranean dishes. Service a bit slow, especially in the afternoon.

Cafés, Teahouses and Snack Foods

Ever since the rise of the City coffee house in the 17th century, London has been addicted to the relaxed charm of café culture. These days it seems to be labouring under one of its periodic illusions that Britain enjoys a Mediterranean climate: pavement cafés, along with al fresco dining, are all the rage. You will soon discover the new vogue for coffee, whether at one of the city's many Italian-style espresso bars or at the even newer chains offering much the same thing Pacific Northwest style: skinny wet caps and the rest, sweetened with a flavoured syrup if you so desire. Back indoors, you will still find a cosy kind of establishment geared towards the English ritual of afternoon tea and cakes. Tea, being the quintessential English drink, tends to be delicious; you'll be given a bewildering choice of varieties.

Soho and Covent Garden

Bar Italia, 22 Frith St, W1 (*open Mon–Thurs 7am–5pm; 24 hrs Fri–Sun*). The café with the best coffee in town and it knows it. The mirrored bar, complete with TV showing Italian soccer games, could have come straight from Milan or Bologna. The seating is a bit cramped, but at least there are tables on the pavement. Better to stand.

Pâtisserie Valerie, 44 Old Compton St, W1 (*open Mon–Sat 8–8; Sat 8–7, Sun 10–6*). Excellent French cakes and coffee.

Bunjie's Coffee House, 27 Litchfield St, WC2 (*open 12pm–11pm, exc Sun*). Eccentric beatnik café, named after the founder's cousin's hamster. Vegetarian food and good coffee.

Maison Bertaux, 28 Greek St, W1 (*open Mon–Sat 9am–8pm; Sun 9–1, 3–8*). Mouthwatering pastries in a slightly cramped upstairs tea-room which is always crowded.

Java Java, 26 Rupert St, W1 (*open Mon–Thurs 9.30am–10pm; Fri–Sat 10.30am–11pm; Sun 1pm–9pm*). Old French haunt frequented by international youth reading free magazines. Good coffee, unusual cakes.

Freuds, 198 Shaftesbury Ave, W1. Trendy basement bar with young, studenty atmosphere and intriguing menu design.

Beatroot, 92 Berwick St, W1 (*open 9–7*). Cheerful, down-to-earth vegetarian eat-in/take-away café where you choose your size of food box and have it filled with any selection of hot dishes and salads from the food bar. Great puddings too.

Mayfair, Kensington, Chelsea

The Ritz, Piccadilly, W1, ℗ (020) 7493 8181. Tea sittings at 3pm and 4.30pm daily. The fanciest, most indulgent tea in town, served in the sumptuous Edwardian Palm Court. Worth splashing out, but you'll definitely need to book.

Browns Hotel, Dover St or Albermarle St, W1. Tea served 3–6pm daily. Very traditional English hotel serving tea to all-comers, as long as you dress to fit the part. A snip cheaper than the Ritz.

Harry's, 19 Kingly St, W1 (*open all night*). London's only all-night diner, with hearty fry-ups and reasonable coffee, featuring an eccentric cast of weirdos and insomniacs. During the day and early evening it serves Thai food. There's often a queue.

Pâtisserie Valerie, 215 Brompton Rd, SW3. Branch of the Soho French pâtisserie.

Muffin Man, 12 Wright's Lane, W8. Quaint all-day café just off Kensington High St. A variety of set teas include, as you would expect, homemade muffins galore.

Stravinsky's Russian Tea House, 6 Fulham High St, SW6. Enormous selection of teas, plus eastern European pastries, at very reasonable prices.

Notting Hill and Around

Julie's, 137 Portland Road, W11. Multi-levelled and multi-purpose establishment with eccentric décor that is part café, part wine bar and part restaurant. The place is at its best for afternoon tea when it is neither too expensive nor pretentious.

Grove Café, corner of Portobello Rd and Westbourne Park Rd, W11. First floor café with a terrace overlooking the market. Good coffee and newspapers to browse in the morning or afternoon.

The City and East End

Brick Lane Beigel Bake, 159 Brick Lane, E1. Round-the-clock bagels. Always crowded, even at three in the morning.

Whitechapel Café, 80 Whitechapel High St, E1. Wholefood café inside the Whitechapel Art Gallery.

Café Rongwrong, 8 Hoxton Square, N1. Beatnik café in one of London's trendiest east London squares. An old warehouse, full of graphic designers and video artists. Atmospheric.

North London

Louis Pâtisserie, 32 Heath St, Hampstead, NW3. Famous Hungarian tea-room which has been a haunt of middle-European emigrés for decades. Wonderful cheesecake and cream cakes brought on a tray for you to choose from.

Everyman Café, Holly Bush Vale, Hampstead, NW3. Atmospheric basement café beneath north London's best established rep cinema.

The Coffee Cup, 74 Hampstead High St, NW3. Dazzling menu including delicious raisin toast. Good for watching the beautiful people walk by.

Carmelli's, 128 Golders Green Rd, NW11. The best bagels in London, in the heart of Jewish Golders Green, though you can't eat them on the premises.

South of the River

Annabel's Pâtisserie, 33 High St, Wimbledon, SW19. Old-fashioned tea-room-cum-brasserie in the genteel atmosphere of Wimbledon.

Kew Greenhouse, 1 Station Parade, Kew. Cakes and pastries near Kew Gardens.

Pubs

The London pub—gaudily decorated with gleaming brass, ornate mirrors and stained glass—is still an essentially Victorian establishment, at least to look at. Even recently built pubs eschew modern décor in favour of mock-Tudor beams, leaded windows and reproduction hunting prints. Licensing hours, although now much extended, are still rigorously enforced; the landlord usually rings a bell when it is time to drink up, like a fussy schoolmaster. Gone, however, are the days when the pubs closed just when you were feeling thirsty; you can now drink without interruption between 11am and 11pm every day except Sunday, when there is still a break from 3–7pm. Many pubs in outer London still close every afternoon, however.

Beer is still the drink of choice. British beer is admittedly an acquired taste—stronger, darker and flatter than lager and served luke-warm rather than stone cold—but easy to get hooked on in time. Unfortunately, London pubs are being swamped, like everywhere else, with generic multinational lagers—Carlsberg, Heineken, Budweiser and the rest. This is far from good news for traditional local breweries, who are fighting an energetic rearguard campaign with the help of CAMRA, the Campaign for Real Ale. CAMRA's influence has been greater in country pubs and the cities of northern England than it has in London, where wine and American-style cocktails are more popular than in the rest of the country; in the capital you will nevertheless find decent bitters like Fullers London Pride and Youngs, and creamy, full-bodied ales like Theakston's, Abbot and Ruddles.

The following list is necessarily short, since few London pubs really shine above the rest. Most of them make the list because of their location—overlooking the river, maybe, or in a quiet row of Georgian houses—or because of a particular historical association. You'll notice their eccentric names, which date from a time when most drinkers were illiterate and recognized pubs only by their signs. Hence the preponderance of coats of arms (King's Arms, Queen's Arms, Freemasons' Arms etc) and highly pictorial appellations (Wheatsheaf, Dog and Duck, Nag's Head, Slug and Lettuce, etc). One thing to look out for is the name of the brewer that owns the pub. If the sign says 'Free House', that means the pub is independent and generally has a better range of beers. Quite a few London pubs are venues for theatre or concerts; where the entertainment is the main attraction, you will find them in the 'Entertainment' chapter rather than here.

Soho, Covent Garden, Fitzrovia

Lamb and Flag, 33 Rose St, WC2. One of few wooden-framed buildings left in central London, dating back to the 17th century, with low ceilings and a lively atmosphere. The pub was for a long time nicknamed the Bucket of Blood because it staged bare-knuckled fights. Now you just have to knuckle your way past the crowds at the bar.

Dog and Duck, 8 Bateman St, W1. Soho's smallest pub. Customers spill out on to the pavement in the summer, and huddle round the log fire in the winter.

The French House, 49 Dean St, W1. Meeting-place for De Gaulle's Free French during the Second World War; now adorned with pictures of famous Frenchmen.

The Sun, 63 Lamb's Conduit St, W1. A beer-lover's paradise: 15 real ales and the chance to tour the cellar with the landlord.

Fitzroy Tavern, 16 Charlotte St, W1. Dylan Thomas's main drinking haunt; see the literary mementoes on the walls downstairs.

Holborn and Fleet Street

Cittie of York, 22 High Holborn, WC1. The longest bar in London. Cosy, separate booths, ideal for winter lunchtimes.

Ye Olde Cheshire Cheese, Wine Office Court, 15 Fleet St, EC4. Dr Johnson's old haunt, with atmospheric beams but disappointing food.

The Eagle, 159 Farringdon Rd, EC1. New wave pub with less emphasis on drinking and more on food, good atmosphere and general hanging out.

East End

Ten Bells, 84 Commercial St, E1. The original Jack the Ripper pub, with oodles of memorabilia. Marred by the tourist coaches who drop in during the evening but friendly enough at lunchtime.

The Ship and Blue Ball, 13 Boundary St, E2. First-rate organic beer from the independent Pitfield brewery. Try the brand called Dark Star.

Town of Ramsgate, 62 Wapping High St, E1. The pub where the merciless 17th-century Judge Jeffreys finally got his come-uppance. Friendly East

End atmosphere, with a riverside garden and view of the post where smugglers and pirates used to be condemned to hang in chains for the duration of three high tides.

Southwark, Rotherhithe, Greenwich

Anchor Inn, 1 Bankside, SE1. Superior food and excellent river views in this ancient Bankside institution where fugitives from the Clink prison next door used to hide in cubby holes.

Old Thameside Inn, Clink St, SE1. Shantymen perform sea shanties at lunchtime on the last Sunday of the month at this pub with attractive riverside views from a concrete terrace.

The Angel, 101 Bermondsey Wall East, Rotherhithe, SE16. The pub where Captain Cook had his last drink before sailing to Australia. Notable for its ship's wheel, smugglers' trapdoor and balcony overlooking Tower Bridge and Execution Dock.

The Mayflower, 117 Rotherhithe St, SE16. Inn from which the Pilgrim Fathers set out for America, and the only place in Britain where you can buy US postage stamps. There's a long jetty from which to admire the river. Avoid the indifferent food.

Trafalgar Tavern, Park Row, Greenwich, SE10. Famous for its Whitebait Dinners, at which cabinet ministers and senior public figures would hold informal chats over seafood from the Thames. River pollution ended the tradition in 1914, though you can still eat rather indifferent whitebait from the pub menu. Nice views.

Islington, Highgate, Hampstead

King's Head, 115 Upper St, Islington, N1. Popular Islington pub, where the money is still counted according to the old pre-decimal system of pounds, shillings and pence. The pub theatre is excellent and the atmosphere is very genial.

Canonbury Tavern, 21 Canonbury Place, Islington, N1. Delightful garden pub with an unusual court for playing *pétanque*.

The Flask, 77 Highgate West Hill, N6. Friendly pub dating back to the 17th century at the top of Highgate Hill, with a garden and good food.

The Bull, 13 North Hill, Highgate, N6. A large tree-lined garden and patio are the most attractive features of this former drinking haunt for painters such as Hogarth and Millais.

Spaniards Inn, Spaniards Road, Hampstead Heath, NW3. Reputed as a highwayman's pub patronized by Dick Turpin and a host of scurrilous scribblers including Byron and Shelley. Wonderful garden and, of course, the expanse of Hampstead Heath just across the road.

The Holly Bush, 22 Holly Mount, Hampstead, NW3. Idyllic pub with five low rooms grouped around an old wooden bar.

Freemasons Arms, 32 Downshire Hill, Hampstead, NW3. Huge garden and terrace, fountain and pitch to play the ancient game of pell-mell. Gets crowded.

West London

Ladbroke Arms, 54 Ladbroke Rd, Notting Hill, W11. Very popular pub with flower-lined patio. Don't bring the car as there's a police station next door and they'll nick you for drink-driving.

Queen's Head, Brook Green (West Kensington), W6. Old coaching inn overlooking a green, with a beer garden at the back.

Anglesea Arms, 15 Selwood Terrace, SW7. Good beer in this local Chelsea haunt.

Havelock Tavern, 57 Masbro Road, W14. Popular pub serving high-quality pub food.

King's Head and Eight Bells, 50 Cheyne Walk, Chelsea. Enjoy the antiques displays in this 16th-century building. There are views of the Battersea peace pagoda across the river.

Dukes Head, 8 Lower Richmond Rd, Putney. Fine views along the river, though you have to put up with plastic cups if you sit outside.

The Ship, Ship Lane, Mortlake. The place to watch the end of the Oxford and Cambridge boat race in April. Fine river views and a tranquil setting the rest of the year.

The White Cross, Cholmondeley Walk, Richmond. A pub that turns into an island at high tide. Enjoy the real fires and good food.

Hotels	163
Bed and Breakfast	167
Student Halls of Residence	168
Youth Hostels	168
Self-Catering	168

London: Where to Stay

There is only one word to describe London's hotels and that word is *nightmare*. Accommodation, although improving slowly, is on the whole shamelessly expensive and shamelessly shoddy. You can pay up to £80 for an ordinary double room with no guarantee of quality or even basic hygiene; and you can pay up to twice that without even approaching the luxury category. There is no universal rating system, and the variously sponsored star or crown systems are so unreliable as to be virtually useless. So your best bet is to dust down your address book and see if there isn't anybody in London who might be able to put you up. If that fails, don't lose heart: there are some cheap deals available, and some surprisingly enjoyable establishments. You must, however, be very wary of the pitfalls.

If at all possible, try to arrange accommodation from your home country. Flight and accommodation packages cover a wide price range and can work out to your advantage. Otherwise, try the numbers below. You can usually confirm your booking by giving a credit card number or sending a fax. The London Tourist Board also operates a telephone credit card booking service on ✆ (020) 7824 8844 which is open Mon–Fri 9.30–5.30. If you turn up in London without a room in your name and you get nowhere ringing the numbers listed below, you can line up outside a tourist office and try your luck there. Try Victoria station forecourt, Liverpool St station, the underground concourse at Heathrow Terminals 1–3, or one of the following local tourist offices: Greenwich (✆ (020) 8858 6376), Islington (✆ (020) 7278 8787) or Richmond (✆ (020) 8940 9125). Commission for all booking services is around £5. If you are travelling out of high season (i.e. not the summer), try haggling a bit and you might negotiate your own discount. Weekend rates are common, and if you stay for a week you might get one night free. You can further save your pennies by declining breakfast (a possible £10 saver, *see* Food and Drink for other places to go) or by asking for a room without a bath. In the cheaper establishments, the corridor bathrooms are usually better than the *en suite* kind, so this is not much of a sacrifice. The following Internet address may also be useful: hotels *www.demon.co. uk/hotel-uk/excindex.html.*

Most hotels are in the West End and around, Kensington, Chelsea, Earl's Court and west London. Try to avoid streets like Sussex Gardens in Bayswater, which is something of a hotel ghetto and rather miserable for it. Finding somewhere quiet can be a problem, especially in the busy summer months, but as a broad rule of thumb you will be disturbed less the further you are out of the centre. The best places to stay are in districts like Notting Hill and Holland Park, or else by the river—don't forget the newer hotels in the Docklands. Bloomsbury offers some excellent bargains as well as the proximity of the British Museum.

Prices given below are for a normal double room for one night, but—again—find out about discounts before dismissing a place as too dear. Remember that space is tight, so book as far in advance as possible, whatever the category of accommodation. Hotels are graded by price, as follows:

        ෲෲෲෲෲ   luxury (£200 and over)
        ෲෲෲෲ   very expensive (£150–200)
        ෲෲෲ   expensive (£100–150)
        ෲෲ   moderate ((£60–100)
        ෲ   cheap for London (under £60)

Hotels

Mayfair

∞∞∞ **Brown's**, 19–24 Dover St W1, ✆ (020) 7493 6020. Old fashioned English establishment, with the air of a country house and impeccable, stiff-collar service. Attractive if smallish rooms. £250–750 + VAT.

∞∞∞ **Claridges**, Brook St W1, ✆ (020) 7629 8860. Art deco bedrooms, black and white marbled foyer and a touch of royal class at London's most celebrated smaller luxury hotel. £280–£3,500 + VAT (the latter for a 2-floor penthouse).

∞∞∞ **Connaught**, 16 Carlos Place W1, ✆ (020) 7499 7070. Attentive service commands a troupe of loyal devotees. An air of calm exclusivity presides. Outstanding restaurants; personalised formality. Book in writing well in advance. £215–360 + VAT.

∞∞∞ **Dorchester**, 53 Park Lane W1, ✆ (020) 7629 8888. Triple-glazed rooms (to foil the Park Lane traffic) and views over Hyde Park, plus a dazzling choice of fine restaurants and acres of gold and marble. £295 + VAT.

∞∞∞ **Ritz**, Piccadilly W1, ✆ (020) 7493 8181. Marble galore, gorgeous rococo carpets, plus glorious views over Green Park if you pick your room right. *Ancien régime* luxury. £260–300 + VAT.

West End

∞∞∞ **Savoy**, Strand WC2, ✆ (020) 7836 4343. A sleeker, more business-like luxury here. *Fin de siècle* dining room: a favourite venue for afternoon tea. Many restaurants and bars and discreet good service. £325 + VAT.

∞∞ **Bryanston Court**, 56–60 Great Cumberland Place W1, ✆ (020) 7262 3141. Business-like hotel with few frills but a pleasant atmosphere and an open fire in winter. £110.

∞∞ **Durrants**, George St W1, ✆ (020) 7935 8131. A former 18th-century coaching inn preserving many old-fashioned touches including silver plate covers in the restaurant. Rooms are simple, a few on the small side. £135.

∞∞ **Hazlitt's**, 6 Frith St W1, ✆ (020) 7434 1771. Small Georgian rooms with some four posters and claw-footed iron baths in the former home of essayist William Hazlitt. Palm trees and classical busts adorn the premises. £170 + VAT.

∞∞ **Blandford**, 80 Chiltern St W1, ✆ (020) 7486 3103. Simple bed and breakfast style hotel, offering decent rooms and a copious morning meal, in a quiet side street near Baker St station. £85.

∞∞ **Concorde**, 50 Great Cumberland Place W1, ✆ (020) 7402 6169. Plain and inexpensive but light and efficient, under the same management as the Bryanston Court. With self-catering options. £85 + breakfast + VAT.

∞∞ **Edward Lear**, 28–30 Seymour St W1, ✆ (020) 7402 5401. Named after the nonsense-verse writer. Small hotel with a homey feel. Informal but efficient. £70.

∞∞ **Fielding**, 4 Broad Ct, Bow St WC2, ✆ (020) 7836 8305. A pretty good deal for central London, right opposite the Opera House. Smallish rooms and a tiny reception area: a parrot greets you on your way in. £85.

∞∞ **Georgian House Hotel**, 87 Gloucester Place W1, ✆ (020) 7935 2211. Spacious rooms with personality; quietly high standards and good prices. Great discounts on 'student' rooms up 3 or 4 flights of stairs. £90.

∞∞ **Hallam Hotel**, 12 Hallam St W1, ✆ (020) 7580 1166. Quiet, businesslike hotel just around the corner from the BBC. Some rooms have views of the Telecom Tower. £102.50.

∞∞ **Hart House Hotel**, 51 Gloucester Place W1, ✆ (020) 7935 2288. Superbly run hotel in a Georgian mansion overlooking Portman Square, with remarkably large rooms for the area. £95.

- **Parkwood**, 4 Stanhope Place W2, ✆ (020) 7402 2241. Family-run hotel with slightly worn furniture but attractive prices. Charming Georgian mansion near Hyde Park. £87.50.

Bloomsbury

- **Bonnington**, 92 Southampton Row WC1, ✆ (020) 7242 2828. Renovated Edwardian establishment with bland furniture but warm management. Plenty of beds, relatively easy to book. £75–140.
- **Russell**, Russell Square WC1, ✆ (020) 7837 6470. Extravagant Gothic Revival architecture and an atmosphere to match. A renovated ballroom. Friendly service. £185.
- **Academy**, 17–21 Gower St WC1, ✆ (020) 7631 4115. Enjoy the atmosphere of a Georgian townhouse. Cosy library and small paved garden. An antique charm. £125.
- **Crescent**, 49–50 Cartwright Gardens WC1, ✆ (020) 7387 1515. Use of the garden and tennis courts a big plus here, as is family atmosphere. Old-fashioned and good value. £80 inc. breakfast and tax.
- **Harlingford**, 61–3 Cartwright Gardens WC1, ✆ (020) 7387 1551. Floral-print wallpaper adorns the simple rooms. Access to tennis courts possible. £82 all inclusive.
- **Mabledon Court**, 10–11 Mabledon Place WC1, ✆ (020) 7388 3866. Clean but unexciting hotel near King's Cross with reasonable rates. £75.
- **Morgan**, 24 Bloomsbury St WC1, ✆ (020) 7636 3735. Beautifully furnished bed and breakfast style hotel, with warm atmosphere and excellent breakfast. Near British Museum. £78.
- **St Margaret's**, 26 Bedford Place WC1, ✆ (020) 7636 4277. Clean, fresh hotel with a plant-filled dining room and a wide variety of large, well-proportioned rooms. £58.50 all inclusive.
- **Tavistock**, Tavistock Square WC1, ✆ (020) 7278 7871. Large rooms, a good location, art deco finishes but impersonal atmosphere and tour-group clientele. Views over Tavistock Square garden a plus. £75.
- **Arran House**, 77–9 Gower St WC1, ✆ (020) 7636 2186. Wonky floors and a lovely rose garden add charm to this otherwise no-frills guest house. In-house laundry and use of kitchen including microwave. £50.
- **Avalon**, 46–7 Cartwright Gardens WC1, ✆ (020) 7387 2366. Bright, old-fashioned Georgian house in a beautiful crescent packed with similar establishments. Drying and ironing facilities. £58.
- **Celtic**, 61–3 Guildford St WC1, ✆ (020) 7837 9258. Simple, unexciting family-run bed and breakfast. No private bathrooms but cheap at around £50.50. Street rooms can be noisy.
- **Elmwood**, 19 Argyle Square WC1, ✆ (020) 7837 9361. Basic but very cheap, in a lovely square near the new British Library. Not far from King's Cross. £40, discount for three-day stays.

Bayswater, Notting Hill

- **Hempel**, 31–5 Craven Hill Gardens W2, ✆ (020) 7298 9000. luxury hotel designed by Anoushka Hempel. Takes minimalism to its logical, most exotic extreme. Pure white blank foyer interrupted only by otherworldly flames and Thai ox-carts. £235–1200 + VAT.
- **Halcyon**, 81 Holland Park, W11, ✆ (020) 7727 7288. Modern but traditional, in a large, renovated Holland Park mansion house. Popular with showbiz and media people. Rated restaurant and bars. £270 inc. VAT.
- **Pembridge Court**, 34 Pembridge Gardens W2, ✆ (020) 7229 9977. Elegant Victorian townhouse, fastidiously deconstructed; but flourishing vegetation and an interesting collection of Victoriana in frames. Next to Portobello market. £270.
- **Whites**, 90 Lancaster Gate W2, ✆ (020) 7262 2711. Stucco palace overlooking

Kensington Gardens. Rebuilt behind the façade for modern tastes in traditional guise. Deferential service. £245 inc VAT. Breakfast is extra.

∞ **Portobello**, 22 Stanley Gardens W11, ✆ (020) 7727 2777. Victorian Gothic furniture conceals all-mod cons comfort including a health club. Idiosyncratic rooms. A touch poky. £155–260 inc VAT and breakfast.

∞ **Ashley**, 15–17 Norfolk Square W2, ✆ (020) 7723 9966. Maniacally clean and quiet hotel, ideal for families or business people looking for peace. Party animals stay away. Bulletin board has hints on sightseeing. £58–69.

∞ **Byron**, 36–8 Queensborough Terrace W2, ✆ (020) 7243 0987 (toll-free number in US ✆ 1-800-448 8355). Young, friendly atmosphere in this smart hotel full of sunshine and flowers, just a stone's throw from Kensington Gardens. £96.

∞ **Delmere**, 130 Sussex Gardens W2, ✆ (020) 7706 3344. Smart building on an otherwise miserable street of hotels. Some tiny rooms, but others are spacious and comfortable. £98 inc. VAT and breakfast.

∞ **Gate,** 6 Portobello Rd W11, ✆ (020) 7221 0707. Well-appointed, flower-bedecked no nonsense hotel in plum location among the antique shops of Portobello Rd. £80–85.

∞ **Kensington Gardens**, 9 Kensington Gardens Square W2, ✆ (020) 7221 7790. Attractive rooms, good bath facilities and a light, pleasant breakfast room make this a good mid-range choice. £80 inc breakfast and VAT.

◊ **Abbey House**, 11 Vicarage Gate W8, ✆ (020) 7727 2594. Simple, spacious rooms in this delightful Victorian town house in a quiet square. Preserves many original features. Cheap at around £60.

◊ **Border**, 14 Norfolk Square W2, ✆ (020) 7723 2968. No-nonsense hotel with simple, cheap facilities, in a square full of other similar hotels. £59.

◊ **Garden Court**, 30–31 Kensington Gardens Square W2, ✆ (020) 7229 2553. Simple bed and breakfast with nice views over the square at the front and gardens at the back. Well located next to Queensway and not far from Portobello. £52 inc VAT and breakfast.

◊ **Lancaster Hall (German YMCA)**, 35 Craven Terrace W2, ✆ (020) 7723 9276. Sounds grim and looks awfully generic, but the rooms are clean, the location excellent. £72 (twins only).

◊ **Mornington**, 12 Lancaster Gate W2, ✆ (020) 7262 7361 (toll-free number in US 1-800-528 1234). Scandinavian-run hotel with serious but professional staff. Nice library. Next to the Football Association, so lots of soccer types around. £120.

◊ **Ravna Gora**, 29 Holland Park Avenue W11, ✆ (020) 7727 7725. Palatial Holland Park mansion turned slightly dilapidated bed and breakfast, with a talkative Serbian owner. £54.

South Kensington

∞∞∞ **Blakes**, 33 Roland Gardens SW7, ✆ (020) 7370 6701. Richly decorated hotel with four-poster beds and antique lacquered chests. Birdcages and carved giraffes to boot. £220–310 + VAT.

∞∞∞ **The Gore**, 189 Queen's Gate SW7, ✆ (020) 7584 6601 (toll free in USA ✆ 1-800-528 1234). Gothic and Edwardian décor, plus hundreds of old prints, make this an atmospheric stopover. £165 + VAT.

∞∞∞ **Number Sixteen**, 16 Sumner Place SW7, ✆ (020) 7589 5232. Charming Victorian house with a garden and fountains, plus large reception areas and rooms with balconies. Posh B&B. £160.

∞∞ **Aster House**, 3 Sumner Place SW7, ✆ (020) 7581 5888. Silk-wall décor and lots of flowers all over this award-winning hotel. Light breakfast alternatives to the usual bangers, bacon and egg. £125–45.

∞∞ **Claverly**, 13–14 Beaufort Gardens SW3, ✆ (020) 7589 8541. Lovingly detailed and award-winning hotel, with attractive rooms and an imaginative breakfast featuring waffles and fresh juices as well as bacon and eggs. £130.

- **Cranley**, 10–12 Bina Gardens SW5, ✆ (020) 7373 0123 (toll free in US ✆ 1-800-553 2582). American-run hotel converted from three elegant town houses. Style, great attention to detail thanks to antiques and designer fabrics, and a view from the top of the pinnacle of St Paul's. £150.
- **Five Sumner Place**, 5 Sumner Place SW7, ✆ (020) 7584 7586. The feel of a country home in the heart of London, with a stunning conservatory-style breakfast room. Smart but unpretentious. Quiet. £120 + VAT.
- **Hotel 167**, 167 Old Brompton Rd SW5, ✆ (020) 7373 0672. Attractively decorated Victorian corner house with young clientele. £99 inc breakfast + VAT.

Knightsbridge

- **Hyatt Carlton Tower**, 2 Cadogan Place SW1, ✆ (020) 7235 1234. De luxe mod cons, marble bathrooms, a stone's throw from Harrods, with a well-equipped health club, swimming pool and spacious rooms. £270 + VAT.
- **Diplomat**, 2 Chesham St SW1, ✆ (020) 7235 1544. Elegant rooms and suites up and down a glass-domed stairwell. Copious buffet breakfast and just a short walk to Beauchamp Place and Harrods. £125 inc breakfast + VAT.
- **Wilbraham**, 1 Wilbraham Place, Sloane St SW1, ✆ (020) 7730 8296. Very English establishment just off Sloane Square, with Victorian décor and attractive wood panelling. £106 inc VAT.

Victoria/Pimlico

- **Ebury Court**, 28 Ebury St SW1, ✆ (020) 7730 8147. Labyrinthine corridors connect the beautifully laid out rooms in this long-established neighbourhood favourite. £140 inc breakfast + VAT.
- **Collin House**, 104 Ebury St SW1, ✆ (020) 7730 8031. Clean, hospitable bed and breakfast behind Victoria station. Homey but fresh. £62–73.
- **Enrico**, 77–9 Warwick Way SW1, ✆ (020) 7834 9538. Basic but comfortable hotel in Pimlico. £40.
- **Oak House**, 29 Hugh St SW1, ✆ (020) 7834 7151. Small rooms with basic catering facilities for only £35. Breakfast is in your room. No advance booking, so roll up early.

Earl's Court/Fulham

- **Hogarth**, 35–37 Hogarth Rd SW5, ✆ (020) 7370 6831 (toll free in US ✆ 1-800-528 1234). Part of Best Western chain, a hotel with full amenities near Earl's Court Exhibition Centre. Busy but friendly. £110–130.
- **Beaver**, 57–9 Philbeach Gardens SW5, ✆ (020) 7373 4553. Simple, attractive establishment, pool table and cheap car parking. Plush lounge with polished wooden floors. Lovely street. £80 inc breakfast + VAT.
- **Pippa Pop-Ins**, 430 Fulham Rd SW10, ✆ (020) 7385 2458. A real oddity: a hotel for children aged 2–12. Leave them here and they will play to their heart's content. Available also for daytime child-minding. £50 per child. (Max stay: 3 days.)

Elsewhere

- **Tower Thistle**, St Katharine's Way E1, ✆ (020) 7481 2575. Not a great beauty, but ideally placed next to the Tower overlooking the river. Ultra-modern fittings and every conceivable comfort (including meeting rooms). £185.
- **Clarendon**, 8–16 Montpelier Row, Blackheath SE3, ✆ (020) 8318 4321. A bit of a way out, but a comfortable Georgian hotel with all mod cons including free parking and a beautiful view over Blackheath and Greenwich Park. £79 inc breakfast + VAT.
- **Dorset Square**, 39–40 Dorset Square NW1, ✆ (020) 7723 7874 (toll free in US ✆ 1-800-543 4138). Restored Regency building between Madame Tussaud's and Regent's Park with beautiful furniture and a strong cricket theme because of the nearby Lord's ground. £130 + VAT.

∞ **La Gaffe**, 107 Heath St, Hampstead NW3, ✆ (020) 7435 4941. Charming bed and breakfast above an Italian restaurant in a former shepherd's cottage. Bedrooms reached via a precipitous stairway. £85 inc breakfast + VAT.

∞ **Swiss Cottage**, 4 Adamson Rd NW3, ✆ (020) 7722 2281. Olde worlde atmosphere with lots of antiques, reproduction furniture and even a grand piano. Good location near Hampstead and Camden. £100 inc breakfast + VAT.

○ **Hampstead Village Guesthouse**, 2 Kemplay Rd NW3, ✆ (020) 7435 8679. Family household just a step away from Hampstead Heath. Lots of books and pot plants, plus fridges in your rooms. £60–100.

Bed and Breakfast

The bed and breakfast is a British (and Irish) tourist institution: you get to stay in someone's house, enjoy their company and eat a slap-up breakfast for a fraction of the cost of a hotel. In London the system works less freely than in the rest of the country, and you will have noticed that some of the hotels listed above have a distinctly B'n'B flavour to them. The least certain way of finding a B'n'B is by going to one of the tourist offices listed at the top of this chapter. A safer bet is to go through one of the following agencies:

∞ **Bulldog Club**, 15 Roland Gdns SW7, ✆ (020) 7341 9295. Will fix you up in palatial surroundings in the city or the country—at a price of course.

∞ **Uptown Reservations**, 50 Christchurch St SW3, ✆ (020) 7351 3445. Offers homes in Knightsbridge, Chelsea and similar neighbourhoods.

○ **Host and Guest Service**, 103 Dawes Rd SW6, ✆ (020) 7385 9922. Agency with 3000 homes on its books all over London. £18 per person per night.

○ **London Homes**, 6 Hyde Park Mansions, Flat G, Cabbell St NW1, ✆ (020) 7262 0900. A wide range to choose from, for as little as £18 per person.

○ **London Homestead Services**, Coombe Wood Rd, Kingston, Surrey, ✆ (020) 8949 4455. Minimum stay three nights for as little as £15 per person. Book early.

○ **Stayaway Abroad**, 71 Fellows Rd, Hampstead NW3, ✆ (020) 7586 2768. Slightly more expensive, but a classier service as a result.

Student Halls of Residence

A number of university halls of residence throw open their doors to foreign visitors during the long summer holiday from July to September and can be excellent value (£25 for a double room per night). Conditions are obviously a bit spartan, and you won't be able to cancel bookings very easily, but try the following addresses:

King's College Campus Vacation Bureau, 552 King's Rd SW6, ✆ (020) 7928 3777. Agency for seven halls of residence all over London.

John Adams Hall, 15–23 Endsleigh St WC1, ✆ (020) 7387 4086.

Walter Sickert Hall, 29 Graham St N1, ✆ (020) 7477 8822.

Ramsey Hall, 20 Maple St W1, ✆ (020) 7387 4537.

International Students House 229 Great Portland St W1, ✆ (020) 7631 8300. Strictly for students only, but excellent value for money, with access to a whole range of student amenities.

Youth Hostels

Not necessarily much cheaper than the cheapest B'n'Bs. You can get a full list of addresses from the **YHA Shop** in Covent Garden (14 Southampton St, ✆ (020) 7836 1036).

The most scenic locations are without doubt **Holland House**, ✆ (020) 7937 0748, slap bang in the middle of Holland Park in a converted Jacobean mansion, and **Highgate Village** (84 Highgate West Hill, ✆ (020) 8340 1831).

Self-Catering

Only really worth it if you are numerous, or if you are staying for several weeks. Try the following agencies:

Aston's, 39 Rosary Gardens, South Kensington, SW7 ✆ (020) 7370 0737.

Kensbridge Hotel Group Flat Rentals, ✆ (020) 7589 2923. Flats all over South Kensington.

Butlers Wharf Residence, Gainsford St, ✆ (020) 7407 7164. A chance to stay in one of the luxury flats built in the failed Docklands property boom of the 1980s. Very close to Tower Bridge and bang next to the Design Museum.

Theatre	170
Opera and Classical Music	172
Dance	174
Jazz	174
Rock, Pop and World Music	175
Comedy Clubs	176
Cinema	177
Nightclubs and Discos	178
Gay Bars	179

London: Entertainment and Nightlife

The indispensable guide to the week's events is the listings magazine *Time Out*, which appears on Tuesday afternoon or Wednesday morning; it provides addresses, descriptions and reviews of everything that moves or is scheduled to move over the following seven days. The magazine isn't perfect, tending to overhype celebrities and the latest fashion fads, but it has no serious competition.

Most of the West End theatres, as well as a good smattering of cinemas and nightclubs, are clustered around Soho and Shaftesbury Avenue. Some of the most interesting nightlife, however, takes place well away from the centre of town: jazz and fringe theatre in Islington, nightclubs in North Kensington or Brixton, comedy way up north in Crouch End or down south in Clapham. If you venture far afield, or if you have a long way to get home, you'll need to think carefully about transport. The Underground system dries up soon after midnight, and taxis can be hard to find in more remote parts of London. Night buses head to and from Trafalgar Square. If these aren't convenient, you may have to resort to a minicab. Don't let yourself be cajoled into taking a minicab off the street; not only is it illegal for drivers to solicit business this way, it may not be safe either. *See* p.7 for some safe compromises.

Theatre

Foreign visitors will find the cast lists of plays showing in London disconcertingly familiar: it looks as though the villains and eccentrics of Hollywood have mounted a takeover. In fact, the London stage is where actors like Anthony Hopkins, Ralph Fiennes and Alan Rickman come home to roost when they are not making megabucks in the movies. Those Californian casting directors know very well that London boasts the best serious stage acting anywhere, a reputation it has built up meticulously over several centuries. Its playwrights have pioneered no theatrical movements—England boasts no equivalent of Pirandello or Brecht—but have nevertheless turned out compelling and challenging dramas of a quality not seen in any other European city. Likewise, West End actors have rarely become major international stars, but still command enormous respect on Broadway and in Hollywood.

What to See and Where to Go

The major commercial theatre companies are concentrated in the West End, just as the main New York stages are grouped together on Broadway. Two distinct traditions are forever jostling for attention, the straight play and the musical. Shakespeare is of course a perennial favourite, along with Chekhov, Shaw and Noel Coward, but in pure terms of seat numbers the darling of the British musical, Andrew Lloyd Webber, is way ahead in the popularity ratings. Lloyd Webber's shows, from *Joseph and the Amazing Technicolour Dreamcoat* through to *Phantom of the Opera*, have been running without interruption in London for the past quarter century. Lloyd Webber's flagship theatre, the Palace on Cambridge Circus, has for the past few years been showing a musical he did not write himself, the smash hit *Les Misérables*. Just across the road at the St Martin's is the longest-running show in London, Agatha Christie's *The Mousetrap*, which has been on in one theatre or another since 1952. Longevity is no guarantee of quality, and you'd do well to give this wooden and outdated tourist attraction a wide berth.

Established playwrights, such as Tom Stoppard, David Hare, Harold Pinter, Tony Kushner and David Mamet, are increasingly turning to the off-West End theatre companies to stage their work. The most consistent and reliable of these is the three-stage **Royal National Theatre** on the South Bank, which puts on superb versions of the classics as well as showcasing high-quality new writing. The RNT is followed closely by the **Royal Shakespeare Company**, based at the Barbican, which concentrates mainly on the Bard and his contemporaries. The **Royal Court** in Sloane Square and **Lyric** in Hammersmith are excellent venues for new work, while experimental shows and reworkings of established plays are the hallmark of the **Almeida** in Islington, the **Hampstead Theatre** or the **Donmar Warehouse** in Covent Garden.

The **fringe** is always active, and occasionally you can find first-rate shows in draughty halls or upstairs rooms in pubs. If you are in London during the summer, don't forget about open-air venues like the **Globe Theatre**, **Regent's Park**, **Holland Park** and the garden of the **Royal Observatory** in Greenwich, where you can enjoy Shakespeare (particularly *A Midsummer Night's Dream*) and lively modern comedies.

Practical Details

Most performances start at 7.30pm or 8.00pm, with matinées usually scheduled on Wednesdays and Saturdays. By far the best way to book is through the theatre itself. At most places you can pay by credit card over the phone, then pick up the tickets just before the curtain goes up. **Ticket agents** charge stinging commissions, usually 22 per cent, although they can be a necessary evil to get into the big musicals (try Ticketmaster on ✆ (020) 7344 4444 or First Call on ✆ (020) 7420 0000). The Royal National Theatre offers a limited number of cheap tickets from 10am on the day of the performance (get there early as there are often long queues), and the Society of London Theatre has a ticket booth in Leicester Square (*open 2.30–6.30pm, or noon–6pm on matinée days*) with half-price tickets for West End shows that night. If all else fails, you can try for returns in the hour before the performance starts; students can get a hefty discount this way.

A Few Addresses

There's not a lot of point recommending individual theatres, as the quality of each production cannot be guaranteed, but the following addresses—most outside the West End—should give you some pointers. The telephone numbers are for the box office.

Royal National Theatre, South Bank, ✆ (020) 7452 3000. The National has three stages—the large apron of the Olivier, the conventional proscenium at the Lyttleton and the smaller, cosier Cottesloe. An evening here not only guarantees top-notch theatre; you can enjoy foyer concerts, browse through the bookshops and linger in the cafés with views out over the Thames. Highly recommended.

Barbican Arts Centre, Silk St, Barbican, ✆ (020) 7638 8891. The Royal Shakespeare Company, based both in London and in Shakespeare's birthplace, Stratford-upon-Avon, has two stages here, the conventional Barbican Theatre and the more experimental Pit. Standards are excellent and well worth the byzantine complications of finding the venue in the first place (*see* p.61). The RSC tours the country Mar–Oct and you'll need to go to Stratford to see them in summer.

Royal Court, Sloane Square, ✆ (020) 7565 5000. The major venue for experimental or counter-cultural writing, made famous by Shaw and Granville-Barker in the 1920s and kept prominent by the likes of Edward Bond, Caryl Churchill, Howard Brenton and Hanif Kureishi. The Theatre Upstairs on the first floor is one of the better fringe venues in town.

Old Vic, Waterloo Rd, ✆ (020) 7928 7616. The former home of the National Theatre has come down in the world a bit, but still puts on good productions. Recently refurbished. Peter O'Toole caused a sensation here in the early 1980s by playing Macbeth for laughs in a near-incoherent drunken slur. The theatre was packed out every night, but the management was scandalised.

Theatre 171

Wyndham's, Charing Cross Rd, ✆ (020) 7369 1736. One of the more reliable West End addresses, with plenty of serious productions that attract big-name foreign actors like John Malkovich and Dustin Hoffman.

Theatre Royal Haymarket, Haymarket, ✆ (020) 7930 8800. Unadventurous choice of plays, but impeccable production and acting standards in this early 19th-century theatre built by John Nash. Maggie Smith, Vanessa Redgrave and Ian McKellen are regular stars here.

Donmar Warehouse, Earlham St, Covent Garden, ✆ (020) 7369 1732. Excellent venue where many distinguished young directors have cut their teeth.

Lyric Hammersmith, King St, ✆ (020) 8741 2311. Hosts many regional and foreign theatre companies. Home also to the smaller, experimental Studio, ✆ (020) 8741 8701.

Hampstead Theatre, Avenue Road, ✆ (020) 7722 9301. Actors and audiences often mingle in the bar after the show at this friendly neighbourhood theatre, which is often a springboard for prestigious West End productions.

Theatre Royal Stratford East, Gerry Raffles Square, Stratford, ✆ (020) 8534 0310. High-quality drama in a crumbling Victorian palace in the midst of grey tower blocks. Worth the long trip out east.

King's Head, 115 Upper St, Islington, ✆ (020) 7226 1916. Eccentric pub (*see* 'Food and Drink', p.160) with popular theatrical tradition in a charming back room. Serves a 3-course dinner in the theatre just before the curtain rises (metaphorically speaking, because there is no curtain).

Almeida, Almeida St, Islington, ✆ (020) 7359 4404. A fringe theatre that has acquired a formidable reputation. Stages different productions every six or seven weeks. Often produces its own plays but also reworks classical pieces.

The Gate, 11 Pembridge Road, Notting Hill, ✆ (020) 7229 0706, *gate@gatetheatre.freeserve.co.uk*. Excellent pub theatre that features new plays as well as ambitious reworkings of the classics, including Greek tragedy.

BAC (Battersea Arts Centre), 176 Lavender Hill, ✆ (020) 7223 2223. Lively theatre venue south of the river.

Shakespeare's Globe, 21 New Globe Walk, ✆ (020) 7401 9919. Opened for business in 1997, this lovingly reconstructed version of Shakespeare's original London theatre puts on three or four Elizabethan productions each year, most of them by the Bard, in a season that lasts from May until September. It's proving popular, so book early (box-office opens around January once the programme has been fixed). Lots of audience participation and period high jinks (like jesters with firecrackers attached to their feet). Watch out for rain and cold, though, as the theatre is open to the skies (*see* p.33 for more on the theatre itself).

Regent's Park Open Air Theatre, Inner Circle, Regent's Park, ✆ (020) 7486 2431. Open-air theatre from May to September. Bring a blanket and umbrella to keep the worst of the English summer at bay.

Holland Park Theatre, Holland Park, ✆ (020) 7602 7856. Has a shorter open-air season, from June to August, but puts on all manner of productions. *See* p.112.

Opera and Classical Music

London has classical music coming out of its ears: two major opera companies, five world-class orchestras, lunchtime concerts, summer festival concerts, open-air concerts. For generations, classical music in Britain was tinged with class prejudice, being a pursuit of the educated upper-middle classes who turned up their noses at the philistine hordes who couldn't tell their Handel from their Haydn. You'll still find the snobs lurking in the foyers of the Festival Hall and on the rarefied airwaves of the BBC's classical station Radio 3. But you'll also find a wealth of unpretentious, dedicated young performers and audiences, especially in smaller concert venues like the Wigmore Hall. London's weakness is undoubtedly in contemporary and avant-garde music; programmers tend to play very safe, with a preponderance of Mozart, Beethoven and Brahms.

The following addresses are for the main concert and opera venues; again, you should check *Time Out* to see what is playing.

Royal Opera House, Covent Garden, ✆ (020) 7304 4000. Britain's leading opera venue is right up there with the Met, the Staatsoper and La Scala, but constant financial and political problems have not only pushed up prices almost as high as the top C in the Queen of the Night's bravura aria from Mozart's *Magic Flute*, they have put the very future of the theatre in doubt at times: the House's financial deficit means it will not be producing opera during summer for the foreseeable future. After an exciting and long overdue renovation it is due to reopen in December 1999. *See* p.64.

London Coliseum, St Martin's Lane, ✆ (020) 7632 8300. Home to the English National Opera, which performs in English to high musical standards and with infectious enthusiasm. Much cheaper (from £5, top price around £50) and far less pretentious than Covent Garden. *See* p.65.

South Bank Centre, South Bank, Belvedere Rd, ✆ (020) 7960 4242. Three first-rate concert halls under the same roof: the Royal Festival Hall, boasting its own organ and room for as many musicians and singers as any musical work might demand; the Queen Elizabeth Hall, which is smaller and a little more adventurous in its programming; and the Purcell Room, for chamber music only. The larger halls also host occasional jazz, rock, dance and even small-scale opera performances. *See* p.83.

Barbican Centre, Silk St, ✆ (020) 7638 8891. Home to the London Symphony Orchestra and English Chamber Orchestra. Excellent acoustics make up for the out-of-the-way venue. *See* p.61.

Royal Albert Hall, Kensington Gore, ✆ (020) 7589 8212. Hosts the Promenade concerts, or Proms, which run every year from July until early September. The Proms are an eclectic platform for music old and new, and for unknown as well as established performers. The seats are removed from the area in front of the stage, leaving an open space in which people either stand or sit on the floor for as little as £3 per person. Queues form in the hours before the performance begins; bring a cushion to soften the bum-numbing effects of the Kensington pavements. You can also book conventional seating in advance, at regular concert prices (up to around £30). The Last Night of the Proms is a raucous affair at which the all-English orchestra plays all-English music, and the all-English audience sings along to the national anthem and *Rule Britannia*. *See* p.28.

Wigmore Hall, 36 Wigmore St, ✆ (020) 7935 2141. An intimate venue with excellent acoustics that attracts solo performers like guitarist Julian Bream or prima donna Jessye Norman. The tickets are very cheap—between £6 and £20—and sell out very fast.

Sadler's Wells, Rosebery Ave, ✆ (020) 7278 8916. A somewhat unfashionable venue for all kinds of music, including the infectious if supremely silly late Victorian operettas of Gilbert and Sullivan performed by the D'Oyly Carte company in April and May.

St John's Smith Square, Smith Square, Westminster, ✆ (020) 7222 1061. This fine Baroque church is one of the best lunchtime concert spots in town. Other good church venues, whether for lunchtime or evening concerts, include St James Piccadilly (usually on Mondays at 1pm); St Martin-in-the-Fields in Trafalgar Square (which boasts its own excellent chamber orchestra); St Bride in Fleet St; St Michael's Cornhill (organ recitals); St Anne and St Agnes, Gresham St; St Giles Cripplegate, Silk St; St Sepulchre-without-Newgate (mainly piano recitals on Fridays); the magnificently restored St Helen's, Bishopsgate; and St Johns Waterloo. Some concerts charge admission, others are free but ask for donations.

Kenwood House, Hampstead Lane, ✆ (020) 7413 1443. From June to September, enjoy idyllic outdoor concerts beside a lake at the top of Hampstead Heath. Highly recommended. Other open-air summer venues include Hampton Court and Marble Hill House in Twickenham (Sunday evenings only). *See* p.103.

Holland Park Theatre, Holland Park, ✆ (020) 7602 7856. Open-air season, from June to August, with all manner of productions including opera.

Dance

London puts on everything from classical ballet to performance art. Covent Garden (*see* above) is home to the highly accomplished Royal Ballet, which is cheaper and much less snooty than the Royal Opera in the same building; while the London Coliseum (*see* above) hosts the English National Ballet, at least for now. Sadler's Wells (*see* above) used to have its own ballet company too, but it decamped to Birmingham in 1990; the theatre nevertheless puts on an eclectic dance programme that has recently included both the mime artist Lindsay Kemp and the National Ballet of Cambodia. Two other addresses worth knowing about are the **ICA** on the Mall (✆ (020) 7930 3647), arguably the most avant-garde address in town; and **The Place Theatre** (17 Duke's Rd, Bloomsbury, ✆ (020) 7380 1268), in The Place building, which is also home to the London Contemporary Dance School. Every autumn, from mid-October to early December, London stages a festival called Dance Umbrella, which provides a showcase for performers from around the world.

Jazz

Jazz came to London in the 1950s, largely thanks to the effort of the late Ronnie Scott and his excellent club in Soho, and it has gone from strength to strength ever since. Venues used to be poky, smoky and cheap; now they are smartening up, perhaps a shade too much since they are starting to offer fancy food and drink at extraordinarily high prices. The music has not suffered yet, however, and continues to flow until the not-so-early hours of the morning. Check *Time Out* for jazz concerts in pubs and foyers of the larger theatres. Note that many clubs charge a (usually nominal) membership fee. You may find it hard to book for the more popular shows at Ronnie Scott's, for example, if you are not already a member.

Ronnie Scott's, 47 Frith St, W1, ✆ (020) 7439 0747 (*closed Sun*). The prime jazz venue in town, with a steady flow of big names and a suitably low-key, laid-back atmosphere. Book if you have time, and get there early (around 9pm) to ensure a decent seat. Admission is £15 Mon–Thurs, £20 Fri–Sat, or more for a very big name band.

100 Club, 100 Oxford St, W1, ✆ (020) 7636 0933. Lively basement venue with an eclectic mix of trad and modern jazz, as well as blues, swing and rockabilly. The Sex Pistols gave one of their first performances here in the mid-1970s.

606 Club, 90 Lots Rd, Fulham, ✆ (020) 7352 5953. Seven-nights-a-week basement club featuring many local musicians, with emphasis on contemporary jazz. Late-night restaurant licence and good modern food. 8.30–2am.

Jazz After Dark, 9 Greek St, Soho, ✆ (020) 7734 0545. Jazz, Latin jazz and salsa, with a bar and restaurant (licensed to 2am, 3am at weekends). Admission free before 11pm on weekdays.

Jazz Café, 5 Parkway, Camden, ✆ (020) 7344 0044. Typical of the new-style jazz club, a slick venue with plush dinner-table seating (food optional). The music is first-rate.

Bull's Head, 373 Lonsdale Rd, Barnes, SW13, ✆ (020) 8876 5241. Top-notch bands in a riverside setting.

Vortex, Stoke Newington Church St, ✆ (020) 7254 6516. Friendly first-floor jazz bar featuring many local north London bands.

Pizza Express, 10 Dean St, Soho, ✆ (020) 7439 8722. Be-bop to accompany your pizza; an unlikely setting, but a congenial one which boasts its own resident band as well as many prestigious visitors. Branch at **Pizza on the Park**, 11 Knightsbridge, off Hyde Park Corner, ✆ (020) 7235 5273.

Soho Pizzeria, 16–18 Beak St, ✆ (020) 7434 2480. Another pizza place with live music as you eat; no extra charge and the pizza is good too.

Rock, Pop and World Music

By and large, the big Madonna/Michael Jackson venues like Wembley Stadium are impersonal and have terrible acoustics, while smaller, more specialized clubs like the Africa Centre or the Mean Fiddler are infinitely more rewarding and cheaper too. Posters and press adverts will tell you how to buy tickets. You'll probably have to go through a ticket agency (*see* Theatre section above) for the bigger acts, otherwise go directly to the venue. Once again, *Time Out* will have all the details, including reliable recommendations on the week's best shows.

Wembley Stadium, Empire Way, Wembley, ✆ (020) 8902 0902. Appalling views, appalling acoustics, appalling transport links. If the big acts insist on coming here, it is mainly because of the seating capacity (up to 100,000); but as Madonna would be the first to tell you, size isn't everything. Only the Live Aid concert of 1985 and the Free Nelson Mandela bash of 1988 generated something approaching atmosphere. Otherwise, only the sledgehammer lyricism of U2 or Bruce Springsteen can ever get through to audiences. Bring a telescope.

Wembley Arena, same address as above. The indoor neighbour of the stadium, with all of its problems but with a seating capacity of only 13,000.

Royal Albert Hall, Kensington Gore, ✆ (020) 7589 8212. The iffy acoustics and somewhat grandiose Victorian architecture are more than compensated for by intelligent programming—folk-rock and R'n'B by the likes of Bonnie Raitt, Eric Clapton etc.

Brixton Academy, 211 Stockwell Rd, Brixton, ✆ (020) 7771 2000. Much more like it. Raw, raucous music in a crumbling art deco setting. Sweaty but exhilarating.

Forum, 9–17 Highgate Rd, Kentish Town, ✆ (020) 7344 0044. Formerly known as the Town and Country Club and arguably the best rock venue in town; an excellent blend of high-quality facilities and first-rate bands.

Shepherds Bush Empire, Shepherds Bush Green, ✆ (020) 7771 2000. Similar-sized venue to the Forum, with seats upstairs. Attracts big names; great atmosphere.

The Grand, Clapham Junction, St John's Hill, ✆ (0800) 783 7485. Newish rock venue with great view of the stage from the bar.

Subterania, 12 Acklam Rd, Ladbroke Grove, ✆ (020) 8960 4590. Funk, jazz, soul and rap, interspersed with new songwriter nights, make this one of the more unpredictable and enjoyable spots in west London. Hot rubber rooms.

The Rock Garden, 6–7 The Piazza, Covent Garden, ✆ (020) 7836 4052. Restaurant venue with live music. the night will have a theme (indie rock, pop/funk, new bands). No big names, but can be good, if expensive.

Africa Centre, 38 King St, Covent Garden, ✆ (020) 7836 1973. Groovy atmosphere and infectious African music. Cheap and great fun.

Camden Palace, 1a Camden Rd, ✆ (020) 7387 0428. Tuesday night features new indie bands. Dancing the other nights of the week.

Dingwalls, Camden Lock, ✆ (020) 7267 1577. Decent if grubby venue featuring a variety of bands, from rock to country.

Hammersmith Apollo, Queen Caroline St, ✆ (020) 7416 6080. A big-name venue, which puts on stage shows as well. Excellent sound and good views of the stage.

The Mean Fiddler, 24–28a High St, Harlesden, ✆ (020) 8963 0940. Ace setting for Irish folk and new country artists. Well worth the schlepp out to north-west London.

The Venue, 2a Clifton Rise, New Cross, ✆ (020) 8692 4077 (*open Fri, Sat*). Specializes in indie music, with dancing late into the night.

Comedy Clubs

Comedy has been all the rage in London since the early 1980s, and clubs have been sprouting with amazing speed all over town. Traditionally, stand-up comedy was restricted to music halls or to working-men's clubs in the industrial towns of northern England. Performers were generally fat and male, and cracked jokes in dubious taste about blacks, big tits and mothers-in-law. The only 'sophisticated' comedy was the zany brand pioneered by the Footlights revue at Cambridge University and developed by the likes of Peter Cook, Dudley Moore and Monty Python. These were middle-class, well-educated performers who despite a strong anti-establishment streak appealed mostly to their own kind. Comedy, like everything else in Britain, was divided along class lines.

All that changed with the advent of the Thatcher government in 1979. A new counter-culture of politically aware comedy sprang up, making what jokes it could out of industrial decline, growing gulfs between rich and poor and the 1980s culture of greed and self-advancement. Performers from a broader social and racial spectrum, including Lenny Henry, Rowan Atkinson, Harry Enfield, Ben Elton, Rik Mayall and Jo Brand, soon became established stars, both on television and in some cases in feature films too. All of them started out in London's comedy clubs, particularly the Comedy Store in Leicester Square (since transferred to new premises) which opened in 1979, the year of Thatcher's election. The comedy club circuit has expanded considerably since then, and established performers mingle easily with new talent in more than 20 major venues. Sit in the front rows at your peril, as you are likely to be roped into the act and insulted or humiliated. Some of the humour is a bit parochial, revolving around British adverts and television programmes, but many acts are truly inspired. Usually several artists will contribute to a single evening, so if you don't like one there's not long to wait for something better. Look out for hilarious Boothby Graffoe, political radical Mark Thomas, Al Murray's Pub Landlord and very funny Rob Newman; but going to a good club to see acts you've never heard of can be just as rewarding as following the big names.

Comedy Store, 1a Oxendon St, ✆ (020) 7344 0234. Improv on Wed and Sun by the Comedy Store Players, otherwise stand-up. The most famous comedy club of them all has got a bit slick for its own good and the hefty admission fee (£8/12) reflects that. The standard remains very high, however.

Bound and Gagged, Tufnell Park Tavern, Tufnell Park Road, ✆ (020) 7483 3456. Saturday night above-pub club with unusual, interesting acts.

Jongleurs, Battersea, The Cornet, 49 Lavender Gardens, Clapham; Bow Wharf, 221 Grove Rd; Camden Lock, Dingwalls Bldg, Middle Yard, Chalk Farm Rd. All ✆ (020) 7564 2500. Top acts on Fri/Sat nights. Book in advance.

Meccano Club, Finnegan's Wake, 2 Essex Rd, ✆ (020) 7813 4478. This intimate, sweaty cellar bar is one of the great London clubs, always worth a visit.

Hackney Empire, 291 Mare St, Hackney, ✆ (020) 8985 2424. Comedy with a political edge in a fine Victorian theatre.

East Dulwich Cabaret, East Dulwich Tavern, 1 Lordship Lane, Thurs–Sat, ✆ (020) 8299 4138. Pub venue.

Downstairs at the King's Head, 2 Crouch End Hill, ✆ (020) 8340 1028. Warm atmosphere encouraged by the very funny compères. Open Sat, Sun.

Red Rose Comedy Club, 129 Seven Sisters Rd, Finsbury Park, ✆ (020) 7281 3051. Top acts at knock-down prices in a slightly iffy area. Open Fri, Sat.

Cinema

London cinemas are a bit like the British film industry—bursting with potential, forever on the verge of a real breakthrough, but poorly looked after and often disappointing. The mainstream cinemas are on the whole unfriendly and very expensive (£7 or more for a ticket, regardless of whether the venue is a plush auditorium with THX Dolby sound or a cramped backroom with polystyrene walls). The multiplex has hit London in a big way, for example at the Warner and Empire in Leicester Square or at Whiteleys in Queensway. For no discernible good reason seats tend to be numbered, which means confusion breaks out just as the main feature is starting, and the audience rarely settles down until 10 minutes into the first reel. There has been a flurry of interest in new British and independent cinema in recent years, thanks to *Four Weddings and a Funeral*, *The Full Monty* and the darkly humorous work of the Scottish director Danny Boyle (*Shallow Grave*, *Trainspotting*, etc). But Hollywood blockbusters still grab more than their fair share of the market, and the work of some of the most challenging British directors— Mike Leigh, Nicolas Roeg or Ken Loach—might not make a first-run cinema at all.

On the plus side, the arthouse and repertory sector is reasonably healthy, showing subtitled foreign-language films as well as the classics of American and British cinema. Prices are lower than first-run cinemas—£4–5 is normal—and can be lower still if you pay a membership fee and return regularly. The National Film Theatre offers the broadest range, while clubs like the Everyman attract a fiercely loyal clientele.

Film censorship in general is very strict, and in some cases the British Board of Film Classification cuts out footage it finds offensive without alerting the audience. Films are graded U (family films), PG (parental guidance recommended), 12 (nobody under that age), 15 (ditto) or 18 (ditto). The system is governed by crazy pseudo-puritanical rules that border on paranoia—the very first film to be censored in Britain, back in 1898, was a close-up of a piece of Stilton cheese. Don't ask why. Steven Spielberg's dinosaur thriller *Jurassic Park* was given a PG rating despite its self-evidently disturbing effect on children, while an intelligent classic like Robert Altman's *McCabe and Mrs Miller* is lumped along with pornography and Kung Fu in the 18 bracket.

Odeon Leicester Square, Leicester Square, ✆ 0870-5050 007. London's plushest venue, which premières major Hollywood productions, often with royals and film stars in tow. Even more expensive than the average mainstream cinema, with interminable adverts before the main feature.

Prince Charles, Leicester Place, ✆ (020) 7437 8181. This former soft-porn cinema has smartened up its act and shows a constantly changing schedule of cult classics at £3.50 a seat. Surely this can't go on... take advantage while you can.

Curzon Mayfair, 38 Curzon St, ✆ (020) 7369 1720. Cinema showing art or foreign films. A more relaxed venue is its sister-cinema, the **Curzon Soho** at 93 Shaftesbury Ave, ✆ (020) 7439 4805.

Metro, 11 Rupert St, ✆ (020) 7437 0757. Two-screen cinema that shuns Hollywood fare in favour of independent productions.

Renoir, Brunswick Centre, Brunswick Square, ✆ (020) 7837 8402. The most adventurous of central London's cinemas, showing lots of foreign films and the best of British and American independents.

Screen on the Hill, 230 Haverstock Hill, Belsize Park, ✆ (020) 7435 3366. Popular first-run and art cinema with excellent coffee at the bar. Affiliated cinemas include the rather cramped **Screen on Baker Street** (96 Baker St, ✆ (020) 7486 0036) and the more commercial **Screen on the Green** (83 Upper St, Islington, ✆ (020) 7226 3520).

Gate, 87 Notting Hill Gate, ℡ (020) 7727 4043. Classy west London cinema with lively Sunday matinée line-ups. First-run films and classic revivals.

National Film Theatre, South Bank, ℡ (020) 7928 3232. The mecca of London's film junkies and main venue for the annual London Film Festival each November. Lots of old and new films always showing in rep, with special seasons, for instance of Iranian cinema.

Pullman Everyman, Hollybush Vale, Hampstead, ℡ (0845) 606 2345. The oldest rep cinema in London with an excellent bar. Lots of old favourites and a dedicated, student audience.

ICA Cinemathèque, Carlton House Terrace, The Mall, ℡ (020) 7930 3647. The wackiest film selection in town, with the emphasis on the avant-garde, especially feminist and gay cinema.

Clapham Picture House, Venn St, ℡ (020) 7498 3323. Cheap and appealing cinema showing intelligent recent releases. A rare cinematic high spot south of the river.

Phoenix, 52 High Rd, East Finchley, ℡ (020) 8444 6789. Rather out of the way but very lovable old rep cinema, showing interesting double-bills.

French Institute, 17 Queensberry Place, South Kensington, ℡ (020) 7838 2144. A good place to catch up on Gabin, Godard *et compagnie*.

Goethe Institute, 50 Princes Gate, Exhibition Rd, ℡ (020) 7596 4000. Shows a broad range of German-language cinema, sometimes without subtitles.

Nightclubs and Discos

From the hot and sweaty to the cool and sophisticated, London has about 150 clubs and discos providing anything from big-band swing to rap and techno. The London club scene always used to be hampered by the strict licensing laws. Now you should be able to drink alcohol until 3am at most establishments and carry on dancing until dawn or beyond. (There is a chance that 24-hour drinking may be legalised in or after 2000, but nothing is certain.) The main handicap is price: it usually costs around £10 to get into a club, and £2 or £3 more to buy a drink. Some clubs have dress codes, which may mean no jeans or trainers.

Things change fast in clubland: the following venues are all long-lasting but opening nights and music may change. Check a listings magazine.

Bar Rumba, 36 Shaftesbury Ave, ℡ (020) 7287 2715 (*open 10pm–3am*). Lively bar and club. Latin nights Mon and Tues, soul and R'n'B Sun, funk and house music other nights.

Bagleys Studios, Kings Cross Freight Depot, off York Way, ℡ (020) 7278 2777. This busy multiplex offers trancy techno on Fri, funky house and disco on Sat.

Café de Paris, 3 Coventry St, ℡ (020) 7734 7700 (*open Fri, Sat only 10pm–6am*). Club music all night in this 1920s ballroom. Very glamorous, with lots of red velvet and jacuzzis, but expensive.

Camden Palace, 1a Camden High St, ℡ (020) 7387 0428. Huge main floor and balcony offering space for a loyal, young crowd to dance to garage and techno.

The Complex, 1–5 Parkfield St, Islington, ℡ (020) 7288 1986. A must for the inexhaustible: it has a 24-hour party licence. A multi-level venue offering mainly funk, hip-hop and soul; gay nights with disco/80s/Motown.

The Cross, Goods Way Depot, off York Way, ℡ (020) 7837 0828. Low brick arches add to the hot, sweaty atmosphere. Three bars and a chill-out garden. Friendly crowd, but no jeans or trainers at Serious, the Friday night bash.

The End, 16a West Central St, ℡ (020) 7419 9199. Classic house party tunes at this central venue. *Open Thurs–Sat*.

The Fridge, Town Hall Parade, Brixton Hill, ℡ (020) 7326 5100 (*open Tues–Sat*). Funky music and a packed dance-floor. Mainy gay nights, but open to all.

The Gardening Club, 4 The Piazza, Covent Garden, ✆ (020) 7497 3154 (*closed Sun*). Varied music during the week; house dominates at weekends.

Gossips, 69 Dean St, ✆ (020) 7434 4480 (*closed Sun*). Atmospheric dark cellar with wide range of music. Cheap entry (£5–7).

Heaven, Under the Arches, Craven St, ✆ (020) 7930 2020. Excellent club with multiple bars, dancefloors, laser shows and crazy lighting. The biggest gay club in Europe, but most nights very cool about anyone who wants to come.

Hippodrome, Cranbourn St, ✆ (020) 7437 4311 (*closed Sun*). Vastly popular club attracting a large crowd of non-Londoners. Trapeze artists and fire-eaters.

The Leisure Lounge, 121 Holborn, ✆ (020) 7242 1345. Packed for soul, funk and disco on Fridays with a 20–40s crowd. House on Sat, with R'n'B and swing in the more chilled second room.

Legends, 29 Old Burlington St, ✆ (020) 7437 9933 (*open Wed–Sat*). Cool-paced, elegantly designed club which livens up at weekends with house music.

Limelight, 136 Shaftesbury Ave, ✆ (020) 7434 0572 (*closed Sun*). A converted church blasting out all kinds of music, especially heavy rock.

Madame Jo Jo's, 8–10 Brewer St, ✆ (020) 7734 2473 (*closed Sun*). Outrageous transvestite cabaret. Camp and colourful but a bit touristy.

Ministry of Sound, 103 Gaunt St, Elephant and Castle, ✆ (020) 7378 6528 (*open all night Fri and Sat only*). Expensive (£15), but very trendy and always packed. A New York-style club with lots of garage and house music. Expect long queues.

The Scala, 278 Pentonville Rd, ✆ (020) 7833 2022 4480. Excellent club/live music venue. Far East monthly on Friday offers a dose of jazz to tech house.

Stringfellow's, 16 Upper St Martin's Lane, ✆ (020) 7240 5534 (*open Mon–Sat 9.30pm–3am*). Glamour models and footballers come here, as do lots of tourists dressed up in their smartest togs for this pricey yet somewhat tawdry night spot. Decent food.

Subteranea, 12 Acklam Rd (under Westway), ✆ (020) 8960 4590. Reggae and dub on Wed, funk, jazz and hip-hop on Fri, house on Sat.

Turnmills, 63 Clerkenwell Rd, ✆ (020) 7250 3409 (*open Fri, Sat*). Everything from funky jazz to house and techno at the home of Trade, London's original gay late-nighter (Sat).

Wag Club, 35 Wardour St, ✆ (020) 7437 5534 (*closed Sun*). Everything from live rock to funk and hip hop. A young, fairly trendy club spread over two floors.

Gay Bars

London's main drag centres on Old Compton St and adjoining streets in Soho, where passing media suits mingle freely with shaven headed, body-pierced fashion queens. Past squabbles between restaurateurs and Westminster Council over tables thrust onto wobbly narrow footpaths may have been resolved; the result is an untidy but lively compromise. The tidal pink pound has seen the rise and demise of many places to be seen in; what follows is a snapshot of the current scene. For gay clubs, *see* above.

The Admiral Duncan, 54 Old Compton St (*open Mon–Sat 12–11, Sun 12–10.30*). Traditional gay pub in the heart of Soho. Bombed by a bigot in 1999, it has acquired a certain iconic status as a symbol of resistance to prejudice.

BarCode, 3–4 Archer St, Soho (*open 12 noon–11 daily*). Busy, fun-loving cruise and dance bar on two levels, with pool tables and fruit machines.

The Black Cap, 171 Camden High St (*open Mon–Fri noon–2am, Sat noon–3am, Sun noon–midnight*). Gay disco and cabaret bar famous for its drag shows, with terrace and late licence.

The Box, 32–34 Monmouth St, Covent Garden (*open Mon–Sat 11–11, Sun 12–10.30*). Café by day and lively bar by night, attracting a young, trendy, mixed crowd and some celebs.

The Candy Bar, 4 Carlisle St (*open Mon–Thurs 5pm–midnight, Fri 5–2am, Sat 2–2, Sun 1–11*). Bustling, friendly, vibrant gay women's bar. Cocktails upstairs, dancing downstairs. Men welcome as guests.

The Edge, 11 Soho Square (*open Mon–Sat noon–1am, Sun 1–10.30*). Relaxed, mixed crowd in this four-floor bar.

First Out Café Bar, 52 St Giles High Street, Covent Garden (*open 10am– 11pm*). Great veggie food served at this café bar, the first of its type in the West End. Women only on Fri eve.

Freedom, 60–66 Wardour St, Soho (*open 11am–3am*). Large café bar serving good food and cocktails to a trendy mixed crowd posing in designer gear. Downstairs club open until 3am.

Ku Bar, 75 Charing Cross Road, Soho (*open Mon–Sat noon–11pm, Sun 1–10.30*). Popular with young, scene-loving crowd.

Kudos, 10 Adelaide St, Covent Garden (*open Mon–Sat 11–11, Sun 12–10.30*). Brasserie and bar, popular with smart or after-work crowd. Big video screen downstairs.

The Retro Bar, 2 George Court, off Strand, Covent Garden (*open Mon–Sat 12–11, Sun 12–10.30*). Karaoke, '70s and '80s music and regular DJs in this friendly, unpretentious, traditional gay bar.

Rupert Street, 50 Rupert St (*open Mon–Sat 12–11, Sun 12–10.30*). Large, stylish, trendy bar, with similarly stylish and upmarket clientele of all ages and both sexes.

The Village, 81 Wardour St, Soho (*open Mon–Sat 2pm–1am, Sun 2pm– 10.30 summer, 4pm–10.30 winter*). Stylish bar on two floors.

The Yard, 57 Rupert Street, Soho. Good food and cabaret attracting mixed stylish crowd. Outdoor courtyard a bonus in summer.

Every year the British Diagram Group holds a competition to find the oddest title of a published book. Recent contenders have included *Thirty Years of Bananas*; *Lights! Catalogue of Worldwide Matchbox Labels with the Word 'Light' in the Title*; and *Construction of an Egyptian Wig in the British Museum*. It was once suggested that the competition should be widened to include CD titles as well, citing as an example the title *Great Moments in Belgian Jazz*.

It is not a joke that most Belgians would understand—not that they can't laugh at themselves: they just would not see the incongruity. The fact is, none of us may find this particularly amusing in a few years' time. Belgium, and Belgian culture, is suddenly being pushed out of the backstage and into the limelight, and undergoing radical reappraisal. Belgian restaurants, Belgian beer, Belgian chocolates have now achieved virtual cult status. New fashion collections by members of the Antwerp Six group of couturiers have buyers and commentators positively salivating beside the international catwalks, where the very name 'Belgique' has acquired a cachet. In 1994 the Royal Academy in London felt brave enough to mount an exhibition devoted entirely to Belgian art, which was warmly received. Nowadays journalists strive to rework the time-worn clichés and produce headlines such as 'Belgium isn't boring any more!' And even the French seem less inclined to make jokes about the Belgians.

This comes as little surprise to anyone who already knows and loves Belgium. But the new mood also brings a tinge of regret: like all aficionados, admirers of Belgium are jealous of the object of their affections. The tired custom of belittling Belgium was—by love's inverted logic—music to their ears: it only served to increase the value of their appreciation, and to keep all but genuine converts outside the temple doors.

Devotees of Belgium have no difficulty in identifying what it is that attracts them. Food is always high on the agenda. Belgian cooking is among the best in Europe—and generally very reasonably priced. Built on a solid foundation of market fare, it is rarely tainted by highfalutin' *gastronomie*: succulent steaks, seafood straight out of the bracing North Sea, unparalleled *frites* (chips/french fries), supreme *pâtisseries*, and, of course, the world-famous chocolates. Belgian beer is the Bordeaux and Burgundy of brewing; many leading brands are still produced under the auspices of Trappist monks, who infuse their brews with a vision of

Brussels: Introduction

heaven. This excellence of Belgian food and drink has not evolved in isolation. It belongs to a long tradition of sociability and *joie de vivre*, captured so infectiously by Flemish artists such as Pieter Bruegel the Elder and Jacob Jordaens. The Dutch have a word for this uniquely Belgian style of life, pronounced with a hint of envy: *Bourgondisch*—Burgundian, reflecting the robust, luxurious and immensely wealthy period when the Low Countries were ruled by the Dukes of Burgundy.

Brussels, Bruges, Ghent and Antwerp all developed as trading cities, fattened on the wealth of the merchants, craftsmen and their guilds, who were responsible for their great collections of art as well as their squares of sparkling, ornamented town halls and guildhouses. Ultimate power may have rested in the hands of the colonial rulers of Belgium—the Burgundians, the Spanish, the Austrians, the French, the Dutch—but the essential character of the nation was shaped by the broad band of the middle classes. A patrician culture dominated feudal Britain and France into the industrial age, producing the palaces and grand stately homes, laden with sumptuous finery. In Flanders, Brussels and Wallonia, by contrast, the arbiter and manufacturer of taste was always the burgher: well-to-do, democratic, moderate in tastes and needs, mindful that pleasure is as important a priority as education, domestic security and social cohesion—and sometimes vociferously independent, idiosyncratic and downright odd. It was this culture that produced the beer, the lace, the luminescent paintings of Jan van Eyck, and it later formed the backdrop to the flourish of Art Nouveau homes for the middle classes, the quirky art of the Symbolists and James Ensor, the surrealism of Magritte and Delvaux, and the Atomium. It also accounts for the way that Belgians have taken the concept of European Union to their heart.

'Capital of Europe' is Brussels' sobriquet, a just claim in view of its role as the focal point of Euro-administration. For some, indeed, Brussels has become a synonym for bureaucratic centralism—and for Eurosceptics the very word can induce a life-threatening rise in blood-pressure. In fact Brussels is not simply the capital city of the EU, but a honeypot which has also attracted a vast number of multinationals, businesses, banks, inter-governmental agencies and media companies from all over the world. It is a truly multicultural city, and it has been successful in its transformation into its modern form because it has been so accommodating. Virtually everyone in Brussels is genuinely pleased that the city has made such a success of it, and foreigners—businessmen and tourists alike—are made to feel welcome. As it turns out, however, the label 'Capital of Europe' paints an oddly inaccurate picture. Brussels is an altogether more modest, down-to-earth and frequently shoddy city than this would suggest—and herein lies its charm. Its attractions are found as much in the lively bars and cafés and welcoming family bistros as in its civic monuments, its art galleries and literally dozens of museums—many of which reflect Belgium's refreshingly skewed vision of the world from the inner rim of European history.

A Note on the Use of French and Dutch

Belgium has two main languages, and in Brussels all street names, place names and the names of museums and so on have both French and Dutch versions. In this volume, however, these names have generally been given in French only. The Dutch equivalents are cited only in exceptional cases. No prejudice or offence is intended: this is for reasons of space, and because it is assumed that readers, for better or worse, are more likely to be familiar with French than Dutch.

Belgium: Key Facts and Figures	184
Children	184
Crime and Police	184
Doctors and Pharmacies	185
Electricity	185
Embassies and Consulates	185
Emergencies	186
Festivals and Events	186
Gay Scene	187
Insurance	188
Language	188
Money and Banks	189
Opening Hours	190
Post Offices	190
Public Holidays	190
Telephones	190
Time	191
Tipping	191
Tourist Information	191

Brussels: Practical A–Z

Belgium: Key Facts and Figures

Belgium is a small country. At 30,000 square km, it's not much bigger than Sicily or Wales. You can drive from north to south in less than three hours. Its population numbers about 10 million. There are *cities* in the world with more people but, given the size of the country, Belgium has one of the highest average population densities, at over 300 inhabitants per square km. Brussels accounts for one-tenth of them, with a population of about 950,000. Antwerp has 486,000, Ghent 231,000, Charleroi 207,000, Liège 196,000 and Bruges 118,000.

The Flemish speakers in the north of the country outnumber the French speakers in the south by 5,848,000 to 3,303,000 respectively; and there are 67,600 German-speaking Belgians in the east, on the German border. These figures, however, do not include Brussels (Bruxelles in French, Brussel in Flemish), which floats like a multilingual bubble in the southern part of the Flemish-speaking region, and is counted as a separate administrative region. Here the French speakers easily outnumber the Flemish—but a full quarter of the population of Brussels is of foreign extraction.

Children

The first thing you notice about Belgian children is how well behaved they are. Belgium has a comparatively close-knit society, where traditional values are maintained not only by parents but also through the kindly guidance of ever-present older cousins, aunts, great-aunts and grandmothers. Just about all children go to the local state-run school, which therefore has the strong backing of Belgium's mighty middle classes. If a child is unacceptably disruptive, the parents will soon be under pressure to do something about it. For all that, this is a child-friendly society, where children are broadly welcomed and generally well catered for. Providing they behave, they will be accepted in all restaurants, cafés and bars. Since lunch in Belgium often lasts well beyond the endurance of most children, many parents wisely take toys, books and colouring kits to the restaurant.

Few of Brussels' attractions are specifically geared to children, apart from the Musée du Jouet. However, most children will probably enjoy the Atomium, the Manneken-Pis and his costumes in the Musée Communal de Bruxelles, the air section in the Musée Royal de l'Armée, the old trams at the Musée du Transport Urbain Bruxellois, and the Musée Royal de l'Afrique Centrale (*see* the Museums chapter).

Crime and Police

Every country seems to think that crime today is much worse than it used to be, and Belgium is no exception. In fact crime in Brussels, and in Belgium generally, is no worse than it is in the rest of Europe, despite a recent rash of highly publicized violent robberies, carjacking (mainly luxury vehicles) and child-abuse scandals. As everywhere, common-sense precautions should see you through. Pickpockets operate among the crowds on public transport, and the Métro has its own breed of nimble handbag slashers who can extricate purses and wallets in a single pass. If you are the victim of crime, go straight away to the Police/Politie (*see* p.186 for emergency numbers). Many officers speak English and you can expect a sympathetic hearing. Remember that you have to report theft to the police in order to claim insurance. Note also that you are obliged to carry your passport or other form of identity at all times, and this is the first thing the police will ask to see. (They can check it, but they are not allowed to take it away from you.) If you are arrested for any reason, you have the right to insist that your consul is informed (*see* 'Embassies and Consulates', below). Proper legal representation can then be arranged.

Doctors and Pharmacies

Belgium has an excellent medical service, with first-class modern hospitals, well-trained staff and a nursing profession founded on the high standards set by the British nurse of the First World War, Edith Cavell. Funded by the state, national insurance and private medical insurance, it has suffered less from growing constraints on government finance than other European nations, notably Britain.

Under the Reciprocal Health Arrangements, visitors from EU countries are entitled to the same standard of treatment in an emergency as Belgian nationals. To qualify you should travel with the E111 form; application forms are available from post offices in the UK. However, the E111 does not cover all medical expenses, and you are well advised to take out health insurance as well.

Hotels have a list of doctors and dentists to whom their guests can apply, but a trip to a pharmacy may be sufficient for minor complaints. Pharmacists have a good knowledge of basic medicine and are able to diagnose: if in doubt they will recommend that you visit a doctor, and can provide you with details. A list of 24-hour duty pharmacies is posted on every pharmacy door, together with a list of doctors on call. To get hold of a dentist in Brussels, call ✆ 426 10 26. For emergency numbers, *see* p.186.

You will be expected to pay for all medicine and treatment. With an E111 you can claim back about 75 per cent of the cost at the local Belgian sickness office; if you have separate health insurance you can claim the entire cost on your policy, but make sure that you ask for the correct documentation to make your claim.

Electricity

The current is 220 volts, 50 hertz. Standard British equipment requiring 240 volts will operate satisfactorily on this current. Plugs are the standard European two-pin type. Adaptors are available locally, but it is easier to buy a multi-purpose travelling adaptor before you leave home. Visitors from the USA will need a voltage converter in order to use their electrical appliances.

Embassies and Consulates

The following embassies are in Brussels.

Australia: 6 Rue Guimard, 1040 Brussels, ✆ 286 05 00
Canada: 2 Avenue de Tervuren, 1040 Brussels, ✆ 741 06 11
Republic of Ireland: 89 Rue Froissart, 1040 Brussels, ✆ 230 53 37
New Zealand: 47–48 Boulevard du Régent, 1000 Brussels, ✆ 512 10 40
South Africa: 26 Rue de la Loi, 1040 Brussels, ✆ 285 44 00
UK: 85 Rue Arlon, 1040 Brussels, ✆ 287 62 11
USA: 27 Boulevard du Régent, 1000 Brussels, ✆ 508 21 11

Emergencies

There are emergency services in every commune or borough of Brussels. The basic ambulance emergency number is ✆ 100. There is always at least one English-speaking operator on call. Or call the English-speaking helpline on ✆ 648 40 14. This can give you names of English-speaking doctors and other useful information.

>   **Accident emergency/ambulance/fire/rescue**, ✆ 100
>   **Police emergency**, ✆ 101
>   **Red Cross Ambulance**, ✆ 105
>   **Emergency line**, ✆ 112
>   **Emergency anti-poisoning centre** ✆ (070) 245 245
>   **Paediatric emergency**, ✆ 477 31 00 or ✆ 477 31 01
>   (Hôpital Universitaire des Enfants Reine Fabiola)
>   **Dental emergencies** (non-surgery hours), ✆ 426 10 26
>   **Brussels standby emergency services**, ✆ 479 18 18.

Festivals and Events

Belgium has a long calendar of events: some are age-old ceremonies and pageants, widely advertised and drawing large crowds; others are religious festivals, including some of disturbing fervour; others still are entirely local excuses for an annual knees-up and binge.

6 January — *Fête des rois.* Epiphany is celebrated with an almond-flavoured cake called the *galette des rois*, which contains a plastic bean. Whoever finds the bean in his or her slice is awarded the paper crown that is sold with the cake.

February/March — Carnival season, with a world-famous costume parade at Binche in western Belgium on Shrove Tuesday.

Easter Sunday — Children look for Easter eggs, which are said to have been hidden in the garden in the early morning by the *cloches de Rome* (the bells of Rome).

First Thursday in July (9–11pm) — *Ommegang* (literally, 'walk-around'). The grand pageant of Brussels, when some 2,000 participants dressed in Renaissance costume—as nobles, guildsmen, mounted soldiers, flag-throwers, jesters, peasants—go on a procession through the Grand' Place before the King and the royal family. The ceremony dates back at least as far as 1549, when it was performed in front of Charles V and the infant Prince Philip; it has now become little more than a costume parade and photo opportunity. Nonetheless, seats are at a premium and have to be booked in advance (from early June onwards) through the tourist office (935–1,335 BF).

Mid-July–3rd week in Aug — *Foire du Midi.* The great summer funfair of Brussels, which fills one side of the Boulevard du Midi between the Porte de Hal and the Place de la Constitution. It brings together a mass of noisy, gaudy attractions, from rifle galleries and halls of mirrors to dodgems and the big wheel. Good-humoured fun for all the family: there are plenty of children's rides, and grown-ups can always retreat to the mass of makeshift bars and restaurants serving seafood, beer and wine at trestle tables (the fair is often seen as the beginning of the shellfish season).

9 August	*Plantation du Meiboom.* A deracinated may tree is paraded around the centre of Brussels amid much jollity, then planted at the corner of the Rue du Marais and Rue des Sables.
13–14 August	*Tapis de Fleurs.* The Grand' Place in Brussels is covered in an elaborate 'carpet of flowers' (biennial, 2000, 2002).
Second Sunday in September	*Journée du Patrimoine.* All kinds of historic houses, private collections, businesses and craft workshops throw open their doors to the public for a day, in celebration of the national heritage. Ask at the tourist office.
Sept/Oct	*Beer festivals* throughout Belgium, for instance at Diksmuide (near Ostend, to the north of Brussels). Bands, marquees and litres of good beer.
1–2 Nov	*Toussaint* (All Saints' Day and the following day). A time when the Belgians honour their dead by tidying up the cemeteries and filling them with flowers in preparation for 2 November, known as the *Jour des Morts.* An estimated 55 million flowers are sold during this period.
6 December	*Fête de Saint-Nicolas* (Feast of St Nicholas). St Nicholas, a.k.a. Santa Claus, walks the streets and markets and enters schools in his guise as the Bishop of Myra. He is usually accompanied by his jolly sidekick, the blacked-up and decidedly un-PC Zwarte Piet. This is when many Belgian children receive their main Christmas gifts, as well as traditional *speculoos* biscuits.
24 December	*Réveillon.* Christmas Eve is the main feast day of Christmas: the centre-piece is a sumptuous evening meal, after which good Catholics stagger off to Mass.
25 December	Christmas Day. A day of family visits and more gifts.

Gay Scene

Brussels may not rank as one of the gay centres of Europe, but nonetheless it has an active, if discreet, gay scene. There are three gay listings magazines (all in French), giving details of events, bars, contacts, accommodation and so forth: *Gay mag* (every other month; 35 Rue Marché aux Herbes, 1000 Brussels); *Regard* (every other month; BP 215, 1040 Brussels—apply using address only, without the name *Regard*); *Tels Quels* (monthly; 81 Rue du Marché au Charbon, 1000 Brussels). *Tels Quels* also has a café and meeting point, 81 Rue du Marché au Charbon, open every day 5pm–2am (4am at weekends), © 512 32 34.

Two further sources of information are: Infor Homo, 57 Avenue de Roodebeek, 1040 Brussels, © 733 10 24, which also has a Gay Switchboard; and AIDE INFO SIDA, © 514 29 65 (hotline 511 45 29) which gives information and support about AIDS (SIDA in French) and also publishes a free Gay-Safe brochure listing bars, clubs, associations and so on.

The main area for gay bars in the centre of Brussels is around the Bourse and southwards down Boulevard Lemonnier—for example, there is Le Belgica, 32 Rue de Marché au Charbon; Why Not, 7 Rue des Riches Claires; Le Soum, 44 Rue du Marché au Charbon; Le Cancan, 55 Rue des Pierres (bar, disco and karaoke); Wing's, 3 Rue des Cyprès (lesbian); L'Incognito, 36 Rue des Pierres; Le Gémou, 12 Rue de Laeken (older clientele); Chez Maman, 12 Rue des Grands Carmes (many transvestites); Le Comptoir, 26 Place de la Vieille Halle au Blé.

Last, but by no means least, the English-speaking Gay Group (EGG), © 537 47 04, or email *tomhoemig@skynet.be*, is an informal club for men and women of all nationalities which offers the opportunity to make new friends at relaxed, informal gatherings and monthly parties. It now has a mailing list of 700 members. You can also write to EGG, BP 198, 1060 Brussels 6.

Insurance

All travellers are strongly advised to take out insurance as soon as they book their tickets. Insurance packages for European travel are not expensive compared to the total cost of a holiday, or the cost of replacing stolen goods or paying any medical bills yourself (*see* 'Doctors and Pharmacies', p.185). Standard packages include insurance to cover all unrefundable costs should you have to cancel, compensation for travel delays, lost baggage, theft, third-party liabilities and medical cover.

Language

Belgium has two main languages: French and Dutch. (Until recently the Dutch spoken in Belgium was referred to as Flemish or *Vlaams*, while Dutch, or *Nederlands*, was reserved for the pure form taught in schools. But now the correct, official term is Dutch.) On a language map of Belgium, the border between the French-speaking and the Dutch-speaking parts runs east to west and roughly slices the country in two, with the Dutch speakers to the north and the French speakers to the south. The north is generally referred to as Flanders (Vlaanderen) and the Dutch-speakers are the Flemish or Flemings; the French-speaking south is called Wallonia (La Wallonie), which is inhabited by Walloons, a few of whom still speak the dialect form of French called *wallon*. The people of Brussels are 85 per cent French-speaking, but Brussels is not part of Wallonia. The third official language, German, is spoken in the small eastern territories of Eupen, Malmédy and Moresnet ceded to Belgium in 1918 by the Treaty of Versailles.

French was imposed as the language of the ruling classes by the Burgundians in the 14th century, and by the 19th century the French-speaking population held political and economic ascendancy over the Flemish. This equation has changed radically since the Second World War, partly because of the decline of heavy industry in the south and the growing strength of modern light industries in the north, and partly because to succeed in administration it is now essential to be bilingual. Remarkably few French-speakers have made the effort to be conversant with Dutch, while a larger proportion of the Flemish have learned French. The result is that the Flemish have now gained the upper hand in the civil service, as well as in public services such as the post office and railways.

However, many of the Flemish appear to preserve a residual distaste for the French language. When you address a Belgian—particularly a civil servant—in the north of the country or in Brussels, do not assume that he or she will want to speak in French: if you happen to be talking to a Dutch-speaker, you are likely to be met with a decidedly cool response, and would be better advised to start off in English. It may subsequently turn out that French is, in fact, your most effective common language, but at least you will have established the rules of play.

Naturally enough, Dutch speakers in Brussels use the Flemish names for streets and the main sights, and may not volunteer the French equivalent. Hence be ready to be directed to the Grote Markt as opposed to the Grand' Place, the Muntplein as opposed to the Place de la Monnaie, or Nieuwstraat as opposed to Rue Neuve.

There is one final complication. The true Bruxellois, whose family has lived in Brussels for generations, may be at home in both Dutch and French, and often occupies a linguistic world somewhere in between, switching from one language to another without even being aware of it. Over time this has given rise to dialect forms of both French and Dutch, generally referred to as *bruxellois*. Although primarily Dutch in origin, *bruxellois* provides a common pool of linguistic inheritance from which both language groups draw, adding spice to their vocabulary. Few people, however, now speak pure *bruxellois*, although efforts are being made to save it from complete extinction. The Toone puppet shows (*see* p.272) are performed in *bruxellois*, for example.

Money and Banks

The currency of Belgium is the Belgian franc (abbreviated to BF or simply F), divided into 100 centimes. At the time of writing, the exchange rate is just over 60 BF to £1, or 35 BF to US$1. There are coins of 50 centimes and 1, 5, 20 and 50 BF, and notes of 100, 200, 500, 1,000, 2,000, 5,000 and 10,000 BF.

Belgium is part of the **European Monetary Union** (EMU) which has come into effect as an exchange rate. However, Euro-banknotes and coins will not replace local currency until 1 January–1 July 2002. Meanwhile, prices are quoted in both Belgian francs and Euros.

You will find no shortage of banks offering exchange facilities. **Banking hours** are not absolutely rigid but are usually 9.15–3.30 Mon–Fri, although some branches stay open until 5pm. Some branches close for lunch between 12 and 2, and a number of banks in the centre of Brussels are open on Saturday mornings. Exchange bureaux have extended opening hours, including weekends, but tend to charge higher commission rates than banks. There are **exchange bureaux** at:

> **Gare Centrale**: 7am–9pm daily
> **Gare du Nord**: 7am–10pm daily
> **Gare du Midi**: 7am–10pm daily
> **Crédit Général**: 7 Grand' Place. 24hrs Mon–Sun

Cards: Visa, Mastercard/Eurocard, Cirrus and Switch cards can be used to draw cash from banks, but usually only through automatic cash dispensers, which means you must come armed with your PIN code. Visa, Mastercard/Eurocard, Diners Club, American Express and a handful of other leading cards are all widely accepted in shops, restaurants, hotels and petrol stations, but you should always check this first: you are sure to find the occasional surprising exceptions.

Traveller's cheques are widely accepted not only for exchange, but also in lieu of cash. Eurocheques, backed by a Eurocheque card, can be used in the same way up to a limit of 7,000 BF per transaction.

> **American Express**: 100 Boulevard du Souverain, 1170 Brussels, ✆ 676 26 26 (lost cards: ✆ 676 23 23 or 676 21 21)
> **Diners Club**: 151 Boulevard Emile Jacqmain, 1210 Brussels, ✆ 206 97 99 (lost cards: ✆ 206 9800)
> **Mastercard/Eurocard/Visa**: 159 Boulevard Emile Jacqmain, 1210 Brussels, ✆ 205 85 85 (lost cards: ✆ (070) 34 43 44)

Opening Hours

The standard opening hours for **shops** are 9–5.30, but many boutiques open 10–6 or 7. Department stores have late-night shopping once a week: in Brussels this is Friday, when they stay open to 8 or 9pm. On Sundays, supermarkets and high-street shops are closed but *pâtisseries* and other specialist food shops open in the morning to cater for the tradition of Sunday lunchtime indulgence. For **bank** opening hours *see* 'Money and Banks', above; for post offices *see* below.

The large public **museums** and **galleries** are generally open over the weekend but closed on Mondays; other museums are often open on Mondays but may be closed at other times.

Post Offices

The postal service in Belgium can claim to date back to the beginning of the 16th century, and today the PTT provides a reliable service. Post offices are generally open 9–5, Mon–Fri, but the following branches have extended opening hours:

Brussels X, 1 Avenue Fonsny: open 24 hours a day, including weekends (but for fax services normal working hours only).

Centre Monnaie: 8.30–7, Sat 9–3; special office (for postal services and stamps only) open Mon–Fri 8–9am and 5–7pm, Sat 8–9am and 12–7pm. The Centre Monnaie also offers fax services (charged by the page, and very expensive) and is Brussels' main poste restante address (Poste Restante, 1000 Bruxelles 1, Belgium).

Stamps are also available from tobacconists and shops selling postcards; however, for reliable information about the cost of postage, it is best to ask at a post office.

Public Holidays

Belgium has a generous number of public holidays. On these days all banks and post offices are closed, as are most shops, bars and cafés and many of the museums and galleries. Where a public holiday falls on a Sunday, the following Monday is taken as a public holiday in lieu.

1 January	New Year's Day (*Nouvel An/Nieuwjaar*)
March/April	Easter Monday (*Pâques/Pasen*)
1 May	Labour Day (*Fête du Travail/Feest van de Arbeid*)
May	Ascension Day (6th Thurs after Easter) (*Ascension/Hemelvaart*)
	Whit Monday (seventh Mon after Easter) (*Pentecôte/Pinksteren*)
21 July	Independence Day (*Fête Nationale/Nationale Feestdag*)
15 August	Assumption (*Assomption/Maria Hemelvaart*)
1 November	All Saints' (*Toussaint/Allerheiligen*)
11 November	Armistice Day (*Armistice/Wapenstilstand*)
25 December	Christmas Day (*Noël/Kerstmis*)

Public offices and institutions are also closed on 15 November (Dynasty Day) and 26 December (Boxing Day).

Telephones

Telephoning in Belgium presents few problems. If you are staying in a hotel the switchboard can connect your call, but this is usually far more expensive than using a public telephone. These take 5 BF and 20 BF coins, but if you intend to make a lot of calls a 'Telecard' is a good investment. Telecards are available from tobacconists, newsagents, post offices and public transport ticket offices and cost either 200 BF for 20 units or 1,000 BF for 105 units. They can be used in any public telephone bearing the Telecard sign; telephone boxes showing a row of foreign flags on the window can be used for international calls. The illustrated instructions in telephone boxes are easy enough to follow, and a liquid-crystal display tells you how many units you have left on your card.

The area code for Brussels from elsewhere in Belgium is ✆ (02), but this does not have to be used within the city. All phone numbers in this book that are not preceded by a bracketed code are Brussels numbers. The country code for Belgium is 32 and if you are calling Brussels you should then dial 2 instead of 02.

To make an international call from Belgium dial 00, then the country code, then the area code without the initial 0, then the number. The country code for the UK is 44, for Ireland 353, for the USA and Canada 1, for Australia 61 and for New Zealand 64.

There is a specialist telephone centre at the head office of Belgacom at 17 Boulevard de l'Impératrice, 1000 Brussels, 8am–10pm daily, from where you can make or receive phone calls, send faxes, telexes or telegrams.

In Brussels: directory enquiries within Belgium: ✆ 1307
directory enquiries within Europe: ✆ 1304
directory enquiries outside Europe: ✆ 1324
person-to-person reverse charge/collect calls: ✆ 1324

For collect calls, dial ✆ 0800100 + country code. Exceptions are USA (✆ 080010010) and Canada (✆ 0800 10019).

Time

Brussels is on Central European Time and is one hour ahead of Britain throughout the year. It is six hours ahead of US Eastern Standard Time, nine hours ahead of California and nine hours behind Sydney.

Tipping

On the question of tipping, relax. Except in the few circumstances listed here, it is not generally expected. In restaurants a 16% service charge is usually included in the bill, along with 21 per cent TVA (Value Added Tax), and so additional tipping is not expected. If you have had table service at a bar or café, it is usual (but not essential) to leave any small change (say 20 BF for a small order). Service is included in hotels, so there is no need to tip porters or staff providing room service. In taxis it is usual to round up the total by 10–15 per cent, but note that in metered taxis the tip is included in the fare. Ushers taking your ticket or showing you to your seat in cinemas will expect a tip of about 10 BF per seat. Similarly, cloakroom attendants may expect 10–50 BF. Lastly, attendants in public lavatories will expect 10 BF or so; minimum charges are posted at the entrance, and the attendant herself will usually be there to enforce it.

Tourist Information

The main tourist office in Brussels is a tiny room beneath the arches of the Hôtel de Ville. The staff can offer all kinds of advice about what to see and when, and about special activities and guided tours; they will make hotel reservations for you, and also offer a reservations service for theatres and concerts. They publish various annual brochures, including their useful Guide and Map (100 BF), and a free weekly programme of events. For information about Flemish Belgium, there is a separate office in the nearby Rue du Marché aux Herbes, where copious literature about the various regions is available. There is also a tourist office at the airport.

The Belgian tourist board has offices in London and New York, which can supply you with information before you leave home.

Brussels: Office de Tourisme et d'Information de Bruxelles (TIB), Hôtel de Ville, Grand' Place, 1000 Brussels, ✆ 513 89 40, ✉ 514 45 38. Open daily 9–6, Sundays in winter 10–2.

Belgium: Commissariat Général au Tourisme/Commissariat General voor Toerisme, 63 Rue du Marché aux Herbes/Grasmarkt, 1000 Brussels, ✆ 504 03 90, ✉ 504 02 70 Open Mon–Sat 9–6 (until 7pm in summer), Sun 1–5 (9–7 in summer).

Belgian Tourist Office, 31 Pepper Street, London E14 9RW, ✆ (0171) 458 2929.

Belgian Tourist Office, 780 Third Avenue, Suite 1501, New York 10017, ✆ (212) 758 8130, ✉ (212) 355 7675.

On the **Internet** there is an enormous amount of disparate information on the official website of the Brussels Capital Region at *www.bruxelles.irisnet.be*. The Walloon-Brussels Tourist Board also has a site at *www.belgium-tourism.net*.

Atomium	194
Cathédrale St-Michel	194
Centre Belge de la Bande Dessinée	195
The Grand' Place	196
Manneken-Pis	199
Musée du Cinéma	200
Musée du Cinquantenaire	201
Musée Horta	202
Musée de l'Hôtel Charlier	203
Musée des Instruments de Musique	204
Musées Royaux des Beaux-Arts	204
Musée Wiertz	207
Palais de Justice	208
Rue des Bouchers	209
Tour Japonaise, Pavillon Chinois, Japanese Art Museum	209
Waterloo	210

Brussels: Essential Sights

Atomium

Boulevard du Centenaire. Ⓜ *Heysel.*

Open Sept–March 10–6, April–Aug 9–8; adm 200 BF, children 3–12 years old 160 BF. Combined ticket with Mini Europe 540 BF, with Océade 630 BF.

The Atomium was designed as the centrepiece of the Exposition Universelle et Internationale de Bruxelles of 1958—a showpiece of the then-powerful Belgian metal industry. During the 1950s the atomic structure, the foundation stone of the New Jerusalem of atomic power, was a popular design theme, first seen on a grand scale at the Festival of Britain Exhibition of 1951 and popularized in the form of 'cocktail-cherry' motifs (coloured plastic beads) found on clocks, coat hangers and record racks of the era. In 1958 a group of Belgian designers went the whole hog, creating this giant-sized version of an iron atom. This is architectural kitsch on a grand scale. Sorely compromised by the practical necessity of grounding the structure to earth with fire escapes, it looks more like a Dan Dare space station than a conceptual image from particle physics. To underline the absurdity of its scale, the Atomium often flies a Belgian tricolour from its top sphere. Yet the Atomium is a remarkable thing: with its nine giant steel balls interconnected by metal tubes (containing escalators) and rising to 102m, it is the Eiffel Tower of Brussels. (A programme of renovation is planned for the year 2000 or 2001, during which time it may be temporarily closed.)

Inside, a glass-topped lift whisks you up the central shaft to the Panorama at 100m. From here you can see right across Brussels (assisted by strategically placed maps) to Altitude 100 at Forst, the highest point of the city (100m) way over to the south. You can look down on the Parc de Laeken and over Bruparck. Beside Bruparck, at the top of the Boulevard du Centenaire, is the Parc des Expositions, a huge complex built for another international exhibition in 1935. To its left is the famous Heysel football stadium, a name familiar to all British and Italian football fans, for it was here, in 1985, at the European Cup Final between Juventus and Liverpool, that 'running' (a British football-hooligan expression meaning to charge at opposing fans) by Liverpool fans caused a wall to collapse in the old and crumbling stadium, killing some 40 people (39 of them Italians). It has since been renamed King Baudouin Stadium.

Cathédrale St-Michel

Rue de Treurenberg. Ⓜ *Gare Centrale.*

Open daily 8–6; adm free.

Brussels' cathedral is currently undergoing a massive programme of restoration, which is bringing its creamy-grey stone back to life, but unfortunately this means that large portions of the interior have been closed off for many a year. Renovations are due to be completed in January 2000. It may seem unfair to criticize a building still in the midst of restoration, but sadly this is not Brussels' greatest church. Its twin towers struggle to be noticed among the modern buildings that surround it, and it seems isolated from the real centre of the city. (The spire of the Hôtel de Ville can be seen from the parapet.)

If it seems disappointing as Brussels' cathedral, that may be explained by the fact that it was ravaged twice—by Protestant iconoclasts in 1579 and French revolutionaries in 1793. Furthermore, it only became a cathedral in 1962, when the archbishopric of Mechelen-Brussels was created. In the past it was a collegiate church dedicated to St Michael (the male patron saint of Brussels) and Ste Gudule (the female equivalent).

Ste Gudule, an 8th-century lady of royal blood, was celebrated for her piety. She is often portrayed holding a lamp, since the most famous tale about her concerns her battle with the devil, who kept on blowing out her light when she attempted to reach her isolated chapel in the marshes to pray. Through the power of prayer, however, she was able to rekindle the flame. Her venerated remains were brought to this church from the chapel on Ile Saint-Géry in the 11th century. When the church became a cathedral, however, it was named after St Michael alone because Ste Gudule was not on the official papal register, but the people of Brussels still obstinately refer to the cathedral as 'Sainte-Gudule'.

The original Romanesque church was replaced after 1226 by the present Gothic one, which then took three centuries to complete. The towers were designed by Jan van Ruysbroeck, the 15th-century architect of the Hôtel de Ville; they contain a 50-bell carillon, most of which was installed in 1975.

The interior is light and airy, with some spectacularly delicate stone tracery in the clerestory. A series of 17th-century statues of the apostles attached to the columns of the nave seem incongruous—albeit that they were commissioned from notable sculptors such as Luc Fayd'herbe and Jérôme Duquesnoy the Younger (son of the creator of the Manneken-Pis). For Baroque ponderousness, however, the monumental oak pulpit is supreme: it is a riot of figures and foliage. Adam and Eve stand beneath the Tree of Knowledge, berated by St Michael and a skeleton; the serpent snakes upwards to the firmament, where its head is crushed with a cross held by the Infant Jesus under the protective arms of the Virgin Mary. Baroque pulpits such as this are found throughout Belgium, and this is one of the most celebrated, created by the sculptor Hendrik Verbruggen (c. 1655–1724) in 1699.

The stained glass windows in the transepts date from 1537 and 1538 and were designed by the gifted painter Bernard van Orley. They depict (north) the king of the day, Charles V (1500–58), and his wife, Isabella of Portugal; and (south) Mary of Hungary, sister of Charles V, and her husband. Stairs in the nave lead down to what appears to be a crypt, but in fact simply shows the recently excavated foundations of the Romanesque church (*open 10–5pm, except during Mass on Sun; adm 40 BF*).

Centre Belge de la Bande Dessinée

(Comic-strip Museum), 20 Rue des Sables. Ⓜ *Rogier/Botanique.*

Open 10–6, closed Mon; adm 200 BF.

This shrine to the comic strip is housed in an old Art Nouveau textile megastore designed in 1903 for Les Magasins Waucquez by Victor Horta, and stylishly renovated in the 1980s.

The comic strip is an art form which is far better developed—and far more popular and widely appreciated—in Belgium, France and Italy than in any English-speaking nation. However, the Belgians credit an American cartoonist, Winsor McCay, with the origins of the European comic-strip tradition. He created 'Little Nemo in Slumberland' for the *New York Herald* in 1905, and when *Les Adventures du Petit Nemo au Pays des Songes* appeared in French in 1908 it proved a wild success. Belgian artists soon became leaders of this new field, and as their characters became better known, their escapades became more ambitious and the magazines more substantial. By far the most famous of these characters is Tintin, whose creator, Hergé, began producing novel-type adventures in book form after the Second World War.

Tintin, naturally enough, is accorded a special place in this museum, with original drawings, historical notes and some 3-D models of famous Tintin scenes. Other characters, such as Lucky Luke the lackadaisical cowboy (by Maurice de Bevere), are only vaguely recognized by the English-speaking public, but are known to every Belgian. There are hundreds more: Gaston Lagaffe (by André Franquin), Petit Biniou (by Dupa), Boule et Bill and the Ribambelle gang (by Jean Roba), the wily Brussels kids Quick et Flupke (by Hergé), and numerous other characters from the hugely popular magazine *Spirou*. Asterix, by the way, is French. More recently comic-strip artists and their publishers have created a new genre of more adult works. The museum bookshop contains thousands of comic-strip books, almost all in French or Flemish, and is a measure of the scale of this industry: 850 new titles are published every year in Belgium alone.

This spacious museum is beautifully presented, with pristine Art Nouveau stairways, a superb Art Nouveau lamp in the entrance hall and cantilevered glass roofs; yet it has a strangely serious air, given its subject. The people poring over the comic strips are not children but adults. It is a window on the extraordinary talents of comic-strip artists, and rewarding for devotees of Tintin and Victor Horta (the museum includes a section devoted to his work, with an audiovisual on Art Nouveau design)—but others may find that the cultural gap is just too wide to justify the admission charge. (Annotation is in French and Flemish only.)

In the late 1990s the museum supported the setting-up of a 'comic-strip route' in the city centre. From the Gare du Midi/Zuid Station to the Gare du Nord you can follow a trail of murals, façades and statues depicting Belgian comic-strip heroes, and at the same time discover hidden streets in the heart of the city.

The Grand' Place

Ⓜ *Bourse.*

Quite what Brussels would be without the Grand' Place does not bear thinking about. The good burghers of Brussels looked this prospect in the face in 1695. Having failed to raise the siege of Namur by William III of England, Marshal de Villeroy, leading the French troops of Louis XIV, issued an ultimatum: Brussels would be bombed unless the English and Dutch lifted their blockade of the French ports. He gave the authorities just six hours to consult all parties, then on the night of 13 August his troops opened up a great barrage, demolishing the Grand' Place along with nearly 4,000 houses and 16 churches. The splendid tower of the Hôtel de Ville was practically the sole survivor—something of a paradox, since this was what the artillery had used as their principal target. What you see, then, is not quite what it seems. The Grand' Place looks like a perfect Flemish Renaissance-Baroque square, but much of it was built at the very end of the 17th century, within five years of the bombardment, in a style that was already outmoded and retrospective.

The Grand' Place was Brussels' main marketplace from the very beginnings of the city's history. The names of the streets that lead into the square today bear witness to this past: Rue au Beurre (butter street), Rue Chair et Pain (meat and bread), Rue des Harengs (herrings), and so on. These streets once threaded past various halls and covered markets occupied by butchers, bakers, cheesemongers, fishmongers and other traders.

The rising stars of civic power in medieval times were the *échevins*, assistants to the burgomaster. In the 1390s they permitted the formation of *corporations*, guilds of craftsmen and traders which became the backbone of the economy. Then during the 15th century the *échevins* organized the building of a grand Hôtel de Ville—a bold statement of the city's wealth and pride which confirmed the Grand' Place's central role in the public life of Brussels. This was where all important public decrees would be announced; it was the setting for colourful pageants and jousting tournaments—and also the scene of public executions. The guilds wanted to be near the seat of civic authority, and during the 16th century the borders of the old market square started to fill up with their guildhouses, first in wood, then in stone.

The Grand' Place was now less a market, more the city's gathering place, busy with ladies and gentlemen parading in their finery, gilded carriages, carts, stray dogs, mobile theatres, hawkers, quacks and charlatans. The centre of Brussels earned a reputation for lively taverns, reckless spending and licentiousness—and the *échevins* were soon struggling to formulate legislation to curb this behaviour. The role of the Grand' Place as the city centre survived even after the guilds were disbanded in the 1790s by French Revolutionaries.

With the large-scale renovations to the Hôtel de Ville and the Maison du Roi during the 19th century and in recent decades, the Grand' Place could have become a museum piece, but it hasn't: today the old guildhouses are occupied by cafés, banks, hotels, lace shops—even a pet-supply store. Now that all traffic has been outlawed, a daily plant and flower 'market' (actually just a couple of stallholders) occupies the centre stage, and every Sunday morning (*8–12.30*) this is joined by a bird market.

A Tour of the Grand' Place

Our tour of the Grand' Place starts in the northwest corner, where the Rue du Marché au Charbon (coal-market street) enters the square.

Like most of the buildings lining the Grand' Place, **No. 7** has a picturesque name, Le Renard (The Fox). Many of the guildhouses' names date back to the earliest building occupying the site and have no link with the guilds themselves. The name Le Renard (Flemish: *De Vos*) predates the acquisition of the building by the haberdashers' guild in the 15th century; it was later elaborated by the carving of the fox over the doorway. A statue of St Nicholas, patron saint of haberdashers as well as of merchants generally, stands on the crest of the gable.

No. 6 is Le Cornet (The Horn), the most successful of the buildings designed by one of the main architects of the Grand' Place, Antoon Pastorana. This was the boatmen's guildhouse and is encrusted with marine symbols. The gable resembles the stern of a galleon, and the horn that gives the building its name can be seen over the central window.

No. 5 is La Louve (The She-Wolf), so named because there is a statue over the entrance of Romulus and Remus suckling the wolf. This was the house of the archers, a kind of city militia raised to the rank of a corporation. This connection made the house the target of assault in 1793 by *sans-culottes* inspired by the French Revolution, who pulled down the statues on the third storey. Since restored to their plinths, these represent Truth, Falsehood, Peace and Discord; the medallions set high on the façade show Emperors Trajan, Tiberius, Caesar Augustus and Julius Caesar, who are held to be symbols of each of these properties. The gable is topped by a phoenix rising out of the ashes.

No. 4 is Le Sac (The Sack). Over the door two jolly-looking characters are standing with an open sack, one with his head in it. This became the guildhouse of the cabinet-makers and coopers in 1444, and the lower two storeys, constructed in 1644, survived the bombardment of 1695. The later upper storeys—richly adorned with cherubs, barley-sugar balustrades, cornucopiae, garlands and urns—are another example of the work of Antoon Pastorana.

No. 3 is La Brouette (The Wheelbarrow), with the forerunners of the modern wheelbarrow pictured over the door. This belonged to the tallow merchants—demonstrating their power in the days before petrol-based lubricants and electric lighting. A statue (1912) of their patron saint, St Gilles, stands over the gable.

Nos. 1 and 2 form La Maison des Boulangers (The Bakers' House), the grandest of the guild-houses, distinguished by its elegant domed lantern in place of a gable. The golden head over the door is St Lambert, patron saint of bakers. The six figures lining the balustrade represent the elements needed to make bread: energy, grain, wind, fire, water and prudence. The bust in the middle of the upper storey is the King of Spain ('Den Coninck van Spaignien'), Charles II (r.1661–1700). The kings of Spain were effectively rulers of this country from 1517 to 1713, during which Spain was one of the most powerful lands on earth. Their reputation as imperial rulers is given a somewhat backhanded compliment by the two figures flanking the bust of the king, an American Indian and a Moor in a turban, both looking dejected with their hands tied behind their backs. The canons and flags are rather misplaced symbols of imperial glory: Charles II was both mentally and physically handicapped and furthermore had no direct heir. During his reign the Spanish empire began to falter. Medallions of the Roman Emperors were used for both decorative effect and to imply a moral message: here Antoninus Pius and Trajan represent long and just rule; Nerva and Decius, by contrast, had dubious claims to power and ruled for only a couple of years. The gilded figure of Fame, perched on the top of the dome, is one of the most delightful statues in the Grand' Place.

The Rue au Beurre enters the Grand' Place at the northern corner. To the right there is a series of less elaborate houses, dated 1696–7 and now occupied by cafés and lace shops. No. 37, Le Chêne (The Oak), was once the guildhouse of the weavers, the most powerful guild of the medieval period. Moving clockwise, you come to the Rue Chair et Pain and the **Maison du Roi**. For over a century now the Maison du Roi has housed the city museum, the Musée Communal de la Ville de Bruxelles (*see* p.214).

Next to the Rue des Harengs is **No. 28**, La Chambrette de L'Amman (The 'Little Room' of the Amman). The Amman was the Duke of Brabant's representative to the council of *échevins*, and also a senior legal officer. His main office was over the other side of the square, at L'Etoile (*see* below). **No. 27** shares a frontage with **No. 26** and is known as Le Pigeon (The Pigeon), acquired by the Guild of Painters in 1510 and reconstructed after 1695. Plaques on either side of the door of No. 26 announce the fact that Victor Hugo lived here in 1852. A bitter critic of Louis Napoleon, who had just declared himself Emperor Napoleon III, Victor Hugo had been forced to flee from France. He stayed in this house for several months, protected from the intrusions of an admiring public by his landlady, Madame Sébert, who owned the tobacconist's on the ground floor. When Victor Hugo, by his continued vitriolic outpourings against Napoleon III, became a security risk and embarrassment to the Belgian government, he went to live in the British Channel Islands, but returned frequently to Brussels.

Next door is another double-fronted house, **Nos. 24 and 25**, designed by another of the great architects of the Grand' Place, Willem de Bruyn. Called La Maison des Tailleurs (The Tailors' House), it has a bust of the patron saint of tailors, St Barbara, over the entrance, and St Boniface on the gable, beneath whom you can see a plaque bearing tailor's shears.

Nos. 22 and 21 form another pair. The two houses are known as Anna-Joseph from the inscription over the lower windows. (The reference is to Joseph, husband of the Virgin Mary, and Anne, her mother.) The iron pulley on the gable is a survivor from the days when stores and furniture were raised to the upper storeys on ropes, rather than up the internal stairs. **No. 20** is known as Le Cerf (The Stag); the stag in question can be seen sculpted in relief around the corner in the Rue de la Colline.

The entire south of the Grand' Place is occupied by **La Maison des Ducs de Brabant**—in fact a series of six houses unified by a single façade and designed as a whole in 1698 by Willem de Bruyn. The building was conceived in palatial style, and is decorated by the busts of the dukes of Brabant (which gave the building its grand name). **No. 13** houses the Cocoa and Chocolate museum, *see* p.252.

The last stretch of gabled buildings begins with **Nos. 12 and 11**, dating from 1699 and 1702 respectively and called Le Mont Thabor (Mount Thabor) and La Rose (The Rose)—so named because it belonged to the Van der Rosen family and was used as a private house.

No. 10 is La Maison des Brasseurs (The Brewers' House), for this was the headquarters of the brewers' guild, and is the only house in the Grand' Place still occupied by the guild which built it, now called the Confédération des Brasseries de Belgique. It houses a small museum of brewing, the Musée de la Brasserie, *see* p.252. This is one of the most striking buildings of the Grand' Place—a reflection of the wealth and standing of brewers since medieval times. Beer was the most common drink in Europe before the development of safe piped water in the late 19th century. The crew of a man-of-war in Napoleonic times, for example, were given 4.5 litres of the stuff as part of their daily rations. Statistics for the Belgian brewing industry today are no less impressive: the industry's total annual output is 14,000 million litres, more than 1,000 litres per head of population. Designed by Willem de Bruyn, the Maison des Brasseurs is unusual in that the columns rise right through the second and third floors to a simple but effective semi-circular pediment. Note the hop vines and grain stalks entwined around the lower sections of the columns.

No. 9 is Le Cygne (The Swan), so named after the sculpture of a swan, wings outstretched, over the door. This elegant, classical-style house was rebuilt as a private dwelling in 1698 but became the butchers' guildhouse in 1720. It differs from others in the Grand' Place by having a dome-shaped roof pierced by dormer windows in place of a gable. Le Cygne is now an expensive restaurant, an ironic twist of fate given that Karl Marx used to hold meetings of the Deutscher Arbeitverein (German Workers' Union) in a café on this site during the period that he was writing the *Communist Manifesto* with Friedrich Engels.

No. 8 is L'Etoile (The Star), built over the arched arcade that leads into the Rue Charles Buls. This was the main office and residence of the Amman, one of whose duties was to oversee executions as the king's representative. It is said that his balcony gave him a good view of executions taking place in the Grand' Place. The original building was demolished in 1850 to given better road access to the Grand' Place, and the present building was erected over an arcade in the 1890s, to redress the lost sense of architectural balance.

For the **Hôtel de Ville**, *see* p.217.

Manneken-Pis

Intersection of Rue des Grands-Carmes and Rue de l'Etuve. ⓜ *Bourse/Anneessens.*

Manneken is *bruxellois* for little man; Pis speaks for itself. This bronze statue of a little naked boy peeing with happy abandon has long been held in great affection by the people of Brussels and has become a symbol of their city. No one can quite explain why—which must be part of his charm.

Endless legends have evolved to fill this gap in human knowledge. One is that the statue celebrates a little boy who prevented a great fire during the time of the Burgundian dukes by extinguishing a firebomb in this manner. Another relates how a wealthy citizen lost his son in the carnival crowds. When the child was found, his grateful father decided to have a statue made of the boy in the pose—and erected in the place—in which he was discovered. In another version, relating back to the 12th century, the infant Godfrey, future Duke of Brabant, was taken to the battlefield where Brussels was fighting against Mechelen. He was placed in the branches of an oak tree to watch the battle, where he was discovered by one of the enemy. Godfrey's response was to piss in his face, a gesture of scorn that so demoralized the whole Mechelen army that they fled.

Here's another idea. One day the infant son of Duke John III of Brabant exposed himself to a company of women in the Rue de l'Etuve. This coincided with a period during which the 14th-century mystic philosopher Jean de Ruysbroeck was having a great public debate with another Brussels mystic called Bloemaerdinne. Bloemaerdinne argued that there was no sin involved in fulfilling the natural impulses of love—an idea that appealed to the hedonistic Bruxellois. A statue of the child served as an apt symbol of Bloemaerdinne's cause.

Perhaps, more prosaically, it was just a rather apt and charming adornment for a public fountain in a district where there were public baths during medieval times (*étuve* means 'steam-bath').

Whatever, when the first bronze statue was cast by Jérôme Duquesnoy the Elder in 1619, it was probably based on an earlier model. Duquesnoy's version was already held in great affection when French soldiers tried to carry it off in 1747. The citizens of Brussels were furious, and to make amends Louis XV had a brocaded suit made for the Manneken-Pis—the first in his splendid collection of costumes (a selection of which can be seen at the Musée Communal de la Ville de Bruxelles, *see* p.214). In 1793 he was given a Revolutionary bonnet by the Paris Convention. When an ex-convict stole the Manneken-Pis in 1817 the town was distraught; the culprit was caught and branded in the Grand' Place, then sentenced to eleven lifetimes' hard labour. But the statue was in ruins and had to be recast. This, then, is the statue you see today. It is much smaller than you expect, perched on his plinth behind high railings. A programme listing which costume he will be wearing over the current period is posted on the railings.

Musée du Cinéma

Palais des Beaux-Arts, 9 Rue Baron Horta. Ⓜ *Gare Centrale.*

Open daily, 5.30pm–10.30pm; adm 90 BF, or 60 BF if pre-booked 24 hours in advance; children under 16 not admitted.

The Musée du Cinéma has two auditoriums, one screening a programme of three 'art films' every evening starting at 6.15pm (most shown in their original language with French subtitles), the other showing old silent films at 7pm and 9pm every evening, accompanied by live piano music. The museum publishes a leaflet each month (20 BF) giving details of its programme. Tickets are valid for 2 hours and include entrance to the auditoriums. However, possession of a ticket is no guarantee that you will get a seat: the auditorium for silent films has only 30 seats, so for a popular movie you have to hover near the entrance for some time before the film starts to be sure of a place. Alternatively you can reserve a seat by telephoning, ✆ 507 83 70, after 9.30am on the day itself (or on Friday for the weekend). Reserved seats have to be taken up at least 15 minutes before the start, otherwise they are offered to waiting hopefuls in the foyer.

Laid out in the restful, dimly lit foyer are numerous ingenious exhibits to demonstrate the early history of the moving image, including such early wonders as the Phénakisticope (1832) and Zoetrope (1834), in which series of images pasted to spinning drums and discs appear to move. Eadweard Muybridge's experiments of the 1870s, using multiple cameras triggered by people or animals in motion, demonstrated the potential of photography to show movement, a concept pursued in conjunction with the magic lantern by Emile Reynaud in 1881. But the breakthrough was made ten years later by Thomas Edison with his Kinetograph using celluloid film. This history is succinctly explained through working models and various historic exhibits, many of them set up to operate at the push of a button.

Musée du Cinquantenaire

Parc du Cinquantenaire. (Formally known as the Musées Royaux d'Art et d'Histoire.)
Ⓜ *Schuman/Mérode.*
Open Tues–Fri 9.30–5, Sat and Sun 10–5, closed Mon; adm 150 BF, students 100 BF and children 50 BF. Note that the Salle aux Trésors (Treasure Room, see below) is open 10–12 and 1–4 (entry restricted to 50 visitors at a time).

Since its foundation in 1835, this collection has accumulated a wealth of historical and anthropological artefacts, in the tradition of the great European capitals—from Phoenician glass and Hoplite helmets to medieval tankards and Renaissance armillary spheres, from *netsuke* and Chinese Buddhas to Brazilian Indian headdresses and erotic Art Nouveau sculptures.

Under the new and inspired direction of Francis van Noten, the museum has been transformed in recent years from a dusty and lifeless exhibition into one of Europe's truly great museums. It is primarily a question of presentation: the exhibits have been beautifully rearranged in well-lit glass cases, and redistributed in a way that makes full use of the grandeur of this extraordinary building, with its palatial halls and corridors and clusters of smaller rooms, separated by sweeping marble staircases, domed lobbies topped by glass lanterns and courtyards filled with greenery. The building, the Hall Bordiau, is the sole survivor of a pair of exhibition halls designed by Gédéon Bordiau for the 1880 *Cinquantenaire* (jubilee celebrations of the Belgian nation)—a huge canopy of glass and blue-painted cast-iron, and a monument to 19th-century industrial ingenuity. (Bordiau, it might be noted, was also the architect of the sumptuous Métropole Hôtel, *see* p.265.) Because of the eclectic nature of the contents, the museum holds out the constant promise of discovery as you proceed around it. Restoration and reorganization are likely to continue for several years, but the bulk of the work has been achieved. The reorganized Art Nouveau and Art Deco sections will be open in spring 2000, and an entirely new collection of Islamic art should be open in November 2000.

You cannot hope to see everything. The best policy is to decide what you want to see, then use the somewhat confusing colour-coded map of the museum's three levels to plan your route. Note that the **Treasure Room** has limited opening hours, so head here first if open. Dramatically lit in a darkened circular room with massive pillars, like a crypt, it contains a superb collection of medieval treasures—gilded and bejewelled reliquaries and medieval church treasures, ivories, jewellery and textiles.

Particularly worth seeking out are the 'Arts Décoratifs' of the Middle Ages, Renaissance and Baroque periods on Level 1. This includes superb Brussels tapestries designed by Bernard van Orley (c. 1499–1541), a remarkable collection of carved, painted and gilded retables (altarpieces) for which Brussels was famous, as well as church treasures and reliquaries, and fragments of medieval houses.

Level 1 also includes a series of rooms displaying 19th-century furniture, one of which contains some superb examples of the Empire style—the form of neoclassicism favoured by Napoleon, ornamented by ormolu sphinxes, lion's feet and palmette motifs. Also in this group is 'La Salle Wolfers', in which Art Nouveau and Art Deco artefacts are displayed in glass-fronted cases from the Magasins Wolfers, designed by Victor Horta in 1909. Art Nouveau had a special line in sensuous female statues for the mantelpiece, made of ivory, silver and bronze—a theme later given a more overtly erotic twist by Art Deco designers. *Le Sphinx Mystérieux*, a helmeted female bust made of ivory and cupro-silver, might be seen as a kind of icon of the age.

Other rewarding rooms on this level are devoted to ornate carriages, ornamental clocks, and a supreme collection of Mesoamerican pottery and sculpture.

Musée Horta

25 Rue Américaine. Ⓜ *Horta.*

Open Tues–Sun 2–5.30, closed Mon and public holidays; adm 150 BF on weekdays, 200 BF at weekends.

Victor Horta was the father of Art Nouveau architecture, and this museum was his home and studio. The son of a Ghent shoemaker, Horta was something of a child prodigy. He attended architecture courses at the Académie des Beaux-Arts in Ghent from the age of 13, and won a gold medal for his work two years later. He spent three influential years as an apprentice in Paris (1878–81) before returning to study at the Académie des Beaux-Arts in Brussels. Here he joined the practice of Alphonse Balat (1818–95), Leopold II's favourite architect, who is best remembered for the huge royal glasshouses, the Serres de Laeken. In 1884 Horta won the Prix Godecharle for architecture, and the following year he began to design houses on his own account. In 1889 he created the Edicule Lambeaux (now called the Pavillon Horta), a temple-like pavilion in the Parc du Cinquantenaire which was built to house relief sculptures by Jef Lambeaux (*see* p.241). It demonstrates Horta's strong feeling for neoclassical proportion.

The Hôtel Tassel (in nearby Rue Paul-Emile Janson), built in 1893, was his breakthrough—the first house in the style soon to be dubbed 'Art Nouveau'. For a decade or so Horta reigned supreme in the world of house-design. He was an '*ensemblier*'—an architect who conceptualized not only the building but everything within it. It was an exacting task, requiring great imaginative and practical energy from himself and his team of draughtsmen. After 1898 he was working on both his home and the Maison du Peuple (built 1898–9), an ambitious complex near the Sablon, demolished in 1965.

In the early 1900s, however, a new vogue began to take over, led by the architects and painters of the Vienna Secession. Like Mackintosh in Scotland, they adopted a more symmetrical, angular, upright look, prefiguring Art Deco. The Palais Stoclet outside the city centre is the outstanding example of this in Brussels. The sensuous, organic lines of Art Nouveau began to look outmoded to private clients, and from now on Horta did little domestic architecture.

Instead, he concentrated on a number of new department stores, to which he applied his usual attention to detail. These included L'Innovation (1900–03), in the Rue Neuve, which was destroyed in 1967 by a horrific fire that killed 251 people; the Magasins Waucquez (1903–06), now the home of the Centre Belge de la Bande Dessinée (see p.195); and the Magasins Wolfers (1909), Rue d'Arenberg, whose salvaged display cases can be seen in the Musée du Cinquantenaire (see p.201). His major projects of the inter-war period were the Palais des Beaux-Arts and the Halte-Centrale in the Quartier Ravenstein. As a widely respected figure in the architectural world, holding eminent positions at various institutes, he was made a baron in 1932. He died in 1947.

Victor Horta built this museum building as his home and studio in 1899–1901, when he was at the pinnacle of his powers. It was bought by the Commune de Saint-Gilles in 1961, and opened as the Musée Horta in 1969. The interior, which had remained more or less intact, has been carefully restored and is now furnished with pieces Horta designed for the house, as well as others from his buildings elsewhere. As soon as you walk through the front door, the Art Nouveau motifs in the mosaic flooring and the flowing shapes of the coathooks, hatstand and door furniture tell you that you are entering a manicured environment. As in the jewellery of René Lalique, the glassware of Emile Gallé, or the furniture of Louis Majorelle, the genius of good Art Nouveau design is not just in the grace of these sensuous shapes but in the element of surprise. Look out, for instance, for the ribbed, angular shapes of some of Horta's details, as in the brass, columned pier of the entrance lobby and the supports for the arches in the dining room—a room which, with a stroke of inventive daring, he lined with white-enamelled industrial brick. Much of the furniture is in American ash, a pale, matt-surfaced wood far removed from the typically sombre and heavy furniture of the late Victorian period.

One of the distinctive features of a Horta house is his use of light, particularly in stairwells lit by an overhead canopy of glass. Here the stairs rise to a crescendo of gold, white and copper beneath the glass canopy, enhanced by pond-shaped mirrors, abstracted floral designs on the walls, and the ribbon-like wrought-iron of the light fittings (originally gas) and banisters. The overall effect is one of elegance, comfort and uplifting joyousness.

Musée de l'Hôtel Charlier

16 Avenue des Arts. Ⓜ *Madou.*

Open Mon 10–5, Tues, Wed 1.30–5; Thurs, Fri 1.30–4.30; closed Sat, Sun and public holidays; adm 100 BF; ring on the brass doorbell to gain entry.

The Hôtel Charlier is a grand *maison de maître*, built in the 19th century in neoclassical style. In 1890 it was bought by the wealthy and cultivated Henri van Curtsem, who commissioned Victor Horta (*see* above) to replan the interior. A great patron of the arts, Van Curtsem effectively adopted a poor young sculptor called Guillaume Charlier, and gave the house to him when he retired to the country. Charlier maintained Van Curtsem's tradition that had made the house a cultural meeting point, and he left the house to the surrounding commune, Saint-Josse-ten-Noode, when he died in 1925. Preserved as a museum since 1928, it offers an exceptional insight into the décor of a house where the well-to-do of the late 19th century entertained their friends.

This was a period in which interest in antique furniture was growing, and the house includes a series of rooms in period style, such as the Salon Louis XV, with its fine marquetry bombé chests, and the Salon Chinois, with coromandel lacquer furniture. The Empire-style bedroom contains an excellent collection of furniture and accessories, decorated with ormolu plaques, sphinxes and caryatids. Contemporary late 19th-century taste is represented by paintings by James Ensor, Fernand Khnopff, Léon Frédéric and others, and sculpture by Rik Wouters and Charlier himself. Look out for the glass display case by Victor Horta, an ingenious and typically elegant solution to a design problem.

A room at the top of the house provides a historical perspective on the commune of Saint-Josse: old prints show the city walls that once ran along the street below.

Musée des Instruments de Musique

> *(Musical Instruments Museum). Old England, 2 Montagne de la Cour.* Ⓜ *Gare Centrale.*
>
> *Closed until June 2000. Opening hours and adm charges will be announced in spring 2000.*

This museum contains over 6,000 items from all over the globe and is one of the biggest of its kind in the world. The European collection includes numerous interesting oddities, such as the 18th-century kits or pochettes—tiny violins which dancemasters could carry about in their pockets. The vast tromba marina, dated 1680, is a single-stringed cello-like instrument that can only produce harmonics—amplified by 20 sympathetic strings inside the triangular body—creating the unearthly sound that gave it its misleading name, 'marine trumpet'. The glass harmonica designed by the American statesman and inventor Benjamin Franklin (1706–90) produces a similarly eerie humming sound by employing the same principle as running a wet finger around the rim of a wine glass. Beethoven and Mozart both wrote music for it.

The museum is housed in a former department store called **Old England**; the name is a throwback to the late 19th century when the British Arts and Crafts movement and Liberty style were all the rage. A classic Art Nouveau building, it was designed by Paul Saintenoy (1862–1952) and completed in 1899. As part of its recent restoration as the new home for this museum, it was stripped to its essentials—cast-iron pillars with characteristic swirling Art Nouveau motifs, and steel joists painted with floral decoration. When the museum reopens, there will be a roof-top café and terrace offering panoramic views of the capital, just as it did in the late 19th century.

Musées Royaux des Beaux-Arts

> *3 Rue de la Régence. From spring 2000 the museum will have two entrances: 3 Rue de la Régence for the Musée d'Art Ancien, and 1–2 Place Royale for the Musée d'Art Moderne.* Ⓜ *Gare Centrale.*
>
> *Open Tues–Sun 10–5, closed Mon and public holidays; adm 150 BF, free 1–5 on first Wed of every month. Note that galleries of the 15th, 16th and 19th centuries close for lunch 12–1pm; 17th, 18th and 20th centuries close for lunch 1–2pm.*

By the standards of most major national art collections, the Musées Royaux des Beaux-Arts are refreshingly single-minded. The main focus is squarely on Belgian art—or at least the art of the Low Countries for those centuries before Belgium came into existence. Italy and Spain, even France, barely get a look in, but nonetheless the collection is a ravishing *tour de force* and a monument to the technical virtuosity and distinctive mood of North European art. What you see here in fact represents only about 20 per cent of the museum's total collection, most of which is in storage.

Stop for a moment to plan your visit. At the reception desk you can pick up a schematized map, which lays out the colour-coded chronological paths leading from room to room.

An excellent way to start your visit is with the 35-minute **audiovisual**, which is effectively an introduction to the history of Belgian art from the 15th to 17th century, focusing on selected works in the collection. The audiovisual is presented more or less continuously (including over the lunch hour) in Auditorium B on the ground floor, and you can pick up a set of radioactivated headphones in the language of your choice at the reception desk beforehand, if you leave some form of identity as security.

Early Flemish Paintings: 15th and 16th Centuries

Blue section on the first floor, rooms 10 to 45.

The earliest 'Flemish primitive' work concentrates primarily on religious subjects, since the Church was the main patron of the arts up to and during the Renaissance. Early Flemish artists depicted these with intense colour and detail, reminiscent of the illuminated manuscripts that were a major influence on their style. One of the most celebrated paintings of this section is *La Justice d'Othon* (The Justice of Otto) (Room 13), a huge narrative diptych by **Dirk Bouts** (1415–75), which tells the tragic story of the German Holy Roman Emperor Otto II (r.973–83). Secular art, particularly portraiture, becomes increasingly prominent as the decades progress. The influence of the Italian Renaissance can be detected in the growing prevalence of classical architectural settings, meticulously rendered in perspective, and the introduction of subjects from Roman mythology.

Pride of place in this section is given to **Pieter Bruegel the Elder** (c.1525–69) (Room 31), who lived in Brussels during the later part of his life. What this collection lacks in quantity it makes up for with quality, with the famous *Fall of Icarus* and *The Census in Bethlehem*, one of Bruegel's most endearing works. There are also numerous examples of the work of Bruegel's son, **Pieter Bruegel the Younger** (1564–1638), whose subjects, often copied from works by his father, are equally powerful but whose more polished style lacks the immediacy of his father's painting.

17th and 18th Centuries

For this collection, follow the brown arrows on the next floor. The star of this section is **Pieter Paul Rubens** (1577–1640) (Rooms 52, 62). For anyone who knows him mainly for his well-fed, rose-pink nudes, this large collection is a revealing insight into his versatility. The paintings in Room 62 are vast, full of drama, and painted with a swift, dynamic touch. *La Montée au Calvaire* (The Ascent to Calvary) and *Le Martyre de Saint Liévin* (The Martyrdom of St Livincus) are extraordinarily stirring works. A visit to this museum is justified by this room alone.

More representative images of the times are provided by the portraits of the well-to-do by **Antoon (Anthony) van Dyck** (1599–1641) (Room 53) and **Cornelis de Vos** (1584–1651), full of solid burgher virtues and gravitas. The paintings of **Jacob Jordaens** (1593–1678), by contrast, are brimming with ebullience and *joie de vivre*.

19th Century

This yellow section climbs through five floors. This is effectively where Belgian art (i.e. after Belgian independence) begins, and it contains some of the most fascinating work of the last 19th-century Belgian post-impressionists and Symbolists. It starts off with the neoclassical era, and work by the influential French painter **Jacques-Louis David** (1748–1825), who died in exile in Brussels. The famous *Marat Assassiné* portrays the French Revolutionary Jean-Paul Marat (1743–93), slumped dead in his bath. There is also work on this level (–2) by the French Romantic painters **Théodore Géricault** (1791–1824) and **Eugène Delacroix** (1798–1863), and the great Belgian odd-ball **Antoine Wiertz** (1806–65, *see* p.207).

Level –1 is devoted to Realism and includes some rather gloomy landscapes, typical of the celebrated Brussels-based artist **Hippolyte Boulenger** (1837–74). There are also a few good works by French realists **Jean-Baptiste-Camille Corot** (1796–1875) and **Gustave Courbet** (1819–77).

On the right-hand side of Level +1 is 'Social Art', heralded at the entrance by the strong social-realist work *A l'Aube* (Dawn) by **Charles Hermans** (1839–1924), in which young and flushed gentlemen spill out on to the street with their women in the early hours under the pious gaze of a family of labourers on their way to do an honest day's work. On the left-hand side of the same level is a section devoted to Belgian Impressionism, which includes work by **Théo van Rysselberghe** (1862–1926) and **Henri Evenpoel** (1872–99). The right-hand side of Level +2 takes you through Luminism, the post-impressionist movement founded by **Emile Claus** (1849–1924), who has few rivals in his ability to evoke the sweetness of the rural idyll.

Continue around this level in a clockwise direction to reach the first part of one of the great collections of Symbolist painters in Europe. There are several classics here, including *Des Caresses/L'Art/Les Caresses* or *The Sphinx* by **Fernand Khnopff** (1858–1921), in which, in a mood of dreamy sensuality set vaguely in antiquity, a male/female figure stands cheek to cheek with a similarly ill-defined personage, whose head is attached to the body of a cheetah. His *Memories/Lawn Tennis* portrays seven women tennis players in an empty green landscape, calm, silent but filled with unspoken thought and pent-up emotion. By contrast, the unrestrained, psychedelic side of Symbolism can be seen on the landing of Level +2 in *Les Trésors de Satan* (Satan's Treasures) by **Jean Delville** (1867–1953), in which a demonic figure with octopus tentacles for wings steps over a sub-aqua stream of naked damsels and youths lying in sleepy abandon.

Level +3 has a collection entitled 'Pre-Expressionism' with work by the sculptor and painter **Rik Wouters** (1882–1916) and the sculptor **George Minne** (1806–1941). Continue clockwise on Level +3 through a small but good collection of French Impressionists and post-impressionist paintings, including work by **Monet**, **Sisley**, **Seurat**, **Signac**, **Gauguin**, **Vuillard** and **Bonnard**.

This then brings you into a room devoted to one of Belgium's most extraordinary painters, **James Ensor** (1860–1949), a fascinating and enigmatic precursor of Expressionism. His early paintings, such as the portraits of his mother and father (1881 and 1882) are well executed in a rapid, grainy, impressionistic style, but comparatively controlled and conformist. Within ten years, however, he had taken the imaginative leap into the bizarre personal world for which he is renowned—a world of masks, skeletons and Punch-and-Judy characters painted in bright, feverish slabs of paint. The small oil *Squelettes se disputant un hareng-saur* (Skeletons arguing over a pickled herring) shows the drift.

20th Century

The building in which this collection is housed is an ingenious solution to the problem of finding space to exhibit a growing collection of 20th-century art while preserving the integrity of the 18th-century Place du Musée. The answer (subsequently adopted by the Louvre): bury it. Completed in the 1980s, it drops downwards from street level through a series of gently spiralling ramps and stairs.

The collection (Level –2, green tour) is essentially laid out chronologically and includes a spattering of big names such as **Dufy**, **Rouault**, **Picasso**, **Braque**, **Matisse**, **Nolde**, **Kokoschka**, **Chagall**, **Ernst**, **de Chirico**, **Dali**, **Francis Bacon** and **Henry Moore**. In the opening section there is a selection of recent acquisitions by **Claus Oldenburg**, **Robert Rauschenberg**, **Christo**, **Allen Jones** and so on.

But take this opportunity rather to study the Belgians. The collection for instance includes more paintings and sculptures by **Rik Wouters** (1882–1916), post-impressionist in style, bright, cheering, and with a deft sense of finish. **Léon Spilliaert** (1881–1946) produced sombre, melancholic works, implying a remote and inward-looking world yet shot through with a unique sense of design. The extensive selection devoted to work by the Sint-Martens-Latem school includes most notably the earth-toned, thickly pasted Expressionist work of **Constant Permeke** (1886–1952).

Belgium produced two major Surrealist painters. **Paul Delvaux** (1897–1994) is well represented here, with several large paintings of tram and railway stations peopled by nudes with body hair, and skeletons. The collection of work by **René Magritte** (1898–1967), mainly the legacy of his wife, Georgette, is a little disappointing, given his huge output (the bulk of his work is in the USA). Nonetheless it includes plenty of the usual visual puns and incongruities, in sketches, sculptures and paintings—among which is the famous *L'Empire des Lumières*.

The post-war collection includes work from the 1940s group **La Jeune Peinture Belge**—a highly disparate movement which included the lyrical abstraction of **Louis van Lint** (1909–89), and the geometric abstraction of **Anne Bonnet** (1908–60). The influential group **Cobra**, founded in 1948, is best represented by the near-abstract expressionism of **Pierre Alechinsky** (b.1927).

Musée Wiertz

62 Rue Vautier. Ⓜ Luxembourg.
Open April–Oct 10–12 and 1–5, Nov–March 10–12 and 1–4, closed Mon and alternate weekends (Ⓒ 648 17 18); adm free.

This is one of the truly original sights of Brussels. For one thing, it offers the rare possibility of seeing inside a 19th-century artist's studio. But this was not just any 19th-century artist—this was Antoine Wiertz, who from an early age liked to compare himself to Rubens and Michelangelo. His ambitions and delusions were on a truly epic scale.

Wiertz (1806–65) had the misfortune to win the Prix de Rome in 1832, after which he felt he was on course for true greatness. He set about painting a series of vast canvases (11m tall, 8m wide) depicting melodramatic biblical or classical scenes and using ambitious perspectives in the style of Rubens—but unfortunately without his genius. Notwithstanding, Wiertz had his admirers in Brussels, and he hatched a grand plan to enable him to make the most of his talents. In 1850 he approached the government with a proposal: if the state would build a studio large enough for him to carry out his projects, he would bequeath the studio and his works to the nation as a museum. The state agreed—a measure of Wiertz's standing in Brussels in his day—and here you see the consequences.

Antoine Wiertz saw himself as a visionary, a socialist, a breaker of taboos. He was ruled by obsessive ideas, one of which was inspired by the rejection of a painting by the Paris Salon of 1839. Stung by this, he launched a campaign calling for the development of Brussels as a giant metropolis—a vast, glittering city of magnificent buildings, industry and commerce, arts and literature, which would render Paris a mere *ville de province* by comparison. He wrote a tract entitled 'Bruxelles Capitale et Paris Province' (his hand-written version hangs in the passageway outside the studio). Amongst the ravings of his overwrought mind, one reads this impassioned address to the city of Brussels: '*Vous vous appelez capitale de la Belgique; votre position géographique est belle; celle que vous occupez dans l'industrie et les arts est plus belle encore; osez dire ceci et sans trembler: je veux être capitale de l'Europe.*' ('You call yourself the capital of Belgium; you have a fine geographical position; your position in industry and the arts is even better; dare to say without hesitation: I want to be the capital of Europe.') Crackpot or visionary? Antoine Wiertz would have been deeply gratified to see the capital of Europe now blossoming on his very doorstep.

The main part of the studio is an aircraft-hangar of a room, just high enough to hang several immense canvases. These are rather crudely executed (supposedly in imitation of fresco) and instantly forgettable. Wiertz's more remarkable works are on a smaller scale, technically very uneven, but stamped with his own peculiar vision. Some are a bizarre combination of the macabre and erotic; others are loaded with a crushingly blunt moral message. (If you are being charitable, you can say he prefigured the Symbolists and Surrealists). *Le Suicide* graphically illustrates a young man blasting his brains out with a pistol under the covetous gaze of good and bad angels. In *Une Scène d'Enfer* (A Scene from Hell) distraught men and women present severed limbs to a smouldering (literally) figure of Napoleon.

There are some real gems in the smaller rooms to one side of the studio. The criminal laxity of doctors is paraded in *L'Inhumation Precipitée* (The Overhasty Burial), in which a body is seen emerging from a coffin in a crypt—despite an inscription scribbled on the coffin affirming that doctors had certified the victim well and truly dead. *La Liseuse de Romans* (The Reader of Novels) shows what happens if you have the wrong kind of bedtime reading: a woman lies reading in naked abandon, while a horned devil pushes corrupting literature towards her.

Palais de Justice

Place Poelaert. Ⓜ *Louise.*
Open Mon–Fri 8–5, also at other hours; adm free.

The Palais de Justice is a monumental hulk of a building—dream architecture for a megalomaniac. The area that it covers, 180m by 170m, made it the largest construction in continental Europe in the 19th century. Its dome—an elaborate confection of copper and gilt that is dwarfed like a pincushion on an overstuffed sofa—rises to 105m. It cost 50 million francs to build, a huge sum in its day, contested as sheer folly by many of the citizens of Brussels. The plan was initiated under Leopold I in 1833 but was not undertaken until the reign of Leopold II. It was the crowning achievement of Joseph Poelaert, a distinguished architect, who paid for it with his sanity. Building started in earnest in 1866 and was not completed until 1883, by which time Poelaert had died in a mental asylum—the victim, according to legend, of a witch from the Marolles (the working-class district at the building's foot, part of which was steam-rollered by the construction).

You are free to wander the public hallways, staircases and galleries of this extraordinary building at your leisure. The entrances alone show that subtlety was not Poelaert's strong card. Using just about every trick in the neoclassical book, the ranks of giant columns that line the portico seem specially designed to belittle anyone who passes between them. But this is nothing compared to the interior, which consists mainly of one colossal atrium, with broad marble stairs rising on either side to the galleries and lit from windows somewhere close to the firmament. Two typically bizarre and sensuous allegorical canvases by the visionary Symbolist Jean Delville, painted in 1914, hang at either end of the first-floor gallery. The main waiting hall of a building like this is known as the *Salle des Pas Perdus* ('Hall of Lost Footsteps'), particularly appropriate here in the face of its disorientating scale, but if you were standing trial you might think it was an oblique reference to your cause.

Almost as an afterthought, there are 25 courtrooms tucked away in the walls of this building, including the *Cour de Cassation*, the highest court in the land. Groups of lawyers and their anxious clients pepper the floor, speaking in hushed, staccato tones; waiting jurors gaze vacantly into the mid-distance from scattered benches or hang about outside the courtrooms, reading scruffy handwritten instructions attached to the oak doors with sticky tape. All around them, and over the city outside, the architecture booms imperiously: 'Justice Shall Be Done!'

Rue des Bouchers

Ⓜ *Bourse.*

The Rue des Bouchers is a visual feast: wall-to-wall restaurants with gaily painted awnings, fronted by spectacular displays of fish, shellfish and fruit laid out on ice-strewn trestles—and patrolled by importuning waiters. Pretty it may be, but no self-respecting Bruxellois would dream of eating in such places: the displays, in their view, are in inverse proportion to the quality of the cooking.

Turn off the Rue des Bouchers into the Petite Rue des Bouchers. Halfway down, on the left-hand side, is a tiny alleyway, the Impasse Schuddeveld. At the bottom of this atmospheric little alleyway is the remarkable Toone puppet theatre (*see* p.272) in a house built in 1696. Shows take place only in the evening at 8.30pm, but you can make reservations after 12 noon in the bar. There is also a Toone Theatre Museum, with a collection of the distinctive elongated puppets used in the show, but this is only open in the intervals during performances. It is nonetheless worth coming down this alley, if only to glimpse this famous Brussels institution and its medieval surroundings.

Tour Japonaise, Pavillon Chinois and Japanese Art Museum

44 Avenue van Praet. Ⓜ *Stuyvenbergh.*

Open 10–4.45, closed Mon; adm 120 BF (combined ticket), free first Wednesday afternoon of each month.

Following his visit to the Paris Exhibition of 1900, Leopold II hatched a grand plan of lining this street near the Laeken royal palace with exotic architecture for the enlightenment of his nation. He commissioned Alexandre Marcel (1860–1928), a specialist in oriental architecture, to devise the plan. The **Pavillon Chinois** was designed in 1901–2, and its constituent parts were made in Shanghai over the following two years. The final assembly of the pavilion was completed in 1910, after Leopold's death. Restoration has returned this remarkable two-storey building to its original splendour—an intricate jigsaw of gilded wood, polychrome ceramics, carved screens and balustrades, and dainty finials. The equally lavish interior contains a collection of Chinese porcelain and furniture.

By walking around to the right of the pavilion, you reach the entrance (via a tunnel under the road) to the newly restored **Tour Japonaise**. This complex consists of a set of Japanese halls leading up to the base of the five-tiered tower. The entrance halls are the work of Japanese architects and builders, and were designed and built in Japan and then shipped over for the 1900 Exhibition. They now contain an admirable collection of Japanese samurai armour and weaponry. The staircase is pure, unashamed 'Japanoiserie'—a stunning marriage of Art Nouveau and Japanese design. It includes luminous stained-glass panels by J. Galland based on Hokusai and other Japanese printmakers, and superb chandelier lamps by Eugène Soleau consisting of entwined foliage and glass lampshades in the form of petalled flowers. The tower itself was designed by Marcel along the lines of a 17th-century Buddhist pagoda; today only the lower level can be visited, an impressive room decorated with Japanese lacquer panels.

In December 2000 a third building will be opened, displaying the Japanese art collection of the Musée du Cinquantenaire.

Waterloo

> There is a regular bus service from Brussels to Waterloo and the Butte du Lion which departs from Place Rouppe about once every hour. For organized coach trips, ask at the Brussels Tourist Office. Trains leave for Waterloo from Bruxelles Nord, Central and Midi; the station is about 1km from the centre at Waterloo. Or travel by car (see below).

The Battle of Waterloo represents one of the great turning points of European history, when Napoleon's Empire was finally demolished after two decades of tumult and radical change across the continent. For all that, Napoleon remained a great European hero (even today, most Belgians regard the battle as the defeat of Napoleon rather than the victory of Wellington and the Allies). In the more settled years that followed, industrialization gathered pace and the modern shape of Europe began to emerge, yet many people still yearned for the élan and the sense of new horizons which had died when the Napoleonic era ended.

The significance of the battle of Waterloo, the romantic tales of bravery and tragedy that emerged from it and Napoleon's enduring fascination, made the battlefield a scene of touristic pilgrimage almost before the bodies had been carted off for burial. The site, therefore, can claim over 150 years of tourism. This heritage accounts to some degree for the strangely amateur and tacky nature of many of the museums connected with the battlefield, but their musty, antique air is part of the unique flavour of the place. The exception is the brand new Visitors' Centre at the battlefield site—but even that is barely able to cope with the hordes of tourists who swarm through it. As a result, this can be a disappointing visit unless you know what you are looking at: you have to do a little homework and then let your imagination flow. If you can get away from the crowds it is not difficult to people the landscape with soldiers in your mind's eye. A short walk from the Butte du Lion to the Ferme de Hougoumont, for instance, will help you to get a feel for the lie of the land, and allow you to contemplate in peace the momentous events that took place in this unlikely rural landscape one Sunday in the middle of June 1815.

The Battle itself didn't take place at Waterloo at all. Wellington sent a dispatch announcing his victory over Napoleon from the small town of Waterloo, some 15km south of Brussels, and as was the custom, the battle took this name. In fact the fighting was closer to Braine-l'Alleud, about 4km south of the centre of Waterloo. The battlefield covers a considerable area, so it is best to visit Waterloo with a car. There are two principal sites: the old inn in the centre of Waterloo where Wellington had his headquarters, now signposted the Wellington Museum, and the battlefield itself, clearly identifiable from a distance by the Butte du Lion, the mound with a statue of a lion on top (follow signs marked 'QG Napoléon' then 'Butte de Lion' to the south of Waterloo on the Charleroi road, the N5). The Waterloo Visitors' Centre, the main exhibition site, is clustered around the Butte du Lion.

The Wellington Museum

147 Chaussée de Bruxelles. Open 1 April–30 Sept 9.30–6.30, 1 Oct–31 March 10.30–5; adm 100 BF.

The old Bodenghien Inn at the centre of Waterloo was chosen by Wellington as his headquarters. He stayed here on the night of 17 June before the battle, making meticulous plans with remarkable composure and sending out dispatches and correspondence. It's an evocative old building, now converted into a small museum of the history of the town of Waterloo and the battle. Displays include weapons, pieces of uniform, engravings, and the bed in which Sir Alexander Gordon died. To the rear is a modern exhibition with panels giving blow-by-blow plans of various stages of the battle. In fact this information is also available in a booklet called *Waterloo 1815* that can be bought at the museum shop—a good investment as it provides an excellent source of information when visiting the battlefield itself.

The Visitors' Centre and the Butte du Lion

254, Route du Lion, Braine-l'Alleud. Open April–Sept 9.30–6.30, Oct 10.30–5, Nov–March 10.30–4; adm Lion 40 BF, children 20 BF; Lion plus film 275 BF, students 220 BF, children 170 BF; Lion plus film plus Panorama 300 BF, students 250 BF, children 190 BF.

The Visitors' Centre is at the heart of the battlefield, 4km south of the centre of Waterloo itself. It is a modern complex fronted by a brash and shameless souvenir shop. Tickets come in the form of *jetons*, which you push into ticket barriers to gain entry to each section. The film is in fact a two-part show. First there is a kind of miniature *son-et-lumière* based on a model of the battlefield—far from perfect but at least it gives an insight into how the battle developed. Next there is a 15-minute film in which children are seen wandering the battlefield, imagining the battle. The battle scenes used in this come from Sergei Bondarchuk's film *Waterloo* (1970), which starred Rod Steiger as Napoleon and Christopher Plummer as Wellington. Neither is exactly a classic work of cinema, but the Bondarchuk film contains powerful footage of the battle, graphically portraying the sheer weight of numbers and the violence of the conflict, which is otherwise hard to picture.

The **Butte du Lion** is the most prominent monument of the battlefield. Rising 143m and with 226 steps leading up to the top, it was built in 1824–26 and dedicated to the Prince of Orange, who was wounded at the battle. The large bronze lion on the summit was cast in the Liège workshops of the British entrepreneur John Cockerill, and it was female workers from his factory who piled up the earth into the mound—all 300,000 cubic metres of it—in wicker baskets. The lion stands at about the mid-point of the Allied lines and the view from the summit offers a magnificent panorama of the battlefield. There is very little documentation at the summit so if you want to study the view in detail, bring your own map.

Ferme de Hougoumont

Private property; visitors may walk in the yards but are expected to behave discreetly.

A narrow road, the Chemin des Vertes Bornes, leads along the ridge to the southwest of the Butte du Lion. From here it is a 20-minute walk to the Ferme de Hougoumont, past the points at which Allied defensive squares were drawn up during the battle. Hougoumont is a large and attractive fortified farmhouse—but a modest prize considering that 6,000 soldiers died here. It was defended by the British against Prince Jérôme's persistent attacks from the very start of the battle, and their valiant resistance was a major contribution to the Allied victory. Inside the farmyard is a tiny chapel where many of the defenders expired.

Dernier Quartier Général de Napoléon

(Napoleon's Last Headquarters), 66 Chaussée de Bruxelles, Vieux-Genappe. Open April–Oct 10–6.30, Nov–March 1–5, closed Mon and Jan; adm 60 BF.

This farm was Napoleon's base, where he worked on his battle plans with Marshals Ney and Soult on the night of 17 June and morning of 18 June. The house (much altered since 1815) now serves as a Napoleonic Museum, with uniforms, furniture, plans and battle mementoes.

Other Monuments and Sites

Napoleon directed the battle from a farm called **La Belle Alliance** (named after a marriage between a farmer and his servant in the preceding century), which lies a little to the north of Napoleon's last HQ. The **Ferme de la Haie-Sainte**, which stood at the centre of the battlefield, lies on the main Waterloo–Namur road to the south of the Butte du Lion. Just to the north of this is **Gordon Monument**, a single broken pillar in memory of Wellington's loyal aide-de-camp, who was fatally wounded on this spot. Further north, also on the Waterloo–Charleroi road, is the **Ferme de Mont-Saint-Jean**, where British military doctors working behind the lines in the most crude conditions did what they could to save the wounded—without, of course, the aid of anaesthetic. On either side of the Ohain road (once a deep ditch that formed a part of Wellington's defensive strategy), to the east of the Butte du Lion, are two monuments to the fallen. To the south is the sober Hanoverian Monument, erected in 1818. Hanover came under British control after 1814; the German Legion, consisting of troops from Hanover, Nassau and Brunswick, fielded a contingent of 20,000 men at Waterloo and played a significant role in the centre of the battle, around La Haie-Sainte.

To the north of the road is the **Monument to the Belgians**. The Belgians played a somewhat equivocal role in the events leading up to the Battle of Waterloo. By and large the nation welcomed the defeat of Napoleon and the French forces that had occupied their territory between 1794 and 1814. Yet there were also many Belgians who had come of age in this period, who had gained much from it and remained committed Bonapartists. The nation was divided in its reaction to Napoleon's comeback in 1815. Some Belgians joined the French army while others joined the Allies and in some cases brother fought brother. Wellington was unsure about the commitment of the Belgians. Nonetheless about 6,000 took part in the battle, and some played a decisive role in the defence of La Haie-Sainte and the defeat of the Imperial Guard.

Brussels: Area by Area

The Grand' Place and the Heart of Brussels	214
The Coudenberg and Parc de Bruxelles	219
The Sablon and Marolles	223
North-central Brussels	229
Quartier Léopold	237

The Grand' Place and the Heart of Brussels

The Grand' Place is the jewel in Brussels' crown—and such a splendid jewel that the rest of the crown might just as well be made of iron. Of course, it is on just about every postcard, brochure, poster of the city. But nothing can quite prepare you for the sense of elation you feel when you emerge from the warren of surrounding streets into this spacious, gilded arena.

Here, at the heart of one of Europe's great cities, you are barely bothered by traffic or by the aggressive intrusion of modern business and its architecture. The Grand' Place is Brussels' top tourist attraction, so it is almost permanently overrun by tourists and the neighbouring streets are tacky with tourist tat; despite all this it glows with an atmosphere of infectious, easy-going pleasure, suggesting the more sedate pace of bygone eras and providing as convincing a link with the past as its medieval street plan.

The Grand' Place

Brussels' main market and gathering place since medieval times, the Grand' Place is still the focal point of Brussels' grand civic traditions today. In early July it is taken over by the Ommegang (see p.186), a spectacular costumed pageant which dates back over at least four centuries. Every two years (even-numbered), during one weekend in mid-August, it is filled with the *'Tapis de Fleurs'*—a carpet of flowers. On 31 December it is the traditional gathering place for thousands of revellers who come to this great floodlit stage to welcome in the New Year.

See p.196 for a history and tour of the Place.

Musée Communal de la Ville de Bruxelles

Maison du Roi, Grand' Place (open Mon–Fri 10–12.30, 1.30–5, closes at 4pm Oct–Mar; Sat, Sun, public holidays 10–1 only; adm 100 BF).

The **Maison du Roi** is a bizarre construction, a confection of arches and loggias, finials, crestings, crockets and steep-pitched roofs topped by statues of knights waving banners and swords. This is 19th-century Gothic run riot, now blackened by city grime to look like something from the House of Horrors. It should not belong, but somehow it does.

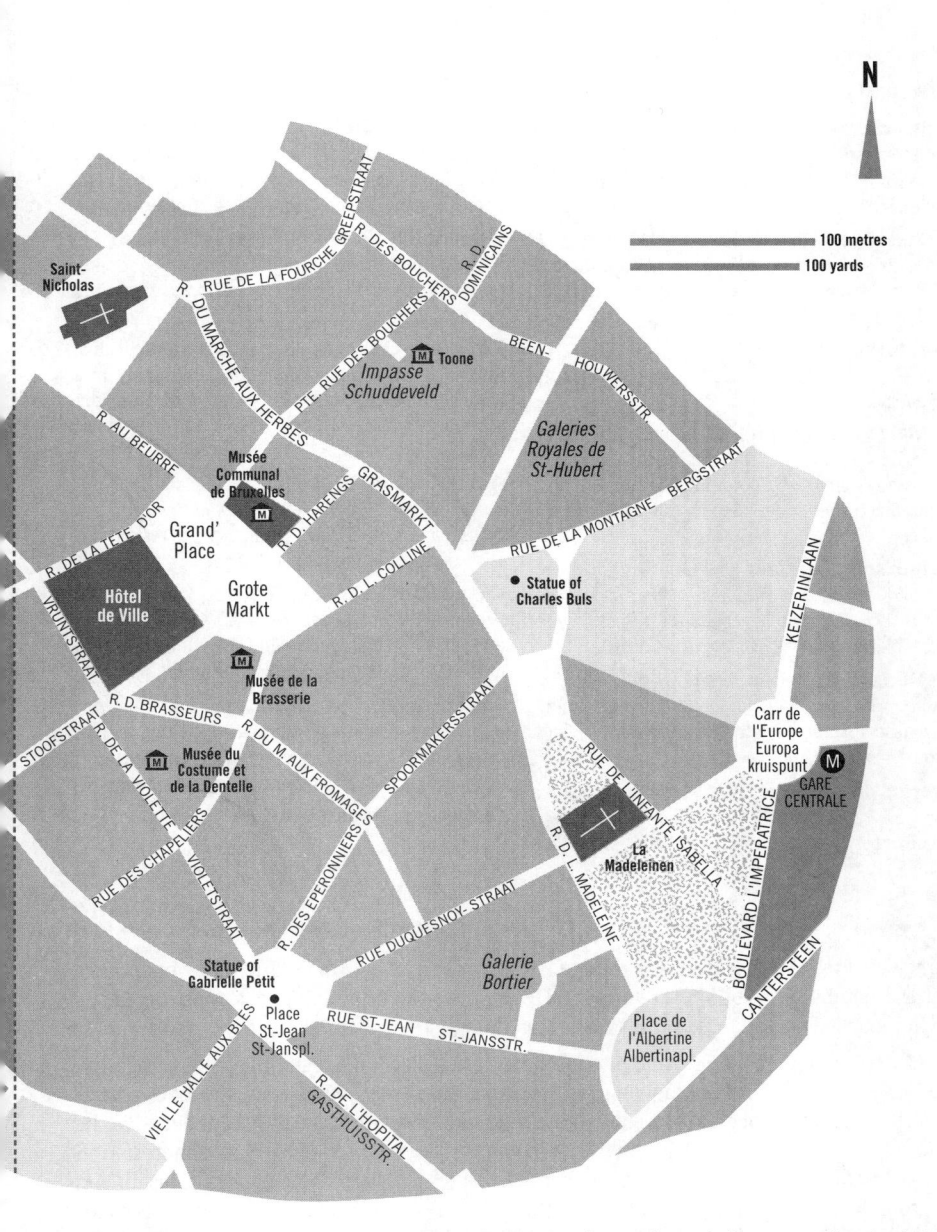

This building has changed its skin at least five times. It was first of all a centre for the bakery trade, the Brodhuis; then in the 15th century a new building was erected on this site to house the Duke of Brabant's high court, hence it became known as the Duke's House. The high court was supplanted in the 16th century by the Royal Assizes, so it became known as the King's House. (The loaf and crown on the weathervane refer to this history.) The Counts Egmont and Hornes (*see* p.226) were held here before their execution in the Grand' Place in

The Grand' Place 215

Cafés and Lunches

Le Roy d'Espagne, 1–2 Grand' Place, ✆ 513 08 07. *10am–1am daily.* This atmospheric bar/restaurant is an institution. You pay for its magnificent position in the Grand' Place, but not excessively.

La Chaloupe d'Or, 24–25 Grand' Place, ✆ 511 41 61. *9am–1am daily.* Another celebrated Grand' Place bar/restaurant, popular with locals. Light meals at marginally inflated prices.

't Kelderke, 15 Grand' Place, ✆ 513 73 44. *12 noon–2am daily.* Medieval cellar setting for hearty *bruxellois* food at reasonable prices.

La Maison du Cygne, 2 Rue Charles Buls, ✆ 511 82 44. *Closed Sat lunch, Sun and the first three weeks in Aug.* Sumptuous restaurant in a Grand' Place guildhouse, serving top-notch French cuisine.

Restaurant Chez Jean, 6 Rue des Chapeliers, ✆ 511 98 15. *Closed Sun, Mon.* Admirably down-to-earth Brussels-style bar/restaurant, just off the Grand' Place.

Taï–Hon, 45 Rue des Eperonniers, ✆ 514 50 58. *Closed Monday.* Tiny but deliciously authentic Taiwanese restaurant which puts freshness and fervour back into Chinese cooking.

Taverne du Passage, 30 Galerie de la Reine, ✆ 512 37 31. *Closed Wed–Thurs in June and July.* Classic old-style restaurant, specializing in Belgian cuisine.

A la Mort Subite, 7 Rue Montagne aux Herbes Potagères. *Open 11am–1am daily.* This famous bar, decked out like a large rococo boudoir, borrows its name ('Sudden Death') from a type of *gueuze*.

L'Ogenblik, 1 Galerie des Princes, ✆ 511 61 51. *Closed Sun.* Small, friendly brasserie serving elegant—if pricy—dishes of scallops, *gâteau de homard*, wild duck, etc.

Rôtisserie Vincent, 8 Rue des Dominicains, ✆ 511 23 03. Totally *bruxellois* atmosphere in a colourfully tiled restaurant entered through the steaming kitchen past a window hung with meat. Good, solid cooking.

Aux Armes de Bruxelles, 13 Rue des Bouchers, ✆ 511 55 50. *12 noon–11.15pm, closed Mon and from 15 June–15 July.* Sophisticated restaurant, always busy, with impeccable service.

Chez Léon, 18 Rue des Bouchers, ✆ 511 14 15. *Open 11.30am–11pm, till 11.30 Sat.* The jam-packed, multi-storeyed original (founded in 1893) of the famous chain, specializing in *moules-frites*.

Falstaff, 19 Rue Henri Maus, ✆ 511 87 89. *Open daily 8am–4am (food served till 2am).* Large, classic Art Nouveau café serving light meals of Belgian cuisine. Now under new management.

La Fleur en Papier Doré, 55 Rue des Alexiens, ✆ 511 16 59. *11am–1am daily, till 3am Fri/Sat.* Splendid old *estaminet* (pub). Good beers from the barrel, plus light snacks.

1568. This first King's House was replaced by another in the 17th century and yet another after the bombing of 1695. Lastly, in the 1870s, the present building was constructed, its design modelled on etchings of the 16th-century building.

The Musée Communal de Bruxelles is a rather oddball collection of painting, pottery, tapestry, historical documents, models showing the evolution of Brussels, and—its most famous possession—the vast wardrobe of clothes tailormade around the world for the Manneken-Pis. Its sombre, neo-medieval halls will prove rewarding for anyone who is seriously interested in Brussels' history, and there are also a number of treasures to delight the more casual visitor. On the ground floor are some superb retables (the ornate, sculpted and painted altar-pieces for which Brussels was renowned) dating from 1480 to 1510. In the same room is a delightful painting attributed to Pieter Bruegel the Elder, who lived in Brussels from 1563 to 1569: *Le Cortège de Noces* (The Wedding Procession) is an affectionate caricature of peasant life. Neighbouring rooms contain fine examples of Brussels' tapestries from the 16th and 17th centuries, and porcelain, which was produced in Brussels (at Tervuren, Schaerbeek, Etterbeek and Ixelles) from 1767 to 1953.

The historical models on the first floor show how Brussels has developed through the ages. In the model of the old walled city, for instance, you can see the old path of the River Senne, the Ile Saint-Géry (the site of the original settlement), the Grand' Place, the city walls, and the Coudenberg. A good collection of paintings serve to illustrate notable historical landmarks, such as the magnificent Coudenberg Palace, destroyed by fire in 1731.

The second floor includes a series of displays relating to the traditional crafts of Brussels—lace-making, printing, weaving and so forth. A further large room has been devoted to the costumes of the Manneken-Pis, where about 100 of his 630 or so outfits are on display. The earliest here dates from the 1920s, but most are modern. They include regimental uniforms, sporting kits (including a sub-aqua outfit), tradesmen's working clothes (plumber, beekeeper, etc.) and samurai armour—all carefully designed so the little chap can continue the activity for which he is so well known.

Hôtel de Ville

Grand' Place (guided tours, in English, German, Dutch or French, last about 45 mins; English tours Tues 11.30 and 3.15, Wed 3.15, and April–Sept Sun 12.15; adm 75 BF).

Although the Hôtel de Ville, or Town Hall, was originally built in the early 15th century, what you see now is really what 19th-century romantics thought a medieval town hall should look like—for almost all the arches, statues, crocketed spires, turrets and balustrades date from a restoration programme that was begun in 1821. Its real glory, however, is the vast tower, which stood alone amid the rubble after the French bombardment of 1695.

Buildings on this site were used as a town hall as early as 1327, but after 1380 the area was cleared to make way for a grand new building. Work proceeded on an ever more ambitious scale during the 15th century, culminating in the tower, by Jan van Ruysbroeck. It rises 96m and is topped by the splendid, primitive 15th-century gilded statue of St Michael (the patron saint of Brussels) killing the devil.

After the destruction of 1695, a new town hall was built around a central courtyard in the neoclassical style associated (ironically) with Louis XIV of France. The star in the cobbles in the middle of this courtyard marks the official centre of Brussels, from which all measurements are made. The 18th-century marble statues set against the west wall represent the two main rivers of Belgium, the Meuse (by Jean de Kinder), and the Scheldt (by Pierre-Denis Plumier).

The guided tour takes you through just one level of the building, which consists mainly of grand public rooms. The 18th-century Council Room is a dazzling confection of tapestries, gilt mirrors and ceiling paintings, and seems like a cross between a royal bedchamber and a funfair roundabout. In the Antechamber of the Burgomaster there is a series of interesting oil paintings by Jean-Baptiste van Moer, dated around 1874. They were based on his earlier watercolours depicting the River Senne flowing through Brussels before it was covered over. Most of the remaining rooms are grandiose examples of municipal Neo-Gothic.

Galeries Royales de Saint-Hubert

Rue du Marché aux Herbes.

This beautiful and recently restored marbled shopping arcade, designed by J.P. Cluysenaar and built in 1847, was the first of its kind in mainland Europe. It is divided into two halves, the Galerie de la Reine and the Galerie du Roi (with a further spur called the Galerie des Princes), intersected by the Rue des Bouchers. It is a celebrated shopping precinct, with ostentatiously expensive clothes shops, dainty *chocolatiers*, and elegant cafés providing excellent coffee and the day's newspapers. With their air of 19th-century elegance, the Galeries Saint-Hubert are the picture of established calm. Yet their construction was highly controversial, and involved the destruction of a considerable swathe of traditional housing. A famous barber called Pameel was driven to kill himself in protest by slitting his throat in his own salon.

Galerie Bortier

17–19 Rue St-Jean.

This cavernous 19th-century shopping arcade was designed (like the far more glamorous Galeries Royales de Saint-Hubert) by J.P. Cluysenaar. Beneath a canopy of glass and ornate ironwork, it is now a dimly lit shrine for bibliophiles, lined with shops selling second-hand books (mainly in French), prints and postcards.

Eglise Saint-Nicolas

Rue au Beurre (usually open 7.45–6.30).

This is one of the oldest and most atmospheric churches in Brussels, with its dim, candlelit interior and quaintly crooked aisle. A church has been on this site virtually since Brussels' foundation, closely linked to the market activities on the Grand' Place. St Nicholas, said to be a 4th-century bishop of Myra in Turkey, is the patron saint of merchants—although he is better known as Santa Claus. Most of the present structure dates from the 14th and 15th centuries.

The church suffered from vandalism at the hands of Protestant iconoclasts during the 1570s and was damaged in the 1695 bombardment. A cannonball is still preserved in one of its walls as a reminder of these more tempestuous times. Restoration gave it its Baroque flourishes. The impressive reliquary of the Martyrs of Gorcum dates from 1868; the martyrs were tortured to death by the Protestant '*gueux*' (rebels) in 1572.

La Bourse

Rue de la Bourse.

La Bourse, the former stock exchange, is an impressive rectangle in neoclassical style but with little sense of neoclassical restraint. Decked with garlands of stone flowers and cherubs playing at horticulture, it is typical of the retrospective style used for many of the grand buildings in the Brussels of Leopold II. Though it looks much earlier, the Bourse dates from 1873. It is a significant monument in central Brussels, but is only occasionally open for special exhibitions.

Eglise Notre-Dame de Bon Secours

Rue du Marché au Charbon (open 9–5, closed Sun pm Oct–June).

This modest little gem, with the coat of arms of Charles of Lorraine over the door, was built between 1664 and 1694 in Flemish Baroque style. The body of the church is based on an octagonal plan soaring to a domed ceiling, made all the more impressive by a nave that has been compressed to virtual non-existence.

Also see: **The Grand' Place**, see p.196; **Manneken-Pis**, p.199; **Rue des Bouchers**, p.209.

The Coudenberg and Parc de Bruxelles

The Coudenberg is the high ground south of the city centre which was once an enclave for the ruling classes and the aristocracy. It is still a very grand, breezy part of town, with long vistas, stately architecture and a large, formally planned park, the Parc de Bruxelles, overlooked by the royal palace. This is the area where 18th-century grandees strutted and preened, and where the arty crowd of the late 19th century lounged and clinked their Art Nouveau glasses, surrounded by chinoiserie and the bright colours of Belgian post-impressionism. The Musées Royaux des Beaux-Arts (*see* p.204) sits on the summit of the Coudenberg.

Cafés and Lunches

Musée d'Art Ancien. Stylish museum cafeteria serving light refreshments at rather inflated prices.

Au Jour le Jour, 4 Rue de Namur, ✆ 502 80 00. *Closed Sat lunch, Sunday and four weeks in July–Aug*. Low lights, friendly service and a faithful following of habitués for dishes such as *carpaccio* and *cuisse de canard à l'Ardennaise*.

New York, 8 Rue de Namur. A *snack*, offering sandwiches, pizza and basic lunch dishes.

Pablo's, 51 Rue de Namur, ✆ 502 41 35. *Closed Sunday lunch*. Upbeat Mexican restaurant with a bar the size of a bowling alley. *Tacos, enchiladas, arroz con pollo,* etc., with pitchers of margaritas.

Bernard, 93 Rue de Namur, ✆ 512 88 21. *Closed Sat and Sun and evenings July–Aug*. Entered through the marbled hallway of an upper-crust delicatessen, this is a hallowed shrine to fish.

The Lunch Company, 16 Rue de Namur, ✆ 502 09 76. A chic and refined salad and sandwich bar that serves Fortnum & Mason teas.

The Parc de Bruxelles

This is Brussels' most attractive formal park. Ranks of mature trees stand over the broad avenues, which lead past statues and fountains to vistas of the palaces at either end. The Dukes of Brabant once owned a famous Renaissance pleasure park on this site, known as the Warande, or warren. It is said that its ingenious fountains inspired the architects of the gardens of Versailles. Following the fire which destroyed the Coudenberg Palace in 1731, the park fell into ruin until it was renovated in French style after 1778. The unusual layout has invited speculation that it represents the symbols of freemasonry. Certainly from a map or aerial view it is possible to trace out the shapes of several of the masonic symbols, such as the compass, set-square and the bricklayer's trowel. The park was designed during the heyday of freemasonry and, like many of his contemporaries, Charles of Lorraine—governor of the Austrian Netherlands—belonged to a freemason's lodge, so such speculation may have some basis in fact.

The park witnessed a series of dramatic events in the early 19th century. On the eve of the Battle of Waterloo, it was used as an assembly point for Allied troops, who were summoned by bugles ringing out over the city throughout the night. (Wellington was staying at the corner of the Rue Montagne du Parc and the Rue Royale.) In September 1830, during the Belgian Revolution, troops from the Dutch garrison holed up in the park, surrounded by revolutionary barricades and sniped at by insurgents from the windows of houses in the Rue Royale. On the morning of 27 September, however, a party of revolutionaries crept into the park to find it deserted: the Dutch had fled. A joyous mob assembled and invaded the royal palace (at the southern end of the park), where they inspected the royal wardrobe and destroyed portraits of King William of Orange. They also brought out a marble bust of the king, crowned it with a

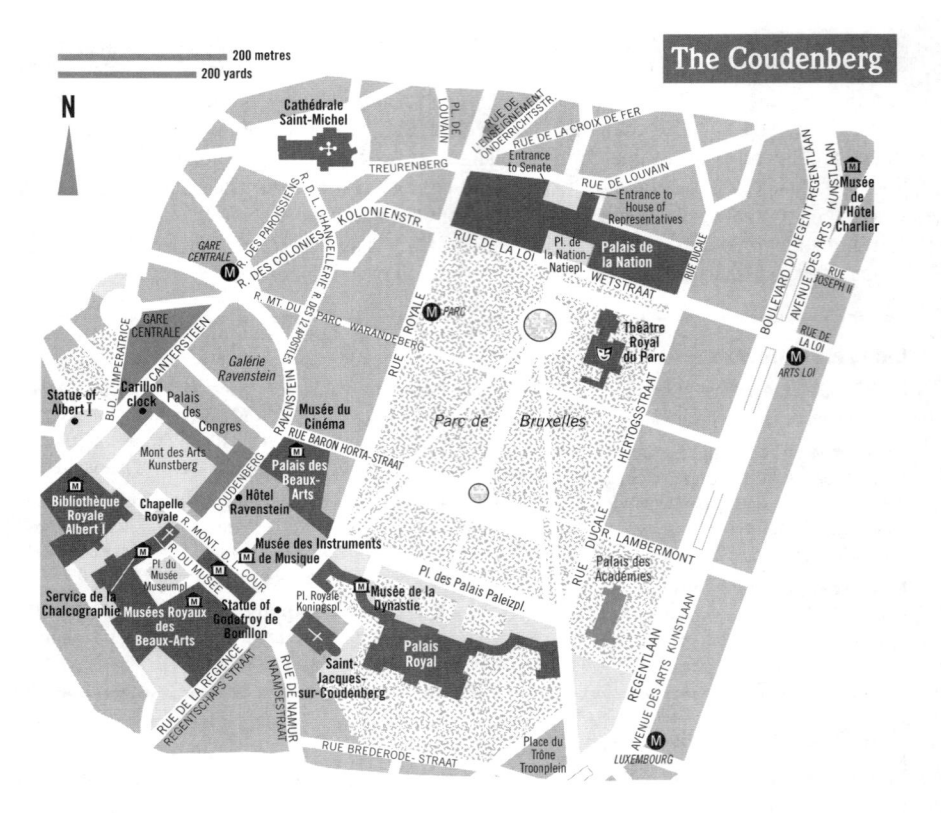

Dutch cheese, and chanted, 'Down with the first and last King of the Netherlands.' Moderation is a Belgian virtue, even in a revolution.

Place Royale and Mont des Arts

This busy yet intimate neoclassical square was laid out on the site of the splendid 15th-century Coudenberg palace, built by Philip the Good as a successor to the original fortress. Contemporary paintings (notably in the Musée Communal de Bruxelles, *see* p.214) indicate that this palace was the crowning glory of Brussels' architecture—until 1731, when it was completely destroyed in just six hours by a fire which apparently started in the kitchens. Charles of Lorraine commissioned the French architect Barnabé Guimard to create a new square over the 'Cour Brûlée', and it was built between 1772 and 1785. For the sake of economy, the foundations were laid on top of the cellars and underground passageways of the old palace, which still run beneath the cobbles of the square.

An equestrian statue, erected by Leopold I in 1848, now dominates the centre of the Place Royale. This is **Godefroy de Bouillon** (1061–1100), a medieval hero and the subject of numerous legends. He was one of the leaders of the First Crusade (1096–9) and succeeded in wresting Jerusalem from the Muslims, after which he was asked by the crusading kingdoms to take the title of King of Jerusalem. Contrary to the inscription on this statue, he refused, preferring the more modest title 'Avoué du Saint-Sépulcre' (Defender of the Holy Sepulchre).

Under an ambitious renovation programme, due to be completed by May 2000, the old passageways beneath the Place Royale will interconnect: a passageway under the pavement of the Rue Royale will lead to the Bellevue building; and the Gresham and Argentau buildings on the corner of the Rue de la Régence and the Place Royale will connect with the Musée d'Art Ancien. This renovation project will encompass the entire Mont des Arts area: the central garden, next to the Royal Library, will be recreated following the original design of René Pechère, and the patio of the Royal Library will be opened to the public, with a passageway leading to Sablon.

Eglise Saint-Jacques-sur-Coudenberg

Place Royale (open Mon 3–6, Tues–Sat 10–6, Sun 9–12).

The original 18th-century façade of this church was an uncompromising reconstruction of a Graeco-Roman temple. Perhaps it was too pagan a concept for 19th-century sensibilities, for on to this was grafted an incongruous, squat, octagonal bell-tower. You have to block this out in your imagination to visualize the restrained elegance of the original conception. Despite this mongrel exterior, Saint-Jacques-sur-Coudenberg is one of the loveliest 18th-century churches in Brussels, with a barrel-vaulted nave leading up to the half-domed apse dotted with floral cartouches. There has been a church on this site since the 12th century, when it served as a stopping-off point for pilgrims on their way to Santiago de Compostela in Spain, hence its connection with St James (Iago, Jacques).

Saint-Jacques-sur-Coudenberg is directly connected to the Royal Palace next door. Members of the royal entourage can cross the palace gardens, take a seat in the royal box on the left-hand side of the choir and peer at the service from behind glass.

Two monumental paintings by Jan Frans Portaels (1818–85) hang on either side of the nave. The one on the right depicts people of all nations gathering around the Cross, while the *Crucifixion and Transfiguration of the Heart* on the left centres upon the symbol of the heart, representing charity—an image explored and celebrated in the remarkable Musée Boyadjian du Cœur (*see* p.250). The beautiful white and gold statue of the Virgin to the right of this painting was brought here from s' Hertogenbosch in the Netherlands in 1629 as a gift from Archduchess Isabella. It survived both the fire which destroyed the Coudenberg Palace in 1731 and the deconsecration of the church during the Napoleonic era (when the building served as a 'Temple of Reason' and a 'Temple of Law'), and was restored to its place in 1853.

Palais Royal

Place des Palais (the state rooms are open to the public only from 22 July to 27 Sept, Tues–Sat 10.30–4.30; adm free).

The Palais Royal is a grand if rather cold-looking building, set too close to the road for comfort and with only a sunken formal parterre garden to relieve the weight of its deadening architecture. The interior is spacious, glittering with chandeliers, brocade curtains and polished marble, but rather soulless. It is no surprise that the royal family prefer to live at their other palace at Laeken. The two wings date from the 18th century, but the central section was rebuilt in the French 18th-century neoclassical style of Louis XVI—in 1904–12, no less. It looks more impressive at night, under its soft pink floodlights. On special occasions the royal family presents itself on the balcony to crowds assembled in the Place des Palais.

Chapelle Royale

2 Place du Musée (opening times vary; usually Sunday morning only).

This small chapel has only limited opening hours but it is worth seeing if you are in the right place at the right time. It is a pearl: a white-painted, ornate neoclassical sanctuary, full of light. It was built in the 1760s by Charles of Lorraine (you can see the double Cross of Lorraine on the capitals and balustrades), but in the 1790s it was turned into a stable by the French revolutionary army. In 1802, under a decree issued by Napoleon, Protestants were given freedom of worship in Belgium, and the chapel was restored as a Protestant church in 1804. The interior was then pasted with copious layers of whitewash, which preserved the delicate plasterwork until its renovation to pristine condition in 1987.

In 1831 it became the private chapel of King Leopold I, a Protestant. (The uncomfortable situation of a Protestant king in a Catholic country was soon put right when Leopold married a Catholic, and hence his offspring were Catholic.) Charlotte Brontë, a fervent Protestant, also came to worship here during her stay at the nearby Pensionnat Héger in the 1840s.

Palais des Beaux-Arts

9 Rue Baron Horta.

This was designed in Art Deco style by Victor Horta (*see* p.202) and completed in 1928. It is now a cultural centre, and home to the Philharmonique de Bruxelles. Horta had to contend with a highly restrictive brief: in order to preserve the view from the Palais Royal he was not allowed to build above the level of the parapet. You can gain a better idea of this building by walking a short distance up the Rue Royale then taking the first left, the Rue Baron Horta. Walk to the top of the stone steps. The Palais des Beaux-Arts stretches down the left-hand side of the street—a bold, angular exterior, very different from those of Horta's Art Nouveau heyday. The Palais des Beaux-Arts was to be part of a grand urban redevelopment plan referred to as the Quartier Ravenstein, stretching from here to the Gare Centrale, but it remained unfinished at Horta's death in 1947. (The Musée du Cinema is in the Palais des Beaux-Arts, *see* p.200.)

Until the first decade of this century there was a large house and garden where the Palais des Beaux-Arts now stands. This had once been the Pensionnat Héger, a girls' boarding school which Charlotte Brontë attended as pupil then teacher in 1842–3, and where she developed an unrequited passion for the husband of the principal.

Hôtel Ravenstein

The Coudenberg.

An attractive red-brick building with a stepped gable, the Hôtel Ravenstein is the only substantial survivor of the old Coudenberg quarter, dating from the 15th century. It formed part of the palace of the Princes of Cleves-Ravenstein and was the birthplace of Anne of Cleves (1515–57), fourth wife of Henry VIII of England. This was a disastrous political marriage: Henry found her not to his taste and declared that he could 'never in her company be provoked and steered to know her carnally'. He divorced her the same year as he married her, 1540.

Also see: **Musées Royaux des Beaux-Arts**, p.204; **Cathédrale St-Michel**, p.194; **Musée du Cinéma**, p.200; **Musée de l'Hôtel Charlier**, p.203; **Musée des Instruments de Musique**, p.204.

The Sablon and Marolles

'*Faire du lèche-vitrines*' ('window-licking') is an activity indulged in with much relish by the Bruxellois. 'Window-shopping' sounds much more prosaic, and quite inadequate to describe that pleasurable, hopeless yearning that so many of Brussels' classier shops seem designed to inspire. You can window-lick to your heart's content here because the charming Sablon district, with its spacious ease and its beguiling step-gabled houses, is an old residential quarter which is now the focus of Brussels' upmarket antiques trade, with a number of chic art galleries thrown in. From here it is only a short walk to the area called Porte Louise (around Place Louise), which is Brussels' answer to the Champs-Elysées, a showpiece of Euro-commerce with a roll call of the world's most revered designer names.

In the shadow of the Palais de Justice lies the Marolles district. This is the old artisans' quarter, with a long and ragged history, its own dialect, its own inalienable scruffiness, and a breed of rough, anarchic characters who reluctantly acknowledge the daylight hours as a necessary evil. It is now undergoing a phase of redevelopment, encouraging a flourish of arty bric-a-brac shops, small galleries and design studios which bring a new touch of colour and vitality to the area. However, detractors deplore this development at the expense, as they see it, of the real character of the Marolles.

Cafés and Lunch

Le Pain Quotidien, 11 Rue des Sablons, ✆ 513 51 54. One of the largest of this successful and alluring chain of upmarket sandwich and pastry cafés. Sandwiches made with the best ingredients on excellent bread, eaten on large shared tables in country-style kitchen. A Belgian institution.

Trein de Vie, 18 Rue Sainte-Anne. An invigorating, modern café that still has one foot firmly in tradition. Sandwiches, salads, and standards such as *waterzooi*. Small open terrace to the rear.

L'Ecailler du Palais Royal, 18 Rue Bodenbroeck, ✆ 512 87 51. *Closed Sun, public hols, 10–18 April and Aug.* Celebrated fish restaurant: classy and welcoming, with absolutely *comme il faut* cuisine.

Maison du Bœuf, Hilton Hotel, 38 Boulevard de Waterloo, ✆ 504 13 34. Its high standards of Belgian and French cuisine have earned this restaurant a seriously good reputation. On the first floor overlooking the Jardin d'Egmont.

Café Le Perroquet, corner of Rue Watteeu and Rue Charles Hanssens. A genuine Art Nouveau setting for the young in-crowd. Simple, wholesome lunch dishes posted on the blackboard.

Comme Chez Moi, 140 Rue Haute. *Closed Mon.* Intimate restaurant specializing in Russian and Romanian cuisine.

Brasserie Ploegmans, 148 Rue Haute. Dingy 1930s wood panelling, gravel-voiced card players and their dogs, pinball machines, and cellar-cool *kriek* and *faro* served from the barrel. A real *marollien* dive.

Indigo, 160 Rue Blaes. *Open till 2.30am daily and till 4am weekends.* Busy, arty café decorated with miscellaneous *brocante* (junk), which is for sale along with well-crafted salads (avocado, Roquefort and bacon), wine and mouthwatering slabs of cake.

De Skieven Architek, 50 Place du Jeu de Balle. *Open 6am–1am.* Welcoming modern bar-café with a sense of history. Sandwiches, home-baked pastries, Belgian *plats du jour* and evening meals.

Les Salons de l'Atalaïde, 89 Chaussée de Charleroi. *Open noon–2am.* Gigantic auction hall, refurbished in exuberant oriental style. This is where the chic set hang out. The food is not great but the setting is. Ideal for tea and cake.

A Malte, 30 Rue Berckmans. *Open 10am–3am.* Trendy café in a picturesque mixture of oriental, Mediterranean and attic style. Refined snacks at reasonable prices.

't Warm Water, 19 Rue du Renard. *Open 8am–5pm.* Authentic Marollien café that serves tasty, healthy and inexpensive Brussels' breakfasts and snacks.

Eglise Notre-Dame du Sablon

38 Rue de la Régence. Open 8–6, Sat 9.30–6, Sun 10–6.

Notre-Dame du Sablon (also known as Notre-Dame des Victoires) is Brussels' most beautiful Gothic church. Unfortunately the grime-blackened external masonry is in such a decrepit state that an unsightly, semi-permanent metal canopy has had to be erected around it to protect passers-by from any stray bits of falling stonework. The interior, however, is like a magic lantern. Soft light filters through the stained glass to settle on the delicate, cream-coloured flagstones. The semi-circular choir is particularly lovely, lit by 11 towering lancet windows.

The Gothic church of today was built in the 15th and 16th centuries to accommodate the cult surrounding Baet's Madonna. Baet (Béatrice) Soetken was a hemp weaver from Antwerp, who in 1348 heard celestial voices instructing her to steal a wooden statue of the Madonna at which she worshipped and take it to Brussels. She set off on the mission with her husband, bringing the statue to Brussels in a boat. The statue itself, however, was destroyed by iconoclasts in 1580. A large model of the boat, complete with Baet Soetken, her husband and the statue, was given to the church in around 1600 by an Italian doctor at the court of Archduke Albert and the Infanta Isabella, and this has been placed on top of the entrance porch (south transept) inside the church.

The wealth and standing of the church's congregation can be judged by the elegant family tombs and the coats of arms in the stained glass. Two marbled Baroque chapels were erected in the 17th century by the Turn and Taxis family, one in the south transept (which now contains the church shop), the other in the north transept, the Chapel of St Ursula, which contains the family vault and a sculpture of St Ursula by Jérôme Duquesnoy the Younger. Various valuable altarpieces that used to adorn this church have since been removed to the safety of the Musée Communal in the Grand' Place (*see* p.214) and the Musées Royaux des Beaux-Arts (*see* p.204). However, next to the Chapel of St Ursula is a triptych of *The Resurrection (and donors)* by Michiel Coxie (1499–1592), who trained in Rome then returned to Brussels to become painter to the court of King Philip II.

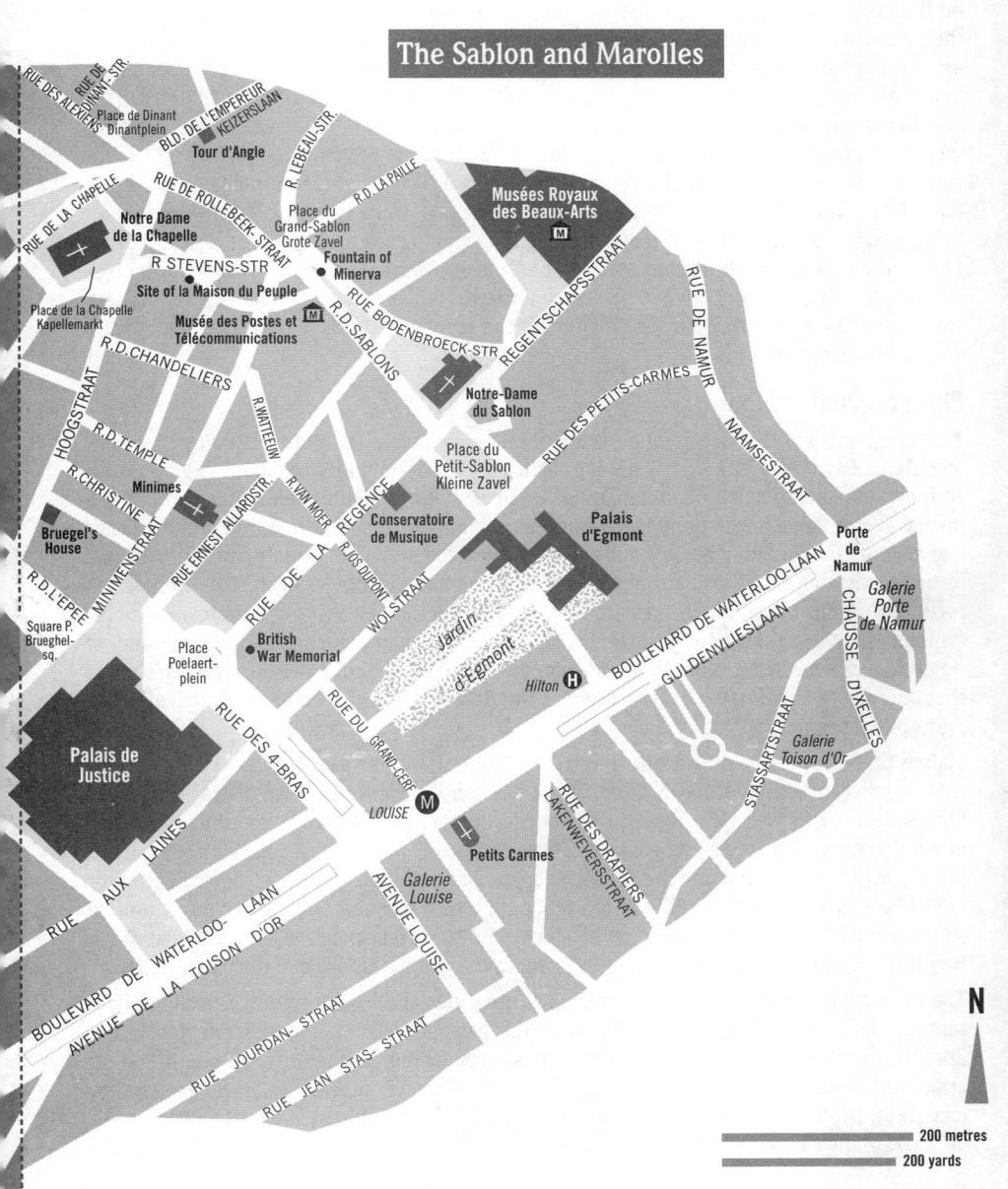

Place du Grand-Sablon

This large triangular square is fronted by enough quaint old step-gabled façades to indicate how it looked when it was first laid out in the late 17th century. It's also famous for its concentration of choice antique and picture galleries, and the splendid *chocolatier* Wittamer on the northeastern side. The Eglise Notre-Dame du Sablon (*see* above) stands at the top of the square. At weekends a superior antiques market, set out beneath striped awnings, clusters around the foot of the church, making the square look like an encampment for a medieval jousting tournament. Halfway up the square, in the centre, is the Fountain of Minerva. This weatherbeaten statue of the Roman goddess of war was built on the site of an earlier fountain, whose very practical function was to drain the water from the Sablon marshes. The new fountain was endowed by the will of an Englishman, Thomas Bruce, third Earl of Elgin and second Earl of Aylesbury. He spent 45 years in exile in Brussels, from 1696 to 1741—the price of being a supporter and friend of James II, who had been forced to flee the English throne in 1688 in favour of the Protestant William of Orange. Married twice to continental noblewomen, the Earl of Aylesbury lived comfortably in a *hôtel* on the square (at Nos. 23–6) and was buried in the nearby Eglise des Brigittines. The fountain was his way of thanking the city and its Austrian overlords.

Place du Petit-Sablon

The formal gardens that occupy the middle of this square were laid out in 1890 by the architect Henri Beyaert (1823–94). They are dedicated to the memory of Counts Egmont and Hornes, and to the spirit of the struggle for liberty and enlightenment that marked the medieval and Renaissance periods. During the reign of Charles V both Egmont and Hornes had distinguished military records and they were respected establishment figures in their late forties by the time that William of Orange led a rebellion of nobles against the repressive régime of Philip II. Although they sided with the rebels, they were moderates. Notwithstanding, they were singled out by the Duke of Alva, who had them arrested, found guilty of treason, and beheaded in front of the Maison du Roi in the Grand' Place in 1568. This made them heroes to a nation which saw them as unjustly punished for defending the legitimate rights of the people.

Statues of the counts stand over the fountain in the centre of the garden. These same statues, cast in 1864, originally stood in front of the Maison du Roi in the Grand' Place, but—as photos show—this was not a happy arrangement. In this garden they are joined by sculptures of other luminaries from the same epoch of Belgian history. Most of these have since returned to obscurity, but they include the Flemish geographer and mathematician Gérard Mercator (1512–94), who is credited with the projection on which most school maps of the world are still based. Such historical statues crop up all over Brussels, reflecting the concerted bid of the Belgian authorities in the 19th century to establish the cultural heritage of their new nation.

The most endearing feature of these gardens is the series of 48 small statues depicting representatives of the various medieval guilds of Brussels—also noted defenders of their liberties—each standing on his individual pillar around the perimeter. Here you'll find an armourer, bleacher, wood-turner, hatter, leather chairmaker, shoemaker, dyer, blacksmith, locksmith, barber-surgeon, cutler and so on—all easily identifiable by the distinctive tools or products of their trade.

Porte Louise

The area between the former sites of two city gates—the Porte Louise (in Place Louise) and the Porte de Namur—forms one of Brussels' most impressive shopping zones, not so much for the shops on the streets but for the covered modern *galeries* that lead off the Avenue de la Toison d'Or to the south—the **Galerie Louise**, the **Galerie de la Toison d'Or** and the

Galerie Porte de Namur. This is where Eurocrats in blazers and snappy tweeds come in their shiny cars to spend Euromoney. Smart cafés spill out over the pavements, where bejewelled friends hail each other across the throngs of shoppers and the constant hubbub of traffic.

Around the top of the **Avenue Louise** the concentration of famous names thickens: Chanel, Versace, Gucci. Avenue Louise—a grand boulevard shaded by chestnut trees—is considered the smartest street in Brussels. Lining the pavements are galleries, showrooms for exclusive furniture designers, and the kind of couturiers' boutiques where you wonder if the decimal point has been left out of the prices.

The **Galerie Louise**, a 20th-century Aladdin's Cave, occupies the ground floor of a 1960s office block, but it has been through ceaseless facelifts and does not show a wrinkle of age. It is a showcase of elegant style, packed with shops selling mainly *haute couture*, jewellery, and shoes that smell sweetly of fine leather—all of which will be delicately giftwrapped and emblazoned with prestigious shop names to make you feel especially good about parting with your money.

A recently opened walk can leads here from the Sablon area: on the pavement of the Rue aux Laines, grey tiles inscribed with text by Marguerite Yourcenar mark a new entrance to the Jardin d'Egmont. Walk through the park and you will reach the Boulevard de Waterloo and Avenue de la Toison d'Or.

Eglise Notre-Dame de la Chapelle

Boulevard de l'Empereur (open 1–4 daily, except public holidays).

The fortress-like grandeur of this church, with its orbed and black-shingled clock tower and its massive creamy-white stone walls, has made it one of the great landmarks of Brussels. However, it has been off-limits for many years because of a massive ongoing restoration programme. Built originally in the 13th century, the church belongs to that transitional period when the pointed Gothic arch was beginning to emerge from the intersection of rounded Romanesque arches. The choir and transept are essentially Romanesque and transitional, whereas the nave and aisles are Gothic, added in the 15th century. The curious clock tower was a later addition by Antoon Pastorana, one of the main architects of the Grand' Place, after the church was damaged by the French bombardment of 1695.

The interior is a bright, elevating space of arching stone vaults, lit by Gothic windows of clear glass set between delicate stone tracery. Much of the church was decorated in the 15th century with polychrome paintings, and remains of these served to guide restorers during the 19th century, notably in the choir. The statues of the apostles attached to the columns of the nave are a typical 17th-century device, less discordant here than elsewhere. The sculptors include Jan Cosyns (later noted as a major architect of the Grand' Place), Luc Fayd'Herbe (designer of Notre-Dame des Riches Claires), and Jérôme Duquesnoy the Younger, son of the original sculptor of the Manneken-Pis. The wooden pulpit, topped by palm trees and cherubs, is another example of exuberant Baroque carving. This one, dating from 1721, is by Pierre-Denis Plumier, who also sculpted the statue representing the River Scheldt at the Hôtel de Ville.

Notre-Dame de la Chapelle is noted most of all as the burial place of Pieter Bruegel the Elder, and the third side-chapel of the south aisle is dedicated to his memory. Born in Flanders, he trained in the studio of Pieter Coecke in Antwerp, but moved to Brussels in 1563. That same year he married Maria Coecke, the daughter of his old master, in this church. They lived on the Rue Haute in the Marolles district, and she bore him two sons before his death in Brussels in 1569, at the age of 44.

Eglise des Minimes

62 Rue des Minimes (open Mon–Sat, 10–1).

The Eglise des Saints-Jean-et-Etienne des Minimes was built between 1700 and 1715 in a period when the neoclassical style was taking over from Flemish Baroque. Hiding behind an unpromising façade is a church of elegant, cool simplicity, as befitted the Minimes, a mendicant order of monks. Founded in Cosenza, southern Italy, in the 15th century, the order came to Brussels in 1616 and built a convent on this site—a site which was formerly occupied by the house of the great anatomist Andreas Vesalius (1514–64). The convent was closed down in 1796 during the French occupation and the buildings were used as an artillery store, workhouse and a tobacco-processing factory. The church was restored to use in 1819.

The small chapel of Notre-Dame de Lorette to the right of the nave reveals a more surprising Italian connection. In wild contrast to the rest of the church, the walls are painted with naïve murals bright with Mediterranean colour. The chapel was built as a reconstruction of the *Santa Casa*, Christ's family home in Nazareth, which according to legend was brought to Loreto, near Ancona in eastern Italy, by angels in 1294. By association, Our Lady of Loreto is patron saint of aviators and air-travellers. The earlier murals fell into decay and were replaced in 1987 by scenes depicting Christ at different ages in his house at Nazareth, which evidently looked very similar to a Greek taverna. The black Madonna over the altar is said to date from 1621 and to be made out of wood from the oak tree that grew from a stick planted by Saint Guidon at Anderlecht.

Palais and Jardin d'Egmont

Rue aux Laines.

The palace behind the large wrought-iron gates is known as the **Palais d'Egmont**, for this was the site of a mansion built in the 16th century by the parents of the unfortunate Count Egmont. In the 18th century it was replaced by the neoclassical palace of the Duke of Arenberg, who had married the Egmont heiress and was one of the leading socialites in the elegant court of Charles of Lorraine. Louis XV of France numbered among his guests here. After being destroyed by fire in 1891, the palace was rebuilt in the same style, and now belongs to Belgium's Ministry of Foreign Affairs. This was where, in 1972, Great Britain, Ireland and Denmark signed the treaty that brought them into the European Community.

The old **garden** of the Palais d'Egmont (now accessible from the Rue aux Laines as well as the Boulevard de Waterloo to the south and the Rue du Grand-Cerf) is now a shady public park which wears a slightly forlorn air. But it affords a good view of the palace, albeit now rather over-restored in kitsch shades of pink and grey. The park has a 1924 copy of the statue of Peter Pan that stands in Kensington Palace Gardens in London, and also a statue of Charles-Joseph, Prince de Ligne (1735–1814). Diplomat, statesman, writer and friend of both Charles of Lorraine and the unpopular Joseph II, the Prince de Ligne was the personification of the cosmopolitan ruling class of the Austrian Netherlands. His family seat was the splendid château of Beloeil in western Belgium, and he was dubbed the 'Prince Charming of Europe'. He is remembered for his epigram: '*Chaque homme a deux patries: la sienne et puis la France*' ('Every man has two fatherlands: his own, and France').

Also see: **Palais de Justice**, p.208.

North-central Brussels

A walk around this area peels back some of the layers of history across the northern sector of the 'Pentagon'—the heart of Brussels. The opera house is where the modern state of Belgium was born; or you can go to the spot where the very first settlement of Brussels was built over a thousand years ago.

The Pentagon of Brussels was first created when its great city walls were erected around it in the 14th century. Since then layer upon layer has been added to the space within, and very little is quite what it seems. Beneath a modern boulevard flows the river on which the city was founded, buried and out of sight; in a courtyard behind a row of shops stands a pristine 17th-century façade; beneath a sedate, neoclassical square lie the bodies of hundreds of Revolutionaries.

Cafés and Lunches

Café de l'Opéra, 4 Place de la Monnaie. Welcoming 1920s-style café, with pavement terrace, offering *petite restauration* such as Parma ham with melon.

Le Pain Quotidien, 16 Rue Antoine Dansaert. This branch was the very first of this chain of tasteful sandwich bars founded in 1991 and now something of an institution. Country décor and inventive rustic sandwiches, such as *bœuf au basilique*.

Kasbah, 20 Rue Antoine Dansaert, ✆ 502 40 26. *Open 11–2, 7–11 daily.* Wondrously theatrical Arabian Nights setting, under dozens of glowing glass lanterns, for top–notch Moroccan cooking. The *tajine aux pruneaux* (spiced Moroccan stew with prunes) is particularly recommended.

Bonsoir Clara, 22–6 Rue Antoine Dansaert, ✆ 502 09 90. *Closed for lunch Sat and Sun.* Deliciously stylish restaurant in Paul Klee colours with low-key lighting, animated by the in-crowd. Inventive cooking from the open kitchen.

La Marée, 99 Rue de Flandre, ✆ 511 00 40. *Closed Mon and June.* Charming family-run fish restaurant.

La Belle Maraîchère, 11 Place Sainte-Catherine, ✆ 512 97 59. *Closed Wed and Thurs.* One of the great fish restaurants of Place Sainte-Catherine. The changing three-course menu includes such wonders as *saumon braisé au champagne*.

La Villette, 3 Rue du Vieux Marché aux Grains, ✆ 512 75 50. *Closed for lunch Sat and Sun.* A decidedly meat-orientated restaurant in a fish-dominated district. Charming, intimate and stylish. Light meals of salads, *pavé façon bruxelloise sauce Villette*, plus serious steaks, and other dishes for the less meat inclined.

Le Métropole, 31 Place de Brouckère, ✆ 217 23 00. One of the grandest and most elegant cafés in Brussels. *Petite restauration* at reasonable prices for the location.

Le Corbeau, 18 Rue Saint-Michel. Salads and *plats chauds*.

Brasserie de la Botanique, in the glasshouse of the Jardin Botanique. Pleasant rendezvous spot.

De Ultieme Hallucinatie, 316 Rue Royale, ✆ 217 06 14. *Closed Sat and Sun lunch.* Drinks and bar food in the stylish bar; full and adventurous menu (*duo de terrine de foies d'oie et de canard chaud*) in the ultimate Art Nouveau restaurant.

P. P. Café, 28 Rue Van Praet, ✆ 514 25 62. *Open daily 11.45am–3am.* One of Brussels' first cinemas, the Pathé Palace, splendidly refurbished in pre-1940s style. Art Deco bar, velvet cinema seats, film music. One of the trendiest cafés in the trendiest part of town.

Zebra, 35 Place St-Géry, ✆ 511 09 01. *Open daily 11.45am–2am.* Trendy café-bistro in the most booming part of the city. Brick walls, candlelight, jazz music. Inexpensive tasty snacks; nice terrace in summer.

Eglise Saint-Jean-Baptiste au Béguinage

Place du Béguinage (open Tues–Fri and Sat 9–5, Sun 10–1, closed Mon, and 2nd and 4th Sat of month).

With its Baroque façade, this is one of Brussels' loveliest churches. It was once the hub of Brussels' largest *béguinage* dating from 1250, when it was established by four wealthy sisters with the blessing of the Bishop of Cambrai. In its heyday it possessed most of the land in the northwestern corner of Brussels, up to the outer city walls—a self-contained area filled with orchards and fields and dotted with the houses of some 1200 *béguines*. Some of these lived in style, in large houses with servants; the less well-off lived in communal houses. They ran a laundry, a windmill and a hospital serving the community at large. By the 14th century the *béguinage* was rich enough to build a large Gothic church on this site.

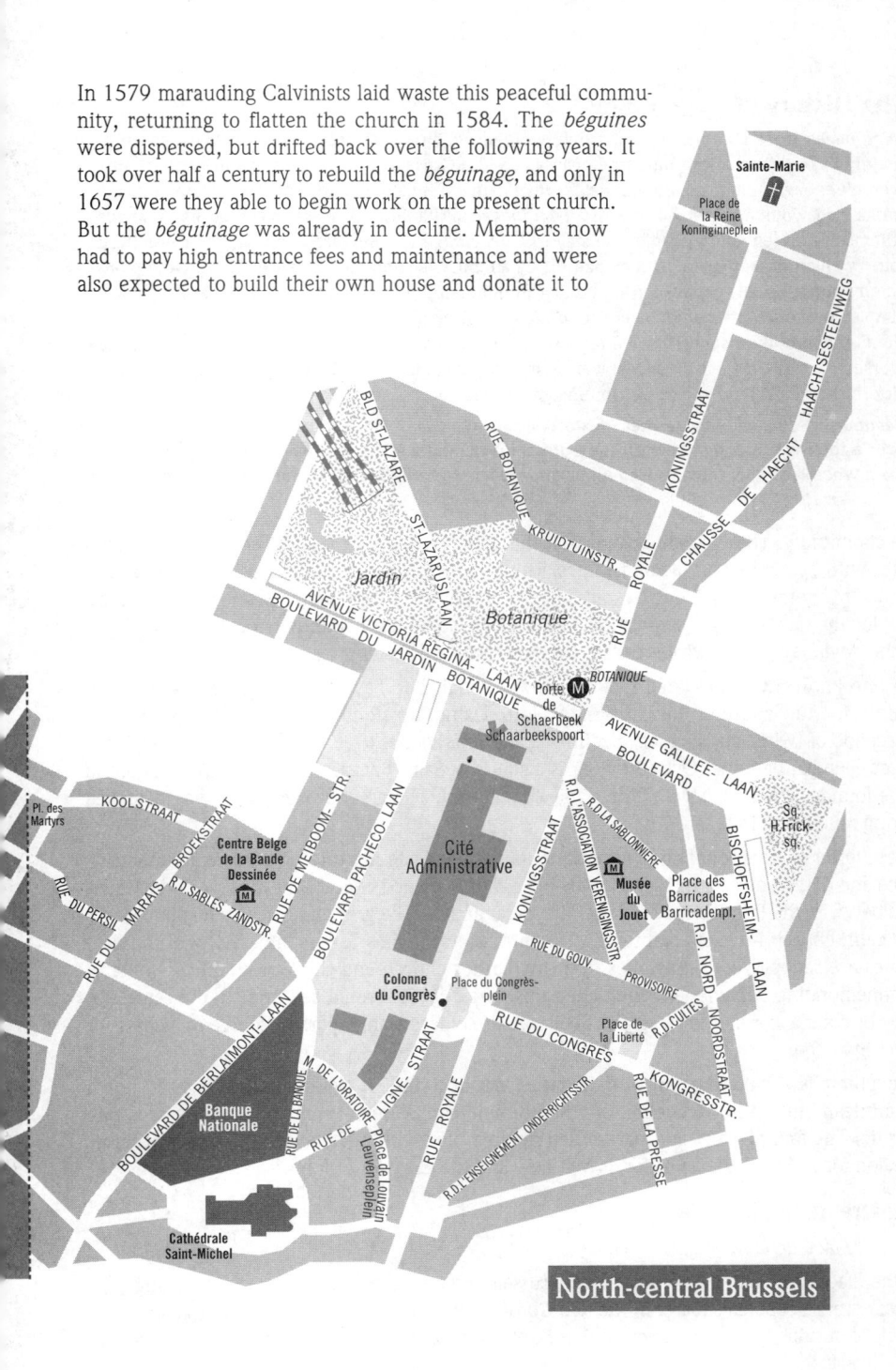

In 1579 marauding Calvinists laid waste this peaceful community, returning to flatten the church in 1584. The *béguines* were dispersed, but drifted back over the following years. It took over half a century to rebuild the *béguinage*, and only in 1657 were they able to begin work on the present church. But the *béguinage* was already in decline. Members now had to pay high entrance fees and maintenance and were also expected to build their own house and donate it to

The History of Béguinages

Béguinages were communities of single women which developed during the 13th century, mainly in response to the imbalance caused by the Crusades: for several centuries there just weren't enough men to go around. Rather than living in isolation or with married relatives, many unmarried women preferred to join a *béguinage* until a suitable partner turned up. Widows (themselves often young) could also stay in a *béguinage*. By and large, the women came from fairly well-off backgrounds, as they had to pay an entry fee and maintenance. These were pious communities, usually closely connected to a church, but the *béguines* were not nuns. They made simple vows of chastity and obedience to their superiors (the elected *maîtresses*), applicable for the duration of their stay. They led modest but comfortable lives, assisted by servants and estate workers, and spent their time in prayer, in making lace, biscuits and sweets, in looking after the sick in their infirmary, and in distributing gifts to the poor.

Béguinages remained a widespread feature of society in the Low Countries—the larger ones had over a thousand members—until the 18th century, and a few continue to operate to this day. Even when deserted, they have a unique atmosphere of care, moderation and tranquillity.

the community. These conditions made it the preserve of the rich, and it soon became out of kilter with contemporary life and values. The number of *béguines* declined, and in the early 19th century the Conseil des Hospices had to intervene, handing empty houses out to aged people who had fallen on hard times. The last *béguine* of this community died in 1833. Little of the *béguinage* has survived, except the streetplan and the church.

No one knows who designed this church, although Luc Fayd'Herbe has been suggested, mainly for the church's similarities to Notre-Dame aux Riches Claires. The façade is a crescendo of twirls, curls, finials, pediments and *œils de bœuf*—a triumph of the Italian-influenced Flemish Baroque. Over the door is a statue of Saint Begga, who is thought by some to have founded the first *béguinages* in the 7th century. The great bronze doors were installed during renovation in the 1850s.

The interior is a model of cool, grey tranquillity, a delicate mixture of massive architectural force and deft stone-carving, seen for example in the winged cherubs' heads that fill the intervals between the Romanesque-style semi-circular arches. The grey and black stone floor recalls the calm church interiors painted by Dutch masters such as Saenredam. Many of the flagstones are redeployed tombstones from the earlier church and the surrounding cemetery, commemorating *béguines* and their chaplains. The *béguines* could be buried in the cemetery, nave or choir according to an established structure of fees—an important source of income for the *béguinage*.

The pulpit is a supreme piece of Baroque woodcarving. It was sculpted in 1757 for a Dominican church in Mechelen, and St Dominic can be seen with his foot on a prostrate heretic. The four apostles are represented by their old medieval symbols: the ox for St Luke, the lion for St Mark, the angel for St Matthew and the eagle for St John.

Théâtre de la Monnaie

Place de la Monnaie.

In the Place de la Monnaie old and new Brussels come squarely face to face, confronting each other across a cobbled square. In the Red Corner is the vast Centre Monnaie, a huge X-shaped block of curving glass and concrete that houses a shopping mall, the central post office and various municipal offices. It stands on the site of the old mint, built in 1420, which has given the square its name. Dwarfed in the Blue Corner is the Théâtre de la Monnaie, built in 1819 to resemble a robust Greek temple. But this contender has form. On 25 August 1830 an excitable audience was stirred into a frenzy by the provocative text of the opera *La Muette de Portici*. Dressed in their opera finery, they burst out of the theatre, rushed to the Grand' Place and raised the flag of Brabant over the Hôtel de Ville, yelling defiance at the Dutch authorities. It was the start of the Belgian Revolution and—after a scrappy, sometimes bloody conflict—led directly to the declaration of Belgian independence just one month later.

There has been a theatre on this site since 1698. After struggling for decades in a moral climate that denigrated all theatre as immoral, this 'Hôtel des Spectacles' began to flourish during the era of Charles of Lorraine (1741–80). In 1766 a company called the Théâtre de la Monnaie was set up, modelled on the Comédie Française in Paris—i.e. with no star system. The theatre was soon all the rage with members of the court: it had gambling tables, and furthermore the cast-list provided the nobility with a string of beautiful and much contested mistresses.

The old building was demolished in 1810 to make way for a new version. The interior of this, however, was gutted by a fire in 1855 and then remodelled to designs by Joseph Poelaert, just before he began his *magnum opus*, the Palais de Justice (*see* p.208). With only 1,200 seats, this is a small opera house. It has a deliberate policy of not contracting the megastars of the opera world, preferring instead to nurture rising stars and to concentrate on the staging and theatrical qualities of opera, for which it has earned a high reputation. The theatre also maintains a resident ballet company, separate from the opera. For three decades until the late 1980s it was the home of the Twentieth Century Ballet of Maurice Béjart, king of the big spectacle in modern dance. When Béjart left after a series of disagreements, he was replaced for a brief but mercurial spell by the troupe formed by the celebrated American dancer Mark Morris; his effusively camp antics and risqué comments succeeded in ruffling the feathers of crustier season-ticket-holders while delighting the avant-garde. The slot has now been filled by Anne Teresa De Keersmaeker, who has successfully held the middle ground.

Boulevard Anspach

Many a great city has its own splendid river or harbourfront; Brussels has the River Senne. Unfortunately this was never a great river. Instead, it was small and sluggish, wending its way through marshland punctuated by low, damp islands, prone to flooding, contamination and stench. Maps of the 1860s mark its course, entering the city near the Gare du Midi and leaving it close to the Gare du Nord. Contemporary paintings show picturesque, lopsided houses and workshops cramming the river's edge, gently sinking into the sludge.

After repeated outbreaks of cholera, the Senne was identified as a health hazard, and in 1867 the city fathers decided that it had to go. A vast building project was initiated in which the Senne was channelled underground, vaulted over and linked into a new city sewage system. Over the top of the river a new thoroughfare was built, running straight through the city, of which Boulevard Anspach forms the central section. It was inaugurated in 1871 and named after Jules Anspach, burgomaster from 1863 to 1879.

Place Saint-Géry

This square once stood in the middle of the Ile Saint-Géry, one of a cluster of islands formed by the River Senne. Some time in the late 6th century, as tradition has it, St Géry (Bishop of Cambrai) founded a chapel here. This became the focus of a small settlement which remained obscure for 400 years until AD 977, when Charles, Duke of Lorraine, built a castle on the island, and the history of Brussels began. St Géry's original chapel was destroyed in about AD 800, but a succession of churches stood on this spot until 1798, when the last became a victim of French Revolutionary zealots. The red-brick covered market, Les Halles de Saint-Géry, which now occupies the middle of the square, was built in 1881 as a meat market. It was recently restored as a shopping arcade, but the venture failed and it now houses a permanent exhibition on the history of the city's urbanization, temporary exhibitions on Brussels' parks and nature, and temporary art exhibitions.

Ile Saint-Géry has now become fashionable, and the developers have moved in to subject the area to what is jocularly referred to as *'façadisme'*: the façade of an old building is propped up and preserved while everything behind it is demolished to make way for rebuilding.

Eglise Sainte-Catherine

Place Sainte-Catherine (open summer 8.30–6, winter 8.30–5).

You might be forgiven for thinking that this grime-coated church has been here longer than the old Willebroeck canal over which it is built (*see* below). In fact it is a piece of 19th-century neo-Gothic designed in 1854 by Joseph Poelaert. Formerly the canal ended in a T-shape, the top of the T being formed by the Bassin Saint-Catherine. After this was covered over in 1853 a new church was built over it. An earlier Eglise Sainte-Catherine, dating from the 13th century, was pulled down in 1893, but its ruined belfry can still be seen close to the west door of the new church, on the other side of the street.

The interior of the Eglise Sainte-Catherine Mark II now has the air of a neglected greenhouse, with peeling paint, the whiff of decay and the odd pigeon flitting about the vast vacant spaces beneath the roofing vaults. On a grey winter's day it looks decidedly down-at-heel, in tune with the pious gloom of the wooden statues of suffering saints. In contrast it comes to life in bright weather, when light streams in through the pale yellow and blue windows: perhaps there simply aren't enough such days in Brussels to make this church much loved.

At the top end of the north aisle there is a famous 'Black Virgin', a 15th-century limestone statue depicting the Virgin in a beautifully observed pose, holding her child on her hip. The statue was dumped into the River Senne by Protestants in 1744, and by the time it was recovered the stone had turned black.

In the south aisle there is a painted wooden statue of St Catherine, a 4th-century Christian from Alexandria. Although they ended up beheading her, the Romans first attempted to martyr her on a wheel, from which she was miraculously saved—hence the name of the firework called the Catherine wheel. In this statue her wheel can be seen beneath the folds of her dress.

The Willebroeck Canal

Open space between the Quai aux Briques and the Quai au Bois à Brûler.

From its inauguration in 1561, the old Willebroeck Canal brought goods from Antwerp and the North Sea to the city centre—a vital element in Brussels' burgeoning prosperity. The tree-lined strip of grass in the centre of the avenue to the north and the cobbled area running south were once filled with water and packed with barges, sailing ships, rowing boats and, latterly, small steamships. On either side were the quays lined with warehouses, an antheap of activity as dockers in their wooden clogs loaded and unloaded shipments of salt, timber, barrels of herrings, sacks of grain, cases of Chinese porcelain, and squealing pigs.

The canal, however, suffered from repeated flooding, and by the 1850s the railways had begun to usurp its role. So in 1853 it was closed and covered over. The quays retained their old titles from the days when merchants of a kind clubbed together: Quai à la Houille (coal), Quai au Bois de Construction (building timber), Quai au Bois à Brûler (firewood), Quai aux Briques (bricks). The newly created square was occupied by a fishmarket, moved from its old site by the River Senne. This was demolished in 1955, but there is still a tang of fish in the air, emanating from the few surviving fishmongers' warehouses and from the many restaurants that now line the old quays. This area, referred to loosely as Place Sainte-Catherine or the Marché aux Poissons, is still *the* place to eat fish in Brussels.

Notre-Dame du Finistère

Rue Neuve (open Mon–Fri 8.30–5.45, Sat 8.30–7, Sun 8.30–12).

Most of this church was built between 1708 and 1730, although the upper portion of the façade was added in 1828. The Baroque interior includes another example of the extraordinarily lavish pulpits of the period—featuring a grotto, the Tree of Life and the Tree of Death—as well as a revered Madonna and Child in azure robes with gilded crowns, the Notre-Dame du Bon Succès, which was brought from Aberdeen in 1625.

Place des Martyrs

Compared with the brash hurly-burly of the nearby Rue Neuve, this charming neoclassical square comes as a refreshing surprise. Designed by Claude Fisco (1736–1825), it was built in 1775 and preserves the stylish, genteel air that characterized the rule of Charles of Lorraine. However, having fallen into almost total disrepair the square is currently undergoing radical renovation behind its façades. Its original character was transformed between 1830 and 1840 when it was dedicated to the memory of the 445 'martyrs' killed in the critical days (23–26 September 1830) of the Belgian Revolution. The centre of the square was turned into their mausoleum, a kind of subterranean cloister faced with commemorative marble slabs. The white marble statue rising above this depicts 'Belga', and is one of many notable public monuments by Willem Geefs (1805–85). The combination of the location and the architectural understatement of this mass grave makes it a curiously powerful memorial.

The renovation of the Place des Martyrs has become the subject of heated contention. The Flemish regional government has been buying up property with the intention of making this their headquarters, and indeed the *Kabinet van de Minister-President* of the Flemish government now occupies the restored northern end of the square, draped in Flemish flags. The effect could hardly be more inflammatory to the majority of Bruxellois, who see themselves as increasingly under threat from Flemish nationalism.

Jardin Botanique

236 Rue Royale.

The botanical gardens themselves have been transferred to the medieval estate of Meise; the beautiful domed glasshouse in the Jardin now serves as the Centre Culturel de la Communauté Française Wallonie-Bruxelles (Cultural Centre of the French Community of Wallonia and Brussels, *open 11–6; adm free*).

This glasshouse was built for the Brussels Horticultural Society in 1826–9 following drawings by a painter and theatre designer called Pierre-François Gineste (1769–1850). Although the exterior was cleverly preserved, the glasshouse was converted into a cultural centre in the early 1980s, and now contains a series of spaces for temporary exhibitions, concerts and plays, as well as a cinema and brasserie. Only the main corridor retains its hothouse atmosphere, with its small fishponds, ferns and papyrus plants. In the huge hollow in front of the glasshouse is a formal garden with box hedges and statuary, some of which is by the noted Brussels sculptor and painter Constantin Meunier (*see* p.251).

The Boulevard du Jardin Botanique, running along the south side of the Jardin Botanique, is another part of the 'Petite Ceinture', the rim of the 'Pentagon' which follows the course of the 14th-century city walls. At this junction between the Rue Royale and the Boulevard du Jardin Botanique there once stood one of the great city gates, the Porte de Schaerbeek, which led to the outlying community of Schaerbeek, now part of the city sprawl.

It was from here that the charismatic early photographer 'Nadar' (Félix Tournachon, 1820–1910) launched his Montgolfier balloon in a series of flights in the mid 1860s, during which he took aerial photographs of the city. On one occasion the unhappy French poet Charles Baudelaire was due to join him, delighting in the opportunity to '*fuir ce sale peuple en ballon, aller tomber en Autriche, en Turquie peut-être, toutes les folies me plaisent, pourvu qu'elles me désennuient*' ('to flee from these filthy people, go and land in Austria, or in Turkey maybe, any mad idea would please me, provided that it relieved my boredom'). However, the balloon was not able to take off with his extra weight, so he had the humiliating experience of having to disembark before a large crowd, which included King Leopold I.

Eglise Sainte-Marie

Place de la Reine.

This is the most beautiful 19th-century church in Brussels, worth the visit even if you can usually see only the exterior. It was designed by a 25-year-old architect from Ghent, Louis van Overstraeten (1818–49), who died of cholera just four years after building work commenced in 1845. Its style is best described as neo-Byzantine: the octagonal ground plan is topped by a star-spangled copper dome and offset by semicircular side-chapels, buttresses, pepperpot spires, rose windows and fretted, receding arches. The builders have used a traditional Brussels mix of stone, cream-coloured for the body of the church and grey for the detailing—the beauty of which has now been restored by cleaning.

Colonne du Congrès

Place du Congrès.

Designed by Joseph Poelaert and built in 1850–9, the handsome 47m-high Colonne du Congrès celebrates the foundation of Belgium's constitutional monarchy after the Revolution of 1830. The statue of Leopold I on the top is by Willem Geefs. Strangely, he has his back to the city—but turned the other way round he would have his back to the administrative district, including the Palais de la Nation (parliament), which might have been even less diplomatic. The inscriptions at the base of the column include extracts from the constitution and lists of the members of the Provisional Government (September 1830–February 1831) and the first National Congress (November 1830–July 1831). Between the outsized bronze lions is the flame to the Unknown Soldier of both world wars.

Also see: **Centre Belge de la Bande Dessinée**, p.195.

Quartier Léopold

Belgium burst upon the economic and world stage in the latter part of the 19th century when it began to reap the rewards of its new, coal-driven industries, its reawakened trading links across Europe, and its wholesale pillage of raw materials from the Belgian Congo. No one stamped this era more decisively than the king, Leopold II (r.1865–1909), who on ascending the throne promised to create '*une Belgique plus grande et plus belle*'. Brussels boomed, and a swathe of wealthy suburbs began to spread out from the old centre, notably in the area just south of the Palais Royal, named after Léopold I. In 1880 Belgium celebrated 50 years of independence with an International Exhibition in the newly laid out Parc du Cinquantenaire. This now forms a grand setting for a series of museums including the Musée du Cinquantenaire (see p.201), which ranks as one of Europe's great museums of archaeology and the decorative arts.

This very same part of town was adopted by the headquarters of the European Union (EU)—an area still locked in an extended and unsettled phase of transformation. Much of this centre of European operations is incongruously surrounded by dilapidated buildings awaiting demolition and some as-yet-unspecified conversion to the Euro-cause. Casual tourists can only stand on the outside of European buildings and look in—only authorized visitors can penetrate their security systems and mystifying barriers of bureaucratic silence.

Cafés and Lunches

The Pullman, 12 Place du Luxembourg. One of a set of unpretentious bars around the Gare du Quartier Léopold. Bar food such as *assiette Américaine-frites* (steak tartare and chips).

Vimar, 70 Place Jourdan, ✆ 231 09 49. *Closed Sat and Sun lunch and Monday.* A stylish setting of sparkling glasses and crisp linen for serious fish cuisine.

L'Esprit du Sel, 52 Place Jourdan, ✆ 230 60 40. One of a cluster of small restaurants and lunch stops now clamouring for attention in the up-and-coming Place Jourdan. Stylish backdrop to good Belgian and French cooking: *salade tiède, waterzooi,* salmon, rabbit.

Taj Mahal, 12 Avenue des Gaulois, ✆ 703 06 81. *Closed Sat and Sun lunch.* Tandooris and tikkas served in the Raj-like splendour of a *tous-les-Louis* salon in a *maison de maître*.

Cafétéria, at the Musée du Cinquantenaire. Elegantly refurbished rooms with rattan chairs and old paintings, serving snacks and more substantial salads (prawn, soused herring) and sandwiches. Eat early; it starts getting busy at 12.

Maison Paul Cauchie

5 Rue des Francs. Open 11–6 on 1st weekend of the month only, or by appointment.

This is one of the most spectacular Art Nouveau façades in the city, brought to life by a large, gilded mural of togaed maidens painted in a style reminiscent of Alphonse Mucha and Gustav Klimt. The design of the house shows the clear progression towards sterner, more angular shapes that took place after the turn of the century under the influence of the Vienna Secession. The emphasis is on strident verticals and horizontals and clean-cut geometric shapes—far removed from the effusion of curves on the Maison Saint-Cyr (*see* below).

This was the private house—and the only architectural work—of its creator, Paul Cauchie, a little-known neo-impressionist and Symbolist painter. It was also his studio and workplace, as the painted inscriptions by the door imply: '*M. et Mme Cauchie décorateurs: cours privé d'art appliqué*'. They could hardly have made a more convincing advertisement of their skills.

European Parliament

'Espace Leopold', 43 Rue Wiertz.

This glossy building—behind a 300m façade of undulating granite, travertine, glass and faintly Aztec-looking ornaments of polished steel—is the new Brussels headquarters of the European Parliament. The 626 Members of the European Parliament (MEPs) usually meet in Strasbourg, but once every month or two, they head for Brussels *en masse* for six two-day mini-sessions per year; meanwhile a number of parliamentary committees have their base in Brussels, close to the two other main EU institutions, the Council of Ministers and the European Commission.

Note how the Rue Wiertz, named after a megalomaniac visionary (*see* p.207), drives through the centre of the new Parliament buildings. On your left is the 'Mail Building', otherwise known by the code D3. Completed in 1997 at a cost of £530 million, it contains 2,600 offices for the MEPs and administrators, 16 conference rooms and 52 meeting rooms. On your right is an oval block called the 'Leopold Building'—D1 and D2. This houses the offices of the President of the parliament, the General Secretariat, press facilities and the 720-seat semi-circular assembly chamber. These buildings were designed by a consortium, on the instructions of a committee, and it shows. They are never likely to appear in the annals of great architecture. In winter, vicious winds funnel through the huge archways. (Incidentally, you do not have to be too sensitive about criticizing these buildings to Belgians: they are not Belgian buildings, but European Union buildings on Belgian land.)

Council of the European Union
80 Rue Belliard and 175 Rue de la Loi.

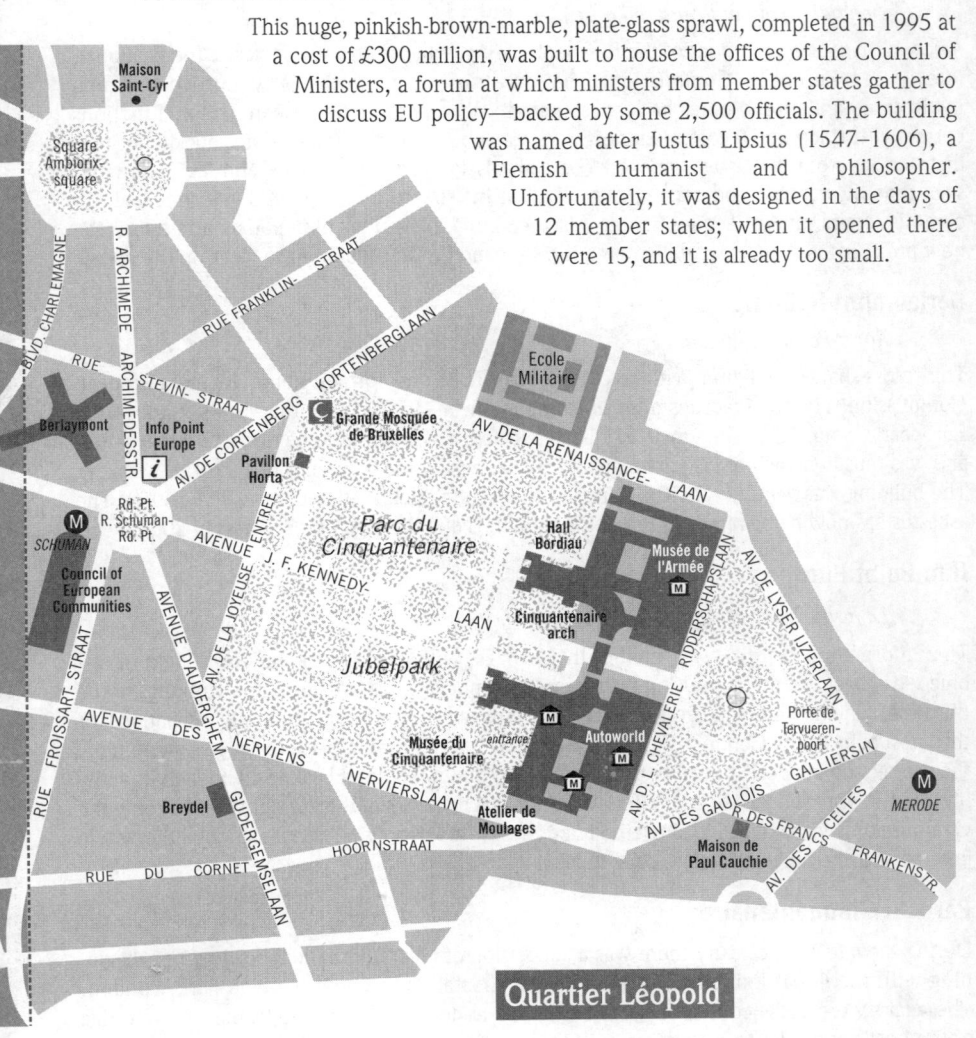

This huge, pinkish-brown-marble, plate-glass sprawl, completed in 1995 at a cost of £300 million, was built to house the offices of the Council of Ministers, a forum at which ministers from member states gather to discuss EU policy—backed by some 2,500 officials. The building was named after Justus Lipsius (1547–1606), a Flemish humanist and philosopher. Unfortunately, it was designed in the days of 12 member states; when it opened there were 15, and it is already too small.

The Council is the main decision-making body of the EU, although the European Parliament is gradually edging into its sphere of action. This therefore remains one of the key forums of the EU, where officials gather to thrash out the burning issues of the day from fish quotas and BSE to immigration policy. The President of the Council changes every six months so each country can have a turn in rotation.

European Commission

Breydel, Avenue d'Auderghem.

A row of flags stands in front of the Breydel building, which currently serves as the headquarters of the European Commission. The Commission is another key European Union institution, an autonomous body designed to see that the European Union functions correctly. It is led by 20 commissioners who are appointed by member states but do not take instructions from their governments. The commission proposes policies and legislation and sees that the treaties are carried out. Scandal hit the commission in 1999 when all 20 commissioners, under Jacques Santer, resigned amid allegations of nepotism and fraud; the new president is the former Italian premier, Romano Prodi, brought in to clear up the mess.

Berlaymont Building

Rond-Point Schuman.

This cross-shaped building with a curving façade is the former home of the European Commission. For two decades after its completion in 1970, it was the very symbol of the European Community. Then in 1991 disaster struck: it was found to be riddled with asbestos, and was thus in breach of the very regulations overseen by the thousands of Eurocrats within it. The building was vacated, and the offices of the Commission scattered about the district. The asbestos has now being removed at vast cost, and it is due to reopen for business in 2000.

Info Point Europe

12 Rond-Point Schuman (open Mon–Fri, 9–4).

This information centre—spattered with EU flags, with the ring of stars on a field of sky blue—has been set up by the Commission to disseminate literature about the workings of the European Union. Here you can get up to date with European health and safety regulations, or the latest edict of the Common Agricultural Policy. It's also a good place to gauge something of the supra-national idealism that was the original inspiration of the EU and still informs its activities. But it won't be able to tell you how the various branches of the EU slot together, only the Commission's view of it. No single body possesses this overview, which can give the whole enterprise something of a Kafka-esque quality.

Parc du Cinquantenaire

During the late 19th century there was a succession of great international exhibitions, beginning with the Great Exhibition of 1851 in the Crystal Palace built in Hyde Park, London. These fairs were designed to promote industry and trade, and above all to trumpet the prestige of the host nation. Huge halls were built to house comprehensive displays of the latest and best manufactured products, from porcelain to steam engines, as well as all manner of gadgets and inventions to delight the public, who thronged to the fairs in their thousands. Brussels played its part. The year 1880 marked the *Cinquantenaire* (the 50-year jubilee) of the Belgian nation. At Leopold II's insistence, an area reserved for military manoeuvres was transformed into a park in which the exhibition halls were built.

The original plan was designed by the architect Gédéon Bordiau (1832–1904), who adapted it over the remainder of his career for further exhibitions in 1888 and 1897. In the 1880s Bordiau's complex consisted of a pair of large, barrel-vaulted exhibition halls linked by a semicircular colonnade which met at a triumphal arch. The rudiments of this concept have survived, although today's triumphal arch was added in 1905 to mark Belgium's 75th anniversary. The copper-green quadriga on the top of the arch is by Thomas Vinçotte (1850–1925), official sculptor to Leopold II: if it looks familiar, no doubt it reminds you of the more famous Brandenburg Gate in Berlin, created over a hundred years earlier. In Leopold's Brussels, originality was not a criterion.

Since 1880 these buildings have had a varied history as exhibition halls and museums. Today they house three museums: the Musée du Cinquantenaire (*see* p.201), the Musée Royal de l'Armée (*see* p.255), and Autoworld (*see* p.252).

Pavillon Horta

Parc du Cinquantenaire.

Also known as the Edicule Lambeaux, this temple-like building in the northeastern corner of the park was designed by the young Victor Horta in 1889, during the period when he was working closely with his neoclassically oriented master, Alphonse Balat. It is, in effect, a straightforward neoclassical temple, with a few streamlined refinements, and was built to house a series of remarkable relief sculptures called *Les Passions Humaines* by Jef Lambeaux (1852–1908). Lambeaux set about his subject with the same graphic realism as his contemporary, Rodin—with the result that the contents of his pavilion earnt a reputation for being shocking. Today they are not easy to see, but for reasons of economy rather than morality—the Musées Royaux d'Art et d'Histoire run occasional tours during the summer months.

Atelier de Moulages

Casting and Moulding Workshop, Parc du Cinquantenaire (open Mon–Fri 9–12 and 1.30–3.30; adm free).

During the 1880s an exhibition of some 5,000 plaster casts of famous statues filled the Hall Bordiau, and was greeted with rapturous enthusiasm. A workshop attached to the exhibition could supply copies from the moulds—so members of the public, government institutions and schools were able to order fine art on demand. The Atelier de Moulages has survived since that time, and still has about 4,000 moulds, many taken from originals in great art collections around the world. Some are newly created, but others date back to the 19th century. (Their Venus de Milo mould was made in 1893.) In cases where the original has been lost or destroyed, the moulds represent a unique archive.

Over the years, demand has tapered off, but the workshop has been preserved by the state—though now in this less prominent position beneath Autoworld. You are free to wander the workshops and watch a small number of craftsmen produce their pristine-white casts. Behind them are deep, cavernous storerooms where the shapeless moulds lie piled high on wooden racks. Another storeroom contains a jumble of miscellaneous casts: here cultures and historical ages collide in a surreal encounter between nude Greek athletes, Egyptian cats, busts of 19th-century royalty, Madonnas and saints, Roman friezes, horses' heads, Dante and Voltaire, dismembered limbs, Buddhas and death masks.

You can buy casts from the small showroom or order them from the catalogue (allow 3–4 months). Prices vary according to the size and complexity of the piece, but start at 1800 BF.

Statue of Leopold II

Place du Trône.

Belgium's second king was driven by the ambition to raise his country to the status of a great nation. He was dismissive of the Belgians' natural inclination to modest ambitions—'*Petit pays, petites gens*,' ('small country, small people') he grumbled. Before ascending the throne he embarked on a series of voyages to India, China and North Africa which ignited his growing desire to acquire colonies—a dream eventually realized when he established the Belgian Congo as a personal fiefdom, then ran it with a disregard for human suffering unmatched by any of his colonial rivals. Meanwhile he instigated an ambitious building programme, notably in Brussels and Ostend. This equestrian statue is a solemn, dignified portrait of a powerful, determined and obstinate monarch, who is immediately recognizable by his voluminous beard, square-cut like a bib.

Maison Saint-Cyr

11 Square Ambiorix.

This extraordinary building takes the Art Nouveau idiom to its ultimate conclusion: the façade is a veritable cascade of looping carved stone, swirling wrought iron and entwined woodwork. Glass occupies almost the entire width of its narrow groundplan, veiled by the web of intricate balustrades lining the curving balconies. There is barely a straight line in sight. One would not call the Maison Saint-Cyr beautiful: in fact the overall effect is almost unsettling. Here Art Nouveau drifts towards the sickly, degenerative art deplored by the more functionalist designers of the Arts and Crafts movement and the Vienna Secession. Such elaborate fantasies, however, were the hallmark of the architect, Gustave Strauven (1878–1919). This is his most famous work, all the more remarkable considering that he was just 20 years old when he designed it.

Maison Van Eetvelde

4 Avenue Palmerston (visitable only through ARAU, see p.251).

This house was designed by Victor Horta in 1895–7. Compared with the Maison Saint-Cyr, the façade is very strait-laced. However, it is typical of Horta, who applied Art Nouveau sparingly and with rigid discipline (for more about him, *see* p.202). The very restraint of this design, with its cast-iron columns and pronounced horizontals, was novel for the time. Art Nouveau embellishments can be seen in the curved brackets beneath the first-floor projection and the decorative panels between the windows. Horta was particularly renowned for his interiors—in this case an ingenious design arranged around an octagonal well and lit by an overhead glass canopy.

On the opposite side of Avenue Palmerston, at No. 3, is the **Maison Deprez-Van de Velde**, also by Horta. It was built at the same time as the Maison Van Eetvelde, and its exterior is even more conventional.

Also see: **Musée du Cinquantenaire**, p.201; **Musée Wiertz**, p.207.

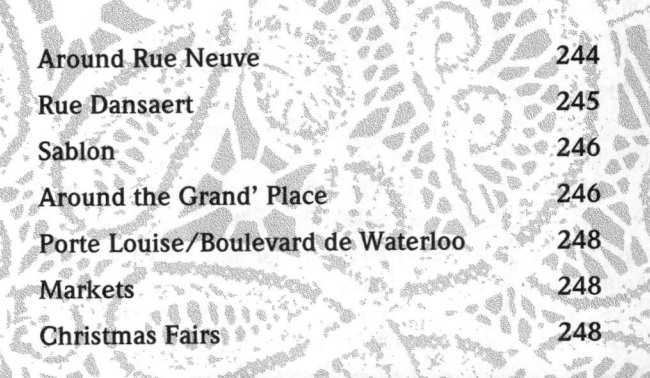

Around Rue Neuve	244
Rue Dansaert	245
Sablon	246
Around the Grand' Place	246
Porte Louise/Boulevard de Waterloo	248
Markets	248
Christmas Fairs	248

Brussels: Shopping

What will you take home from your trip to Brussels? Fresh-cream chocolates for the neighbours, a few bottles of Belgian beer? A tablecloth of the finest hand-made Brussels lace? A set of Tintin classics to help improve your French? How about a 19th-century engraving of Brussels, an Art Nouveau lamp, or a party mask of Gilles de Binche?

Remember, the very character of Belgium was forged by the strong traditions of its artisans and traders. Shops and stores are in the mainstream of Belgian life, and the Belgians love to shop. To enhance the feel-good factor for those parting with their money, there are numerous elegantly styled *galeries*—covered arcades filled with shops, as well as restaurants and cafés for those who need refuelling between bouts of spending. You could pass most of the day in one: many Belgians do.

Value Added Tax

All shop prices include Value Added Tax (TVA/BWT) where applicable. At the time of writing this stands at 21 per cent. Non-European Union visitors may claim back the VAT on purchases in excess of 7,000 BF made in any one shop. This is a fairly complex procedure, most effectively dealt with if you are departing from Brussels international airport (Zaventem). When making your purchase, ask the shop for a form called a 'Tax-free Shopping Chèque'. Staple the receipt to it and fill out your personal details. When you reach the airport, have the Shopping Chèque stamped by customs (who may wish to inspect the goods), then take it to the refund office in the departure hall, which will refund to you the VAT paid.

Refunds are also available at the Interchange offices in central Brussels (88 Rue du Marché aux Herbes). If you prefer, you can apply for a refund by post through Interchange. For further information ask at any major shop, the tourist office, or the specialist agency Europe Tax-free Shopping, 13/1 Jan Sobieskilaan, 1020 Brussels, ✆ 479 94 61.

Around Rue Neuve

Rue Neuve is one of the Brussels' busiest shopping streets, with many of the capital's more upmarket chainstores, such as Hennes & Mauritz and Marks & Spencer. The narrow pedestrianized thoroughfare is often so packed that it is hard to cross the flow. The Passage du Nord shopping arcade, off the Rue Neuve, was built in 1882.

Boulevard Adolphe Max is named after the burgomaster who held the post for a total of three decades, from 1909 to 1939. He is fondly remembered for his dignified and spirited resistance to the oppressive policies of the Germans in occupation during the First World War—for which he was deported and imprisoned—and as an advocate of universal suffrage, including votes for women.

100% Design, 30 Boulevard Anspach. Witty and fun domestic wares, especially inflatables—picture frames, waste-paper bins, armchairs.

Anticyclone des Açores, 34 Rue Fossé-aux-Loups. The best selection of maps, guidebooks and travel literature in Belgium.

Cartes, 25 Rue Neuve. Postcards and greetings cards of all kinds and descriptions, featuring everything from work by classic photographers to filmstars, joyous kitsch and the outrageously lewd.

Centre Belge de la Bande Dessinée, 20 Rue des Sables. Thousands of comic-strip titles—in French and Dutch.

Christiaensen, City 2 (top of Rue Neuve), and 36 Rue Marché aux Herbes, and other branches. Comprehensive selections of international toy brands, anything from Barbie to radio-controlled speed-boats.

City 2, top of Rue Neuve, off Place Rogier (Galerie). A warren of shops, restaurants and cinemas. Its wide range of quality shops includes the mega-book-and-record store FNAC, and the department store Inno.

Esprit, 4–6 Rue Neuve. Large store of the American quality casual wear brand.

FNAC, City 2, 123 Rue Neuve. French megastore selling a huge selection of books (in French, English and other languages), CDs and cassettes, and computers. Also has a ticket agency for concerts, etc.

Free Record Shop, Gaîté Theatre, 18 Rue du Fossé aux Loups. Impressive recently converted record/CD and videocassette megastore in a venerable old music hall.

GB, City 2, top of Rue Neuve. One of a vast chain of standard supermarkets, specializing in food and drink—good-quality, competively priced.

Hennes & Mauritz, 36, 80, 123 Rue Neuve and 80 Rue St-Michel. Amazingly inexpensive fashionable clothes, each of the huge stores offering a different assortment. Swedish chain that has become the most popular of its kind since it entered the Belgian market in the early 1990s.

Inno, 111 Rue Neuve. The best-known department store in Brussels: clothes, sports goods, furnishings and domestic appliances, perfumes, textiles—the great department-store mix.

In den Olifant, 47 Rue des Fripiers. A branch of this small chain of toy stores known for its tasteful range and sympathetic shop designs. Particularly strong in wooden toys.

Leonidas, 46 Blvd Anspach; also 34 Rue au Beurre. Good value, and, in many people's opinion, as good as the more expensive Neuhaus and Godiva.

Marks & Spencer, 17–21 Rue Neuve. A well-stocked representative of the British chain: clothes, toiletries and some food.

M&S Lighting, 45 Boulevard Anspach. All kinds of lighting—grand, ultra-modern, exotic, outrageous.

Peek & Cloppenburg, 30 Rue Neuve. One of a group of stylish general clothing stores at the lower end of the Rue Neuve.

Virgin Megastore, Anspach Centre, Blvd Anspach. CDs, videos, videogames.

W. H. Smith, 71–75 Boulevard Adolphe Max. Unlike most of the British chain of the same name, this is much more than just a stationer with a stock of popular books: this is a serious English-language bookshop, with a huge range of titles.

Zara, 48 Rue Neuve. Trendy Spanish chain that offers stylish clothes at surprisingly low prices. For those who like Gucci but not Gucci's prices.

Rue Dansaert

Ten years ago Rue Dansaert was a scruffy street on the 'wrong' side of Blvd Anspach; now it is a trendy centre for serious avant-garde fashion. The fashion shops include Rue Blanche, Virgin Shoes (with Dirk Bikkembergs shoes), Kat en Muis children's clothes (with lines by Dries Van Noten) and, in the stretch between Marché aux Grains and the Place du Nouveau Marché au Grains, Idiz Bogum II (second-hand), and Stijl, which carries many of the great Antwerp names.

Comme des Garçons—Yohji Yamamoto, 6 Place du Nouveau Marché aux Grains. Outlet for top couturier Rei Kawakubo and several Japanese associates.

Espace Bizarre, 19 Rue des Chartreux. Beautiful, stylish Japanese furniture and furnishings (futons, tatamis, etc.), plus work by other leading designers in the same mould.

Le Grenier de la Bourse, 2 Rue Antoine Dansaert. *Brocanteur* near the city centre, specializing in metal office furniture of the 1920s, pine,

Art Nouveau and anything witty and stylish which takes his fancy.

Idiz Bogum I, 162 Rue Blaes; **Idiz Bogum II**, 76 Rue A. Dansaert. Chic second-hand clothes of the 1940s–70s, frequented by fashion-hounds and theatrical costumiers.

Kat en Muis, 32 Rue Antoine Dansaert. Stylish off-the-peg children's clothes. Knitwear, smocks and winning woolly hats, for 0–14 years. Now owned by Stijl up the road, it carries children's clothes by Dries van Noten.

Les Précieuses, 83 Rue Antoine Dansaert. An exquisite collection of bags, jewellery, knitwear and candles. Just staring at the shop window will soothe your soul's craving for beauty. **Rue Blanche**, 35 Rue Antoine Dansaert. Outlet for this label, known for its tasteful elegance in a modern idiom.

Stijl, 74 Rue Antoine Dansaert. Well-established avant-garde fashion boutique in an 18th-century converted butter wrapping factory, with changing rooms in the carriage block. Stijl has exclusive rights in Brussels over a number of top names, so this is the place to hunt for your new outfit by Dries van Noten, Ann Demeulemeester, Dirk Bikkembergs, Martin Margiela, Raf Simons, or a wedding gown by David Fielden.

Virgin, 10 Rue Antoine Dansaert and 13 Rue des Eperonniers. Gritty, modish boots and shoes, where black rules. For those who want street cred with style, and are prepared to pay for it. Exclusive retailers for Dirk Bikkembergs' shoes.

Sablon

The Place du Grand-Sablon is one of the main areas for antiques and the fine art trade, and is home to a number of small art galleries.

Anne de Beaujeu, 7 Rue de Sablons. Fine quality 19th- and 20th-century furniture, furnishings and ornaments in the heart of the antiques district.

Antiques fair and flea market: Place du Grand-Sablon. A small, well-established, and rather upmarket antiques fair: old prints, books, 18th-century furniture, porcelain, Art Deco figurines, bakelite. Sat 9–6, Sun 9–2.

Les Caves de Colette, 59 Rue des Minimes. An antique shop with a lived-in look because it is also Colette's home. A huge cellar, with an open fire, kitchen, beds and 101 other things all for sale.

Cento Anni, 31 Place du Grand-Sablon. Classic, florid Art Nouveau glass and metalware.

Louise Verschueren, 16 Rue Watteeu. Part exhibition, part shop, and a reliable source for real hand-made Belgian lace.

Musées Royaux des Beaux-Arts, 3 Rue de la Régence. Good selection of art books, particularly on Belgian painters.

Philippe Denys, 1 Rue des Sablons. Fine silverware of the streamlined Art Nouveau/Art Deco kind by such luminaries as Jean Puiforcat and Georg Jensen, plus furniture and ceramics of the same era.

Sablon Shopping Gardens, 36 Place du Grand-Sablon. A cluster of some 40 sophisticated antique and art shops.

Service de Chalcographie, 1 Place du Musée. Over 5,000 historical and contemporary prints from the royal library collection of plates; *see* p.255.

La Vaisselle au Kilo, 8A Rue Bodenbroeck. Crockery of all grades sold by weight, from 75 BF to 200 BF per kilo. Also cutlery and glasses.

Le Village d'Antiquaires, 22 Rue Bodenbroeck. A warren of ten dealers at the top end of the Place du Grand-Sablon selling 18th- and 19th-century furniture, bric-a-brac, prints and glassware.

Wittamer, 12–13 Place du Grand-Sablon. The most celebrated *pâtisserie* in Brussels. Eat one of their chocolate cakes and you'll see why: angels will dance on your tongue.

Around the Grand' Place

There are numerous outlets selling lace around the Grand' Place—anything from glass-mats and handkerchiefs to tablecloths; you only have to watch it being made to understand why there is no such thing as cheap Belgian lace. Down the Rue du Midi, from the Bourse to the Place Rouppe, there are stamp shops of all kinds and levels.

Belgasafe, 24 Rue du Midi. One of a cluster of stamp shops at the upper end of the street: mainly modern stamps from all over the world, for the general collector.

La Boule Rouge, 52 Rue des Pierres. Artist's materials of every description in neatly ordered stacks and shelves, the very sight of which is inspiration to pick up a brush and have a go.

Boutique de Tintin, 13 Rue de la Colline. T-shirts, models, stationery, plus the books themselves, featuring Tintin, Captain Haddock, Snowy et al.

Corné, 9 Rue de la Madeleine. One of the big names in luxury chocolates.

La Courte Echelle, 12 Rue des Eperonniers. Everything for the doll's house—plus the house itself. A magical world of miniaturization where craftsmanship is the guiding principle.

Dandoy, 31 Rue au Beurre and 14 Rue Charles Buls. Famous for its buttery, crumbly biscuits: *speculoos* and also many other specialities. As wondrous to take home as any chocolates.

Dragées Maréchal, 40 Rue des Chapeliers. Fine old store founded in 1848, specializing in the sugared almonds and fancy porcelain containers that are traditionally offered to guests at christenings.

Elvis Pompilio, 60 Rue du Midi. Hats wild and wonderful, stylish and fanciful—just how far can Elvis go? His most extravagant creations are virtually sculptures fashioned in felt. But don't expect any change out of 6,000 BF.

Euroline, 52 Rue du Marché aux Herbes. One of several Euro-shops, selling postcards, stickers, nailbrushes, flags—and just about anything with a flat surface that can be emblazoned with the be-spangled Euro-flag.

Galerie Agora, off Rue des Eperonniers, Rue de la Colline and Rue du Marché aux Herbes. A surprisingly upmarket setting for this bazaar of subculture: T-shirts, leather, jewellery, baseball caps, body-piercing, and other forms of alternative exotica, all within a stone's throw of the Grand' Place.

Galerie Bortier, between Rue Saint-Jean and Rue de la Madeleine. A 19th-century *galerie*, now a centre for second-hand books.

Galeries Royales de Saint-Hubert, off Rue du Marché aux Herbes. The oldest and most elegant of them all; marbled halls and a relaxed café ambience in which to window-gaze at exquisite shoes and clothes in luxurious boutiques, as well as browse around some excellent bookshops. *See* p.217.

Godiva, 22 Grand' Place; also 89 Boulevard A. Max. Celebrated and expensive *chocolatier*.

Neuhaus, 27 Galerie de la Reine, Galeries Saint-Hubert; also 1 Rue de l'Etuve, 34 Passage du Nord and 27 Ave de la Toison d'Or. Refined, restrained, perhaps *the* place for the chocolate addict.

Lauffer, 26 Rue des Bouchers. Equipment for the chef, professional and amateur alike. Ranks of superb knives, glistening steel saucepans, precison-made spatulas, wooden moulds for *speculoos* biscuits—you can even buy yourself a full chef's outfit and crown yourself with a genuine *bonnet de chef*.

Langhendries, 41 Rue de la Fourche. Supreme selection of beautifully conditioned French, Italian, Dutch and Belgian cheeses from 'dare you to' strong *crottes* to slabs the size of truck tyres, all presented with the true passion of a *maître-fromager*.

Maison Rubbrecht, 23 Grand' Place. Central outlet for good-quality lace, much of it hand-made.

La Manufacture Belge de la Dentelle, 6–8 Galerie de la Reine, Galeries Saint-Hubert. Expensive, but good, lace.

Pandin, 47 Rue de la Fourche. Choose patés, *charcuterie* or delicious ready-made dishes from this ravishing display of the *traiteur*'s art.

Peau d'zèbre, 40 Rue du Midi. Remarkable clothes for younger children, designed and made on the premises. Charming, stylish yet practical, in inspired autumnal colours. Most remarkable of all, they are incredibly good value: dungarees for 700 BF; nothing costs more than 2,000 BF.

Philatelie Corneille Soeteman, 131 Rue du Midi. A major auction house, but also exhibits the *crème de la crème* of stamps for purchase in its showroom.

Tropismes, Galerie des Princes, Galeries Saint-Hubert. Famously elegant bookstore, a joy to browse in. Has some English titles. The only bookstore in town that is open on Sundays.

Williame Baeton, 7 Rue du Midi. August antique stamp dealer and auctioneer, for the expert whose passion means spending serious money.

W. Sand, 28c Rue du Lombard. A long-established dealer in antique sculptures, musical instruments, jewellery and so forth from Africa and the Orient—an anthropological treasure trove.

Around the Grand' Place

Porte Louise/Boulevard de Waterloo

The Boulevard de Waterloo and its twin, the Avenue de la Toison d'Or (Golden Fleece) form part of the busy thoroughfare called the 'Petite Ceinture', which rings the city centre along the course of the ancient city walls. The area between the former sites of two city gates—the Porte Louise (in Place Louise) and the Porte de Namur to its left—is an impressive and fashionable place to shop, as apart from the shops on the streets themselves there are covered modern *galeries* that lead off the Avenue de la Toison d'Or to the south—the Galerie Louise, the Galerie de la Toison d'Or and the Galerie Porte de Namur. The Galerie Louise, in particular, is a showcase of elegant style, packed with shops selling mainly *haute couture*, jewellery and shoes.

Nearby, Avenue Louise is the smartest street in Brussels and is lined with designer names.

Bernard, 93 Rue de Namur. Marbled delicatessen on the ground floor of a celebrated fish restaurant, specializing in mouthwatering fish and seafood preparations.

Bouvy, 52 Avenue de la Toison d'Or. Famous, elegant shop, established over half a century ago, offering a large assortment of contemporary designers' clothes (Armani, DKNY, CK, Versace, Anvers, Rue Blanche…).

Delvaux, 27 Blvd de Waterloo, also 31 Galerie de la Reine and 22 Blvd Adolphe Max. The ultimate sophistication in leather goods.

Dujardin, 82–4 Avenue Louise. This famous shop sells chic children's clothes, all designed and made in Belgium. Recently rescued from oblivion by Delvaux, it is now housed in a vampishly renovated *maison de maître*.

Les Enfants d'Edouard, 175–77 Avenue Louise. Nearly new second-hand clothes by top designers.

Galerie Louise, off Avenue de la Toison d'Or and Avenue Louise. Sleek and tasteful, at the upper end of the shopping spectrum—mainly high-class clothing stores and shoe shops. Expensive, but the throngs of customers include many an average Bruxellois(e) out to buy that little number for the coming season. *See* p.227.

Galerie de la Toison d'Or, between the Avenue de la Toison d'Or and the Chaussée d'Ixelles. Often paired with its neighbour, the Galerie Louise, and of matching high standards. Clothes, accessories and much more.

Serneels, 69 Avenue Louise. Tasteful toys and clothes based on comic-strip heroes such as Babar.

Markets

Gare du Midi. *Sun am*. The biggest market in Brussels, filling the Boulevard de l'Europe and selling everything from couscous to cars.

Grand' Place. *Sun 8am–12.30pm*. Bird market: half the square fills with traders selling parrots, love birds, budgies and fancy chickens. (The daily flower market consists of little more than a couple of stalls.)

Parvis Saint-Gilles. *Tues–Sun 6am–12.30pm*. A busy food market a short walk from the Porte de Hal. Mainly fruit, vegetables and other necessities, displayed in vivid Technicolor—and also some speciality hams and cheeses.

Place du Jeu de Balle. The premier flea market in Brussels. *Daily 7–2, bigger on Sun*.

Christmas Fairs

These take place in the run-up to the Fête de Saint-Nicolas (6 December) and Christmas itself (contact the tourist office for dates and times). The best-known are held in the **Place du Grand-Sablon**, and the **Place Cardinal Mercier** (Jette). The stalls sell decorations, candles, foods associated with the festive seasons, hand-crafted gifts, and so on, but their particular appeal is the joyous mood and vivid colour which bring light and warmth to those chill and gloomy December days.

Art and Architecture Museums	250
Art Nouveau	251
Other Museums	252
Monuments and Other Attractions	255

Brussels: Museums and Monuments

Brussels boasts 70 museums in all. Many of these are tiny, specialist museums of limited interest, open only by appointment or to groups, while others are downright cranky, and disappointing to boot. That still leaves a wealth of hugely varied museums to visit. What follows is a selected list of the best known or more interesting.

The admission charges shown are for adults; there are usually discounts for children under 16, and most museums admit children under 4 for free.

Art and Architecture Museums

Musée d'Art Ancien, see Musées Royaux des Beaux-Arts.

Musée d'Art Moderne, see Musées Royaux des Beaux-Arts.

Musée Bruegel, 132 Rue Haute. *Group tours only, by written request.* This red-brick step-gabled house, much restored, gives a flavour of how this district might have looked in the 16th century when it was a prosperous suburb. So little is known about Bruegel's life that it is not certain that he did live here. However, it does seem that the house belonged to Anne Bruegel, Bruegel's granddaughter (and wife of the painter David Teniers the Younger), who probably inherited it through her father, Jan ('Velvet') Bruegel.

Musée du Centre Public d'Aide Sociale de Bruxelles, Hôpital Saint-Pierre, 298a Rue Haute, ✆ 543 60 55. *Open Wed only 1–5; adm free.* The Hôpital Saint-Pierre was founded in the 12th century as a leprosy hospital. Over time, it received gifts through various legacies, and its small, oddball but valuable collection of treasures can be seen displayed in a corridor and series of conference rooms. It includes 17th-century furniture, Roman coins, tapestries, church treasures and several notable paintings, including the curious *Christ Surrounded by the Sponsors of the Hospital* by Gaspard de Crayer (1584–1669). The gem of the collection, however, is a small folding altarpiece by Bernard van Orley, dated 1520. Entitled *La Dormition de la Vierge*, it is a beautiful early-Renaissance depiction of the deathbed of the Virgin, with accompanying scenes from the beginning of Christ's story, from the Annunciation to the Circumcision, all painted with loving detail and tenderness.

Musée du Cinquantenaire, Parc du Cinquantenaire, ✆ 741 72 11. *Open Tues–Fri 10–6, Sat and Sun 10–5, closed Mon; adm 150 BF, students 100 BF, children 50 BF. See p.201.* Also contains the **Musée Boyadjian du Cœur** (Boyadjian Heart Museum). *Open Tues–Fri 9.30–5, Sat and Sun 10–5, closed Mon; adm 150 BF, students 100 BF and children 50 BF.* This curiosity occupies two small rooms in the Musée du Cinquentenaire. Dr Boyadjian, a leading contemporary heart surgeon, was interested in the way that the heart is used as a symbol, and this interest led to the acquisition of an extensive private collection which he donated to the Musées Royaux d'Art et d'Histoire. The role of the heart in Christian symbolism can be traced to the piercing of Christ's side by the soldier at Calvary; the flaming heart denotes fervent devotion and is the symbol of charity. The collection includes reliquaries, silver ex-voto offerings given in thanks for relief of ailments of the heart (both physical and emotional, no doubt), and church treasures of fabulous vulgarity.

Musée Communal d'Ixelles, 71 Rue J. van Volsem, ✆ 511 90 84 (ext. 1459). *Open Tues–Fri 1–7, Sat and Sun 10–5, closed Mon; adm free to permanent exhibition.* This museum is a delight—a small, informal gallery with all kinds of unusual surprises. The collection was founded in 1892 and includes numerous interesting minor works by great artists, such as sketches by Rembrandt, Boucher, Fragonard and Delacroix, a tiny self-portrait by Jongkind, 15 original posters by Toulouse-Lautrec, a small Cubist painting in acrylic by Picasso, a watercolour of Cannes by Raoul Dufy, and a painted metal work by Frank Stella. Belgian artists are particularly well represented, with paintings by Léon Frédéric, Magritte and Spilliaert. Two works by Rik Wouters (1882–1916) may help to convince you that he was one of Belgium's most endearing artists: one painting of his wife Nel in a red hat, the other called *La Vierge Folle* (The Mad Virgin, 1912)—a bronze statue of a nude dancing with energetic abandon, stepping out, arms akimbo. This sculpture is full of the *joie de vivre* for which Wouters' work is celebrated.

Musée Communal de la Ville de Bruxelles, Maison du Roi, Grand' Place, ✆ 279 43 50. *Open Tues–Thurs (closed Mon & Fri), 10–12.30 and 1.30–5, closes at 4pm Oct–Mar; Sat and Sun 10–1; adm 80 BF. See* p.214.

Musée Constantin Meunier, 59 Rue de l'Abbaye, ✆ 508 32 11. *Open 10–12 and 1–5, closed Mon and alternate weekends; adm free.* The painter and sculptor Constantin Meunier (1831–1905) is best remembered for his bronzes of industrial workers—notably the gaunt forge-workers called *puddleurs* ('puddlers'), with their round leather hats to protect them from sparks. In his early career, Meunier painted only monastic and religious scenes, but between 1879 and 1881 his visits to the industrial regions around Liège and the coal-mining Borinage district (which also so impressed the young Van Gogh at about the same time) left a deep mark. Meunier thereafter became a social realist in the mould of Gustave Courbet and Jean-François Millet.

The museum consists of a collection of Meunier's paintings, drawings and sculpture set out on the ground floor and in his large, north-facing studio to the rear. It includes sketches and trial work on the theme of fecundity for his monument to Emile Zola, which was erected in Paris but destroyed by the Germans during the Second World War. One of his most famous paintings, *Le Retour des Mineurs*, is on show here; look out also for the dramatic preparatory sketch (in the passage to the studio), in which the miners are rendered in skeletal cross-hatching and set against a dismal industrial landscape.

Musée Horta, 25 Rue Américaine, ✆ 543 04 90. *Open 2–5.30, closed Mon; adm 150 BF on weekdays, 200 BF at weekends. See* p.202.

Musée de l'Hôtel Charlier, 16 Avenue des Arts, ✆ 218 53 82. *Open Mon 10–5, Tues–Thurs 1.30–5, Fri 1.30–4.30, closed Sat and Sun; adm 100 BF. See* p.203.

Musée René Magritte, 135 Rue Esseghem, ✆ 428 26 26. *Open Wed–Sun 10–6; adm 240 BF.* The house where Magritte and his wife Georgette lived on the ground floor from 1930 to the mid 1950s. It was bought in 1994 and has been meticulously restored to show how it looked when they lived there, with other exhibits on the upper floors. The Magrittes were noted for living in an almost impossibly middle-class manner, and those seeking traces of the artist's genius are likely to leave disappointed. While Magritte painted thousands of works during his time in Rue Esseghem, the house has only a few sketches and letters, as well as his easel and the trademark bowler hat.

Musées Royaux d'Art et d'Histoire, *see* Musée du Cinquantenaire.

Musées Royaux des Beaux-Arts, 3 Rue de la Régence, ✆ 508 32 11. *Open 10–5, closed Mon; adm 150 BF. See* p.204.

Musée Wiertz, 62 Rue Vautier, ✆ 648 17 18. *Open 10–12 and 1–5, closes at 4pm Nov–Mar; closed Mon & alternate weekends; adm free. See* p.207.

Art Nouveau

In the heyday of Art Nouveau at the turn of the century, there were some 2000 Art Nouveau houses in Brussels; only about half of these have survived. ARAU, a highly professional, non-profit-making organization, can organize trips to Art Nouveau houses which are otherwise inaccessible (*see* list below for a selection of these). Contact them at 55 Boulevard Adolphe Max, 1000 Brussels, ✆ 219 33 45.

Hôtel Solvay, 224 Avenue Louise (Victor Horta).
Hôtel Tassel, 6 Rue Paul-Emile Janson (Victor Horta).
No. 83 Rue Faider (A. Roosenboom, one of Horta's draughtsmen).
No. 48 Rue Defacqz (Paul Hankar).
No. 71 Rue Defacqz (Paul Hankar).
Nos. 53 and 55 Avenue Brugmann (E. Pelseneer).
Hôtel Hannon, Avenue de la Jonction (Jules Brunfaut, interior by Emile Gallé and Louis Majorelle). Contains a gallery open for temporary shows.
Nos. 30, 32, 42, 44 and 46 Rue de Bellevue (Ernest Blérot).
No. 30 Rue du Monastère (Ernest Blérot).
Nos. 38 and 39 Avenue Général de Gaulle (Ernest Blérot).

Nos. 9 and 11 Rue Vilain XIII (Ernest Blérot).
No. 40 Rue de la Vallée (Ernest Blérot).
No. 6 Rue du Lac (Léon Delune).
Maison Saint-Cyr, 11 Square Ambiorix (Gustave Strauven), *see* p.242.
Maison Van Eetvelde, 4 Avenue Palmerston (Victor Horta), *see* p.242.
Maison Deprez-Van de Velde, 3 Avenue Palmerston (Victor Horta), see p.242.
Maison de Paul Cauchie, 5 Rue des Francs (Paul Cauchie), *see* p.237.
Musee Horta, *see* above.

Other Museums

Album, 25 Rue des Chartreux, ✆ 511 90 55. *Open 1–7, closed Tues; adm according to time spent, from 50 BF to 200 BF for over an hour.* From September 1999 Album will hold a 'Zigzag Europe' exhibition, shedding fresh light on the history of the Old Continent, through the stories of a dozen famous Europeans—from Julius Caesar and Leonardo da Vinci to Hitler and the Beatles. Set in a reconstructed 17th-century house in the heart of historic Brussels, the museum is run by an enthusiastic, knowledgeable and friendly couple.

Atelier de Moulages (Casting and Moulding Workshop), Parc du Cinquantenaire (on Avenue des Nerviens), ✆ 741 72 94. *Open Mon–Fri 9–12 and 1.30–3.30; adm free. See* p.241.

Autoworld, Parc du Cinquantenaire, ✆ 736 41 65. *Open April–Sept 10–6, Oct–March 10–5; adm 200 BF, students 150 BF.* Filling a vast space beneath the towering cast-iron arches of this trimly restored exhibition hall is a formidable array of over 300 glistening motor vehicles, dating back to the dawn of the combustion engine. There are rickety old horseless carriages, dashing early sports cars, pre-war breadvans, tail-finned American gas-guzzlers of the 1950s, and various huge limousines which once transported the rich and famous. The core of the collection was put together by a single private enthusiast, Ghislain Mahy, but the museum is run as a joint-venture project assisted by state funds.

Centre Belge de la Bande Dessinée, 20 Rue des Sables, ✆ 219 19 80. *Open 10–6, closed Mon; adm 200 BF. See* p.195.

Hôtel de Ville de Bruxelles, Grand' Place, ✆ 279 43 65. *Guided tours only, in English, German, Dutch or French: English tours Tues 11.30 and 3.15, Wed 3.15 and April–Sept Sun 12.15; adm 75 BF. See* p.217.

Koninklijk Museum voor Midden-afrika, *see* Musée Royal de l'Afrique Centrale.

Musée de la Brasserie, Maison des Brasseurs, 10 Grand' Place, ✆ 511 49 87. *Open 10–5; adm 100 BF.* This brewing museum consists of two rooms: the first contains a variety of traditional paraphernalia from the old days of brewing, while the second gives a flavour of the hi-tech, squeaky-clean world of modern brewing. Touch-screen computers offer a breakdown of statistics about the Belgian brewing industry. A disappointing museum; you would be better off visiting the Musée de la Gueuze (*see* below).

Musée Bruxella 1238, Société Royale d'Archéologie de Bruxelles, Rue de la Bourse, ✆ 279 43 50. *Guided tours only, from La Maison du Roi; adm 80 BF.* Excavations of a 13th-century Franciscan convent, destroyed in the religious wars of the 16th century.

Musée Bruxellois de la Gueuze, 56 Rue Gheude, ✆ 521 49 28. *Open Mon–Fri 8.30–4; Sat 10–4; adm 100 BF; guided tour on request, 2,000 BF.* The atmospheric old brewery where Cantillon, one of the great *gueuze* beers, is made in the traditional way from *lambic*. The beer is brewed only in the winter months (approximately 15 Oct–15 May), but there is still plenty to see outside this period.

Musée du Béguinage d'Anderlecht, 8 Rue du Chapelain (Anderlecht), ✆ 521 13 83. *Open 10–12 and 2–5, closed Tues and Fri; adm 50 BF.* A charming *béguinage* with reconstructed, furnished interiors.

Musée du Cacao et du Chocolat, 13 Grand' Place, ✆ 514 20 48. *Open 10–5, closed Mon; adm 200 BF.* Through video films, info panels and various chocolate samples (yes, you can taste!), this little museum gives a general idea of the origins and history of cocoa and chocolate, from its discovery by the Spanish to modern production processes. On Wed, Thurs and Fri a professional praline-maker gives demonstrations. For all its cosy charms, this museum will only reward serious chocolate enthusiasts.

Musée du Chemin de Fer Belge, Gare du Nord (off the central hall), ✆ 224 62 79. *Open 9–4.30 (upper floor open only 1st Sat of month); closed Sat (except 1st Sat of month) and Sun and public hols; adm free*. A small collection of engines and detailed models of trains and carriages; photographs and railway equipment: for railway buffs.

Musée du Cinéma, Palais des Beaux-Arts, 9 Rue Baron Horta, ✆ 507 83 70. *Open 5.30–10.30pm; adm 80 BF, 50 BF if booked a day in advance*. See p.200.

Musée du Costume et de la Dentelle, 6 Rue de la Violette, ✆ 512 77 09. *Open Mon, Tues, Thurs and Fri 10–12.30 and 1.30–5, open until 4pm Oct–Mar; Sat and Sun 2–4.30, closed Weds and public hols; adm 80 BF*. Housed in an 18th-century building, this small museum contains a small but rich collection of lace and clothing accessories from the 17th century to the present day and hosts well-presented temporary exhibitions about the history of fashion. If you want to make some sense of all the lace that fills so many of the shops in the surrounding streets, this a good place to start. The museum's extensive costume collection forms the basis of a rolling series of temporary exhibitions.

Musée David et Alice van Buuren, 41 Avenue Léo Errera (Uccle), ✆ 343 48 51. *Open Sun 1–6 and Mon 2–6 only; adm 300 BF, children 200 BF*. Dutch banker's elegant private house, with gardens, built and furnished in Art Deco style in the 1930s. It contains a remarkable collection of paintings, including works by Bruegel (a version of the *Fall of Icarus*), Wouters, Van Gogh, and the Sint-Martens-Latem School.

Musée de la Dynastie, 7 Place des Palais (Hôtel de Bellevue), ✆ 511 55 78. *Open 10–6, closed Mon and public hols; adm free*. This museum, laid out in the elegant rooms of a palatial residence, tells the history of the Belgian royal family through a collection of paintings, prints, photographs, furniture, clothing and other mementoes. Even if you are not an avid royal-watcher, it's worth at least a quick visit, if only to be able to put faces to the names of the Belgian royals through their short history and see them in their historical context.

Musée des Egouts, Pavillon d'Octroi, Porte d'Anderlecht (on Boulevard du Midi), ✆ 513 85 87. *Open Wed only, 9am, 11am, 1am and 3pm (you may need to ring bell at door on southeast side); adm 80 BF*. An exhibition with video explaining the history of the Brussels sewer system and the fate of the River Senne, which was covered over in the 1860s. The visit includes descent to see the Senne and a short walk along the main sewer.

Musée d'Erasme, 31 Rue du Chapitre (Anderlecht), ✆ 521 13 83. *Open 10–12 and 2–5, closed Tues and Fri; adm 50 BF*. A collection of books, prints, paintings and furniture focusing on the life and times of the great Humanist Erasmus, who lived in this gabled brick house in 1521.

Musée de l'Imprimerie, Bibliothèque Royale Albert 1er, 4 Blvd de l'Empereur, ✆ 519 53 56. *Open Mon–Sat 9–5, closed Sun; adm free*. This printing museum consists of a collection of old printing presses and equipment, from massive hand-pulled presses and compositors' trays to hot-metal casting machines, bewilderingly complex monotype keyboards and a vast camera on a wooden frame for making early photographic plates. It offers a brief glimpse of the world of printing, which computer technology has rendered archaic in less than two decades.

Musée de l'Institut Royal des Sciences Naturelles de Belgique, 29 Rue Vautier and 260 Chaussée de Wavre, ✆ 627 42 33 or 627 42 38 (24hr line). *Open Tues–Sat 9.30–4.45, Sun 9.30–6, closed Mon; adm 120 BF*. The building's modern shell incorporates a 19th-century museum inaugurated by Leopold II in 1891. The original halls, with their tiled floors and ornate, painted, cast-iron structure, were built to house a major find of iguanodon skeletons at Bernissart (near Mons) in 1870. These have now been joined by a dozen or so life-size, moving, roaring models—the survivors of a temporary exhibition called Dinosaurs & Co. This section is still the highlight, and your life really would not be much the poorer if you gave the museum a miss. (Children, however, seem to enjoy it.) The main body of the museum consists of hundreds of stuffed animals and skeletons displayed in a maze of long rooms, floors and corridors, which are inter-connected by lifts and spiral staircases. It is in a constant state of flux, and even if you invest in a plan of the layout you are likely to find your progress unexpectedly barred by sections that have been cordoned off. There are some redeeming features besides the dinosaurs, however, such as the rooms of glittering, gem-like minerals, and an impressive collection of shells.

Musée des Instruments de Musique, 2 Montagne de la Cour, ✆ 545 01 30. *Opening*

June 2000; opening hours and adm as yet unknown. See p.204.

Musée du Jouet, 24 Rue de l'Association, ☏ 219 61 68. *Open 10–12.30 and 2–6; adm 100 BF.* This museum has the one ingredient that the Centre Belge de la Bande Dessinée lacks: joy. Housed on three floors in a grand but rather dilapidated 19th-century *maison de maître* (gentleman's residence), it is crammed with toys of all kinds and all ages: dolls, teddy bears, cars, trains, farm animals, magic lanterns, puppets. It is run on a shoestring, but the improvised display cases, higgledy-piggledy arrangement of the exhibits, handwritten labels and histories (French and Flemish only) help to create a magical world—a kind of walk-in toy box. Children are genuinely welcome: there is an area where they can play with numerous larger toys, and the display cases have steps so that smaller children can see into them. Grown-ups will be assailed by nostalgia; and there are some unusual curiosities, such as the set of model figures depicting King Baudouin I's visit to the Congo in 1955.

Musée du Livre, Bibliothèque Royale Albert Ier, 4 Boulevard de l'Empereur, ☏ 519 53 57. *Open Mon, Wed, Sat 2–5; adm free.* The museum occupies just one small room—a womb-like interior of dark carpeting and softly lit display cases, containing books of up to 1,200 years old. The 12th- and 13th-century exhibits date from the heyday of the illuminated manuscript, while a printed text from Japan of AD 770 is a salutary reminder that Gutenberg's breakthrough in around 1430 was not so much printing itself but the development of movable type. The earliest European printed book on display, dating from 1474, is so immaculately preserved that it might have been printed 50 years ago, not 500. There are also 16th-century books from Christopher Plantin's famous workshop in Antwerp, and a priceless manuscript by Matisse illustrating a work by the 15th-century poet Charles d'Orléans.

Musée Numismatique et Historique de la Banque Nationale de Belgique, 9 Rue du Bois Sauvage, ☏ 221 22 06. *Open Mon 10–5; July–Aug Tues–Fri 2–4; adm free.* Coins and banknotes.

Musée des Postes et Télécommunications, 40 Place du Grand-Sablon, ☏ 511 77 40. *Open Tues–Sat 10–4.30, closed Sun, Mon and public hols; adm free.* In 1500 the head of the Turn and Taxis family was made Master of the Posts by Philip the Handsome, a job which was assiduously cultivated during the reign of Charles V so that within half a century the family controlled the most effective post and messenger service in Europe, stretching right across the Habsburg empire. Four centuries later, Turn and Taxis is still a society name to be reckoned with, and the family owns a vast palace in Regensburg, Germany. In the 16th century, the Turn and Taxis family lived in a palace up the hill from here, off what is now the Rue de la Régence, and so it is appropriate to find this small museum on their own postal round. It may not sound too thrilling, but it's free, and worth visiting if only to admire the huge boots—like plaster casts—worn by postillions to ward off the weather and passing traffic. Other artefacts from postal history include post-horns, uniforms, historic letter-boxes (dating from their introduction in 1800), models of post coaches and long forks carried by rural postmen to keep dogs and geese at bay. Exhibits in the telecommunications section explain various communications systems that led from the 'visual telegraph' set on hilltops—which linked Brussels to Paris in 1803—to the first electrical telegraph networks introduced with the railways, and from thence to successive generations of telephones and the fax. There is also a philately department.

Musée Royal de l'Afrique Centrale, 13 Leuvensesteenweg, Tervuren, ☏ 769 52 11. *Open 10–5, weekends and public hols 10–6, closed Mon; adm 80 BF.* There was once a pleasure palace on this huge domain where Charles of Lorraine liked to hold hunting parties and other festivities, and he died here in 1780. The vast, domed Louis XV-style château that now dominates the park looks as though it might have been built in that era: in fact it was designed expressly as a museum at the end of the reign of Leopold II.

The museum contains a large and absorbing collection of historical, anthropological and zoological artefacts: fetishes, jewellery, baskets, weapons, sculpture, masks and headdresses, stuffed wildlife—many of which were collected for the Congo exhibit at the Brussels Universal Exhibition of 1897. Among the most memorable exhibits are an enormous pirogue—a 22.5m-long canoe, big enough for 100 men, hewn out of a single tree; a battered trunk used by Dr Livingstone on his last voyage; Stanley's peaked cap; an explorer's tin travelling case that doubled as a hip-bath; slaving manacles; and a pickled coelacanth (the living 'fossil fish', believed to have been extinct for 70 million years until it was discovered off Africa in 1938).

Musée Royal de l'Armée et d'Histoire Militaire, Parc du Cinquantenaire, ✆ 737 78 11. *Open 9–12, 1–4.30, closed Mon; adm free.* This is a huge collection, but fairly easy to assimilate in a quick visit, mainly because the core is packed into a series of rooms close to the entrance. The oldest part of the exhibition (installed in 1923) contains ranks of antique, glass-fronted cabinets stuffed with uniforms, weapons, flags and assorted military mementoes, mainly from the 19th century. Portraits of mustachioed generals, tattered regimental colours and neatly arranged sunbursts of rifles, swords and lances on the walls create the cheery atmosphere of a baronial hall. Running parallel to this hall is an impressive armour collection, including a complete set of horse armour.

Follow signs to the 'Section Air et Espace'. In a vast hall built for the 1910 International Exhibition, big enough to house a Zeppelin, is a jumble of antique and not-so-antique aircraft—from fragile, canvas-winged biplanes of the First World War, which have you reaching for your leather helmet and goggles, to Russian MiGs and a sleek Starfighter. It's a rough and ready display, where children are free to scamper around and rows of worn airliner seats are provided for you to slump into whenever your feet grow weary. Outside, open to the skies, is the 'Section Blindés', a kind of graveyard of tanks and armoured cars.

Musée du Théâtre de Toone VII, 6 Impasse Schuddeveld, ✆ 217 04 64. *Open only in the intervals during performances; adm free. See p.273.*

Musée du Transport Urbain Bruxellois, 364b Avenue de Tervuren, ✆ 515 31 08. *Open weekends and public holidays only, 1st Sat of April–1st Sun of Oct, 1.30–7; adm 150 BF with return trip on historic tram to Tervuren, children 75 BF.* Filling the extensive sheds of this old tram depot are dozens of trams (and some buses)—essential ingredients in the expansion of Brussels in the 19th century. The first trams were the horse-drawn *hippomobiles*, introduced in 1835, just after Belgium's first railway. They went on to dominate urban transport until 1895, when they were superseded by the electric tram. The museum has beautifully restored examples of trams of all ages—including the sleek cream and chrome models of the 1950s and 1960s—plus plenty of tram memorabilia, guaranteed to pluck the strings of nostalgia somewhere along the line.

Pavillon Chinois, 44 Avenue van Praet (Laeken), ✆ 268 16 08. *Open 10–4.45, closed Mon and public hols; adm 120 BF (combined ticket with Tour Japonaise). See p.209.*

Planétarium National, 10 Avenue de Bouchout (Laeken), ✆ 474 70 50/474 70 60. *Open according to a timetable of audio-visual-style presentations; adm 120 BF.* Primarily an educational institution.

Service de Chalcographie, 1 Place du Musée, ✆ 519 56 31. *Open Mon–Fri 9–12.45 and 2–4.45, closed Sat and Sun; adm free.* Chalcography is a fancy name for the art of engraving using copper plates. This department of the Bibliothèque Royale Albert I owns a collection of 5,400 engraving plates which include everything from old views of Brussels to abstract art. You can buy prints over the counter or select others from their catalogue, which will then be printed using traditional presses.

Tour Japonaise, 44 Avenue van Praet (Laeken), ✆ 268 16 08. *Open 10–4.30, closed Mon and public hols; adm 120 BF (combined ticket with Pavillon Chinois). See p.209.*

Monuments and Other Attractions

Atomium, Boulevard du Centenaire (Laeken), ✆ 474 89 77. *Open Sept–Mar 10–6; April–Aug 9–8; adm 200 BF, children 160 BF. See p.194.*

Basilique Nationale du Sacré Cœur, 1 Parvis de la Basilique (Koekelberg), ✆ 425 88 22. *Easter–early Nov 8–6, winter 8–5; adm free. Panorama from dome Mar–Oct Mon–Fri 11am and 3pm; adm 100 BF.* The green-copper dome that dominates northwestern Brussels belongs to what is often cited as the city's least loved building. Begun in 1905 (another brainchild of Leopold II) and eventually completed in 1930, it belongs to the 'bring-your-own-spirituality' school of ecclesiastical architecture: if you don't, you'll find it about as inspiring as a public swimming bath.

Bois de la Cambre, southern end of Avenue Louise. *Always open.* The wooded park that until 1842 formed the northern tip of the Forêt de Soignes. A favourite spot for walks and picnics, the park includes a large artificial boating lake, cafés and a roller-skating rink.

Brasserie Belle-Vue, 43 Quai du Hainaut, ✆ 410 19 35. *Tours Mon–Fri at 9.30, 11, 1.30, 3pm and Sat at 2pm; adm free.* Guided tours of Interbrew's *lambic* and *gueuze* brewery, with free sample drinks; telephone appointments essential for individual visitors as you have to join a group.

Bruparck, Boulevard du Centenaire (Laeken), ✆ 474 83 77. *Free admission to village.* A pleasant reconstructed gabled village of restaurants and boutiques, which acts as the hub for a variety of leisure attractions: **Mini Europe** (*see* below), **Océade** (indoor swimming-pool complex in a tropical setting), and **Kinepolis** (multi-screen cinema complex with an IMAX theatre for 3D films).

Cathédrale St-Michel et Ste-Gudule, Parvis Sainte-Gudule, ✆ 217 83 45. *Open daily 8–6; adm free, 40 BF to enter crypt.* See p.194.

Forêt de Soignes. Vast beech forest bordering southeast Brussels, covering 4,000 hectares; a remarkably wild area given its proximity to the city, and ravishingly beautiful in its golden colours of autumn. Plenty of good paths for walkers—take your own picnic. A popular starting point is the Abbaye du Rouge-Cloître, a former 14th-century monastery at Auderghem. The forest includes two major tree collections, the **Arboretum Géographique de Tervuren** (Old and New World trees), and the **Arboretum de Groenendaal** (400 forest species).

Jardin Botanique National, Domaine de Bouchout (Meise), ✆ 269 39 05. *Park open 9am–sunset; adm free. Palais des Plantes (greenhouses) open from Easter to last Sun of Oct 1–6.30pm, Sun and public hols 9–6.30, winter 9–5, closed Thurs; adm 120 BF.* Park and national botanical collection in the grounds of a château that belonged to Charlotte, Empress of Mexico (sister of Leopold II).

Kasteel van Beersel, Beersel (8km south of Brussels), ✆ 331 00 24. *Open Mar–mid Nov 10—6; mid Nov–Dec and Feb weekends and public hols only 10–6; closed Sun and Jan; adm 100 BF.* Robust medieval castle on a small lake. It consists of three massive towers joined by a curtain wall; the interiors are stark but atmospheric.

Mini Europe, Bruparck, Boulevard du Centenaire, ✆ 474 13 11. *Open April–June and Sept 9.30–6, July–Aug 9.30–8 except mid-July to mid-Aug, when closing is extended to midnight, Oct–Mar 10–6; adm 390 BF, children under 12 years old 290 BF, children under 1m20 free.* Some 300 architectural landmarks of Europe—the Acropolis, Colosseum, Leaning Tower of Pisa, Eiffel Tower, etc.—reduced to head-height models.

Palais de Charles de Lorraine, 1 Place du Musée, ✆ 519 53 71. *Closed for renovation; due to open April 2000.* Elegant, fully furnished, 18th-century apartments in palace of fashionable Austrian governor.

Palais de Justice, Place Poelaert, ✆ 508 64 10. *Mon–Fri 8am–5pm; adm free.* See p.208.

Palais Royal, Place des Palais, ✆ 551 20 20. *Open 22 July to 27 Sept, Tues–Sun 10.30–4.30; adm free.* See p.221.

Porte de Hal, Blvd du Midi, ✆ 534 25 52. *Closed until October 2000.* When it reopens, the Musée du Cinquantenaire will hold a permanent exhibition entitled 'History and Traditions of the City of Brussels'.

Serres Royales de Laeken, Domaine Royal (Laeken), ✆ 513 89 40. *Open for guided tours in April–May only, when the flowers are in bloom; consult the tourist office and book early.* The Serres Royales are a complex of eleven huge barrel-vaulted galleries and glass domes, the largest of which rises to 25m, set in the grounds of the royal palace of Laeken. This extraordinary 'city of glass' was built for Leopold II during the 1870s by Alphonse Balat (Victor Horta's teacher). Inside are extensive collections of tropical and subtropical plants, some dating back to the 19th century. If you are here in spring when the glasshouses are open to the public, it is well worth making a visit.

Central Brussels	259
East Brussels	260
South Brussels	260
West Brussels	261
North Brussels	261
Bars and Cafés in Brussels	262

Brussels: Food and Drink

It is now a well-known secret that Belgium's food ranks among the best in Europe—and that even the French are prepared to admit it. Belgians have a great enthusiasm for eating out. This means that decent restaurants are well patronized and are able to keep their prices competitive. Standards are invariably high—in the humble *friterie* on a street corner as well as at the dizzying pinnacles of *haute cuisine*. The foundations of this impressive tradition are laid by the quality of produce. Everyone in the food production chain takes immense pride in their profession, and they are likewise held in high regard by their clients, provided that the Belgians' fastidious standards are met.

The preoccupation with quality extends even to the large supermarket chains, such as Delhaize and GB, where standards are almost as good as in the numerous specialist high-street, family-run concerns. All the while, a fair amount of Belgium's food is grown in the back yard, where small *potagers* are coaxed into producing immense quantities of nutrition from tightly packed rows of carrots, sprouts, beans, endives, artichokes, asparagus, celery and tomatoes.

Pâtisseries offer an array of glistening *tartes aux fruits*, light and fluffy *tartes aux fromage*, elaborate gâteaux and chocolate extravaganzas. Good pastries are considered an inalienable part of Belgian living, and *pâtisserie* has been raised to an art form.

Given this *embarras du choix*, how do you decide where to eat? The Bruxellois have the same problem: most of them end up with their own selection of favourite restaurants, usually near where they live. Here are a few tips to avoid disappointment. Look out for busy restaurants, patronized by locals; avoid restaurants that appear to cater mainly for tourists. And don't be afraid to ask for recommendations—all Belgians are experts on food and happy to advise.

Restaurant hours are generally 12–2.30 and 6–10.30 or 11, although many of the smaller *bistrots* and brasseries serve *cuisine* non-stop from about 11am to midnight. Many restaurants are closed for Saturday lunch and on Sunday, and some shut down completely in July or August. Always phone first to check opening times. It's advisable to make a reservation for the more upmarket establishments. There are restaurants to suit all palates and appetites; menus at the door will show what's on offer. The fixed-price *menu du jour* or *plat du jour* is often a bargain, and you will find that even luxury restaurants usually feature a cheaper menu at lunchtime. Many cafés serve a limited range of light dishes for lunch and supper, and bars may offer '*petite restauration*'—snacks of sandwiches, *croque monsieur* (grilled cheese and ham on toast), *toast cannibale* (raw minced steak on toast) and so forth. Such food is usually also available in the *estaminets*—a class of rare, old-world taverns celebrated for their antique clutter and relaxed atmosphere.

Value Added Tax (TVA/BTW) at 21 per cent is generally already included in the price of restaurant meals. In principle, if you eat in a restaurant you must insist on a VAT receipt and take this out of the restaurant with you. VAT officials may demand to see your receipt, and failure to produce one can entail a fine, and a penalty for the restaurant owner. However, this recently introduced, uncharacteristically officious regulation appears to have had little impact in Belgium.

The price categories used here indicate the cost of a three-course meal (without wine), for one person, from the à la carte menu.

∞∞∞ *expensive*	—	over 1,500 BF
∞∞ *moderate*	—	700–1,500 BF
∞ *inexpensive*	—	below 700 BF

Central Brussels

∞ **Bonsoir Clara**, 22–26 Rue Antoine Dansaert, ℡ 502 09 90. *Open till 11.30pm daily*. Deliciously stylish restaurant in Paul Klee colours with low-key lighting, animated by the in-crowd. Inventive cuisine with lunch menu at 450 BF.

∞ **Gazebo**, 5 Place du Nouveau Marché aux Grains, ℡ 514 26 96. *Open daily exc Wed*. Classic American cuisine reinvented by a New Yorker who has lived in Brussels for 23 years. Classy food in a stylish decor. After 11pm, you pay only 990 BF for the menu.

∞∞ **Chez Marius en Provence**, 1 Place du Petit-Sablon, ℡ 511 12 08. *Closed Sun and public hols*. Stylish, much-loved restaurant specializing in southern French food and famous for its *bouillabaisse*. Prices can escalate to 3000 BF, but there are set menus at around 1,100, 1,600 and 2,000 BF.

∞∞ **Comme Chez Soi**, 23 Place Rouppe, ℡ 512 29 21. *Closed Sun , Mon and July*. Owned and run by Pierre Wynants, one of Europe's most fêted chefs, this is Brussels' premier restaurant—but with just 40 places you need to book weeks in advance. Exquisite concoctions of snipe, eel, truffle, lobster, beautifully presented. Expect no change out of 5,000 BF.

∞ **L'Ecailler du Palais Royal**, 18 Rue Bodenbroeck, ℡ 512 87 51. *Closed Sun, public hols and Aug*. One of Brussels' most celebrated fish restaurants: classy and welcoming, with absolutely *comme il faut* cuisine. Bargain *plat du jour* at 1,000 BF.

∞ **Kasbah**, 20 Rue Antoine Dansaert, ℡ 502 40 26. *Open 11–2, 7–11 daily*. Wondrously theatrical Arabian Nights setting, under dozens of glowing glass lanterns, with top-notch Moroccan cooking. The *tajine aux pruneaux* (spiced Moroccan stew with prunes, 550 BF) is particularly recommended.

∞∞ **La Maison du Cygne**, 2 Rue Charles Buls or 9 Grand' Place, ℡ 511 82 44. *Closed Sat lunch, Sun and three weeks in Aug*. Sumptuous and justly famous restaurant in one of the Grand' Place guildhouses, serving top-notch French cuisine at matching prices. Lunch menu at 1,450–1,750 BF; dinner would set you back at least three times as much.

∞ **Le Quai**, 14 Quai aux Briques, ℡ 512 37 36. Tiny restaurant with a dozen tables, but *the* place to eat lobster.

∞ **Au Thé de Pékin**, 16–24 Rue de la Vierge, ℡ 513 46 42. *Open noon–3 and 7–11*. Large, better than average Chinese restaurant, where the local Belgian Chinese come to eat. Menus upwards of 650 BF.

∞ **Neos Kosmos**, 50 Rue Dansaert, ℡ 511 80 58. Probably the most refined Greek cuisine you will ever eat. Stylish decor and very fashionable.

∞ **Aux Armes de Bruxelles**, 13 Rue des Bouchers, ℡ 511 55 98. *Open noon–11, closed Mon*. Sophisticated busy traditional French restaurant, with impeccable service.

∞ **La Belle Maraîchère**, 11 Place Ste-Catherine, ℡ 512 97 59. *Closed Wed, Thurs*. With its elegant late-19th-century air, this is one of the great fish restaurants. The changing three-course menu, 950–1,150 BF, includes such wonders as *saumon braisé au champagne*.

∞ **In 't Spinnekopke**, 1 Place du Jardin aux Fleurs, ℡ 511 86 95. *Open 11am–3pm and 6pm-11Pm, Sat 6–12 midnight*. One of Brussels' oldest *estaminets* (its name means 'at the head of the little spider'), dating back to 1762, now a charming restaurant noted for traditional Belgian cuisine. *Coquilles Saint-Jacques* (scallops) cooked in Trappist beer. Bargain weekday *plat du jour* at 295 BF.

∞ **L'Ogenblik**, 1 Galerie des Princes, ℡ 511 61 51. *Closed Sun*. Friendly, stylishly low-key brasserie serving elegant—if pricey—dishes of scallops, *gâteau de homard*, wild duck, game.

∞ **Rôtisserie Vincent**, 8–10 Rue des Dominicains, ℡ 511 23 03. *Closed 2 weeks in Aug*. Bruxellois atmosphere in a colourfully tiled restaurant entered through the steaming kitchen and fronted by what looks like a butcher's window. Good, solid cooking; *menu du patron* at 965 and 1,200 BF.

∞ **Taverne du Passage**, 30 Galerie de la Reine, ℡ 512 37 31. *Open noon–midnight, closed Wed and Thurs in June and July*. Classic old-style restaurant, where elderly ladies speak in hushed voices over crisp linen. Specializes in Belgian cuisine, such as *andouillette grillée* and *waterzooi*.

- **La Villette**, 3 Rue du Vieux Marché aux Grains, ✆ 512 75 50. *Closed Sat lunch and Sun.* Named after the old slaughterhouses of Paris—boldly advertising that this is a decidedly meat-orientated restaurant in a fish-dominated district. Charming, intimate and stylish. Light meals of salads, *américaine maison* (steak tartare), plus serious steaks to satisfy all waistlines, although for these less beef-favoured days the menu includes a variety of other dishes, including fish.
- **Chez Léon**, 18 Rue des Bouchers, ✆ 511 14 15. *Open 11.30am–11pm daily, Sat till 11.30pm.* The jam-packed, multi-storeyed original (founded in 1893) of what has now become a small chain, specializing in *moules-frites* and other Belgian standards. Tourists enthuse, but the Bruxellois remain sniffy.
- **'t Kelderke**, 15 Grand' Place, ✆ 513 73 44. *Open noon–2am.* Medieval cellar setting for authentic shoulder-to-shoulder dining. Hearty *bruxellois* food at reasonable prices.
- **La Marée**, 99 Rue de Flandre, ✆ 511 00 40. *Closed Mon and June.* Charming, family-run fish restaurant with an escalating reputation.
- **Taï Hon**, 45 Rue des Eperonniers, ✆ 514 50 58. *Closed Mon.* Tiny, but deliciously authentic Taiwanese restaurant which puts freshness and fervour back into Chinese cooking. Lunchtime *plat du jour* 180 BF.

East Brussels

- **Mon Manège à Toi**, 1 Rue Neerveld (Woluwe-Saint-Lambert), ✆ 770 02 38. *Closed Sat, Sun, public hols and last three weeks of July.* This rather ordinary-looking suburban house is home to one of Brussels' best known restaurants: presentation sometimes triumphs over content.
- **Moulin de Lindekemale**, 6 Avenue J. F. Debecker (Woluwe-Saint-Lambert), ✆ 770 90 57. *Closed Sat lunch and Sun evening.* A well-known restaurant in a picturesque old watermill. Even if the interior is not as atmospheric as its 15th-century origins would suggest, its French-style cuisine is supremely judged, backed by excellent service. The four-course set menu at 1,650 BF includes wines and is well worth devoting an afternoon to.
- **3Couleurs**, 453 Ave de Tervuren (Woluwe-Saint-Pierre), ✆ 770 33 21. *Closed Sat lunch, Sun evening, Mon and mid Aug–mid Sept.* Comfortable, elegant and justly celebrated for its supreme French cuisine.
- **Colmar Royal**, 71 Blvd de la Woluwe (Woluwe-Saint-Lambert), ✆ 762 98 55. Friendly, well-respected family restaurant.
- **Les Jardins de l'Europe**, Woluwe Shopping Center, 202/98 Rue Saint-Lambert (Woluwe-Saint-Lambert), ✆ 762 61 82. *Open 11–10, closed Sun evening.* Busy and comfortable brasserie-style restaurant serving admirable food—far better than you might expect in a shopping centre! *Menus du jour* at 375 BF and 795 BF.
- **Sukhothai**, 135 Ave d'Auderghem, ✆ 649 43 66. *Closed Sat and Sun lunch.* Friendly rattan-furnished Thai restaurant, with the full range of Thai favourites, such as *tom yam koong* (spicy soup with prawns and lemon grass). Lunch menu at 475 BF.
- **Taj Mahal**, 12 Avenue des Gaulois, ✆ 703 06 81. *Closed Sat and Sun lunch.* Tandooris and tikkas served in the Raj-like splendour of a *tous-les-Louis* salon on the first floor of a *maison de maître*. Set lunch 580 BF.
- **Vimar**, 70 Place Jourdan, ✆ 231 09 49. *Closed Sat lunch and Sun.* A stylish setting of crisp linen for serious fish cuisine. Lunch menu at 940 BF.
- **L'Annexe**, Woluwe Shopping Center (Woluwe-Saint-Lambert), ✆ 771 94 54. *Closed Sun.* Shop and bistro rolled into one, where you can *déguster* meat specialities.
- **Oceanis**, Woluwe Shopping Center, next to L'Annexe (Woluwe-Saint-Lambert), ✆ 771 90 24. *Closed Sun.* Another shop-cum-bistro. Here you can sample oysters, *bouillabaisse* and *anguilles au vert* (eels).

South Brussels

- **L'Amandier**, 184 Avenue de Fré (Uccle), ✆ 374 03 95. *Closed Sat lunch and Sun.* Good French food served amid elegant décor designed by Ralph Lauren: what the Francophones would call *huppé* (very select).

∞ **A'mbriana**, 151 Rue Edith Cavell (Uccle), ✆ 375 01 56. *Closed Sat lunch, Mon eve, Tues and Aug.* Elegant Italian restaurant, one of the best in Brussels. *Carpaccio* 475 BF, grilled prawns, etc. Good-value set menu for 975 BF, including wine.

∞ **La Maison du Bœuf**, Hilton Hotel, 38 Boulevard de Waterloo, ✆ 504 13 34. Its high standards of Belgian and French cuisine have earned this restaurant a seriously good reputation. On the first floor overlooking the Jardin d'Egmont. Set lunch 1,750 BF.

∞ **Tagawa**, 279 Avenue Louise, ✆ 640 50 95. *Closed Sat lunch and Sun.* First-class Japanese food—*sashimi, tempura* and so on. Up to 4,000 BF for a full meal, lunch menu at 1,600 BF.

∞ **Taishin**, Hôtel Mayfair, 381–3 Avenue Louise, ✆ 647 84 04. *Closed Sun.* Japanese food, 1,500–3,000 BF.

∞ **La Villa Lorraine**, 28 Chaussée de la Hulpe (Uccle), ✆ 374 31 63. *Closed Sun and last 3 weeks in July.* Luxurious elegance at the edge of the Bois de la Cambre. Up to 5,000 BF, but lunch at 1,750 BF.

∞ **La Canne en Ville**, 22 Rue de la Réforme, ✆ 347 29 26. *Closed Sat lunch and Sun.* Charming restaurant in three small rooms decorated with 1900s tilework, paintings and walking sticks. Well-known for its first-rate French cuisine. Bargain lunch 380 BF.

∞ **Les Foudres**, 14 Rue Eugène Cattoir, ✆ 647 36 36. *Sat lunch and Sun.* A wine-lover's paradise: a restaurant with wine shop attached (a *foudre* is a large wine cask). Excellent, well-balanced cuisine and fine wines. Set menus at around 1,000 BF.

∞ **Leonardo da Vinci**, 6 Rue du Postillon (Uccle), ✆ 347 02 92. *Closed Sun.* Friendly pizzeria and restaurant serving above-average Italian food. Lunch menu at 595 BF.

∞ **Le Living Room**, 50 Chaussée de Charleroi, ✆ 534 44 34. International, eclectic menu in a handsome townhouse, refurbished in a low-lit plush style. Trendy.

∞ **La Quincaillerie**, 45 Rue du Page, ✆ 538 25 53. *Closed for lunch Sat and Sun.* The name means 'hardware store' and that's what it is—a wonderful, invigorating brasserie installed between the ranks of wooden drawers in an authentic 1900s shop. Well-prepared French cuisine at around 1,500 BF.

∞ **Rick's Café**, 344 Ave Louise, ✆ 647 75 30. *Open 11am–1am.* Best of the new American-chic cafés, noted for its Sunday brunch.

∞ **Shanti**, 68 Ave A. Buyl, ✆ 649 40 96 (*closed Sun, Mon*). Cut-above-the-average vegetarian restaurant, with food inspired by the Orient, Africa and southern Europe.

∞ **Le Paradoxe**, 329 Chaussée d'Ixelles, ✆ 649 89 81. Vegetarian restaurant with similar cuisine to Shanti, above. Live music on Wed, Fri, Sat (jazz, folk, world).

○ **Chez Mustafa**, 79 Rue de l'Eglise (under the Beni Znassen sign). *Open evenings only.* Celebrated cheap couscous restaurant (around 300 BF).

○ **El Yasmine**, 234 Chaussée d'Ixelles, ✆ 647 51 81. *Closed Sun, lunch by reservation only.* Friendly restaurant serving some of the best Tunisian and Moroccan food in Brussels. Couscous for around 350 BF. Claims to be the only restaurant in the world serving its particular speciality, *couscous aux truffes*.

West Brussels

∞ **Bruneau**, 73–5 Avenue Broustin, ✆ 427 69 78. *Closed Tues evening, Wed and Aug.* Famously luxurious, much-garlanded restaurant, with three Michelin stars. Impressive *haute cuisine française*, and prices to match (5,000 BF, but set lunch 1,750 BF).

○ **Le Béguinage**, 3 Place de la Vaillance, ✆ 523 08 44. Stylish, agreeable tavern, serving food all day. *Plat du jour* at 295 BF.

North Brussels

∞ **De Ultieme Hallucinatie**, 316 Rue Royale, ✆ 217 06 14. *Closed Sat and Sun lunch.* Famous Art Nouveau restaurant, with chandeliers, fireplace, side cabinets, ceiling mouldings, stained-glass partitions all of the period. An adventurous menu includes *magret de canard aux figues* and warmed *foie gras* with honey. Lunch menu at 950 BF.

∞ **La Ferme du Wilg**, 164 Chaussée de Wemmel, ✆ 420 56 10. *Closed Tues and*

Wed. Delightful converted 14th-century farmhouse (with garden in summer) known for its buffet meals (650 BF) and Scotch beef.

∞ **Restaurant Adrienne**, at the top of the Atomium, ✆ 478 30 00. *Closed Sun and July*. Copious buffet lunch (690 BF and 840 BF), with unsurpassed views. Good value given that this is a tourist site. Booking advisable; ask for a table on the south side, overlooking Brussels.

Bars and Cafés in Brussels

Central Brussels

A la Mort Subite, 7 Rue Montagne aux Herbes Potagères. This famous bar, designed by Paul Hamesse in 1910 and done up like a rococo boudoir, has had a type of *gueuze* named after it. *Gueuze* from the barrel at 75 BF and *petite restauration*.

L'Archiduc, 6 Rue Antoine Dansaert. Authentic Art Deco gem and core of Brussels' nightlife. Designed like the interior of a cruise ship, it has remained intact since its opening in the 1930s. Jazz and '30s music only; quality concerts.

L'Avant-Nuit, 50 Rue A. Dansaert. *Closed Sun*. One of a growing number of gallery-cafés. Imaginative salads and light dishes for around 300 BF.

La Bécasse, 11 Rue de Tabora. Famous drinking hall, at the end of a passageway; founded in 1793.

La Belgica, 32 Rue du Marché au Charbon. Thrusting rock dive, with standing room only; lip-readers at an advantage.

Café de l'Opéra, 4 Place de la Monnaie. Welcoming 1920s-style café, with pavement terrace over the Théâtre de la Monnaie; offers *petite restauration*.

La Chaloupe d'Or, 24–25 Grand' Place. Celebrated and stylish Grand' Place bar/restaurant, popular with well-heeled locals. Light meals.

Le Cirio, 18 Rue de la Bourse. Classic fin-de-siècle café packed with mirrors and gilt and old ladies with lapdogs.

Falstaff, 19 Rue Henri Maus. Large, classic 1903 Art Nouveau café with sweeping curves of woodwork (by Victor Horta's cabinet maker and decorator) and stained glass. Light Belgian cuisine; lunch menus at 360 BF.

La Fleur en Papier Doré, 55 Rue des Alexiens. Splendid old *estaminet,* once the meeting place of the Belgian surrealists and a favourite haunt of Magritte's. Good beers from the barrel, plus light snacks and sandwiches from around 150 BF.

H_2O, 27 Rue du Marché au Charbon. A candlelit bar playing classical music: the ultimate *'feutré'* (felt-like) environment.

Le Métropole, 31 Place de Brouckère. *Closed Sat and Sun*. One of the grandest cafés in Brussels, dating from 1890. Chandeliered luxury, wicker chairs on the pavement. *Petite restauration* at acceptable prices.

P. P. Café, 28 Rue Van Praet, ✆ 514 25 62. Brussels' first cinema, the Pathé Palace, refurbished in pre-1940s style. Art Deco bar, velvet cinema seats, film music. Trendy.

Le Roy d'Espagne, 1–2 Grand' Place. An institution: a wonderfully atmospheric bar/restaurant, with waiters in starched, medieval aprons. You pay for its magnificent position in the Grand' Place. Light lunch menu for around 600 BF.

South Brussels

Chez Moeder Lambic, 68 Rue de Savoie. Celebrated bar boasting 1,000 different beers.

CyberTheatre, 4/5 Avenue de la Toison d'Or, ✆ 500 78 78, *cyberbar@ arcadis.be*. Futuristic and stylish bar, restaurant and multimedia performance venue, the best among a rash of new cybercafés.

Indigo, 160 Rue Blaes. Busy, arty, joyous café decorated from head to toe in miscellaneous *brocante* (junk), which is for sale along with well-crafted salads. Open terrace to the rear.

Les Salons de l'Ataläide, 89 Chaussée de Charleroi, ✆ 537 21 54. Huge auction hall, refurbished in fairylike, exuberant, oriental style.

North Brussels

De Ultieme Hallucinatie, 316 Rue Royale. Famous Art Nouveau bar. Drinks and light meals from the bar; for the restaurant, *see* above.

Hotels	
Central Brussels	265
Upper Town:	
Congrès and Porte Louise	266
East Brussels: Around the EU	266
South Brussels	267
North-central and	
North Brussels	267
Apartment Hotels	267
Bed and Breakfast	268
Youth Hostels	268

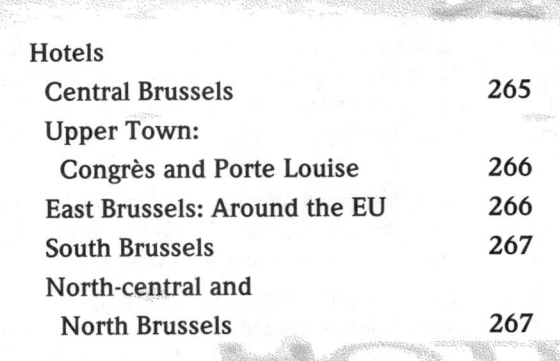

Brussels: Where to Stay

As a major centre for business and tourism, Brussels has scores of hotels, ranging from extremely cheap—and very central—youth hostels to venerable old luxury hotels of the highest standard. In the middle range there are some agreeable family hotels and dozens of good establishments of the international, 'I-could-be-anywhere' sort: a little soulless they may be, but by and large they are competitively priced and efficiently run by staff who manage to welcome their endless turnover of guests with a smile.

Reservations may not always be essential but they are certainly advisable at busy times of the year—such as during the school holidays in the summer, around Easter and Christmas/New Year, and at weekends between May and September. It is so simple to make a reservation—by telephone or fax—that there seems little point not reserving in advance if you can. Almost all reception staff speak good English—or certainly enough English to take a reservation. You may be asked to send a deposit or give a credit-card number to secure the reservation but this is not always the case. You can also make reservations, free of charge, through the central hotel organization BTR (Belgian Tourist Reservation), Boulevard Anspach 111 BF, 1000 Brussels, ✆ 513 74 84, ℻ 513 92 77. If you arrive in the city without a hotel reservation, the tourist office in the Grand' Place (*see* p.192) can offer advice and make reservations for you in return for a small fee.

The hotels in this list have been divided into five categories based primarily on price. These ratings are not the same as the official star ones, which are based on facilities rather than character and comfort. The prices indicated below are for a double room for one night; a light 'continental' breakfast is often included in the overnight price—it is worth establishing this when you make your reservation, as breakfast can otherwise add 250–800 BF to the bill. Prices are only marginally cheaper for single travellers, who will probably occupy double rooms anyhow.

Note that many of the larger hotels frequently offer special discounts for weekends and off-season stays: ask about these if telephoning in advance. Also note that some of the smaller hotels (usually in the one-star category) do not accept credit cards.

These days almost all hotel rooms in Brussels—except the very cheapest—have their own *en suite* bathroom—sometimes squeezed into a space about the size of a telephone kiosk. Most also have a television and telephone, and perhaps a small fridge with 'mini-bar'.

- ∞∞∞∞∞   ***luxury***: 7,000 BF or more—often much more.
- ∞∞∞∞   ***very expensive***: first-class; 7,000 BF or more.
- ∞∞∞   ***expensive***: 4,500–7,000 BF.
- ∞∞   ***moderate***: 2,500–4,500 BF (sometimes more, on account of location).
- ∞   ***inexpensive***: up to 2,500 BF.

Hotels

Central Brussels

∞∞∞ **Métropole**, 31 Place de Brouckère, 1000 Brussels, ✆ 217 23 00, ✉ 218 02 20. Brussels' grandest old hotel: marbled halls and palm court—the picture of Belle Epoque elegance encountered only on film sets; expect to pay at least 11,000 BF for a room.

∞∞∞ **Radisson SAS Hotel**, 47 Rue du Fossé aux Loups, 1000 Brussels, ✆ 219 28 28, ✉ 219 62 62. The most impressive modern hotel in Brussels, with atrium containing waterfalls and fountains. Very polished service—as you come to expect from this chain—and super-luxurious, with prices to match (much cheaper weekend rates).

∞∞∞ **Royal Windsor**, 5 Rue Duquesnoy, 1000 Brussels, ✆ 505 55 55, ✉ 505 55 00. Supreme first-class elegance, all highly modern.

∞∞∞ **Jolly du Grand Sablon**, 2–4 Rue Bodenbroek, 1000 Brussels, ✆ 512 88 00, ✉ 512 67 66. Member of the Jolly chain, with the advantage of its location off the Place du Grand-Sablon.

∞∞∞ **Carrefour de l'Europe**, 110 Rue du Marché aux Herbes, 1000 Brussels, ✆ 504 94 00, ✉ 504 95 00. Central hotel, built in 1992; gabled exterior and international-style comfort inside.

∞∞∞ **Jolly Atlanta**, 7 Boulevard Adolphe Max, 1000 Brussels, ✆ 217 01 20, ✉ 217 37 58. Good, well-appointed and central.

∞∞∞ **Bedford**, 135 Rue du Midi, 1000 Brussels, ✆ 512 78 40, ✉ 514 17 59. Stylish modern international hotel; member of the Best Western chain.

∞∞∞ **Amigo**, 1–3 Rue de l'Amigo, 1000 Brussels, ✆ 547 47 47, ✉ 513 52 77. Elegant modern hotel on the site of the old prison, a stone's throw from the Grand' Place.

∞∞∞ **Le Dixseptième**, 25 Rue de la Madeleine, 1000 Brussels, ✆ 502 57 44, ✉ 502 64 24. Elegant and charming hotel of just 24 rooms occupying the 18th-century residence of the Spanish ambassador, sympathetically restored; close to the Grand' Place.

∞∞∞ **Arenberg**, 15 Rue d'Assaut, 1000 Brussels, ✆ 501 16 16, ✉ 501 17 17, ✉ 501 18 18. Modern, no-nonsense hotel, close to the cathedral; part of the City Hotels chain.

∞∞ **Novotel Off Grand' Place**, 120 Rue du Marché aux Herbes, 1000 Brussels, ✆ 514 33 33, ✉ 511 77 23. Modern hotel dressed in a Flemish-style exterior; efficient, international, and a cut above its neighbour, the Ibis.

∞∞ **Orion**, 51 Quai au Bois à Brûler, 1000 Brussels, ✆ 221 14 11, ✉ 221 15 99. Apartment hotel in the old fishmarket district close to Place Sainte-Catherine; small but adequate accommodation, special rates for the week or month.

∞∞ **Ibis**, 100 Rue du Marché aux Herbes, 1000 Brussels, ✆ 514 40 40, ✉ 514 50 67. Central, efficient, smart-but-no-frills hotel—and competitively priced.

∞∞ **Ibis Sainte-Catherine**, 2 Rue J. Plattéau, 1000 Brussels, ✆ 513 76 20, ✉ 514 22 14. Comfortable, modern, if somewhat characterless hotel, in a good location close to the city centre.

∞∞ **Arlequin**, 17–19 Rue de la Fourche, 1000 Brussels, ✆ 514 16 15, ✉ 514 22 02. Small, friendly, modern hotel in the thick of touristic Brussels: some rooms have a view of the Grand' Place.

∞∞ **Auberge Saint-Michel**, 15 Grand' Place, 1000 Brussels, ✆ 511 09 56, ✉ 511 46 00. This cheap(ish), family-run hotel could not be more central. Every room is different, furnished with character, and some (more expensive) overlook the Grand' Place itself.

∞∞ **La Madeleine**, 22 Rue de la Montagne, 1000 Brussels, ✆ 513 29 73, ✉ 502 13 50. Agreeable small hotel, close to the Grand' Place.

∞∞ **Noga**, 38 Rue du Béguinage, 1000 Brussels, ✆ 218 67 63, ✉ 218 16 03. Welcoming hotel in a quiet street.

○ **Pacific**, 57 Rue A. Dansaert, 1000 Brussels, ℘ 511 84 59. 'Clean and cheap' declares the 3rd-generation owner of this utterly charming, very central hotel—but it is much more than this. More like a private home, every room has bags of old-world character, down to the original 1910 plumbing. A full breakfast (included) is served in an authentic Art Nouveau-style restaurant.

○ **Sleep Well**, 23 Rue du Damier, 1000 Brussels, ℘ 218 50 50, ℻ 218 13 13. Remarkably stylish, brand-new 'youth hotel', friendly, very central and very cheap. Monastic accommodation in rooms with up to six beds; shared bathrooms. Some youth hostel rules apply, such as no access to rooms during the day; no linen (sheets can be rented for 125 BF). Reservation advised.

○ **Windsor**, 13 Place Rouppe, 1000 Brussels, ℘ 511 20 14, ℻ 514 09 42. Quiet, modern, clean, comfortable—a small hotel of just 25 rooms, but with a warm welcome that sets its apart.

Upper Town

Congrès and Porte Louise

∞∞∞ **Astoria**, 103 Rue Royale, 1000 Brussels, ℘ 227 05 05, ℻ 217 11 50. Ranked alongside the Métropole as a grand old hotel of Brussels—timeless elegance, originally opened in 1908 and superbly renovated.

∞∞∞ **Brussels Hilton**, 38 Boulevard de Waterloo, 1000 Brussels, ℘ 504 11 11, ℻ 504 21 11. Ugly modern monolith, but comfortable and with splendid views; noted not only for its service but also for the standards of its restaurants.

∞∞∞ **Conrad**, 71 Avenue Louise, 1050 Brussels, ℘ 542 42 42, ℻ 42 00. Super-luxurious modern hotel in a cocktail of architectural styles designed to impress. Cheaper weekend rates.

∞∞∞ **Royal Crown Hotel**, 250 Rue Royale, 1210 Brussels, ℘ 220 66 11, ℻ 217 84 44. Superlative luxury hotel.

∞∞∞ **Bristol Stéphanie**, 91–3 Avenue Louise, 1050 Brussels, ℘ 543 33 11, ℻ 538 03 07. Has recently come under Norwegian management and has been entirely refubished. Well run and comfortable.

∞∞ **Tulip Inn Delta**, 17 Chaussée de Charleroi, 1060 Brussels, ℘ 539 01 60, ℻ 537 90 11. Functional, with all mod-cons, if short on character; one of the City Hotel chain.

∞ **Argus**, 6 Rue Capitaine Crespel, 1050 Brussels, ℘ 514 07 70, ℻ 514 12 22. Pleasant small hotel offering good-value accommodation close to up-market Porte Louise area.

∞ **Congrès**, 42 Rue du Congrès, 1000 Brussels, ℘ 217 18 90, ℻ 217 18 97. A friendly welcome in a fine *maison de maître*, with *fin-de-siècle* touches.

○ **Duke of Windsor**, 4 Rue Capouillet, 1060 Brussels, ℘ 539 18 19. A tiny hotel with just five rooms, close to the Porte Louise. Strictly non-smoking.

East Brussels: Around the EU

∞∞∞∞ **Montgomery**, 134 Avenue de Tervuren, 1150 Brussels, ℘ 741 85 11, ℻ 741 85 00. Brand new, very splendid hotel with 65 richly upholstered rooms and suites, furnished in antique style of various inspirations; fax machine and video in every room; to the east of the Parc du Cinquantenaire.

∞∞∞∞ **Stanhope**, 9 Rue du Commerce, 1000 Brussels, ℘ 506 91 11, ℻ 512 17 08. Sumptuously elegant hotel with just 50 rooms, decorated in the refined style called *à l'anglaise*; strategically placed between the main EU buildings and the city centre.

∞∞∞∞ **Swissôtel**, 19 Rue du Parnasse, 1050 Brussels, ℘ 505 29 29, ℻ 505 25 55. A new, glittering addition to this respected international chain within a stone's throw of the new European Parliament, with a beautiful indoor swimming pool, sauna and large fitness centre (free for guests). 9,300 BF (without breakfast, 700 BF) for a double during the week; 3,950 BF weekend rate (Fri, Sat, Sun) which includes buffet breakfast.

∞∞∞ **Brussels Europa**, 107 Rue de la Loi, 1040 Brussels, ℘ 230 13 33, ℻ 230 36 82. Conveniently located modern hotel, near the EU and close to Maelbeek métro station, run with aplomb by staff who know what the business community needs.

∞∞ **Clubhouse Park**, 21–2 Avenue de l'Yser, 1040 Brussels, ✆ 735 74 00, 🖷 735 19 67. Business hotel in a renovated townhouse on the other side of the Parc du Cinquantenaire from the main EU buildings.

∞∞ **City Garden**, 59 Rue Joseph II, 1040 Brussels, ✆ 282 82 82, 🖷 230 64 37. Well-appointed, business-orientated apartment hotel, with special rates for minimum one-month stays.

∞∞ **Euro-flat**, 50 Blvd Charlemagne, 1000 Brussels, ✆ 230 00 10, 🖷 230 36 83. Hotel also offering apartments, with rates for the week or month.

∞ **Lambeau**, 150 Avenue Lambeau, 1200 Brussels, ✆ 732 51 70, 🖷 732 54 90. Agreeable family and business hotel to the east of the EU.

○ **Armorial**, 101 Boulevard Brand Whitlock, 1200 Brussels, ✆ 734 56 36, 🖷 734 50 05. For something a little different, at surprisingly low prices: an atmospheric *maison de maître* with just 15 individually furnished rooms; to the east of the Parc du Cinquantenaire.

○ **Derby**, 24 Avenue de Tervuren, 1040 Brussels, ✆ 733 08 19, 🖷 733 74 75. Popular, straightforward business and tourist hotel to the east of the Parc du Cinquantenaire.

South Brussels

∞∞ **Mayfair**, 381–3 Avenue Louise, 1050 Brussels, ✆ 649 98 00, 🖷 640 17 64. East

meets West: classy hotel in the Japanese Chisan chain.

∞∞ **Four Points**, 15 Rue P. Spaak, 1000 Brussels, ✆ 645 61 11, 🖷 646 63 44. Spacious and comfortable accommodation.

∞ **Capital**, 191 Chaussée de Vleurgat, 1050 Brussels, ✆ 646 64 20, 🖷 646 33 14. Pleasant, modest and friendly new hotel; no extras, but comfortable rooms and efficient, helpful staff.

North-central & North Brussels

∞∞∞∞ **Sheraton Towers**, Brussels, 3 Place Rogier, 1210 Brussels, ✆ 224 31 11, 🖷 224 34 56. Huge, top-quality international hotel, as the name would suggest, with swimming pool on the 30th floor—but on the margins of the decidedly iffy Gare du Nord district.

∞ **Art Hotel Siru**, 1 Place Rogier, 1210 Brussels, ✆ 203 35 80, 🖷 203 33 03. 'Art hotel', with every room stylishly decorated by work of contemporary Belgian artists—a lively and commendable concept with mixed results. For the more aesthetically adventurous.

∞ **Albert I**[er], 20 Place Rogier, 1210 Brussels, ✆ 203 31 25, 🖷 203 43 31. Smart, friendly hotel converted in functional modern style, behind an Art Deco façade of the 1930s.

○ **Père Boudart**, 592 Chaussée Romaine, 1853 Stombeek, ✆ 460 74 96, 🖷 460 78 16. Pleasant guesthouse within walking distance of Heysel and the Atomium.

Apartment Hotels

There are several of these in Brussels: by providing bedrooms with small kitchens attached they combine the advantages of self-catering with hotel service, and are particularly useful for families. They are available for stays of just one night, but prices become increasingly competitive the longer the stay. There are over twenty apartment hotels in the city. Three are listed above: the Orion in the city centre and City Garden and Euro-flat in east Brussels.

Bed and Breakfast

It is possible to find accommodation in family homes in Brussels, staying on a bed-and-breakfast basis. The conditions vary from household to household, of course, but it can be a remarkably cheap alternative to hotels (around 1,400 to 2,750 BF per night for two) and can, if successful, provide a rewarding insight into Belgian life. Some of the addresses in Brussels are extremely well located. Details change from year to year, so cannot reliably be published here. There is a useful booklet called *Bed and Breakfast: Benelux Guide*, which is given away free by some of the Belgian tourist offices abroad (*see* p.192). Alternatively, apply directly to the publishers: Taxistop, 28 Rue Fossé aux Loups, 1000 Brussels, ⌀ 223 23 10. Alternatively you could apply to Bed & Brussels, 2 Rue Gustave Biot, B–1050 Brussels, ⌀ 646 07 37, ⌀ 644 01 14, internet *http://www.bnb-brussels.be*.

Youth Hostels

There are four main youth hostels (*auberge de jeunesse/jeugdherberg*) in the city. Prices per head per night range from about 300–620 BF, depending on the number of beds in the room. Auberge de Jeunesse Jacques Brel and the Vlaamse Jeugdherberg Bruegel are both located close to the centre and represent outstanding value for money. You don't really have to be a youth, by the way; young at heart will do.

Auberge de Jeunesse Bruegel, 2 Rue du Saint-Esprit, 1000 Brussels, ⌀ 511 04 36, ⌀ 512 07 11. In a prime position at the foot of the Sablon district. Here you have to be a member of the International Youth Hostel Association.

Auberge de Jeunesse Jacques Brel, 30 Rue de la Sablonnière, 1000 Brussels, ⌀ 218 01 87, ⌀ 217 20 05. In the Congrès area.

Centre Vincent van Gogh (CHAB), 8 Rue Traversière, 1210 Brussels, ⌀ 217 01 58, ⌀ 219 79 95. Close to the Jardin Botanique. The biggest youth hostel in Belgium.

Auberge de Jeunesse Jean Nihon, 4 Rue de l'Eléphant, 1080 Brussels, ⌀ 410 38 58, ⌀ 410 39 05. In Molenbeek, west Brussels, far from the city centre.

Listings	270
Ticket Agencies	270
Cultural Centres	270
Opera and Classical Music	270
Dance	271
Theatre	271
Puppets	272
Jazz, Rock, World Music	273
Nightclubs and Discos	274
Cabaret and Revues	274
Film	275

Brussels: Entertainment and Nightlife

The best entertainment in Brussels is in the restaurants and bars—they are great places to while away the evening and in many of the bars you can drink well into the small hours. Brussels has all the mainstream cultural attractions of a large European city—a wide choice of international films, imported rock concerts, jazz venues and discos. It also has an armful of theatres (fine, if you speak the language), some seriously good classical music and the opera of the Théâtre de la Monnaie, which commands considerable international respect. Unique to Brussels are the famous Toone puppets, which are to theatre what the Manneken-Pis is to sculpture.

Listings

The best listings magazine for the English-speaking visitor is the pull-out supplement called *What's On* (in Brussels and other towns and cities) which comes with the weekly publication *The Bulletin* (out on Thursdays, 85 BF). The magazine itself also contains reviews of what's currently on offer. The most widely available French listings magazine for Brussels is the monthly *Kiosque* (60 BF). The tourist office also publishes a free guide to the main cultural events in the city.

Ticket Agencies

Tickets to mainstream events can be booked (for a small charge) through the TIB tourist office in the Grand' Place, ✆ 513 89 40 (*see* p.192). Other agencies include:

Auditorium 44, 44 Boulevard du Jardin Botanique, ✆ 218 27 35 and ✆ 218 56 30.

FNAC, City 2, 123 Rue Neuve, ✆ 209 22 39.
Info Ticket, ✆ 504 03 90.

Cultural Centres

There are a number of these in central Brussels as well in the suburbs. They put on a broad range of events, such as theatre, performances by foreign dance troupes, and concerts (classical, folk, blues, etc.). The most important are:

Le Botanique, 236 Rue Royale, ✆ 226 12 11. The cultural centre for the French community of Brussels, housed in the elegant domed glasshouses of the old botanical garden, *see* p.235.
Palais des Beaux-Arts, 23 Rue Ravenstein, ✆ 507 82 00. The cultural centre designed by Victor Horta between the wars; *see* p.222.
Beurschouwburg, 22 Rue Auguste Orts, ✆ 513 82 90.

Centre Culturel d'Auderghem, 185 Boulevard du Souverain, ✆ 660 03 03.
Centre Culturel d'Uccle, 47 Rue Rouge, ✆ 374 64 84.
Centre Culturel de Woluwe-Saint-Pierre, 93 Avenue Charles Thielemans, ✆ 773 05 91.
Centre Culturel Jacques Franck, 94 Chaussée de Waterloo, ✆ 538 90 20.

Opera and Classical Music

elgium must be the only country in the world that was born out of an opera. A performance the Théâtre de la Monnaie led directly to the revolution of 1830 (*see* p.232). La onnaie/De Munt is still the jewel in the crown of Brussels' cultural life. Its company is owned for the high quality of its productions, its inventive staging, and as a nursery for nt (while the big stars, and their big fees, are shunned).

Opera tickets may be hard to come by, but there is no shortage of classical music concerts. There are a number of well-established concert halls, but look out also for one-off performances held at other venues, such as the churches (Cathédrale Saint-Michel, Eglise Notre-Dame du Sablon, Eglise Sainte-Catherine, Eglise des Minimes, and so forth).

Le Cercle, 20–22 Rue Sainte-Anne, ✆ 514 03 53. Venue for small-scale classical music and jazz concerts.

Cirque Royal, 81 Rue de l'Enseignement, ✆ 218 20 15. Venue for visiting opera companies and dance troupes—as well as rock groups.

Conservatoire Royal de Musique, 30 Rue de la Régence, ✆ 511 04 27. Brussels' venerable Conservatory, which runs a busy programme, mainly of chamber music.

Forest National, see 'Jazz, Rock, World Music', below.

Maison de la Radio, Place Eugène Flagey. Classical and contemporary music concerts in this outlandish 1930s landmark. It has recently been bought by the Brussels Public Transport Authority (STIB) with the declared intention of continuing to use it as a music venue after several years in limbo.

Musée Charlier, 16 Avenue des Arts, ✆ 218 53 82. Inspirational turn-of-the-century setting for chamber music (see p.203)

Théâtre Royal de la Monnaie, Place de la Monnaie, ✆ 229 12 11. Brussels' most celebrated theatre, devoted to opera, ballet and classical music concerts since 1850; many of the tickets are taken by season-ticket holders, and the rest are snapped up fast—so book early; see also p.232.

Palais des Beaux-Arts, 23 Rue Ravenstein, ✆ 507 82 00. This is the home of the Philharmonique and the Orchestre National de Belgique/Het Nationaal Orkest van België, and is also one of the key venues for visiting orchestras.

Dance

The name Maurice Béjart is still uttered in hushed and reverent tones in Brussels. He created his 'Ballet du XXe Siècle' during his long residence at the Théâtre Royal de la Monnaie, producing his own kind of modern-dance grand spectacle. Like it or loathe it, Béjart's work laid the foundations for an enthusiastic appreciation of modern dance in the city. The Monnaie's resident ballet is now directed by Anne Teresa de Keersmaeker, to considerable acclaim.

Cirque Royal, see above.
Théâtre Royal de la Monnaie, see above.

Théâtre du Résidence Palace, see 'Theatre', below.

Theatre

Brussels has its fair share of theatres and theatre companies putting on a spread of plays ranging from French classics by Molière, Corneille and Racine, to Feydeau farces, to modern classics by Ionesco, Michel de Ghelderode and the like, and works by contemporary Belgian playwrights. For better or worse, however, there is no equivalent of Broadway or London's West End, dominated by musicals that any visitor might appreciate. Theatre-goers in Brussels will need a good grip of French or Flemish—or of *bruxellois* if they are going to enjoy that most famous of Brussels plays, the knockabout comedy *Le Mariage de Mademoiselle Beulemans* (1910) by Frans Fonson and Fernand Wicheler.

Théâtre Les Tanneurs, 75–77 Rue des Tanneurs, ✆ 502 37 43. Engaging venue for high quality, small-scale works.

Espace Delvaux/La Vénerie, Place Keym (Auderghem), ✆ 672 14 39. Specializes in humorous café-theatre performances.

Kaaitheaterstudios, 81 Rue Notre-Dame du Sommeil, ✆ 201 59 59. Leading contemporary and avant-garde Dutch-language theatre.

Koninklijke Vlaamse Schouwburg, 146 Rue de Laeken, ✆ 412 70 70. The main Dutch-language theatre of Brussels, built in grand Edwardian style.

Lunatheater, 20 Square Sainctelette, ✆ 201 59 59. Classical and modern plays in Dutch.**Magic Land Theatre**, no fixed address. Unpredictable and inventive street theatre troupe, worth looking out for.

Rideau de Bruxelles, Palais des Beaux-Arts, 23 Rue Ravenstein ✆ 507 83 60. Intimate theatre with a respected and long-established company, performing classic modern Belgian work by authors such as Michel de Ghelderode and Maurice Maeterlinck, as well as contemporary work.

La Samaritaine, 16 Rue de la Samaritaine, ✆ 511 33 95. Warm-hearted café-theatre currently considered on form.

Théâtre 140, 140 Avenue Plasky, ✆ 733 97 08. For over three decades one of Brussels' leading venues for contemporary theatre and other performances.

Théâtre de la Balsamine, 1 Avenue Félix Marchal, ✆ 735 64 68. Award-winning theatre presenting mainly new and experimental plays and dance.

Théâtre de Poche, 1a Chemin du Gymnase (Bois de la Cambre), ✆ 649 17 27. Widely respected small theatre presenting contemporary, often experimental work in pleasant woodland surrounds.

Théâtre de Quat'Sous, 34 Rue de la Violette, ✆ 512 10 22. Tiny, friendly theatre of 50 seats, performing mainly modern French plays.

Théâtre National de Belgique, Place Rogier, ✆ 203 53 03. Modern francophone plays, often by Belgian authors, located in an ugly tower-block.

Théâtre du Résidence Palace, 155 Rue de la Loi, ✆ 231 03 05. A 1920s Art Deco-style theatre, with resident company; and also a dance venue.

Le Théâtre Royal des Galeries, 32 Galeries du Roi, ✆ 512 04 07. A theatre founded in 1847, with a well-worn tradition of comedies and melodramas, these days supplemented by some more challenging productions.

Théâtre Royal du Parc, 3 Rue de la Loi, ✆ 505 30 30. Splendid 18th-century theatre mounting respected seasons of plays in French, both classical and modern (Pagnol, Pirandello, Ionesco, Ibsen and so forth).

Théâtre Varia, 78 Rue du Sceptre, ✆ 640 35 50. Progressive theatre at the cutting edge of Brussels' avant-garde—often inspired.

Puppets

The Théâtre Toone is a famous Brussels institution, with a history that goes back over 150 years. On a small stage in a loft off an ancient alleyway (*see* p.209), the great works of Aristophanes, Shakespeare and Corneille, as well as more jolly entertainments, are played out with characteristic relish and verve by troupes of large puppets made of wood and *papier mâché*, manipulated by a few rather crude strings. No subject is too elevated for these characters: at Easter they take on The Passion. The first Toone theatre was established in 1830 by Antoine Genty (Toone is a shortened form of Antoine), and the tradition has been handed down from generation to generation (though not always within the family). It started off in the Marolles, but has been in its present home since 1966.

The Toone puppets are famous for their performances in a French-based *bruxellois* dialect, and é Géal, who now leads the 20 or so puppeteers in the 7th generation of this theatre (Toone), is not just a famous face in Brussels but also a noted expert on the language. If you want to r *bruxellois*, this is the place to come—although you should note that for some of the clas- l plays only certain performances are in dialect. Some plays are also performed in English.

ay seem folksy, something to take the kids along to, but it is not. These plays are staged in vening for good reason: they are serious productions, hard to follow and—so say those who can follow them—often outrageously bawdy. However much you can take in, an evening with Toone VII is an unmistakably *bruxellois* experience.

For children, there is the Théâtre Peruchet in Ixelles, a delightful puppet theatre which stages a varied programme based on fairy-tales, in a converted farmhouse; it also has a puppet museum, open during performances. The Théâtre Ratinet also puts on puppet shows for children, mainly new workings of fairy-tales.

Théâtre Toone VII, Impasse Schuddeveld, 21 Petite Rue des Bouchers, ⓟ 511 71 37. *Performances at 8.30pm, not every day. Reservations by telephone or at the theatre bar (estaminet) after 12 noon. The Toone puppet museum is open during the intervals.*

Théâtre Peruchet, 50 Avenue de la Forêt, ⓟ 673 87 30. *Performance times are erratic and need to be checked beforehand, closed July and Aug.*

Théâtre Ratinet, 44 Avenue de Fré (Uccle), ⓟ 375 15 63. *Afternoon performances.*

Jazz, Rock, World Music

Although Belgium does have its own rock culture and some energetic bands, the world still awaits a Belgian band of truly international distinction. Meanwhile, Brussels attracts many of the major international stars, who seem to respond well to their enthusiastic reception, and to the comparatively modest scale of most of the venues.

Jazz has a loyal and devoted following, and blossoms during the annual three-day Brussels Jazz Rally (*end April, early May*), when mainly European artists invade dozens of bars and small venues in and around the city centre in a happy festival of drinking and foot-tapping.

Ancienne Belgique, 110 Boulevard Anspach, ⓟ 584 24 24. Medium-sized key venue for blues, rock and pop, in a refurbished variety hall.

Le Botanique, *see p.270.*

Le Cercle, *see p.271.*

Cirque Royal, *see p.271.*

Fool Moon, 28 Quai de Mariement, ⓟ 410 10 03. Live dance, rock and world music.

Forest National, 36 Avenue du Globe, ⓟ 340 22 11. This is the largest and somewhat soulless rock venue in Brussels—an arena for 6,000 adoring fans; also plays host to opera and classical music events.

Les Halles de Schaerbeek, 22a Rue Royale Sainte-Marie. Formerly the main rock venue. After massive renovation this iron- and glass-covered market has now re-emerged as a key venue for rock, pop and world music.

La Luna, 20 Square Sainctelette, ⓟ 201 59 59. A big rock venue.

Maison de la Radio, *see* 'Opera and Classical Music', above.

Le Paradoxe, 329 Chaussée d'Ixelles, ⓟ 649 89 81. *Closed Sun, Mon and Aug.* Vegetarian restaurant which on Fridays and Saturdays doubles up as a popular venue for jazz, blues, folk and world music.

Sounds, 28 Rue de la Tulipe, ⓟ 512 92 50. Small café that offers live jazz, folk, funk and South American music.

La Soupape, 26 Rue A. de Witte, ⓟ 649 58 88. A café-theatre which specializes in Belgian singer-songwriters.

Travers, 11 Rue Traversière, ⓟ 218 40 86. Café that is one of the key jazz and world music venues, which also hosts occasional theatre.

UGC–De Brouckère, *see* 'Film', below.

Nightclubs and Discos

On Fridays and Saturdays the young-at-heart head for the trendy bars, then those with energy still to burn dance until sunrise. This is a lively and, by and large, amicable scene, but it's the people rather than the venues that make it work. Ask around in the livelier bars for tips about which places are currently on form.

Bazaar, 60 Rue des Capucins, ℡ 511 26 00. *Open 8pm–1am; closed Mon.* Chic, atmospheric nightspot, laid-back ethnic music, two bars, restaurant serving exotic dishes (crocodile et al) and dance floor that avoids the sins of 'tchak-boom-tchak'.

Do Brasil, 88 Rue de la Caserne, ℡ 513 50 28. *Closed Sun, Mon and Tues.* Thumping Brazilian fun: tropical food with flair, and samba music to dance to.

Le Bulex, 11 Rue de Rome, ℡ 537 95 14. *First Sat of the month after 10pm.* Famed organizers of wild mega-parties, throbbing rhythms and massed fun into the early hours. Venues change so phone first.

L'Equipe, 40 Rue de Livourne, ℡ 538 31 84. *Open every night.* Standard-fare, fun disco for all comers.

Fool Moon, 28 Quai de Mariement, ℡ 410 10 03. Quality dance nights with top DJs. From world music to hip hop, techno and house. Only open a few nights per month.

Le Fuse, 208 Rue Blaes, ℡ 511 97 89. *Open Fri and Sat after 11pm.* Hottest techno spot in town, boasting top DJs from the world over. Also a venue for live music during the week. Gay night once a month.

Jeux d'Hiver, Chemin du Gymnase (Bois de la Cambre). *Thurs and Sat; adm free (priority to members).* Disco at the edge of the woods, next to the Théâtre de Poche, frequented by the youthful smart set—*BCBG (bon chic, bon genre).*

Mirano Continental, 38 Chaussée de Louvain, ℡ 218 57 72. *Sat only, after 11pm.* A converted cinema, now one of the city's best and most popular dance spots. Dress up or you won't get in.

La Rose, 21 Rue des Poissonniers, ℡ 513 43 25. *Wed–Sun 5pm onwards.* A splendidly seedy *café/bar-dansant* close to the Bourse, with live band, reflector-globes and toyboys in flares: weird but pure Jacques Brel.

Le Siècle, 41 Rue de l'Ecuyer, ℡ 513 08 10. Theme nights in huge but pleasant hall that looks like a cross between a squat and an oriental palace. Trendy and laid-back. Gay night once a month.

Le Sparrow, 16 Rue Duquesnoy, ℡ 512 66 22. Spacious, funky, latino disco.

Le Sud, 43–45 Rue de l'Ecuyer, ℡ 502 19 81. *Fri and Sat evenings afer 10pm.* Pieced together from a set of abandoned houses around a covered courtyard, this unusual disco and bar provides a variety of *ambiences* under one roof. Grunge, techno and disco.

Cabaret and Revues

Cabaret is always a mixed bag, and no more so than in Brussels. It ranges from small-scale comedy pieces, accompanied by singers and illusionists, to glam shows just this side of sleaze. it is true sleaze that you want, follow your nose around the Gare du Nord.

...ez Flo, 25 Rue au Beurre, ℡ 512 94 96. *...d–Sat only, 8pm.* A ritzy transvestite show with ...er, the classiest of its kind in town. All good, ...fun—after a fashion. Dinner and show 1,470

EU—but looks innocent enough on a credit-card statement.

Le Pré Salé, 20 Rue de Flandres, ℡ 513 43 23. Restaurant serving Belgian cuisine, famous for its jocular 'playback' (mimed) show on Fridays; dinner with show 1,500 BF.

...en's Club, 203 Avenue d'Auderghem, ...7 13 66. Louche '*club intime*' close to the

Film

Belgium's domestic film industry has had a small but devoted following among arthouse audiences for several decades, fuelled by such work as the touching semi-surrealist films of André Delvaux including *L'Homme au crâne rasé* (1965) and *Un Soir, un train* (1968). In 1992, the joint directors Rémy Belvaux, André Bonzel and Benoit Poelvoorde drew wider attention with their acclaimed arthouse movie *Man Bites Dog*. Since then Belgian directors have won a string of accolades: the iconoclastic Jan Bucquoy for *The Sexual Life of the Belgians* (1994), recommended for its witty and cutting portrait of Belgian family life in its opening sequences; Gérard Corbiau for *Farinelli, Il Castrato* (1994); Jaco van Dormael's *Toto the Hero* (1991) and *The Eighth Day* (1996), both starring the Down's Syndrome actor Pascal Duquenne; Alain Berliner's *Ma Vie en rose*; and Jean-Pierre and Luc Dardenne, who won the 1999 Golden Palm at Cannes with *Rosetta*, a realistic sociological portrait of a working-class girl's struggle for survival.

By and large, however, films in Belgium are imported, and the most successful tend to be mainstream Hollywood ones. The new releases are usually shown in their original language *(VO, version originale)* with subtitles in French or Flemish (or both). Older films occasionally have the soundtrack dubbed *(doublé)*. *The Bulletin* gives listings of performances in English. Movies for children are mostly dubbed.

For a comprehensive programme of classic international films, look out for the programme of the Musée du Cinéma; films shown there usually have the original soundtrack with French subtitles.

Remember that in Belgium (as in France) it is customary to tip the cinema attendant who takes your ticket and may show you to your seat (about 10 BF), although many of the newer cinemas have dispensed with this tradition.

Musée du Cinéma, Palais des Beaux-Arts, 9 Rue Baron Horta, ✆ 507 83 70. Daily menu of classic films, and two performances of silent movies with live piano accompaniment; a ticket of 80 BF to the museum entitles you to see a film as well. The museum publishes a monthly schedule of films, usually organized around a central theme; *see* p.200 for further details and how to book.

Other Major Cinemas

Actor's Studio, 16 Petite Rue des Bouchers, ✆ 512 16 96. Mainly art films.

Arenberg-Galeries, 26 Galerie de la Reine, ✆ 512 80 63. Mainly art films.

Aventure, Galerie du Centre, ✆ 219 17 48.

Kladaradatschi Palace, 85 Blvd Anspach, ✆ 501 67 76. The newest cinema, showing a fine selection of the latest international art movies. Pleasant bar downstairs.

Movy Club, 21 Rue des Moines, ✆ 537 69 54.

Nova, 3 Rue d'Arenberg, ✆ 511 27 74. Open Thurs–Mon. Old cinema rescued by a young group of film enthusiasts now presenting mainly art movies, and occasional concerts.

Styx, 72 Rue de l'Arbre Bénit, ✆ 512 21 02.

UGC–Acropole, 8 Avenue de la Toison d'Or/17 Galerie de la Toison d'Or, ✆ (0990) 29 930.

UGC–City 2, 235 Rue Neuve (City 2), ✆ 219 42 46.

UGC–De Brouckère, 38 Place de Brouckère, ✆ (0990) 29 930. Also a venue for jazz concerts.

Vendôme-Roy, 18 Chaussée de Wavre, ✆ 512 65 53.

Index

Numbers in **bold** indicate main references. Numbers in *italic* indicate maps.

LONDON

accommodation **162–8**
Admiral's Walk 102
Admiralty Arch 77
airports 2–3, 4–5
Albert Hall 28
Albert Memorial 28
Anne of Denmark 107
Anne, Queen 79
Apsley House 137–8
Aquarium **28–9**, 140
Asprey's 122
Athenaeum 78
Augusta, Princess 114–15
Baker, Robert 69
Bank of England Museum **58–9**, 135
banks 21–2
Bankside
  Bridge 82
  Power Station 84
  see also South Bank
Barbican Arts Centre 61
Barry, Charles 36
bars *see* pubs and bars
Battersea Park 110
Bayswater 164–5
BBC Experience 139
Beauchamp Place 127
bed and breakfast 167
Bentham, Jeremy 53
Berkeley Square 68
Berwick Street Market 75, **129**
Bethnal Green Museum of Childhood 139
Big Ben 36–7
Birkbeck College 53
Bloomsbury *52*, 52–4
  cafés and lunches 53
  hotels 164
  restaurants 150
Bloomsbury Group 53
Bond Street 66, 68, **122**
book shops 123
Boswell, James 117
Bow Street Magistrates' Court 64–5
Bramah Tea and Coffee Museum 139
Brewer Street 75
Brick Lane 129
Britain at War Museum 136
British Library 54
British Museum 29–31
Brixton 129
Brompton Cross 127–8
Brooks 78
Brown's Hotel 66–7
Brunel, Marc Isambard 136
Buckingham Palace 32–3
Burlington Arcade **72**, 124
Business Design Centre 101
Butler's Wharf 86
Cabaret Mechanical Theatre 63
Cabinet War Rooms 135

Café Royal 71, 121
calendar of events 16–18
Camden *88*, 99
  cafés and lunches 99
  restaurants 155
Camden Lock 99, **129**
Camden Passage 100, **129**
Campden Hill Road 90
Canary Wharf 96–7
Canonbury 101
Carlton House Terrace 77
Carlyle's House **93**, 138
Carnaby Street 120
Caroline of Brunswick 79
Chalk Farm Road 99
Chamber of Horrors 140
Changing of the Guard 77
Channel Tunnel 3
Chapel Market 101, **129**
Charing Cross Road 123
Chelsea *88*, *92*, 92–3
  cafés and lunches 93, 158
  markets 126
  Old Church 93
  Physic Garden 110
  restaurants 152–3
  Riverside 93
Cheyne Walk 93
child-minding services 143
Childhood Museum 139
Chinatown 75
Church Row 102
Church Walk 125
cinema 177–8
City of London 55–61, *56–7*
  cafés and lunches 56, 158
  classical music 172–3
Clerkenwell 61
Clink Prison Museum **84**, 135
Clockmakers' Museum 133
coaches and buses 3, 6, 9
Coliseum theatre 65
Columbia Road 129
comedy clubs 176
Commonwealth Institute 133–4
County Hall 28
Courtauld Institute 132
Covent Garden *62*, 62–5
  cafés and lunches 63, 157, 159
  restaurants 149–50
  shopping 128–9
Crafts Council Gallery 134
cricket 144
crime 18–19
Criterion Restaurant 70
Crown Jewels 45
Cutty Sark 108
cycling 8, 10
dance 174
Davies Street 120
Davy, Humphrey 68

Dean Street 73–4
Dennis Severs' House 139
Deptford 98
Design Centre 101
Design Museum **86**, 134
Diana, Princess 32, 37
Dickens' House 138
disabled travellers 19
discothèques 178–9
Docklands *88*, **94–5**, 94–8
  cafés and lunches 96
Docklands Light Railway 6
Downing Street 43–4
Dr Johnson's House 138
drink *see* pubs and bars
Duke Street 120
Earl's Court 166
Earlham St 129
East End
  cafés and lunches 158, 159–60
  restaurants 156
Economist Building 78
Elgin Marbles 30
Elizabeth I 106
emergencies 20
entertainment and nightlife 21, **170–80**
Eros statue 70
Estorick Collection of Italian Art 132
Etheldreda, Saint 60
Eurostar 3
Execution Dock 97
Fan Museum 140
Faraday Museum 68, **136–7**
Fenton House 102
Festival Hall 82
Fighting Temeraire 98
film 177–8
Fitzrovia 150, 159
Flamsteed, John 108
Flask Walk 103
Fleet Street 159
Floating Lido 82
Florence Nightingale Museum 137
Folgate Street, No.18 139
Fortnum & Mason 71, **124**
free sights in London 20–1
Freemason's Hall 138
French House 73–4
Freud's House 138
Frith Street 73–4
Fulham
  hotels 166
  restaurants 152–3
funfairs 142
Gabriel's Wharf 83
galleries *see* museums and galleries
Garden History Museum 140
gardens *see* parks and gardens
Gatwick airport 2, 4
gay bars 179–80
Geffrye Museum 134

London Index: ACC – GEF

George Inn (South Bank) 84
Gipsy Moth IV 108
Globe Theatre 33–4
Golborne Road 91
Golden Hinde 136
Gower Street 53
Gray's Antique Market 121
Great Fire of London 41
Green Park 111
Greenland Dock 98
Greenwich *88*, 106–8
　cafés and lunches 107, 160
　market 130
　Park 111
Guildhall 58
Ham House 105
Hampstead *88* 102–3
　cafés and lunches 102, 103, 158, 160
　restaurants 155
Hampstead Heath 111
Hampton Court 34–5
Harrison, John 108
Harrods **126**, 127
Harvey Nichols **126**, 127
Hay's Galleria 86
Heath Street 103
Heathrow airport 2, 4
Henry VIII 34–5, 106, 118
Herb Garret 85
Highgate
　cafés and lunches 160
　Cemetery 112
　Ponds 111
Highgate Village 168
Hillgate Street 90
Hogarth's House 138
Holborn 159
Holland House and Park 112–13, 168
Holly Walk 102
Hollybush Hill 102
Horse Guards Parade 77
hotels 163–7
Houses of Parliament 35–7
Howard, Catherine 118
Hyde Park 113
Imax Theatre 83
Imperial War Museum 135
Institute of Contemporary Arts 77
Inverness Street 99
Island Gardens 97
Isle of Dogs 96
Islington *88* 100–1
　cafés and lunches 101, 160
　restaurants 156
Islington Green 101
James Street 120
jazz clubs 174
Jermyn Street 124
Jewish Museum **99**, 138
Jodrell Laboratory 115
Johnson, Dr 138
Judges Walk 102
Keats' House **103**, 138
Kensal Green Cemetery 91
Kensington
　cafés and lunches 158
　Church Street 125
　Gardens 114

High Street 125
　market 125
　Palace **37**, 135
　restaurants 152
Kenwood House **103**, 111, 132
Kew Gardens and Palace 114–15
King's Road 93, **125–6**
Knightsbridge 126–7, 166
Knot Garden 98
Kyoto Garden 113
Leadenhall Market 61
Ledbury Road 91
Leicester Square *69*, 69–70
　cafés and lunches 70
Leighton House 134
Lewis chessmen 31
Liberty 122
Limehouse 97–8
Lindisfarne Gospels 54
Lindow Man 31
Lloyd's of London 60
London Aquarium **28–9**, 140
London Bridge 85
London City airport 2, 4
London Dungeon 85
London Pavilion 71
London Planetarium 137
London Transport Museum 137
London Underground 4, 5, **6**
London Zoo 116
lost property 19
Luton airport 2, 4
Madame Tussaud's 140
Magna Carta 54
The Mall 77
Mansion House 57
maps 21
Marble Hill House 105
Maritime Museum **107–8**, 136
markets **129–30**
　Berwick Street 75, **129**
　Camden Lock 99, **129**
　Camden Passage 100, **129**
　Chapel Market 101, **129**
　Chelsea 126
　Gray's 121
　Kensington 125
　King's Road 93, **125–6**
　Leadenhall 61
　Portobello Road 90, **130**
　Shepherd Market 68
　Smithfield 60
Marx, Karl 75, 112
Marx Memorial Library 61
Mary, Queen 106
Marylebone 150–1
Mayfair 66–8, *67*
　cafés and lunches 67, 158
　hotels 163
　restaurants 151–2
Mayflower 98
Mayflower (Rotherhithe) 98
Methodism Museum 138
Michelin Building 127
Mildenhall Treasure 31
Millennium Dome 38
Millennium Wheel 82
Milton, John 61

money 21–2
　free sights in London 20–1
Monument 60
Moore, Henry 110
More, Sir Thomas 93
Morris, William 135
Moving Image Museum 82
Mudchute 97
Murray, William 105
Museum of London 135–6
museums and galleries 20–1, **131–40**
　Apsley House 137–8
　Aquarium **28–9**, 140
　Bank of England Museum **58–9**, 135
　BBC Experience 139
　Bramah Tea and Coffee Museum 139
　Britain at War Museum 136
　British Museum 29–31
　Brunel Engine House 136
　Cabinet War Rooms 135
　Carlyle's House **93**, 138
　Chamber of Horrors 140
　Childhood 139
　Clink Prison Museum **84**, 135
　Clockmakers' Museum 133
　Commonwealth Institute 133–4
　Courtauld Institute 132
　Crafts Council Gallery 134
　Dennis Severs' House 139
　Design Museum **86**, 134
　Dickens' House 138
　Dr Johnson's House 138
　Estorick Collection of Italian Art 132
　Fan Museum 140
　Faraday Museum 68, **136–7**
　Florence Nightingale Museum 137
　Freemason's Hall 138
　Freud's House 138
　Garden History 140
　Geffrye Museum 134
　Golden Hinde 136
　Hogarth's House 138
　Imperial War Museum 135
　Jewish Museum **99**, 138
　Sir John Soane's Museum 134
　Keats' House **103**, 138
　Kensington Palace **37**, 135
　Kenwood House **103**, 111, 132
　Leighton House 134
　Madame Tussaud's 140
　Methodism 138
　Moving Image 82
　Museum of London 135–6
　National Gallery 38
　National Maritime Museum **107–8**, 136
　National Portrait Gallery 132–3
　National Postal Museum 136
　Natural History Museum **39**, 137
　Percival David Foundation of Chinese Art 133
　Planetarium 137
　Pollock's Toy Museum 54
　Richmond Town Hall 104
　Royal Naval College **106–7**, 136
　Royal Observatory **108**, 111, 137
　St Thomas Operating Theatre Museum **85**, 137
　Science Museum **39–40**, 137, 142

museums and galleries (cont'd)
  Serpentine Gallery 114
  Sherlock Holmes Museum 140
  Spirit of London 140
  Tate Gallery 42–3, 82
  Thames Barrier Visitor Centre 137
  Theatre Museum 140
  Transport Museum 137
  Victoria and Albert Museum **46–8**, 134
  Vinopolis 140
  Wallace Collection 133
  Whitechapel Art Gallery 133
  William Morris Gallery 135
  Winston Churchill's Britain at War Museum 136
music *see* entertainment and nightlife
Nash, John 45–6, 115
National Gallery 38
national holidays 22
National Maritime Museum **107–8**, 136
National Portrait Gallery 132–3
National Postal Museum 136
National Theatre 82
Natural History Museum **39**, 137
Neal's Yard 64
Neal Street 64
Nelson's Column 46
Nereid Monument 30
New Bond Street 68
  shopping 68, **122**
Newgate Prison 59
nightclubs 178–9
Nightingale, Florence 137
nightlife *see* entertainment and nightlife
Notting Hill *88*, 89–91
  cafés and lunches 91, 158
  Carnival 90
  hotels 164–5
  restaurants 153–5
Notting Hill Gate 90
Observatory **108**, 111, 137
Old Bailey 59
Old Bond Street 66, **122**
Old Compton Street 75
Old Royal Observatory **108**, 111, 137
One London Bridge 85
Open Air Theatre 116
opening hours 22
  banks 22
opera 172–3
Oriel Place 103
Oxford Street 120–1
Oxo Tower 83
Palace of Westminster 36
Pall Mall 78
pantomimes 142
parks and gardens **110–18**
  Battersea Park 110
  Chelsea Physic Garden 110
  Green Park 111
  Greenwich Park 111
  Hampstead Heath 112
  Highgate Cemetery 112
  Holland Park 113
  Hyde Park 113
  Kensington Gardens 114
  Kew Gardens 114–15
  Regent's Park 116

Richmond Park 117
St James's Park 117
Syon Park 118
Parliament Hill 111
Pembridge Road 90
pensioners 24
Percival David Foundation of Chinese Art 133
Peter Pan 114
Petticoat Lane 130
Piccadilly *69*, 69–72
  cafés and lunches 70
Piccadilly Circus 70–1
Pimlico 166
Planetarium 137
Poets' Corner 50
police 18–19
Pollock's Toy Museum 54
Portland Vase 31
Portobello Road 90–1, **130**
Portrait Gallery 132–3
post offices 22–3
Postal Museum 136
practical A–Z **16–26**
pronunciation 23
pubs and bars 158–60
  opening hours 22
  see also cafés and lunches
Pugin, Augustus 36
Queen's House 107
Quo Vadis 75
rail travel 3, 5, 7
  Docklands Light Railway 6
  London Underground 4, 5, **6**
Raleigh, Sir Walter 106
Ranger's House 111
Reform Club 78
Regent Street 71, **121–2**
Regent's Park 115–16
religion 23–4
restaurants 146–57
  Bloomsbury 150
  Camden 155
  Chelsea 152–3
  costs 146
  Covent Garden 149–50
  East End 156
  Fitzrovia 150
  Fulham 152–3
  Hampstead 155
  Islington 156
  Kensington 152
  Marylebone 150–1
  Mayfair 151–2
  Notting Hill 153–5
  opening hours 146
  St James's 151–2
  Smithfield 156
  Soho 147–9
  South of the River 156–7
  see also cafés and lunches
Reynolds, Sir Joshua 43
Richmond *88*, 104–5
  Bridge 104
  Palace 104
  Park 117
  Town Hall 104
Ritz Hotel 71
Riverbuses 8

Rock Circus 71
rock and pop music 175
Rosetta Stone 30
Rotherhithe 98, 160
Rotten Row 113
Royal Academy 72
Royal Arcade 66
Royal Exchange 58
Royal Festival Hall 82
Royal Institution 67–8
Royal Naval College **106–7**, 136
Royal Observatory **108**, 111, 137
Royal Opera House 64
rugby 144
Russell Square 53
St Anne Limehouse 97–8
St Christopher's Place 120
St Etheldreda's 60
St George in the East 97
St George's Hanover Square 68
St Giles Cripplegate 61
St James' Piccadilly 71–2
St James's *76*, 76–9
  cafés and lunches 77
  restaurants 151–2
St James's Church 61
St James's market 130
St James's Palace 79
St James's Park 117
St James's Square 78–9
St James's Street 78
St John's church (Hampstead) 102
St Katharine's Dock 97
St Martin-in-the-Fields 65
St Martin's Lane 65
St Mary-le-Bow 59
St Mary's church (Rotherhithe) 98
St Paul's Cathedral **40–2**, 55
St Paul's Church 65
St Thomas Operating Theatre Museum 85, 137
Savile Row 124
School of Oriental and African studies (SOAS) 53
Science Museum **39–40**, 137, 142
Scott, Ronnie 73
self-catering 168
Selfridge's 120
Senate House 53
Serpentine 113
Serpentine Gallery 114
Severs, Dennis 139
Shepherd Market 68
Sherlock Holmes Museum 140
shopping 21, **120–9**
  Asprey's 122
  Beauchamp Place 127
  Bond Street 66, 68, **122**
  book shops 123
  Brompton Cross 127–8
  Burlington Arcade **72**, 124
  Charing Cross Road 123
  Chatila 122
  Covent Garden 128–9
  Fortnum & Mason 71, **124**
  Harrods **126**, 127
  Harvey Nichols **126**, 127
  Jermyn Street 124
  Kensington High Street 125

shopping (cont'd)
   King's Road 93, **125–6**
   Knightsbridge 126–7
   Liberty 122
   New Bond Street 68, **122**
   Old Bond Street 66, **122**
   Oxford Street 120–1
   Portobello Road 90–1
   Regent Street 71, **121–2**
   Savile Row 124
   Selfridge's 120
   Sloane Street 127
   Tiffany's 122
   Tottenham Court Road 123
   toy shops 142–3
   Value Added Tax (VAT) 120
   see also markets
Sir John Soane's Museum 134
Sloane, Sir Hans 110
Sloane Street 127
Smithfield
   Market 60
   restaurants 156
smoking 24
snack foods *see* cafés and lunches
Soane, Sir John 134
Soho 73–5, *74*
   cafés and lunches 74, 157, 159
   restaurants 147–9
Somerset House 132
Sotheby's 122
South Bank *80–1*, 80–6
   cafés and lunches 81, 158
   market 130
   restaurants 156–7
South Bank Centre 82
South Dock 98
South Kensington 165–6
South Molton Street 120
Southwark *80–1*, 80–6
   cafés and lunches 160
   Cathedral 83

Spaniards Inn (Hampstead) 103
Speaker's Corner 113
Spencer House 79
Spirit of London 140
sports 143–4
The Stables 99
Stansted airport 2, 4
Star and Garter Home 117
statues
   Duke of Wellington 58
   Eros 70
   General Wolfe 111
   Peter Pan 114
   Sir Hans Sloane 110
Storm Water Pumping Station 97
students 24
Surrey Docks 98
swimming 143
Syon Park 118
Tate Gallery 42–3, 82
taxis 7, 10
telephones 24–5
Temple Bar 55
10 Downing Street 43–4
tennis 143, 144
Thames Barrier Visitor Centre 137
theatre 142, 170–2
Theatre Museum 140
Theatre Royal Drury Lane 64
Thomas Neal's Arcade 64
Three Standing Figures 110
Tiffany's 122
time 25
tipping 25
Tipu's Tiger 47–8
Tobacco Dock 97
toilets 25
Tottenham Court Road 123
tourist buses 6, 9
tourist information 25–6
Tower Bridge 44, 86
Tower of London **44–5**, 55

toy shops 142–3
Trafalgar Square 45–6
trains *see* rail travel
Transport Museum 137
travel **2–10**
traveller's cheques 22
Trocadero Centre 71
Trooping the Colour 77
Trumpeters' House 104
Turner Collection 43
Underground *see* London Underground
University of London 53
Upper Street 101
Uxbridge Street 90
Value Added Tax (VAT) 120
Vanbrugh Castle 111
Victoria 166
Victoria and Albert Museum **46–8**, 134
Vinopolis 140
visas 5
Wallace Collection 133
Walton Street 127
Wapping 97
Wardour Street 75
Well Walk 103
West End 160, 163–4
Westbourne Grove 91
Westminster Abbey 49–50
Westminster Palace 36
where to stay **162–8**
Whispering Gallery 42
White, Marco Pierre 75
Whitechapel Art Gallery 133
White's 78
Wilkins, William 53
William Morris Gallery 135
Wolsey, Cardinal Thomas 34
Woolf, Virginia 52, 53
Wren, Sir Christopher 41–2, 106
youth hostels 168
zoo 116

---

by the same authors

London   1-86011-971-9   £12.99 $17.95

CADOGAN's city guide to London explores the little-known nooks as well as the sights you know you want to see. From Wren's churches to offbeat toy museums, the ten detailed walks pace the streets with clarity, knowledge and wit, and nine day trips whisk you out of the hustle and into the countryside.

Brussels   1-86011-981-6   £12.99 $17.95

CADOGAN's guide to Brussels uncovers the hidden attractions of the capital of Europe. Six walks lead you through the historic city centre and the home of *Art Nouveau*, and there's advice on where to enjoy Belgium's highly regarded cuisine, beer and chocolate. Includes chapters on Bruges, Ghent and Antwerp.

BRUSSELS

air travel 2–3
  arrivals 4–5
Album, Musée 252
apartment hotels 267
Arboretum Géographique de Tervuren 256
Arboretum de Groenendaal 256
Art Nouveau 251–2
Atelier de Moulages **241–2**, 252
Atomium **194**, 255
Autoworld 252
Avenue Brugmann 251
Avenue Général de Gaulle 251
Avenue Louise 227
Avenue de la Toison d'Or 226–7, 248

banks 189
bars 262
  see also cafés and lunches
Basilique Nationale du Sacré Coeur 255
bed and breakfast 268
beer **181–2**, 187
Béguinage d'Anderlecht 252
béguinages 232
Belgian Revolution 219–20
Berlaymont Building 240
bicycles 8, 10
Bois de la Cambre 255
border formalities 5
Bouillon, Godefroy de 220
Boulevard Adolphe Max 244
Boulevard Anspach 233
Boulevard de Waterloo 248
Bouts, Dirk 205
Boyadijun du Coeur 250
Brasserie Belle-Vue 256
Brasserie, Musée 252
Bruce, Thomas 226
Bruegel, Musée 250
Bruparck 256
Bruxella 1238, Musée 252
Bruxellois de la Gueuze, Musée 252
buses and coaches
  around Brussels 9
  around London 6
  London–Brussels 3–4
  tte du Lion 211–12

aret 274
ao et du Chocolat, Musée 252
s and lunches 262
udenberg 219
and' Place 216
rth-central Brussels 229
artier Léopold 237
on and Marolles 223
ar of events 186–7
rel
g in Brussels 10
g in London 7–8
n–Brussels 4
le St-Michel et Ste-Gudule
  256
Paul 237
ge de la Bande Dessinée
252
lic d'Aide Sociale de Bruxelles
yale 222

Charlier, Guillaume **203–4**, 251
Chemin de Fer Belge 253
children 184
Christmas Fairs 248
churches
  Cathédrale St-Michel et Ste-Gudule **194–5**, 256
  Chapelle Royale 222
  Minimes 228
  Notre-Dame de Bon Secours 218
  Notre-Dame de la Chapelle 227
  Notre-Dame du Finistère 235
  Notre-Dame du Sablon 224
  Saint-Jacques-sur-Coudenberg 221
  Saint-Jean-Baptiste au Béguinage 230–2
  Saint-Nicolas 218
  Sainte-Catherine 234
  Sainte-Marie 236
Cinéma, Musée **200–1**, 253
cinemas 275
Cinquantenaire, Musée **201–2**, 250
classical music 270–1
coaches and buses
  around Brussels 9
  around London 6
  London–Brussels 3–4
Colonne du Congrès 236
Communal d'Ixelles 250
Communal de la Ville de Bruxelles **214–17**, 251
Constantin Meunier, Musée 251
consulates 185
Costume et de la Dentelle, Musée 253
Coudenberg 219–22, *220*
  cafés et lunches 219
  Cathédrale St-Michel et Ste-Gudule **194–5**, 256
  Chapelle Royale 222
  Eglise Saint-Jacques-sur-Coudenberg 221
  Hôtel Ravenstein 222
  Mont des Arts 220–1
  Musée du Cinéma **200–1**, 253
  Musée de l'Hôtel Charlier **203–4**, 251
  Musée des Instruments de Musique **204**, 253–4
  Musées Royaux des Beaux-Arts 204–7
  Palais des Beaux-Arts 222
  Palais Royal **221**, 256
  Parc de Bruxelles 219–20
  Place Royale 220–1
Council of the European Union 239–40
credit cards 189
crime 184–5
cultural centres 270
culture 181–2
customs formalities 5
cycling 8, 10

dance 271
David et Alice van Buuren, Musée 253
David, Jacques-Louis 206
Dernier Quartier Général de Napoléon 212
discos 274
Docklands Light Railway 6
doctors 185
driving in Brussels 10

driving in London 7–8
Dynastie, Musée 253

E111 forms 185
Eglise des Minimes 228
Eglise Notre-Dame de Bon Secours 218
Eglise Notre-Dame de la Chapelle 227
Eglise Notre-Dame du Finistère 235
Eglise Notre-Dame du Sablon 224
Eglise Saint-Jacques-sur-Coudenberg 221
Eglise Saint-Jean-Baptiste au Béguinage 230–2
Eglise Saint-Nicolas 218
Eglise Sainte-Catherine 234
Eglise Sainte-Marie 236
Egouts, Musée des 253
electricity 185
embassies 185
emergencies 186
Ensor, James 206
entertainment and nightlife **270–5**
  cabaret 274
  cinemas 275
  classical music 270–1
  cultural centres 270
  dance 271
  discos 274
  jazz 273
  listings magazines 270
  nightclubs 274
  opera 270–1
  puppet shows 272–3
  rock music 273
  theatre 271–2
  ticket agencies 270
Erasme, Musée 253
European Commission 240
European Monetary Union (EMU) 189
European Parliament 238–9
Eurostar 3

Ferme de la Haie-Sainte 212
Ferme de Hougoumont 212
Ferme de Mont-Saint-Jean 212
festivals 186–7
Fête des rois 186
Fête de Saint-Nicolas 187
film 275
Foire du Midi 186
food and drink 181, **258–62**
  bars 262
  beer **181–2**, 187
  cafés see cafés and lunches
  Central 259–60, 262
  East 260
  North 261–2
  pastries 258
  restaurant opening hours 258
  South 260–1, 262
  tipping in restaurants 191
  Value Added Tax 258
  West 261
Forêt de Soignes 256

Galerie Bortier 218
Galerie Louise 226–7
Galerie Porte de Namur 227
Galerie de la Toison d'Or 226–7
Galeries de Saint-Hubert 217–18

Brussels Index: AIR – GAL

gardens and parks
  Jardin Botanique 235–6
  Jardin Botanique National 256
  Jardin d'Egmont 228
  Parc de Bruxelles 219–20
  Parc du Cinquantenaire 240–1
gay scene 187–8
Gordon Monument 212
Grand' Place **196–9**, *215*
  cafés and lunches 216
  Eglise Notre-Dame de Bon Secours 218
  Eglise Saint-Nicolas 218
  Galerie Bortier 218
  Galeries de Saint-Hubert 217–18
  Hôtel de Ville de Bruxelles **217**, 252
  La Bourse 218
  Manneken-Pis 199–200
  Musée Communal de la Ville de Bruxelles **214–17**, 251
  shopping 217–18, **246–7**
Gudule, Saint 195

health 185, 186
Hôpital Saint-Pierre 250
horse-drawn carriages 10
Horta, Musée **202–3**, 251
Horta, Pavillon 241
hospitals 185
Hôtel Charlier **203–4**, 251
Hôtel Hannon 251
Hôtel Ravenstein 222
Hôtel Solvay 251
Hôtel Tassel **202**, 251
Hôtel de Ville de Bruxelles **217**, 252
hotels 265–7
  reservations 264
  tipping 191
Ile Saint-Géry 234
Imprimerie, Musée 253
Info Point Europe 240
Institut Royal des Sciences Naturelles 253
Instruments de Musique, Musée **204**, 253–4
insurance 188

Japanese Art Museum 209–10
Jardin Botanique 235–6
Jardin Botanique National 256
Jardin d'Egmont 228
jazz 273
Jouet, Musée du 254
Jour des Morts 187
Journée du Patrimoine 187

Kasteel van Beersel 256
Khnopff, Fernand 206
Kinepolis 256
Koninklijk Museum voor Midden-afrika 252

La Belle Alliance 212
La Bourse 218
La Maison des Ducs de Brabant 199
language 182, 184, **188–9**
Leopold II 237, 242
  statue 242
Les Passions Humaines 241
listings magazines 270
Livre, Musée 254
lunches *see* cafés and lunches

Magritte, René 251
Maison Deprez-Van de Velde **242**, 252
Maison Paul Cauchie **237**, 252
Maison du Roi 214–16
Maison Saint-Cyr **242**, 252
Maison Van Eetvelde **242**, 252
Manneken-Pis 199–200
markets 248
Marolles *see* Sablon and Marolles
Métro 8, 9
Meunier, Constantin 251
Mini Europe 256
Minimes 228
money 189
Mont des Arts 220–1
Montgolfier balloon 236
Monument to the Belgians 212
monuments 255–6
museums **250–5**
  Album 252
  Art Nouveau 251–2
  Atelier de Moulages **241–2**, 252
  Autoworld 252
  Béguinage d'Anderlecht 252
  Boyadijan du Coeur 250
  Brasserie 252
  Bruegel 250
  Bruxella 1238 252
  Bruxellois de la Gueuze 252
  Cacao et du Chocolat 252
  Centre Belge de la Bande Dessinée **195–6**, 252
  Centre Public d'Aide Sociale de Bruxelles 250
  Chemin de Fer Belge 253
  Cinéma **200–1**, 253
  Cinquantenaire **201–2**, 250
  Communal d'Ixelles 250
  Communal de la Ville de Bruxelles **214–6**, 251
  Constantin Meunier 251
  Costume et de la Dentelle 253
  David et Alice van Buuren 253
  Dynastie 253
  Egouts 253
  Erasme 253
  Horta **202–3**, 251
  Hôtel Charlier **203–4**, 251
  Hôtel de Ville de Bruxelles **217**, 252
  Imprimerie 253
  Institut Royal des Sciences Naturelles 253
  Instruments de Musique **204**, 253–4
  Japanese Art Museum 209–10
  Jouet 254
  Koninklijk Museum voor Midden-afrika 252
  Livre 254
  Numismatique et Historique de la Banque Nationale de Belgique 254
  opening hours 190
  Pavillon Chinois **209–10**, 255
  Planétarium National 255
  Postes et Télécommunications 254
  René Magritte 251
  Royal de l'Afrique Centrale 254
  Royal de l'Armée et d'Histoire Militaire 255
  Royaux des Beaux-Arts 204–7
  Service de Chalcographie 255
  Toone Theatre Museum **209**, 255
  Tour Japonaise **209–10**, 255

  Transport Urbain Bruxellois 255
  Wellington Museum 211
  Wiertz **207–8**, 251

Napoleon Bonaparte 210–12
night buses (London) 6
nightclubs 274
North-central Brussels 229–36, *230–1*
  Boulevard Anspach 233
  cafés and lunches 229
  Centre Belge de la Bande Dessinée **195–6**, 252
  Colonne du Congrès 236
  Eglise Notre-Dame du Finistère 235
  Eglise Saint-Jean-Baptiste au Béguinage 230–2
  Eglise Sainte-Catherine 234
  Eglise Sainte-Marie 236
  Jardin Botanique 235–6
  Place des Martyrs 235
  Place Saint-Géry 233–4
  Théâtre de la Monnaie 232–3
  Willebroeck Canal 234–5
Notre-Dame de Bon Secours 218
Notre-Dame de la Chapelle 227
Notre-Dame du Finistère 235
Notre-Dame du Sablon 224
Numismatique et Historique de la Banque Nationale de Belgique, Musée 254

Océade 256
Old England 204
Ommegang 186
opening hours 190
opera 270–1

Palais des Beaux-Arts 222
Palais de Charles de Lorraine 256
Palais d'Egmont 228
Palais de Justice **208–9**, 256
Palais Royal **221**, 256
Parc de Bruxelles 219–20
Parc du Cinquantenaire 240–1
parking in Brussels 10
parking in London 7–8
parks *see* gardens and parks
passports 5
pastries 258
Pavillon Chinois **209–10**, 255
Pavillon Horta 241
pedestrian crossings 10
pharmacies 185
Place Cardinal Mercier 248
Place du Grand-Sablon **225–6**, 246
Place des Martyrs 235
Place de la Monnaie 232–3
Place du Petit-Sablon 226
Place Royale 220–1
Place Saint-Géry 233–4
Planétarium National 255
Plantation du Meiboom 187
police 184–5
population of Belgium 184
Porte de Hal 256
Porte Louise **226–7**, 248
post offices 190
Postes et Télécommunications, Musée 254
practical A–Z **184–92**
public holidays 190
puppet shows 272–3

Quartier Léopold 237–42, *238–9*
  Atelier Moulages **241–2**, 252
  Berlaymont Building 240
  cafés and lunches 237
  Council of the European Union
    239–40
  European Commission 240
  European Parliament 238–9
  Info Point Europe 240
  Maison Deprez-Van de Velde **242**, 252
  Maison Paul Cauchie 237
  Maison Saint-Cyr **242**, 252
  Maison Van Eetvelde **242**, 252
  Musée du Cinquantenaire **201–2**, 250
  Musée Wiertz **207–8**, 251
  Parc du Cinquantenaire 240–1
  Pavillon Horta 241
  statue of Leopold II 242

rail travel
  around London 6
  arrivals 5
  Docklands Light Railway 6
  Eurostar 3
  London Underground 6, 7
  Métro 8, 9
  tickets and passes (Brussels) 9
  tickets and passes (London) 7
René Magritte, Musée 251
restaurants 181, **258–62**
  opening hours 258
  tipping 191
  see also cafés and lunches
Réveillon 187
revues 274
Riverbuses 8
rock music 273
Royal de l'Afrique Centrale, Musée 254
Royal de l'Armée et d'Histoire Militaire, Musée 255
Royaux des Beaux-Arts, Musée 204–7
Rubens, Peter Paul 205
Rue de Bellevue 251
Rue des Bouchers 209

Rue Dansaert 245–6
Rue Defacqz 251
Rue Faider 251
Rue du Lac 252
Rue du Monastère 251
Rue Neuve 244–5
Rue de la Vallée 252
Rue Vilain XIII 252

Sablon and Marolles 223–8, *225*
  cafés and lunches 223
  Eglise des Minimes 228
  Eglise Notre-Dame de la Chapelle 227
  Eglise Notre-Dame du Sablon 224
  Palais and Jardin d'Egmont 228
  Palais de Justice **208–9**, 256
  Place du Grand-Sablon **225–6**, 246
  Place du Petit-Sablon 226
  Porte Louise **226–7**, 248
  shopping 223, **226–7**, *246*, 248
Saint-Jacques-sur-Coudenberg 221
Saint-Jean-Baptiste au Béguinage 230–2
Saint-Nicolas 218
Sainte-Catherine 234
Sainte-Marie 236
Senne, River 233
Serres Royales de Laeken 256
Service de Chalcographie, Musée 255
shopping **244–8**
  Boulevard de Waterloo 248
  Christmas Fairs 248
  Galerie Bortier 218
  Galeries de Saint-Hubert 217–18
  Grand' Place 217–18, **246–7**
  markets 248
  Porte Louise **226–7**, 248
  Rue Dansaert 245–6
  Rue Neuve 244–5
  Sablon 223, **226–7**, **246**, 248
  Value Added Tax (VAT) 244

Tapis de Fleurs 187
taxis 7, 9–10
telephones 190–1

theatre 271–2
Théâtre de la Monnaie 232–3
ticket agencies 270
time 191
tipping 191
Toone Theatre Museum **209**, 255
Tour Japonaise **209–10**, 255
tourist buses (London) 6
tourist information 191–2
Toussaint 187
trains *see* rail travel
trams 9
Transport Urbain Bruxellois, Musée 255
travel **2–10**
  arrivals 4–5
  border formalities 5
  getting around Brussels 8–10
  getting around London 6–8
  getting to Europe 2–3
  London–Brussels 3–4
traveller's cheques 189

Underground 6, 7

Value Added Tax (VAT) 244, 258
Van Buuren, David et Alice 253
Van Curtsem, Henri 203
visas 5

walking 10
Waterloo, battle of **210–12**, 219
Wellington Museum 211
where to stay **264–8**
  apartment hotels 267
  bed and breakfast 268
  hotels 265–7
  reservations 264
  youth hostels 268
Wiertz, Musée **207–8**, 251
Willebroeck Canal 234–5

youth hostels 268